Condillac and His Reception

This volume explores the philosophy of Étienne Bonnot de Condillac. It presents, for the first time, English-language essays on Condillac's philosophy, making the complexity and sophistication of his arguments and their influence on early modern philosophy accessible to a wider readership.

Condillac's reflections on the origin and nature of human abilities, such as the ability to reason, reflect and use language, took philosophy in distinctly new directions. This volume showcases the diversity of themes and methods inspired by Condillac's work. The chapters are divided into four thematic sections. Part 1 traces connections between Condillac and his contemporaries to understand the context in which themes and discussions central to Condillac's own philosophical thinking evolved. Part 2 focuses on the different ways in which Condillac's philosophy was taken up, challenged, and further developed in nineteenth-century France, before moving in Part 3 to the discussion of thinkers outside of France. Finally, Part 4 looks at the contemporary applications of Condillac's philosophy in a variety of different fields, such as phenomenology, psychology, and psychopathology.

Condillac and His Reception will appeal to scholars and advanced students working on early modern philosophy, history of science and intellectual history.

Delphine Antoine-Mahut is Professor of Philosophy at the ENS de Lyon. She has widely published on Cartesianism, its historiography and its various receptions. Among other collective works, she co-directed *The Oxford Handbook of Descartes and Cartesianism* with Steven Nadler and Tad Schmaltz (2019). Her last book was *L'autorité d'un canon philosophique. Le cas Descartes* (2021).

Anik Waldow is Professor of Philosophy at the University of Sydney and specialises in early modern philosophy. She is the author of *Hume and the Problem of Other Minds* (2009) and *Experience Embodied: Early Modern Accounts of the Human Place in Nature* (2020).

Routledge Studies in Eighteenth-Century Philosophy

Human Dignity and the Kingdom of Ends
Kantian Perspectives and Practical Applications
Edited by Jan-Willem van der Rijt and Adam Cureton

System and Freedom in Kant and Fichte
Edited by Giovanni Pietro Basile and Ansgar Lyssy

Perspectives on Kant's *Opus postumum*
Edited by Giovanni Pietro Basile and Ansgar Lyssy

Adam Smith and Modernity
1723–2023
Edited by Alberto Burgio

Metaphysics as a Science in Classical German Philosophy
Edited by Robb Dunphy and Toby Lovat

Kant on Freedom and Human Nature
Edited by Luigi Filieri and Sofie Møller

Condillac and His Reception
On the Origin and Nature of Human Abilities
Edited by Delphine Antoine-Mahut and Anik Waldow

For more information about this series, please visit: www.routledge.com/Routledge-Studies-in-Eighteenth-Century-Philosophy/book-series/SE0391

Condillac and His Reception
On the Origin and Nature of
Human Abilities

Edited by
Delphine Antoine-Mahut and
Anik Waldow

NEW YORK AND LONDON

First published 2024
by Routledge
605 Third Avenue, New York, NY 10158

and by Routledge
4 Park Square, Milton Park, Abingdon, Oxon, OX14 4RN

Routledge is an imprint of the Taylor & Francis Group, an informa business

© 2024 selection and editorial matter, Delphine Antoine-Mahut and Anik Waldow; individual chapters, the contributors

The right of Delphine Antoine-Mahut and Anik Waldow to be identified as the authors of the editorial material, and of the authors for their individual chapters, has been asserted in accordance with sections 77 and 78 of the Copyright, Designs and Patents Act 1988.

All rights reserved. No part of this book may be reprinted or reproduced or utilised in any form or by any electronic, mechanical, or other means, now known or hereafter invented, including photocopying and recording, or in any information storage or retrieval system, without permission in writing from the publishers.

Trademark notice: Product or corporate names may be trademarks or registered trademarks, and are used only for identification and explanation without intent to infringe.

ISBN: 978-1-032-36978-5 (hbk)
ISBN: 978-1-032-36979-2 (pbk)
ISBN: 978-1-003-33475-0 (ebk)

DOI: 10.4324/9781003334750

Typeset in Sabon
by codeMantra

Contents

List of Contributors	ix
Acknowledgements	xv

1 Introduction: Condillac and Us   1
DELPHINE ANTOINE-MAHUT AND ANIK WALDOW

PART I
Condillac and His Intellectual Context   9

2 The Materialists (Diderot, La Mettrie, Deschamps) and Condillac's Theory of Knowledge   11
GUILLAUME COISSARD

3 Condillac and the Molyneux Problem   28
PETER R. ANSTEY

4 Reinventing Newtonianism: Hypotheses, Systems and Attraction in Condillac   44
GIANNI PAGANINI

5 Languages of Action, Methodological Signs and Deafness: The Reception of Condillac by the Abbé de L'Épée—Or Was It the Other Way around?   63
MARION CHOTTIN

PART II
Condillac's Reception in Nineteenth-Century France   81

6 Condillac Restored: The Paradox of Attention in Pierre
   Laromiguière's *Lessons on Philosophy* (1815)   83
   PIERRE BROUILLET

7 Madness and Ideologist Philosophy of the Mind: Pinel
   and Condillac on the Dualism of Understanding
   and Will   102
   SAMUEL LÉZÉ

8 "The Only, the True French Metaphysician of the
   Eighteenth Century:" Condillac, Cousin
   and the "French School"   119
   DELPHINE ANTOINE-MAHUT

9 Condillac's Puerile Reveries: The Reception of Condillac
   in Phrenology and in the Philosophy
   of Auguste Comte   137
   LAURENT CLAUZADE

PART III
Condillac's Influence Beyond France   153

10 Between Debate and Reception: Formey
    Reads Condillac   155
    ANGELA FERRARO

11 Rethinking the Human Animal with
    Condillac and Herder   171
    ANIK WALDOW

12 The Reception of Condillac in Argentina: From the
    Nineteenth-Century Professors of *idéologie*
    to José Ingenieros   190
    SILVIA MANZO

PART IV
Contemporary Receptions 213

13 Time, Order and the Concept of a Human Interior:
   Paths towards Condillac 215
   CHRISTOPHER GOODEY

14 Representations of the Body and Self-Knowledge:
   Condillac's *Treatise on Sensations* and Contemporary
   Naturalistic Psychology 232
   ALIÈNOR BERTRAND

15 Reductions and Radicalisation of Reductions: Condillac,
   Michel Henry and Maine de Biran 253
   ANNE DEVARIEUX

Index 273

Contributors

Peter Anstey is Professor of Philosophy at the University of Sydney. He specialises in early modern philosophy with a focus on individual philosophers, such as Boyle, Locke and the French *Philosophes*, as well as broader themes, such as experimental philosophy and the theory of principles. He is the author of *John Locke and Natural Philosophy* (2011) and *Experimental Philosophy and the Origins of Empiricism* (with Alberto Vanzo, 2023).

Delphine Antoine-Mahut is Professor of Philosophy at the ENS de Lyon. She has widely published on Cartesianism, its historiography and its various receptions. Among other collective works, she co-directed *The Oxford Handbook of Descartes and Cartesianism* with Steven Nadler and Tad Schmaltz (2019). Her last book was *L'autorité d'un canon philosophique. Le cas Descartes (2021)*.

Aliènor Bertrand is a research fellow at the *Centre national de la recherche scientifique* (CNRS) in Lyon (IHRIM-ENS de Lyon). Her work stands for the development of a systematic interpretation of Condillac's philosophy in *Logique naturelle et principes de l'action humaine*. She edited several volumes of collected essays on Condillac, such as *Condillac, L'origine du langage (2002)* and *Condillac, philosophe du langage?* (2016), as well as the first volumes of a new edition of Condillac's *Œuvres completes* (Vrin). Her recent publications include several articles on lesser-known aspects of Condillac's work, such as his economic language and political relevance ("Lire *Le Commerce et le Gouvernement*: contre l'interprétation néolibérale de Condillac," 2019/1). Her current work deals with the Condillaquian articulation of the history of metaphysics and anthropology.

Pierre Brouillet is a PhD student at the Institut d'Histoire des Représentations et des Idées dans les Modernités (IHRIM-ENS de Lyon, CNRS UMR 5317) and a teaching assistant at the École Normale Supérieure

x Contributors

de Lyon (ENS de Lyon). His research focuses on the concept of attention in early modern and modern psychology and its interaction with theories of auditory perception (seventeenth to nineteenth centuries). His research interests include philosophy of psychiatry and medicine and the therapeutical use of music in early nineteenth-century mental medicine.

Marion Chottin has been a research fellow at the CNRS since 2015. Her early work focused on theories of perception of the classical age and the Enlightenment, from Descartes to Kant, and was published by Éditions Honoré Champion in 2014 under the title *Le Partage de l'empirisme. Une histoire du problème de Molyneux aux XVIIe et XVIIIe siècles.* More recently, she has specialised in the study of conceptualisations of blindness, mainly in the eighteenth century (Condillac, Diderot, Jaucourt, D'Alembert, etc.) and the twentieth century (Derrida, Lusseyran). She also works on deafness and disability more generally as part of her engagement with the conceptual framework developed in the disabilities studies. She published "Éléments pour une contre-histoire de la cécité et des aveugles" (2014), "La liaison des idées chez Condillac: le langage au principe de l'empirisme" (2014/12), "Penser la surdité. L'histoire du sourd de Chartres et l'empirisme des Lumières" (2018), "La cécité dans les *Mémoires d'aveugle* de Derrida: un renversement paradoxal de sa représentation traditionnelle" (2019/8) and *Jacques Lusseyran entre cécité et lumière* (with Céline Roussel and Zina Weygand, 2019).

Laurent Clauzade is Associate Professor of Philosophy at the University of Caen-Normandy and an associate researcher at the Institute for the History and Philosophy of Science and Technology (IHPST, Paris). He is also the treasurer of the international association "Maison d'Auguste Comte." He is the author of *L'organe de la pensée: biologie et philosophie chez Auguste Comte* (2009). He is currently working on a new edition of Auguste Comte's *System of Positive Polity* and has recently published the "Introduction fondamentale" to this edition (2022).

Guillaume Coissard was a post-doctoral fellow at the Labex CoMod (Constitution de la modernité), hosted at the ENS de Lyon. His thesis entitled "Lectures matérialistes de Leibniz au 18ème siècle" identifies the uses of Leibniz's philosophy in La Mettrie, Diderot, D'Holbach and Helvétius, and led to several journal articles: "Du Châtelet entre monadisme et atomisme: la matière dans les Institutions de physique" (2021), "Penser une radicalité leibnizienne? L'exemple des réceptions matérialistes de Leibniz" (2021), "Spinoza et Leibniz: réceptions et usages croisés dans la pensée moderne et contemporaine" (2021) and "La raison de l'ordre: le double rôle de Leibniz dans la sortie du finalisme chez Diderot" (2018). His current research focuses on the French materialists of the eighteenth century.

Contributors xi

Anne Devarieux is Associate Professor of Philosophy and deputy director of the *Identity and Subjectivity* team (EA 2129) at the University of Caen-Normandy. She is a specialist in Maine de Biran's work and has published several journal articles and a monograph on his philosophy and phenomenology (*Maine de Biran, l'individualité persévérante*, Grenoble, Jérôme Millon, 2004). She edited and prefaced *De l'aperception immédiate*, de Maine de Biran, Librairie générale française, coll. Classiques de la philosophie, 2005, and published her habilitation to direct research on the Henrian reading of Maine de Biran: *L'intériorité réciproque. L'hérésie biranienne de Michel Henry* (2018).

Angela Ferraro is an assistant professor at Université Laval (Quebec, Canada). She works mainly on the history of early modern philosophy, especially on Malebranche and the Enlightenment, but she is also interested in the history of the life sciences as well as philosophical historiography. She has several publications on the Berlin Academy, e.g. "In Search of a 'Golden Mean': Experience and Reasoning According to Louis de Beausobre," in *Philosophy at the Berlin Academy in the Reign of Frederick the Great* (2022) and *Philosophie spéculative à l'Académie de Berlin. Mémoires 1745–1769* (with D. Dumouchel, F. Duchesneau and C. Leduc, 2022). Her main publication on Malebranche is *La Réception de la philosophie de Malebranche en France au XVIIIe siècle. Métaphysique et épistémologie* (2019).

Christopher Goodey obtained his PhD from the Department of History and Philosophy of Science at Cambridge University. He worked at the Social Science Research Unit, University College London Institute of Education, researching government programmes on inclusive education, and was subsequently Staff Tutor in the Arts and Social Science Faculty at the Open University. His academic research for the past three decades has centred on the conceptual history of the mind sciences. As well as being the author of numerous articles and joint editor of several collected volumes, he is the author of the monographs *A History of Intelligence and "Intellectual Disability:" The Shaping of Psychology in Early Modern Europe* (2011) and *Development: The History of a Psychological Concept* (2021).

Samuel Lézé is Associate Professor of Medical Anthropology at ENS de Lyon. He teaches the epistemological history of psychiatry and nineteenth-century French philosophy at the *Department of Human Sciences*. At the *Institut d'Histoire des Représentations et des Idées dans les Modernités* (IHRIM-UMR5317), he has been leading the "Dire la Santé Mentale" (DSM) research team since 2015. His research focuses on "Clinical Judgment Formation," specifically the relationship between Freudianism and clinical practice in France. Since

2015, he has also been co-directing (with Delphine Antoine-Mahut) the *Nineteenth-century French Philosophy Research Program* at the LabEx COMOD at ENS de Lyon. His recent publications include "Madness and spiritualist philosophy of mind: Maine de Biran and AA Royer-Collard on a 'true dualism,' " *British Journal for the History of Philosophy*, 28(5), 2020, 885–902. He is preparing a book on the reception of philosophy in mental alienation medicine in France.

Silvia Manzo is Professor of Early Modern Philosophy at the Department of Philosophy in the University of La Plata (UNLP, Argentina) and a research scholar of the National Research Council of Argentina (CONICET). She is the author of numerous books, articles, chapters and translations on Renaissance and early modern history of philosophy and science, particularly on Francis Bacon, Baconianism, Late Scholasticism, historiography of philosophy, the empiricism-rationalism divide and the history of women philosophers. She is currently writing a book on Francis Bacon and the laws of nature. Her recent publications include the chapter "Monsters, laws of nature, and teleology in Late-Scholastic textbooks" (Springer, 2019) and the co-edited special journal edition (with Delphine Antoine-Mahut) "Debates on experience and empiricism in nineteenth-century France," *Perspectives of Science* 27, 5 (2019), which includes her essay "Historiographical approaches on experience and empiricism in the early nineteenth-century: Degérando and Tennemann." She was an associate editor and contributed entries on early modern empiricism and monsters to the *Springer Encyclopedia of Early Modern Philosophy and the Sciences*, ed. Dana Jalobeanu and Charles T. Wolfe (2020).

Gianni Paganini is Emeritus of History of Philosophy at University of Piedmont (Vercelli). He is the author of many books and articles on early modern philosophy, in particular on Bayle, Hobbes, Hume and the history of skepticism. Recently, he edited *Early Modern Philosophy and the Renaissance Legacy* (with C. Muratori, 2016) and *Clandestine Philosophy* (with M.C. Jacob and J.C. Laursen, 2020). For his philosophical achievements, he received a prize from the Accademia dei Lincei (2011) and his book *Skepsis* (2008) received an award by the Académie Française in 2009. He recently published the monograph *De Bayle à Hume. Tolérance, hypothèses, systèmes* (2023) and was elected a fellow of the Accademia dei Lincei (Rome).

Anik Waldow is Professor of Philosophy at the University of Sydney and specialises in early modern philosophy, with a focus on Hume, Descartes, Locke, Rousseau, Herder and Condillac. She has published articles on the moral and cognitive function of sympathy, early modern theories of personal identity and the role of affect in the formation of the self, skepticism and associationist theories of thought and language. She is the author of *Hume and the Problem of Other Minds* (2009) and *Experience Embodied: Early Modern Accounts of the Human Place in Nature* (2020). She edited several volumes of collected essays, among them a special volume on *Sensibility in the Early Modern Era: From Living Machines to Affective Morality* (2016) and *Herder: Philosophy and Anthropology* (with DeSouza, 2017).

Acknowledgements

We would like to thank the *École normale supérieure* de Lyon for its generous support of the conference "Condillac and His Reception" that was held in March 2022 and provided us with a platform to develop the key themes of this volume. It was organised by IHRIM (Institut d'Histoire des Représentations et des Idées dans les Modernités, CNRS, UMR 5317) and the LabEx COMOD (Constitution et Origines de la Modernité), more specifically the "Blanc" programme "La 'philosophie française' au XIXe siècle." We would also like to thank the programme managers, who did a great job in record time to make the conference a success: Alla Zhuk, Marion Sylla, Afida Madjidi and Diane Laurent.

The collaboration leading to the conference in Lyon was initiated through a previous workshop at the *Séminaire Descartes*, "From Port Royal to Condillac," ENS de Paris in January 2020. We extend special thanks to Martine Pécharman, Laura Kotevska, Denis Kambouchner and Sophie Roux for their initiative, support and dedication in organising this event. We also express our gratitude for the insightful inputs and discussions provided by our speakers and audiences of both events. Without their perceptive comments and questions, this volume would have been much less interesting. We are also grateful for the excellent work and editorial support of Manuel Vasquez-Villavicencio, Iona Gitt-Henderson and Joshua Penney.

The research for this volume was financially supported by an *Australian Research Council Discovery Project* grant on "The Experimental Self in Early-Modern Philosophy" (DP170102670, 2016–2021) and several research support schemes of the *Faculty of Arts and Social Sciences* and the *School for Philosophical and Historical Inquiry* of the University of Sydney.

1 Introduction
Condillac and Us

Delphine Antoine-Mahut and Anik Waldow

This volume seeks to render more accessible the relevance, complexity, and sophistication of Étienne Bonnot de Condillac's philosophical arguments and their various receptions by later thinkers and practitioners. It focuses on the complex contribution of his philosophy, particularly of his conceptualization of the nature and origin of human abilities, to the shaping of the salient features of modern society. Indeed, by re-engaging Bacon and Descartes, and numerous other thinkers who embraced little-known hybrid accounts, Condillac can be seen as having bequeathed to his successors a method of analysis or decomposition, which, in many ways, became a foundational principle, both theoretically and practically. One aspect that renders Condillac's philosophy so peculiar is that it was continuously applied in many different fields of knowledge and human practices. Such applications can be found in the French debate about "alienism," concerned with clinical and medical considerations in managing mental illnesses, but also in the economic and political reflections of the so-called *ideologues* and their *spiritualist* opponents, who sought to found a new metaphysics that would retain the benefits of Condillac's conception of the limits of human reason in Europe and beyond.

To date studies of this critical potential of Condillac's philosophy certainly remain largely minor compared to the numerous works on canonical philosophers. Despite this, research focusing on Condillac has gained momentum in the last five to ten years, with the publication of a new critical edition of his main work, *Essai sur l'Origine des connaissances humaines* (ed. Pariente/Pécharman, Vrin 2014), after André Charrak's seminal study on metaphysics and epistemology in Condillac's *Essay* (2003), a very substantial special journal issue (*Les études philosophiques*, ed. Pécharman, 2019), and two volumes of essays dedicated to Condillac's philosophy of language (ed. Bertrand 2002, 2016). This surge of interest in Condillac is not limited to the French-language context. Numerous recent English publications have also helped to put Condillac firmly on the radar of early

DOI: 10.4324/9781003334750-1

modern scholars (e.g., Orain 2012, Jacquette 2015, Thiel 2015, Dunham 2019, Kaitaro 2020, Waldow 2021).[1] Yet, what is still missing are studies that bring together the different facets of Condillaquian themes and the connections that tie them together in Condillac's own explorations and in the thoughts and practices of those who engaged with his philosophical project.[2] This volume seeks to close this gap by providing the first English collection of essays on Condillac and his reception.

One of the main contributions of this book is to offer a fresh perspective that invites us to transform the binary readings that still dominate our representation and teaching of modern philosophy: Descartes against Locke; "rationalism," "idealism," "spiritualism," and "metaphysics" against "empiricism," "realism," "materialism," and "positivism." That Condillac has the potential to subvert these distinctions and reveal the deficiency of current classificatory schemes becomes immediately clear when reflecting on his place in the history of philosophy. On the one hand, Condillac has long been regarded as continuing the tradition of "empiricism," or even the kind of "sensualism" attributed to Locke and his followers. On the other hand, however, Condillac incorporated into his philosophy a form of "idealism" or even "intellectualism" assigned to Cartesian innatism, whose excesses Condillac nonetheless denounced. The impression that Condillac's work is fragmented in his engagement with various philosophical traditions is reinforced by the fact that there were at least two distinct periods in Condillac's intellectual life—which to some extent might even justify to speak of two different philosophical periods: that of the *Essay on the Origin of Human Knowledge* (1746) where we find a delicate balance between sensation and reflection, which has sometimes been interpreted as a contradiction; and the period which, consecrated by the *Treatise on Sensations* (1754), begins the reign of the absolute primacy of sensation and the resolution of reflection into the genesis of human knowledge.

Despite this fragmentation within his own oeuvre, Condillac set out to identify a common ground for any attempt to know the extent and limits of human faculties. As Delphine Antoine Mahut's chapter shows, his strategy here focused on recharacterizing the opposition between Locke and Descartes as that of "two [kinds] of metaphysics"—one with the ambition "to pierce all the mysteries; the nature [and] the essence of beings, the most hidden causes," and the other which "knows how to contain itself within the limits traced for it."[3] Through this move, Condillac opened the way to unprecedented hybridizations between metaphysical and empirical contents, the originality and impact of which we are only beginning to understand (see also Antoine-Mahut and Lézé eds. 2024).

By describing a pendulum-like movement, from Condillac himself to his receptions and back, the contributions to this volume tackle this paradox in their own way. We present them here based on what unites them, with the understanding that, for the sake of clarity and convenience, the table of contents will be organized chronologically and geographically. Part 1 traces connections between Condillac and his contemporaries to understand the context in which themes and discussions central to Condillac's own philosophical thinking evolved. Part 2 focuses on the different ways in which Condillac's philosophy was taken up, challenged, and further developed in nineteenth-century France, before moving in Part 3 to the discussion of thinkers outside of France. Finally, Part 4 looks at the contemporary applications of Condillac's philosophy in a variety of different fields, such as phenomenology, psychology, and psychopathology.

Focusing on the French debate of the mid-eighteenth century, the volume starts with Guillaume Coissard's discussion of Condillac in the works of Diderot, La Mettrie, and Deschamps. With the intention of justifying their own materialist position, these philosophers added to Condillac's original epistemological claims a new ontological dimension. Presenting him as an idealist who denied the existence of the external world, they argued that only a materialist ontology could address the problems to which Condillac's philosophy gave rise. Turning to Condillac's theory of perception, Peter Anstey demonstrates that Condillac's "volte-face" regarding his answer to the "Molyneux Problem" becomes completely requalified when situating Condillac's treatments in the broader philosophical context of the French reception of this problem. To show this, Anstey considers the writings of Voltaire, La Mettrie and Diderot, as well as the discussion of the doctrine of innate ideas and associations, together with the new empirical observations deriving from William Cheselden's cataract operations.

Gianni Paganini's chapter on the status of hypothesis in Condillac's work further supports the claim that an engagement with Condillac's intellectual context requires us to revisit some of the established interpretative paradigms. Far from rejecting the use of hypothesis—as assumed by most standard historiographies—Paganini demonstrates that Condillac in fact provided a substantial re-evaluation of its function in his construction of systems. Moreover, Paganini argues that the real source of Condillac's approach to the issue of hypothesis in the *Traité des systèmes* (1749) and later on in his *Cours d'études* (1775) was Emilie Du Châtelet rather than Isaac Newton himself.

Marion Chottin's chapter complements this more complex picture of Condillac by pursuing his intellectual engagements into the practical domain. She argues that Condillac's mature reflections on the language of action (as presented in his *Logic*, 1780) evolved through his engagement with Abbé de l' Epée's work in the education of deaf people—which challenges the idea that it was in fact Condillac who inspired de l' Epée. What Condillac realized was that the organization of ideas can either involve linguistic signs or, as L'Epée argued, artificial "methodical signs:" that is, gestures used in the sign language of deaf people. Due to this insight, Condillac's *Logic* substantially requalifies his original account of the *Essay*.

4 *Delphine Antoine-Mahut and Anik Waldow*

If we move from this predominantly French context to the Franco-German milieu of the Berlin Academy of the mid-eighteenth century, it becomes clear that even here Condillac's philosophy was perceived as a major influence, as Angela Ferraro's analysis of Jean Henri Samuel Formey's engagement with Condillac shows. Formey succeeded Maupertuis as the secretary of the Berlin Academy, where Condillac's philosophy was treated as a serious alternative to the paradigm of Leibnizian-Wolffian psychology and as a less dangerous option than Hume's "pyrrhonism." Formey produced several reviews of Condillac's works and engaged in an extended letter exchange with Condillac himself. Although this exchange was marked by a keen interest and mutual respect, Formey also questioned the consistency of Condillac's anti-system stance and objected to the proximity his comparison between human and animal minds established.

Another example of this mixture of respect, curiosity, and rejection can be found in Johann Gottfried Herder's engagement with Condillac's theory of the origin of language. Like many other mid-eighteenth-century thinkers in Germany and France, Herder was spell-bound by Condillac's idea that, during an early phase of their development, humans share with animals fundamental mental capacities from which higher order capacities then evolve. And yet, as Anik Waldow argues in her chapter, one of Herder's main motivations for his engagement with Condillac was to iron out some of the extremes to which his animal-human comparison gave rise. He did so by distinguishing between developments that enabled the emergence of the human species as a whole from developments each individual human must undergo during their lifetime in order to acquire reason and language.

While in Germany Condillac was utilized to advocate alternative philosophical systems and introduce new themes into the debate, in Argentina his reception took a more radical form. As Silvia Manzo demonstrates, in the first half of the nineteenth century, Condillac was here received as a philosopher who integrated the new philosophical canon that would replace the Scholastic canon that had been imposed by the colonial regime. In the early-twentieth century, this development led to a further change when Ingenieros inserted Condillac into a narrative that, starting with Bacon and Locke, culminated in positivism—a current that, in his view, offered the best framework to make Argentina shine in the concert of civilized nations.

As this discussion shows, approaching Condillac through his intellectual connections is not only valuable when considering the genesis of some of his claims and the difference in emphasis characterizing his earlier and later reflections. It can also provide us with a clearer understanding of the different strata of interpretation that have shaped the picture of Condillac to this day.[4] When turning to the French nineteenth-century debate concerning the status of philosophy and its methods, this connection with our present-day perspective becomes particularly clear.

By describing the crucial role of Maine de Biran's criticism of Condillac's sensualism in Michel Henry's material phenomenology, Anne Devarieux's chapter shows to what extent these receptions fit into each other to the point of sometimes disappearing. Restoring each one of them individually is therefore a way of attesting to the presence of Condillac's philosophy in contemporary philosophy, a presence which is diffuse but nonetheless permanent. Devarieux's analysis thus reveals that the relationship between metaphysical theses and empirical content, as thematized by Condillac, remains an all-compassing structure for subsequent debates, even if the connection between the two elements has often been criticized and even been interpreted as regrettable.

Laurent Clauzade's analysis of Auguste Comte's discussion of the status of human abilities in relation to Gall's cerebral physiology—to which Comte fully adhered—further illustrates what is involved in this critique. His chapter describes how Comte's engagement with Condillac led to a marginalization of the sensualist and analytic tradition in French empiricism, a tradition that was designated as stemming from Condillac. But Clauzade at the same time shows that Gall's engagement with Condillac also brought about adjustments within the empiricist camp itself. Pierre Brouillet draws an equally complex picture of Condillac's reception in France by detailing the methods and importance of Pierre Laromiguière's hybridization of Condillac via the philosophy of Descartes. What results from this hybridization is a "correction" of Condillac, one that aims to reassign attention to an active role, which in turn makes it possible to identify Condillac as the founding father of experimental psychology and the new philosophy that France required.

Finally, Philippe Pinel's clinical appropriation of Condillac perfectly illustrates the eminently Condillaquian dimension of his critique of Condillac. Thus, Samuel Lézé shows that for Pinel, the problem to be solved is how the dualism of understanding and will can most appropriately serve as a foundation of a medical science of mental alienation. The "philosophical medicine" that should result corrects Condillac's too intellectualist definition of mental disorder by clinical facts. It thus mobilizes Condillac to correct Condillac.

As we can see, this work on Condillac's paradoxical originality, reinforced by his different receptions, always brings us back to Condillac. It encourages us to read and reread him differently, even when he himself does not seem to have taken a direct position on the questions posed to him. Highlighting this indirect connection with Condillac, Christopher Goodey shows that Condillac's relevance to current developmental psychology becomes all the more meaningful when we remember that from the late sixteenth century onward, the concept of predestined election became prominent in debates about human nature. Over a period beginning with Pascal, a residual concept of election can be detected even in Locke, Montesquieu and Rousseau, since it was the model for change to be interpreted as a stadial development with quasi-secular descriptors.

Further probing into links with contemporary philosophy and psychology, Aliènor Bertrand shows that to appreciate the radical originality of his philosophy of consciousness and self-consciousness it is not only required to abandon the standard comparison between the Condillac of the *Treatise on Sensations* and the Locke of the *Essay*. To understand better his topicality—in this case, his relevance for naturalistic psychology—also requires us to reread Condillac more faithfully by returning to three of his key theses: first, that only human beings have self-consciousness; second, that humans share elementary self-relations with animals, and, third, that representations of one's own body are essential to the formation of self-consciousness.

We can see here the value of revisiting Condillac's philosophy and its reception. Doing so offers new insights into the subtle influences and classifications that have shaped our understanding of the philosophical questions and problems that were bequeathed to us and which we continue to investigate to this day. Exploring this connection promises to provide us with a deeper comprehension of some of the theoretical assumptions underpinning our own philosophical explorations as well as those of other disciplines. After all, many modern disciplines, like sociology and psychology, emerged from philosophy in the nineteenth and twentieth centuries. And they have come to be seen as distinct disciplines, at least partly so because of their methodological choices and empirical orientation. It is in this way that Condillac's reflections on the importance of sensation, perception, method, and analysis in the development of theoretical knowledge offer a promising framework for re-evaluating our own disciplinary commitments.

By covering an extensive range of topics, this volume seeks to acquaint its readers with the diversity of themes and methods inspired by Condillac's philosophical work. It also intends to bring into focus disciplinary reflections that surpass the primary paradigm of philosophy, by engaging the work of thinkers who pioneered new approaches in physiology, medicine, anthropology, psychology, sociology and linguistics. The mix of chapters in this volume reflects this diversity, encompassing a variety of intellectual and cultural traditions. In addition, the chapters illuminate how Condillac's theoretical concepts were applied in practice, revealing the importance of philosophical discourse for political, social, medical, and economic questions, as well as for human life and well-being more generally.

Notes

1 For older works on Condillac, see Aarsleff (1982, 2007) Falkenstein (2005) and Hayes (1999).
2 The few works that have a broader focus are mostly written in French, such as *Étienne Bonnot de Condillac. Les Monades*, edited by Laurence Bongie.
3 Condillac (2014), pp. 59–60. Nigel Briggs's translation.
4 On the construction of philosophical figures, see Antoine-Mahut (2021).

References

Aarsleff, Hans (1982). *From Locke to Saussure*. London: Athlone.
Aarsleff, Hans (2007). "Philosophy of Language," In *The Cambridge History of Eighteenth-Century Philosophy*, edited by Knud Haakonssen, 451–495. Cambridge: Cambridge University Press.
Antoine-Mahut, Delphine (2021). *L'autorité d'un canon philosophique. Le cas Descartes*. Paris: Vrin.
Antoine-Mahut, Delphine and Lézé, Samuel (eds.) (forthcoming 2024). *Metaphysics and Sciences in XIXth Century France*. Leiden: Brill, forthcoming.
Bertrand, Aliènor (2002). *Condillac: L'origine du langage*. Paris: PUF.
Bertrand, Aliènor (2016). *Condillac, philosophe du langage?* Lyon: ENS Éditions.
Charrak, André (2003). *Empirisme et métaphysique: l'Essai sur l'origine des connaissances humaines de Condillac*. Paris: Vrin.
Condillac, Étienne Bonnot de (1992). *Philosophical Writings*. Volume 2. Translated by Franklin Philip and Harlane Lane. London: Lawrence Erlbaum.
Condillac, Étienne Bonnot de (2001). *Essay on the Origin of Human Knowledge*. Cambridge: Cambridge University Press.
Condillac, Étienne Bonnot de (2014). *Essai sur l'Origine des connaissances humaines*. Edited by Jean-Claude Pariente and Martine Pécharman. Paris: Vrin.
Dunham, Jeremy (2019). "Habits of Mind a Brand New Condillac." *Journal of Modern Philosophy* 1(1): 1–18.
Falkenstein, Lorne (2005). "Condillac's paradox." *Journal of the History of Philosophy* 43(4): 403-435.
Hayes, Julie C. (1999). *Reading the Enlightenment*. Cambridge: Cambridge University Press.
Jacquette, Dale (2015). "Condillac's Analytic Dilemma." *History of Philosophy Quarterly* 32(2): 141–160.
Kaitaro, Timo (2020). *Language, Culture and Cognition from Descartes to Lewes*. Leiden: Brill.
Orain, Arnaud (2012). "The Moral Theory of Condillac: A Path toward Utilitarianism." *Revue de philosophie économique* 2(13): 93–117.
Pécharman, Martine (2019). Condillac après l'Essai sur les connaissances humaines. *Les Études philosophiques* 1: 128 (special journal issue).
Thiel, Udo (2015). "Self and Sensibility: From Locke to Condillac and Rousseau." *Intellectual History Review* 25(3): 257–278.
Waldow, Anik (2021). "Condillac on Being Human: Language and Reflection Reconsidered." *European Journal of Philosophy* 29(2): 504–519.

Part I
Condillac and His Intellectual Context

2 The Materialists (Diderot, La Mettrie, Deschamps) and Condillac's Theory of Knowledge

Guillaume Coissard

1 Introduction

According to the historiographical scheme inherited from Victor Cousin, French materialism established a continuity with Condillac's sensualism (Bloch, 1997). On this interpretation, Helvetius, one of its main representatives, deepened a theory of knowledge that was first established in the *Essay on the Origin of Human Knowledge* (1746), and then further developed in the *Treatise on Sensations* (1754). It is true that, for the materialists of the mid-eighteenth century, Condillac was a particularly important author. Helped by the influence of Diderot, the *Essay on the Origin of Human Knowledge* was published shortly before La Mettrie's *L'Homme Machine* (1748) and Diderot's *Lettre sur les aveugles* (1749). However, instead of regarding Condillac as a mentor, they saw him as an interlocutor, whose theses had to be interpreted, discussed, sometimes taken up, and sometimes refuted.

The case of the first paragraph of the *Essay* is emblematic. Condillac opens the work with these famous lines:

§ 1. Whether we raise ourselves, to speak metaphorically, into the heavens or descend into the abyss, we do not go beyond ourselves; and we never perceive anything but our own thought. Whatever the knowledge we have, if we wish to trace it to its origin, we will in the end arrive at a first simple thought, which has been the object of the second, which has been the object of the third, and so on. It is this order of thoughts we must explore if we wish to know the ideas we have of things.

(Condillac, 2001, p. 11)

This is an epistemological statement insofar as it concerns what we can know. It reduces the field of metaphysics to an investigation of the human mind centrally revolving around the question of the origin of ideas and the faculties of the mind. It is not an ontological statement about the inexistence of the external world. Condillac reduces metaphysics to a theory of human knowledge and its development. However, this reduction paradoxically opens his philosophy to ontological interpretations.

Three years later, in a well-known passage of the *Letter on the Blind for the Use of Those Who Can See*, Diderot refers to the *Essay*'s opening statement to compare Condillac with Berkeley and to foreground the idealist character of former's philosophy. He thus provides an ontological reading of the same passage, considering that the statement that "we do not go beyond ourselves" seems to imply the negation of the external world. By contrast, in an extract from *Animals More than Machines*, La Mettrie regards Condillac as a "Machinists" (La Mettrie, 1750, p. 16), a term he takes to be synonymous with "Materialists," for Condillac explains the development of the mind through a mechanism that transforms sensation. On the basis of analogous interpretation, Condillac's opponents accused him of defending materialism (Ricken, 1999). There is, therefore, a debate within the materialist tradition about the ontological meaning of Condillac's theory of knowledge. This debate has its roots in what Coski has called "Condillac's metaphysical paradox," arising from Condillac's struggle to amalgamate the spiritualist and the materialist tendencies of his thought (Coski, 2004, p. 3). In reality, these two readings are based on different elements. The idealistic reading is based on a formulation found in the first paragraph of the *Essay*, according to which the mind never goes beyond itself. Conversely, the materialistic reading insists on the empiricist ambition behind Condillac's program which denies the existence of innate ideas by sketching a genealogy of the soul's operations through the transformations of sensation.

To look at the reception of Condillac's theory of knowledge among materialists does not require us to decide between these two readings: neither La Mettrie nor Diderot claims to provide a commentary on the *Essay*; instead, they use this work strategically, following their own philosophical agenda. It would thus, for example, be a methodological mistake to ask whether Diderot provided an acceptable interpretation of Condillac's philosophy when labeling him as an idealist. Diderot interrogates Condillac's statements not so much for the purpose of identifying their true meaning as to determine their conceptual potential and their theoretical possibilities for the establishment of materialism. In this way, he treats the text of the *Essay* as a resource and not just as a work that requires an interpretation by a historian of philosophy.

If that is the case, we can ask what function Condillac's theory of knowledge played in the construction of Enlightenment materialism. To answer this question, I would like to focus here on the reception of the first paragraph of the *Essay on the Origin of Human Knowledge* by showing that it provided materialists philosophers with the opportunity to construct

The Materialists and Condillac's Theory of Knowledge 13

(a) a more or less fictitious theoretical adversary called the idealist, and (b) a problem that any materialist position had to solve. This problem concerns the proof of the existence of things outside of thought, representation, and sensation. It is constructed by Diderot, but answers can be found in La Mettrie and even more clearly in Deschamps.

2 Is Condillac an Idealist?

The figure of the idealist is already present in Diderot's early philosophical texts. In *The Skeptic's Walk* (1748), the idealist is called an *egotist*, someone who asserts that, apart from the subject of thought and its representations (as well as its ideas and sensations), there is strictly nothing else. This is a radical and subjectivist version of idealism (which I refer to hereafter as solipsism), which consists in denying the existence of the external world.

Diderot is not the first to discuss and define idealism. He continued the use of a typology found in Christian Wolff's *Psychologia rationalis* (§ 36). It describes various types of philosophers, and already defines solipsism as a radical and strange variant of idealism (§ 38). He names as the only representative of this philosophy an almost unknown Malebranchean called Jean Brunet, who lived at beginning of the eighteenth century.[1] So, Diderot's contribution to the construction of the category of idealism consisted in turning one of its possible but absurd conclusions into its essential characteristic: in his hands, the idealist becomes someone who denies the existence of things outside of the mind.

However, it is worth noting that in the texts from the late 1740s, in which Diderot constructs this figure of the idealist as a denier of the external world—*The Skeptic's Walk* and the *Letter on the Blind*—he refers to Condillac and quotes the first paragraph of the *Essay on the Origin of Human Knowledge*. It is often noted that Diderot caricatures Condillac in these passages.[2] He indeed gives an ontological interpretation of a purely epistemological statement by Condillac. The latter never denies the existence of external things, but he states that we only have access to our sensations, which is quite a different claim (Baertsch, 1988). Not being able to know the true properties of things (epistemological statement) doesn't mean that things do not really exist (ontological statement). By using Condillac as a representative of this second (ontological) statement, Diderot modified the meaning of his philosophy.

What I would like to do, for my part, is not to ask whether Diderot is a good or bad reader of Condillac, but rather to interrogate his interpretative strategies. This will allow us to understand how the first paragraph of the *Essay* could turn into a standard source for the development of arguments used to defend ontological solipsism, independently of the question of whether Condillac's text justifies this reading. For I believe that Diderot did not intend to provide an accurate representation of Condillac's ideas. These interpretative strategies are of three kinds: Isolating, Comparing, Problematizing.

a Isolating the first paragraph of the Essay: The first strategy is to isolate a statement or an argument from the rest of Condillac's philosophy. For example, if we read *The Skeptic's Walk*, we see that the narrator represents the sect of solipsists, and does so by using Condillac's own words:

> I am today who I want to be, and I will show you that maybe I am you, and you are nothing; Whether I raise myself into the heavens, or descend into the abyss, I do not go beyond myself, and I never perceive anything but my own thought, he said to me emphatically.
> (Diderot, 1975–, vol. II, pp. 118–119, my translation, emphasis in the original)

When reading this passage, one notices that the first paragraph of the *Essay* is indeed quoted, but that Condillac's name is absent. As it stands, it is not possible to positively assert that the solipsists are meant to represent Condillac, nor that Diderot is proposing here an idealist interpretation of the *Essay on the Origin of Human Knowledge*. It is clear, however, that certain passages in Condillac's text can be used to provide arguments for the solipsist. Therein lies the difference between an idealist interpretation of Condillac and the use of Condillac for the purpose of constructing an idealist position. It is precisely insofar as the first paragraph of the *Essay* is treated in isolation from its context that it can be used as an argument for the solipsist; less so, however, if treated in connection with the other statements of Condillac's theory of knowledge. By using this strategy, Diderot treats the first paragraph of Condillac's text from the point of view of a philosopher with certain ambitions of his own rather than from the point of view of a historian of philosophy who aims to be faithful to the text.

Obviously, Diderot's decision to treat the first paragraph of the *Essay* in isolation from the rest of the text has decisive effects on the interpretation of Condillac's philosophy. Diderot's reconstruction is in fact very complex. While he does not seek to provide a commentary on Condillac's philosophy to demonstrate its idealism (in its solipsistic variant), he nevertheless shows that Condillac's statements, if treated as independent philosophical propositions, may imply solipsism. Diderot is in fact interested in what Condillac refused to develop, that is the ontological consequences of the first paragraph of the *Essay*. This is what one can call the tendencies of Condillac's philosophy: not the theses it explicitly defends but the theses it implicitly allows to build. By tendency, I do not

The Materialists and Condillac's Theory of Knowledge 15

mean that Diderot considers that in the *Essay* Condillac denies the existence of the external world, but rather that some of his statements may offer formulation and arguments in support of solipsism, when interpreted as ontological propositions. Isolating the first paragraph of the *Essay* allows one to draw out the idealist tendencies of Condillac's text, even when Condillac himself pretend not to treat ontological issues. This strategy aims at specifying a possible interpretation of Condillac's philosophy based on the exaggerated meaning of one of his statements.

b Comparing Condillac and Berkeley: I believe that seeing things in this way makes it easier to understand the famous passage in the *Letter on the Blind* where Diderot defines idealism by comparing Condillac and Berkeley, which is the second strategy he uses to read Condillac as an idealist:

Those philosophers, madam, are termed idealists who, conscious only of their own existence and of a succession of external sensations, do not admit anything else; an extravagant system which should to my thinking have been the offspring of blindness itself; and yet, to the disgrace of the human mind and philosophy, it is the most difficult to combat, though the most absurd. It is set forth with equal candour and lucidity by Doctor Berkeley, Bishop of Cloyne, in three dialogues. It were to be wished that the author of the *Essay on the Origin of Human Knowledge* would take this work into examination; he would find matter for useful, agreeable, and ingenious observation—for which, in a word, no person has a better talent. Idealism deserves an attack from his hand, and this hypothesis is a double incentive to him from its singularity, and much more from the difficulty of refuting it in accordance with his principles, which are the same as those of Berkeley. According to both, and according to reason, the terms essence, matter, substance, agent, etc., of themselves convey very little light to the mind. Moreover, as the author of the *Essay on the Origin of Human Knowledge* judiciously observes, whether we go up to the heavens, or down to the deeps, we never get beyond ourselves, and it is only our own thoughts that we perceive. And this is the conclusion of Berkeley's first dialogue, and the foundation of his entire system. Would you not be curious to see a trial of strength between two enemies whose weapons are so much alike?
(Diderot, 1916, pp. 104–105)

In the *Letter on the Blind*, as much as in all passages from the *Encyclopédie* that discuss solipsistic idealism, Berkeley is seen as the perfect representative of this position. If Condillac is summoned, it is insofar as his principles are the same as Berkeley's. For Diderot, the proposition that "we never get out of ourselves" is indeed the "foundation of Berkeley's entire system." Significantly, Diderot's comparison does not focus on Condillac's and Berkeley's entire philosophies but only concerns their foundational principles, particularly the propositions opening the first paragraph of the *Essay*. By building this connection between Condillac and Berkeley, Diderot informs us that Condillac's text shows the same tendency toward idealism as Berkeley's. This tendency is then revealed by comparing the isolated statements. This is the reason why the passage of the *Letter* appears much less affirmative than exhortative: it is in fact an invitation for Condillac to examine Berkeley's work so that he may denounce the idealism that his own text inadvertently advocates. Thus, Diderot does not treat idealism as an explicit thesis of Condillac's philosophy, but something his philosophy may imply, that is, as a thesis that can be constructed from the first paragraph of the *Essay*. In this way, Diderot falls short of identifying Condillac as an idealist, while showing how the *Essay* acts to support idealism.

c Building an ontological problem: The third operation I would like to mention, which is a consequence of the first two, is that Diderot uses Condillac's text to construct a specific philosophical problem that then needs to be answered. This is the problem of establishing the existence of the external world. Of course, Diderot is not the first to raise this issue, but he's the first to link so explicitly idealism with the question of the existence of the external world. How, one could ask, can we be sure of the existence of bodies outside ourselves if we only are aware of our own mental states? Solipsism is indeed a strong objection against the existence of the external world. But it provides at the same time a challenge that is all the more important to take up for materialist thinkers. Condillac's text is therefore not only the bearer of explicit theses or implicit tendencies, but also the resource for building a philosophical problem that stands on its own. In doing so, Diderot strongly modifies the scope of Condillac's statement. In his interpretation, the first paragraph of the *Essay* may imply that the external world does not *exist*. Whereas Condillac prudently affirms that we don't *know* anything about it. Diderot transforms an epistemological statement about what we are able to know into an ontological question about the existence of the external world.

Thus, in Diderot's hand, the first paragraph of the *Essay* is transformed: it no longer serves as the opening paragraph of Condillac's theory of knowledge but as a statement that represents an autonomous proposition, one that is susceptible to an idealist reading and allows for the construction of an ontological problem—is there anything outside what we perceive? Diderot's work should therefore not be seen as a commentary on Condillac but rather as an attempt to use his text to raise objections to which

The Materialists and Condillac's Theory of Knowledge 17

his own philosophy is supposed to be the answer. In this way, Diderot draws on Condillac's ideas for his own philosophical purposes, thus already revealing a style that he would later refer to as Eclecticism. Indeed, six years later, Diderot would define the eclectic philosopher as the one who "admit[s] nothing except on the testimony of his experience and his reason, and from all the philosophies which he has analyzed without deference or partiality, creates an individual and private philosophy which is his own" (Diderot, Denis, Jean Le Rond d'Alembert, and University of Michigan, 2002, 'Eclecticism').[3] Isolating Condillac's statement, comparing it with Berkeley, and drawing out from it an ontological problem are strategies Diderot uses to build his own philosophy.

This transformation of Condillac's text by Diderot has identifiable effects, particularly on the *Encyclopédie*, where the external world problem is discussed in a range of interrelated articles. It can be found, first of all, in an article by Diderot entitled "Pyrrhonic or skeptical philosophy." In the final paragraph of the article, he writes:

What shall I say to the one who claims that, whatever he sees, whatever he touches, whatever he hears, whatever he perceives, it is only his sensation that he perceives: that he could have been organized in such a way that everything happens within him, as it does, without there being anything outside, and that perhaps he is the only being which really is?

(Diderot, 1765, my translation)

Condillac is not cited in this passage, but there are two important elements worth noting. The first is the reference to empiricism as a way of arguing in favor of solipsism. The second is the use of a formulation that relies on the dichotomy between the inner mind and the inaccessible outer world. The occurrence of these elements is not an isolated phenomenon but rather constitutes commonplaces in the *Encyclopédie*. They are also part of articles produced by other contributors, such as the articles 'Evidence', written by Quesnay; 'Existence', by Turgot; 'Égoists' and 'Body', by D'Alembert; and even the *Preliminary Discourse*. All of these articles question the possibility of proving the existence of things outside the mind. When we look closely at the texts of these articles, we realize that Condillac's name almost never appears. However, the first paragraph of the *Essay on the Origin of Human Knowledge*, is reproduced in many formulations and arguments. For example, the article 'egoists' states that egoists are a "class of philosophers who recognize no other truth than that of their own existence, who believe that there is nothing outside us that is real, nor similar to our sensations; that bodies do not exist, etc." (D'Alembert, 1755). The problem the article 'Body' seeks to solve is posed in the following terms: "But how would reason show us the existence of *bodies* outside our mind?⁴" (D'Alembert, 1754) The most explicit statement in relation to this point can be found in the article 'Existence', which mentions idealists and solipsists ('égoïstes') while stating that only a few followers of this sect are known, before adding:

> It is Cloyne's famous bishop, Dr. Berkeley, known by a great number of works all full of wit and singular ideas, who, by his dialogues of Hylas and Philonous, has in recent times awakened the attention of Metaphysicians to this forgotten system.
> (Turgot, 1756)

Although the identity of the 'metaphysicians' in question remains vague, the formulation points to Condillac:

> Will we be not able to get out of ourselves and of this sort of prison, where nature keeps us locked up and isolated amid all beings? Will we have to be reduced with the idealists to admit no other reality than our own sensation?

As one can see, all these articles question the 'existence', the 'reality', and the 'being' of things outside the mind, not simply the possibility of knowing them. This is the consequence of Diderot's ontological interpretation of Condillac's statement.

Idealism and solipsism are not categories used in the *Encyclopédie* to specify Condillac's theory of knowledge; instead, we find Condillac's formulation when portraying the characteristic of idealism. This shows the importance of Diderot in the attempt to isolate the first paragraph from the rest of the *Essay* and to transform it into a textual resource for the idealist, thus giving way to objections, and a theoretical problem, that materialism was supposed to address. In this way Condillac's text was charged with a metaphysical problem. It received an importance that goes beyond the theses Condillac explicitly defends. This fact becomes evident when we place the text in the context of its publication and in relation to the questions it raises. These questions are all the more crucial for authors who claimed to be materialists.

I propose thereafter to examine to what extent materialists indeed replied to the problem Diderot built using Condillac's resources.

3   La Mettrie: Physiologizing Empiricism

The case of La Mettrie is remarkable because he is the first philosopher to claim materialism as his own position. In the opening of *Machine Man* (1748), La Mettrie divides the history of philosophy into two camps:

Materialists, who affirm the materiality of the soul, and Spiritualists, who defend the existence of an immaterial principle, the irreducible subject of thought. Here one may wonder in which camp La Mettrie places Condillac. The answer to this question is not simple.

A few of the claims formulated in La Mettrie's first philosophical work, *The Natural History of the Soul* (1745), directly compare with Condillac's statements. For example, in the sections devoted to sensation, La Mettrie states that sensations are the modifications of the sensitive soul and that "we certainly feel only modifications of ourselves" (La Mettrie, 1745, p. 161, my translation). In *Machine Man*, La Mettrie proposes his own genealogy of the operations of the mind. He treats all of them as modifications and refinements of the imagination. Thus, attention, reasoning, judgment, memory, etc., are all understood as successive transformations of the faculty of imagination: "I always use the word 'imagine' because I believe that everything is imagined and that all the parts of the soul can be properly reduced to imagination alone, which forms them all...." (La Metrtie, 1996, p. 14–15). Similarly, La Mettrie devotes a few pages of the text to the question of signs and their origin. This suggests that thematically speaking, *Machine Man* owes much to the *Essay on the Origin of Human Knowledge*, even though Condillac is not cited.

There is, however, a major difference between the two authors. Indeed, La Mettrie's genealogy of the operations of the mind aims at establishing the continuity between the physical impressions received by the body and the perceptions of the mind. For him, both count, to put it rigorously, as one and the same phenomenon. In this way, *The Natural History of the Soul*, after explaining the mechanism and laws of sensations, proceeds to materialize the soul. La Mettrie states:

> I can only see matter in the brain and only extension, as we have proved, in its sensitive part; when alive, healthy, well-organised, this organ contains at the source of the nerves an active principle spread throughout the medullary substance. I can see this principle, which feels and thinks, being disturbed, failing asleep and dying with the body.... If everything can be explained by what anatomy and physiology reveal to me in the medulla, what need have I to forge an ideal being?
> (La Mettrie, 1996, p. 66)

This is a typical example of the materialist (and clandestine) corpus of text of the eighteenth century, where the author denies the immateriality of the soul. However, in comparison with Condillac, we notice that the genealogy of the operations of the soul is no longer anchored, as in Condillac, to a metaphysics that focuses on the mind and its sensation. Instead, it is anchored to an 'Anatomy' and a 'Physiology' of the human body, of its organization and its tissues. Therefore, sensation does not have the status of an irreducible fact or principle, as in Condillac, because La Mettrie's genealogy examines how sensation is produced by the body. Through this move, the physiologization of sensation serves as a proof of the existence of things outside of thought because it presupposes the existence of the human body, as well as the existence of things causing the body's impressions: "These impressions of outside bodies constitute therefore the true physical cause of all our ideas" (La Mettrie, 1996, p. 63). Similarly, in *Machine Man*, La Mettrie does not content himself with the reduction of the operations of the mind to the functioning of the imagination; additionally, he claims that the workings of the imagination are the "wonderful and incomprehensible result of the organization of the brain" (La Mettrie, 1996, p. 15), which presupposes the existence of cerebral matter and requires the experimental investigation of human anatomy.

The theory of mind proposed by La Mettrie can thus be seen as pursuing the purpose of resolving ambiguities or divergent tendencies within Condillac's philosophy. In fact, there is a text in which La Mettrie mentions Condillac's *Essay*. It is called *Animals more than machines* published in 1750. It is a difficult text (not translated in English) since La Mettrie often takes the point of view of his spiritualist opponents by defending their thesis with the aim of revealing their contradictions. In this context, Condillac, like all representatives of empiricism, is identified as a materialist, whom La Mettrie also calls a 'machinist':

> Let all our learned Machinists tell us, by what mechanism I don't know, what feeling spring put into the substance, and composing it itself, remembers a voice heard only once twenty years ago! Finally, let St. Augustine be answered (I have the right to demand it) when he objects with Tralles and others, more solidly perhaps than those who have read Locke and Condillac can imagine.... [That] all our spiritual ideas do not derive from the senses in any way; but that our soul has the faculty of forming them itself'.... Chimeras therefore forever repudiated, forever relegated to the non-Christian Philosophers, all these traces, these vestiges, these impressions of the bodies in the Brain!
> (La Mettrie, 1751, pp. 16–17, my translation)

As representatives of empiricism, Locke and Condillac are here treated as 'machinists' in opposition to the spiritualists. La Mettrie confirms this interpretation a few pages later, declaring that the doctrine of the "originally clean slate" "leads to materialism." By renouncing any innate faculty, La Mettrie argues here that Condillac used a methodology that allowed him to get rid of the presupposition of spiritual beings whose origin remains principally incomprehensible. It is for this same reason that Auroux states that Condillac is the inventor of a new kind of materialism, which is not based on an explicit ontology. Condillac's materialism lies in the way he states not only the generation of ideas but also the generation of the mind's faculties. In doing so, Condillac does not presuppose any mysterious and immaterial being which would be the subject of knowledge: the mind must be seen as the result of its own history (Auroux, 1992).

Yet this link between empiricism and materialism that was first established is severed again a few pages later. While La Mettrie pretends to defend spiritualism once again, he states:

> No more disputes; I have found the stable point, from which I am going to depose the organs unjustly raised over the debris of the principle which animates them, and to dethrone forever the tyrant usurper of the Empire of the Soul; it is matter, to which it is time to make succeed Spirit.
> The whole domain of our vast understanding has just been reduced to a single principle by a *young philosopher* whom I place as much above Locke as the latter above Descartes, Malebranche, Leibniz, Wolff, etc. This principle is called Perception, and it arises from the sensation that takes place in the brain.
> It is a rather singular thing, that after having denied the propagation of the senses to the brain, I nevertheless admit what supposes it... we authors lose sight of our Principles, we grant what we have denied; we deny what we have granted...
> (La Mettrie, 1751, pp. 295–296, my emphasis, my translation)

This passage is admittedly very complex, since La Mettrie is playing with the reader in order to show the inconsistency of the position he pretends to defend. It seems more than likely to me that the young philosopher referred to is Condillac. I, therefore, propose to explain this passage as follows: by reducing the vast domain of the understanding to one single principle, that of perception and its transformation, Condillac provides the spiritualist with a weapon. He cuts his theory of sensation loose from all physiology, or at least treats bodily movements as occasions for, but not as the real cause of, the modifications of the soul. As a result, the *Essay on the Origin of Human Knowledge* appears to be compatible with the purest spiritualism.

To counter this impression, La Mettrie takes great pleasure in showing the possibility of reading Condillac's theory in a different way: for perception "is born of the sensation that takes place in the brain." For La Mettrie, it is clear that by adopting this cautious occasionalist position, Condillac embraced all the elements necessary for materialism, but then took a step back by distinguishing between perceptions and bodily movements. According to this interpretation, Condillac had all the elements ready at hand to demonstrate the material origin of thought. La Mettrie's genealogy of the operations of the mind thus becomes a means of adjudicating between the different tendencies embodied within the empiricist tradition. The aim here is to physiologize empiricism by showing that Condillac's theory is compatible with and even presupposes the idea that sensations are produced by bodily processes. By doing so, La Mettrie draws Condillac into the materialist camp as he cuts out the metaphysical questions Condillac has left unanswered.

In this analysis, La Mettrie applied the same principle of interpretation that he also employed in his engagement with other thinkers, such as Leibniz: he subverts Condillac's philosophy in such a way as to show that it can, by itself, serve the project of a materialist theory of knowledge. To decide in favor of a materialist interpretation of empiricism, it is enough, for example, to link the analyses of memory and imagination to observations that prove that brain tissue is required to make these operations possible. From this perspective, empiricism no longer appears to conceive of the subject of thought as trapped within the world of his representations. It rather reveals how a physiological process can lead to the transformation of relations between real bodies, so they give rise to impressions, sensations, perceptions, ideas, and signs.

4 Dom Deschamps: Metaphysics and Sensation

Léger-Marie Deschamps is a little-known and understudied author. His works were first published in French in 1993.[5] He was a Benedictine monk who constructed a rather complex metaphysics based on the idea that there is a totality of things, while denying the existence of God—at least if this existence is conceived in line with traditional religious and theological tenets. His main idea was to develop an approach to the human being that understands it in relation to the totality of the universe. He draws moral and political insights from this conception. In one of his most important texts, the *Observations Métaphysiques*, written before 1761, Deschamps devoted a few pages to the question of sensation.[6] This was an opportunity for him to set up a debate with Condillac. This debate concerns the origin of sensation, but it also involves more profound polemical writings on the definition and scope of metaphysics.

Indeed, in Condillac's work, metaphysics is given a new meaning. Already in the Introduction to the *Essay on the Origin of Human Knowledge*, Condillac distinguishes between two types of metaphysics. The first refers to classical metaphysics, whose traditional objects are "nature, the essence of beings, the most hidden causes." Metaphysics in the first sense is an illusion in so far as it claims to be concerned with the things themselves, without taking into account the faculties of the human subject that relate to these things (Condillac, 2001, p. 3). This position is strongly criticized by Condillac, who continues his attacks against this type of metaphysics in the *Treatise on systems* (1749). But Condillac does not entirely give up on metaphysics: if understood in its second and more accurate sense, metaphysics "proportion[s] its research to the weakness of the human mind," and takes the study of the mind as its object. From this point of view, the true metaphysician is Locke. Properly understood, Condillac's theory of knowledge, which takes sensation and its transformations as its first principle, is a form of metaphysics, and indeed the only legitimate one.

Deschamps focuses his discussion precisely on this point by asserting that a true understanding of sensory phenomena requires much more than metaphysics reduced to the domain of the human mind. For Deschamps, one cannot explain the transformations of sensation without reference to the universal totality of things. For example:

It is in The Whole, and as part of The Whole, that we must consider man to thoroughly reason about his mechanics, sensations, and faculty of knowledge to see that all this is only him physically understood, as his science is only him metaphysically understood.
(Deschamps, 1993, p. 380, my translation)

From the point of view of this totality, the human being is one part standing in relation to other parts, and sensation expresses this relationship in the human body. To elucidate the mechanism of sensation, Deschamps introduces the concept of incorporation: "Bodies are constantly incorporate more or less of each other, and it is this incorporation which, taking place in us, causes all the sensations we have of them" (Observation XI). He then immediately confronts these claims with the problem of the existence of the external world. Three times in the *Observations* he returns to this question. First, he states:

It is because we have ignored it [that the human body is constantly exchanging with other bodies], that we have considered the relation between our sensations and the objects which cause them as the greatest mystery. It is for the same reason that everything surprises us when we want to philosophize about ourselves. Indeed, it follows from this ignorance, or, what is the same, from what makes us distinguish our sensations from our body, that nothing is more of a phenomenon for us than ourselves.
(Deschamps, 1993, p. 382, note q, my translation)

In other words, idealist solipsism results when sensation is considered as a principle of thought, without seeing it in relation to the human body and other parts of the universe. A sensation is caused through an action of the bodies surrounding the human being, and it is then processed by the brain. These reflections show that, unlike La Mettrie, Deschamps addressed more directly the question of whether there are bodies outside the mind. This is a result of how the problem had been discussed in the *Encyclopédie* since the 1750s. The texts quoted earlier from La Mettrie had been written before the publication of the first volumes of the *Encyclopédie*, whereas Deschamps wrote the *Observations Métaphysiques* probably during their dissemination. Given the discussion the Encyclopédie initiated, solipsism is therefore a pressing problem for him to which an explicit answer had to be given:

> Through the false idea of believing us a *self*, in the sense that it seems to us that we exist, philosophers absurdly maintain that we are only certain of our existence and that bodies, which are indeed only phenomena, might not exist outside us. Had we been more enlightened, we would know that our body's existence necessarily depends on the existence of other bodies.
> (Deschamps, 1993, p. 385, note r, my translation)

According to Deschamps, a genealogy of the mind which takes sensation as its first principle is flawed by the fact that it isolates the human body from its real (material) relations. At the root of this mistake characterizing Condillac's philosophy lies an abstraction: namely the abstraction of the self from the infinite relations marking its existence in the world. The subject of sensation results from these relations and is not the first principle of philosophy. Deschamps denounces this abstraction and opposes it with a metaphysics of the totality of things which understand the human being as one of part of this totality. This is why one could say that Deschamps replaces one metaphysics with another. The first is the subjectivist metaphysics as defined by Condillac in the Introduction to the *Essay*, whose exclusive object of study is the human mind. But, for Deschamps, this metaphysics invites an impermissible abstraction, in the sense that the mind never exists in nature as an independent entity. When seeking to know what happens within us, we are required to immediately turn to the world outside of the human body, for if we confine ourselves to the purely subjective sphere, we cannot solve the problem of the origin of human knowledge: "We know what happens in us, without knowing how, and we have believed that to know this, and to do metaphysics on this topic, it was sufficient to observe man" (Observation XIII). This understanding of the human place in nature lies at the heart of the second type of metaphysics. By defending it, Deschamps attacks a subjectivist metaphysics and replaces it with a materialist metaphysics that focuses on the totality of things. Reiterating that metaphysics cannot be reduced to an anatomy of the faculties or operations of the soul, he states:

> Most of the observers of men's ideas, perceptions, and sensations have only given us words, believing that they were doing metaphysics. Hence the deplorable state of metaphysics today. The speculative anatomy of man, which has been done so much up to now, never taught anything.
> (Deschamps, 1993, p. 386, note u, my translation)

It is not that Deschamps thought the problem of solipsism unsolvable. But in order to respond to it, Deschamps thought it necessary to change our perspective and adopt a (true) metaphysics. One whose point of departure is not the inner world of the subject of thought, but the external relations that locate the mind within nature. Deschamps' approach thus leads us to a discussion about the methodological orientation of empiricism. He argues that sensation should no longer be considered as a basic explanatory principle but as the result of how external relations affect the mind, which turns sensation from an original into a derived phenomenon.

5 Conclusion

Condillac was an important interlocutor among advocates of an emerging materialism in the late 1740s and 1750s. In his *Essay on the Origin of Human Knowledge* they found resources suitable for the construction of a specific philosophical problem and a fictitious adversary in the persona of the solipsist. It is remarkable, however, that neither Diderot nor La Mettrie explicitly identified Condillac as an idealist, but only pointed to the idealist consequences to which his philosophy gave rise, what I called its tendencies.

Here is my alternative: one of the benefits of engaging with the materialist reception of Condillac is that it brings to light two ostensibly conflicting tendencies in his philosophy. By questioning the ontological presuppositions of Condillac's philosophy, Diderot, La Mettrie, and Deschamps reveal the possibility of interpreting it in opposite ways. It results from the paradoxical consequence of focusing metaphysics on the analysis of the subject of thought and its sensations while professing caution concerning claims of that which lies outside the mind: due to these factors, Condillac's philosophy is susceptible to the various metaphysical interpretations between which he refused to decide.

The preceding discussion thus offers an instructive example of considerations that touch on the relationships between empiricism and materialism. As we have seen, Diderot, La Mettrie, and Deschamps all agree that a theory of mind that takes sensation as its first principle, from which the formation of ideas and the operations of the mind are derived, tends to negate the existence of a world outside of thought. This thesis may seem radical and absurd, and it may be objected that no one in the history of philosophy has ever really defended it, but its reconstruction allows us to identify various ways of interpreting empiricism. Thus, all three argued that, by using a genealogy of the mind that takes sensation as its first principle, Condillac methodologically isolated the mind from its surroundings, whether it be by detaching it from its own body, that is, the locus where its sensation arises, or from other bodies to which the human mind always relates with its perceptual engagements. Through this move, Condillac invited idealists to make use of his theory of knowledge for their very own purposes. To correct what they deemed an abuse of empiricist principles and the idealist consequences to which this abuse gave rise, La Mettrie and Deschamps reattached the mind to the human body and re-located it in the midst of other material entities, thus giving back to it its proper place.

Notes

1 See J. Deprun (1984).
2 This is the expression used by I. Thomas-Fogiel (2017).
3 Diderot, "Eclecticism" *The Encyclopedia of Diderot & d'Alembert Collaborative Translation Project*. Translated by Malcolm Eden and Philip Stewart. Ann Arbor: Michigan Publishing, University of Michigan Library, 2021. Web. [18 January 2023]. http://hdl.handle.net/2027/spo.did2222.0000.843.
4 "Body" *The Encyclopedia of Diderot & d'Alembert Collaborative Translation Project*. Translated by Philip Stewart. Ann Arbor: Michigan Publishing, University of Michigan Library, 2021. Web. [25 January 2023]. http://hdl.handle.net/2027/spo.did2222.0004.246. Trans. of "Corps," *Encyclopédie ou Dictionnaire raisonné des sciences, des arts et des métiers*, vol. 4. Paris, 1754.
5 Passages cited here will be taken from this edition and will use my own translation (there's no English translation).
6 We do not have a more precise date.

References

Auroux, Sylvain (1992). Condillac inventeur d'un nouveau matérialisme. *Dix-Huitième Siècle [Le matérialisme des Lumières]*, vol.24, pp.153–163.
Baertsch, Bernard (1988). Le problème du réalisme chez Condillac. *Les Études philosophiques*, vol.3, pp.371–393.
Bloch, Olivier (1997). Oublier le matérialisme. *Matière à Histoires*, Paris: Vrin, pp. 349–360.
Condillac, Etienne Bonnot de (2001). *Essay on the Origin of Human Knowledge*, translated by Hans Aarsleff, Cambridge: Cambridge University Press.

The Materialists and Condillac's Theory of Knowledge 27

Coski, Christopher (2004). Condillac's Metaphysical Paradox: The Nature of the Soul, versus the Natural Origin of Language and Reason. *Dalhousie French Studies*, vol.67, pp.3–15.
Deprun, Jean (1984). Diderot devant l'idéalisme. *Revue internationale de Philosophie*, vol.38, n.148/149 (1/2) Diderot et l'encyclopédie (1784–1984), pp.67–78.
Deschamps, Marie-Léger (1993). *Œuvres philosophiques*, Paris: Librairie philosophique J. Vrin.
Diderot, Denis (1916). *Diderot's Early Philosophical Works*, translated by Margaret Jourdain, Chicago, IL and London: The Open Court Publishing Company.
Diderot, Denis (1975–...). *Œuvres complètes* [J. Fabre, H. Dieckmann, J. Proust, J. Varloot], Paris: Hermann.
Diderot, Denis et al., (1751–1772). *Encyclopédie, ou dictionnaire raisonné des sciences et des arts, et des métiers*, 17 vol. and 11 vol. suppl., Paris and Neufchâtel.
Diderot, Denis, Jean Le Rond d'Alembert, and University of Michigan (2002). *The Encyclopedia of Diderot and D'alembert: Collaborative Translation Project*. Ann Arbor: Scholarly Pub. Office of the University of Michigan. http://www.hti.umich.edu/d/did/.
La Mettrie, Julien Offray de (1745). *Histoire naturelle de l'âme*, La Haye: chez Jean Neaulme Libraire.
La Mettrie, Julien Offray de (1750). *Les animaux plus que machine* [no other indications].
La Mettrie, Julien Offray de (1751). *Œuvres philosophiques*, À Londres: chez Jean Nourse.
La Mettrie, Julien Offray de (1996). *Machine Man and Other Writings*, edited and translated by Ann Thomson, Cambridge: Cambridge University Press.
Ricken, Ulrich (1999). Condillac et le soupçon de matérialisme. *Être matérialiste à l'âge des Lumières* (B. Fink et al.), Paris: Presses Universitaires de France, pp.265–274.
Thomas-Fogiel, Isabelle (2017). L'opposition entre réalisme et idéalisme? Genèse et structure d'un contresens. *Revue de métaphysique et de morale*, PUF, vol.95, pp.393–426.

3 Condillac and the Molyneux Problem

Peter R. Anstey

1 Introduction

Etienne Condillac changed his mind. In the *Essay on the Origin of Human Knowledge* (hereafter *Essai*) of 1746, he opposed John Locke and George Berkeley's answer to the Molyneux Problem: where they answered "No," he answered "Yes." Then eight years later, in the *Treatise on Sensations* (hereafter *Treatise*), he reversed his position and, in effect, sided with Locke and Berkeley with a definitive "No." Now, sometimes a *volte face* by a leading philosopher is of little consequence, but in this case Condillac's change of mind reflected a deep subterranean shift in his philosophy of perception. So profound was this shift and so self-conscious was he of it that in the prefatory plan (*Dessein*) of the *Treatise* Condillac gestured at an explanation of his change of view: he attributed the change in large part to the influence of the late Mademoiselle Ferrand.[1] Whatever the sources of influence on his new position, our concern here is with the content of those changes. What was it in Condillac's revised philosophy of perception that led him to radically change his position on the Molyneux Problem? Before answering this question, however, it is worthwhile setting Condillac's responses to the Molyneux Problem in the broader context of the French reception of the problem in the years leading up to the publication of the *Essai* in 1746 and *Treatise* in 1754.[2]

2 The Early Reception of the Molyneux Problem in France

In 1688, the Irish natural philosopher William Molyneux, whose wife was blind, was stimulated on reading the "Extrait" of Locke's (yet to be published) *An Essay concerning Human Understanding* to write to Locke and to pose an early version of the eponymous Molyneux Problem to him.[3] Five years later, after they had established a friendship, Molyneux put a fuller question to Locke in correspondence and Locke realized that he could use this thought experiment to illustrate his claim in

DOI: 10.4324/9781003334750-4

Book Two of the *Essay* that in the case of vision alone, the understanding engages in a form of unconscious inference.[4] So, Locke inserted Molyneux's question in the text of the second edition of the *Essay*:

> Suppose a Man born blind, and now adult, and taught by his touch to distinguish between a Cube, and a Sphere of the same metal, and nighly of the same bigness, so as to tell, when he felt one and t'other, which is the Cube, which the Sphere. Suppose then the Cube and Sphere placed on a Table, and the Blind Man to be made to see. Quaere, Whether by his sight, before he touch'd them, he could now distinguish, and tell, which is the Globe, which the Cube.
>
> (Locke, *Essay* II. ix. 8)

This insertion, together with Locke's short response to the question, breaks up the flow of the discussion of unconscious inference. It is hardly surprising then, given its intrinsic interest, that Locke's treatment of the Molyneux Problem is often taken out of context and discussed in its own right, rather than as an illustration of unconscious inference in Locke's broader theory of perception.

Berkeley also introduces the Molyneux Problem in the context of the exposition of a theory of visual perception. In *An Essay towards a New Theory of Vision*, first published in 1709, Berkeley brought out a key premise that was only implicit in Locke, namely, that the ideas of shapes acquired by touch are completely heterogeneous to those acquired by sight.[5] And while there are further differences between Locke and Berkeley, both of them treat the Molyneux Problem merely as a thought experiment and answer it negatively.[6]

It was not until 1728 that the first significant empirical observations to bear on the Problem emerged. The physician William Cheselden, in an article published in the *Philosophical Transactions*, related the observations of a young teenage boy who had had his cataracts removed in a series of successful operations performed by Cheselden himself.[7] Cheselden's article does not mention the Molyneux Problem, and yet the observations seemed to many to be of direct relevance and to confirm the negative answers of Locke and Molyneux. Thus, we see the Molyneux Problem beginning its long journey of transition from a pure thought experiment to an empirically tractable problem to be solved by the natural sciences.

The first to mention the Cheselden experiments in the context of a discussion of the Molyneux Problem appears to have been James Jurin who contributed an essay on the Molyneux Problem to the second volume of Robert Smith's *A Compleat System of Opticks in Four Books* published in 1738.[8] Jurin disagrees with Molyneux, Locke, and Berkeley, giving an affirmative answer to the Problem on the assumption that the newly sighted man knows in advance that what he will see will be a sphere and a cube. Two points are relevant here concerning Jurin's foray into the debate. First, he is also the first person to introduce the blind Cambridge mathematician Nicholas Saunderson into the Molyneux Problem discussion. Saunderson, as is well known, later became the central figure in Diderot's treatment of the Problem in his *Letter on the Blind for the Use of Those Who Can See*.[9] In addition to his essay on the Molyneux Problem, Jurin contributed a longer piece to Smith's textbook entitled "An essay upon distinct and indistinct vision."[10] This essay was subsequently attacked by the mathematician Benjamin Robins and in 1739 Jurin published a rejoinder.[11] And this brings us to the second relevant piece of background information, namely, that from the late 1730s Jurin corresponded with Voltaire about the theory of vision. Thus, probably in 1739, Voltaire sent Jurin his *Elements of the Philosophy of Newton* (1738), which contained a discussion of the Cheselden experiments and the Molyneux Problem, and Jurin responded by forwarding Voltaire a copy of his recent rejoinder to Robins.[12] And while we don't have evidence that they actually discussed the Molyneux Problem, this is an important Anglo-French connection in the background to Condillac's treatment of the Problem.

What then of the continental response to the Molyneux Problem? Locke's *Essay* was widely available on the Continent through Pierre Coste's translation of 1700 and subsequent editions;[13] Berkeley's *New Theory of Vision* was translated into French in 1734 in a version based on the 1732 edition which was appended to Berkeley's *Alciphron*.[14] The first francophone writer to publish on the Problem appears to have been the Dutchman David Bouiller, who in the second edition of his *Philosophical Essay on the Souls of Beasts* (1737) disagreed with Locke,[15] giving an affirmative answer to the Problem and denying Locke's implicit heterogeneity thesis: "the visual idea of the globe, for example, and the tactile idea of the globe are essentially the same idea" (Bouiller 1737, p. 120).[16] Bouiller, however, does not mention the Cheselden observations.

The first mention of Cheselden's cataract operations in French appears in Voltaire's *Elements of the Philosophy of Newton*, published the following year in 1738. Voltaire gives a summary of Cheselden's article and goes on to claim that the observations confirm Locke and Berkeley's answer to the Molyneux Problem. Voltaire's text proved to be the major, though not the only, conduit for knowledge of the Cheselden observations in France. Thus, in 1745, La Mettrie appended a discussion of the Cheselden observations, deriving from Voltaire's discussion, to his *Natural History of the Soul*. La Mettrie uses the Cheselden observations as reported by Voltaire to discuss Locke and the Molyneux problem.[17] One year later Condillac also used Voltaire's *Elements of the Philosophy of Newton* in his discussion of the Molyneux Problem in the *Essai*, quoting it extensively.[18] It is not certain whether Condillac had read either Bouiller's or La Mettrie's discussion of the Molyneux Problem,[19] though he had read Locke's and Berkeley's discussions very closely.

Finally, three years after the publication of Condillac's *Essai* Diderot's *Letter on the Blind for the Use of Those Who Can See* appeared, and it contains a very long discussion of the Molyneux Problem, including a detailed summary of Condillac's treatment of the Problem in the *Essai*.[20] Diderot's work, in turn, was cited in the very same year in the third volume of Comte de Buffon's *Natural History*, in the chapter on the sense of vision. And while Buffon does not mention the Molyneux Problem, he does cite Jurin's second essay on distinct and indistinct vision and Smith's *Opticks*.[21] Thus, by 1749, the Molyneux Problem and the associated empirical evidence supplied by Cheselden had been cited or discussed in works by Voltaire, La Mettrie, Condillac, Diderot, and Buffon. With this background in mind, it is time to turn to Condillac's first pass on the Problem.

3   Condillac's *Essai* and the Molyneux Problem

The Condillac of the *Essai* and especially the *Treatise on Systems* agreed with Locke and Berkeley that there are no innate ideas.[22] So, in answering Molyneux's Problem, one cannot appeal to pre-existing ideas of shapes. Condillac also agreed with his British counterparts that we do not have immediate epistemic access to external objects but only to ideas; he was committed to the veil of perception in both the *Essai* and the *Treatise*.[23] Where he differed from Locke and Berkeley in the *Essai* is that he denied that visual perception is naturally two-dimensional; he followed common sense and claimed that it is three-dimensional.

According to Locke, "[w]hen we set before our Eyes a round Globe, of any uniform colour ... 'tis certain, that the *Idea* thereby imprinted in our Mind, is of a flat Circle variously shadow'd" (*Essay* II. ix. 8). How is it then that we perceive the globe as a three-dimensional object? In order to explain the phenomenology of visual perception in this case, Locke appealed to unconscious inference. He admitted that in the particular case of vision, there are such inferences: "the *Ideas we receive by sensation, are often* in grown People, *alter'd by the Judgment*, without our taking notice of it" (*Essay* II. ix. 8). And although Locke is not explicit about it, his report of Molyneux's response to the Problem implies that these unconscious inferences involve correlating tactile with visual sensations: "though he has obtain'd the experience of, how a Globe, how a Cube affects his touch; yet he has not yet attained the Experience, that what affects his touch so or so, must affect his sight so or so" (*Essay* II. ix. 8; Locke is approvingly quoting Molyneux).

Condillac, for his part, would have none of this. First, he denied that there is such a thing as unconscious inference on the grounds that Locke is, in effect, appealing to a black box.[24] Secondly, he denied Berkeley's heterogeneity thesis, namely, the claim that the ideas of shape acquired by the sense of touch differ from those acquired by vision. Berkeley had argued:

> *The Extension, Figures, and Motions perceiv'd by Sight are specifically Distinct from the* Ideas *of Touch, called by the same Names, nor is there any such thing as one* Idea, *or kind of* Idea *common to both Senses.*
> (Berkeley 1709, §127, pp. 150–151)

Condillac countered in the *Essai*:

> If I see or touch a circle or a rule, the idea of the first can never represent anything other than a curved line and the second that of a straight line. This man born blind will thus distinguish the globe from the cube on sight, because he will recognize in them the same ideas which he has formed by touch.
> (*Essai*, p. 107)[25]

Third, and more important, however, Condillac brings a powerful empirical consideration against the Locke/Berkeley view that visual perception is naturally two-dimensional:

> When I see a bas-relief, I know, without any doubt, that it is painted on a flat surface; I have touched it, and yet this knowledge, repeated experience, and all the judgments I can make do not prevent me from seeing convex figures.
> (*Essai*, p. 103)

This is, actually, a rather beautiful argument. Condillac's point is that if, as Locke and Berkeley would have us believe, touch enables us to see three-dimensionally, how is it that touch is unable to cause us to see a two-dimensional object two-dimensionally? Why cannot touch correct vision's tendency to perceive three-dimensionally in this case, especially given that visual perception is "naturally" two-dimensional?

As for the evidence from the Cheselden operations, Condillac acknowledges that he needs to give an explanation of the reason why it took the boy so long to be able to identify shapes. After quoting Voltaire's summary of the Cheselden report,[26] Condillac gives a physiological explanation of the long delay in the patient's ability to identify shapes. The untrained cornea "was too much or too little convex in relation to the situation of the other parts," and because "the crystalline lens had become immobile, it always reunited the light rays either short of or beyond the retina" and never at the optimal spot; having become stiff over time, "it took many days of exercise to make the springs act in harmony" (*Essai*, p. 110). As for the supporters of Locke and Berkeley, such as Voltaire, they allowed (what we now call) confirmation bias to influence the interpretation of the Cheselden report: "it did not occur to them that reasons could be advanced other than those Locke and Berkeley had imagined" (*Essai*, p. 110).

Yet the bas-relief argument and the major premise it was defending—that vision is naturally three-dimensional—were to be abandoned in the *Treatise on Sensations*[27] (see below), for there Condillac agrees with Locke and Berkeley that visual perception is naturally two-dimensional, and that we do need to correlate the sense modality of touch in order to acquire depth perception in vision. For the Condillac of the *Treatise*, the answer to the Molyneux Problem is "No." What changed and when did this change come about?

Laurence Bongie argued back in 1978 that Condillac had abandoned the position of the *Essai* as early as 1747.[28] In a memorandum to the Genevan mathematician Gabriel Cramer datable to 1747, Condillac claims with regard to the Molyneux Problem, "Locke, Berkeley and I, all three, are wrong" (Condillac 1953, p. 107). Interestingly, possibly around this time, Condillac interviewed a person who was born blind, for he mentions the conversation in *Les monades*.[29] Clearly then, the Molyneux Problem and the epistemology of blindness remained matters for reflection in the years immediately following the publication of the *Essai*, long before the appearance of the *Treatise on Sensations*.

4 Condillac's *Treatise* and the Molyneux Problem

So, what changed for Condillac? In order to answer this question, I want to focus on three features of the content of the theory of perception developed in the *Treatise*. First, however, it is crucial that we get clear on the place of the Molyneux Problem in the work as a whole. When approaching the *Treatise* it is important to appreciate that the Molyneux Problem is not an issue that is confined to a particular section of the work, an issue that is dealt with *en passant* as Condillac sets out his new theory of sense perception through the literary conceit of an "in-sensed" human-shaped statue. Rather, the Molyneux Problem is part of the *problematique* of the whole book; it is a major contributor to the nature and structure of the theory that gradually unfolds as the statue acquires one sense after another. We get an inkling of this in the "Extrait raisonnée" (a précis of the *Essai*) which was published a year later in 1755 in his *Treatise on Animals*, in which Condillac credits Molyneux with disabusing Locke about unconscious inference at least in the case of vision, a clear allusion to the discussion of the Molyneux Problem in *Essay* II. ix. 8.[30] Turning to the *Treatise*, the Molyneux Problem is alluded to in the second paragraph of the book in the description of the plan of the work.[31] The Molyneux Problem is alluded to again in Part II, Chapter 11, where Molyneux is credited as the first one to raise the issue of the relation between touch and vision.[32] And we should also note that Condillac devotes two chapters to William Cheselden's cataract operations in Part III of the *Treatise* and mentions them in the "Extrait raisonnée."[33] Moreover, the perception of spheres and cubes features in a variety of places within the work.[34] To be sure, there is an explicit focus on the Problem itself in Part III, Chapter 4;[35] however, in some sense the Molyneux Problem is the driver for the whole of Part III on the relation between touch and vision. And in broader terms, Condillac's goal in the *Treatise* is to show how the sense of touch is correlated with the other senses in order to bring about knowledge of the nature of external objects, including the perception of three-dimensional shapes such as cubes and spheres. In short, while the Molyneux Problem is not the central focus of the *Treatise*, it is in the warp and weft of the whole project. Let us now turn to the new theory of sensory perception in the *Treatise*.

4.1 Touch, Solidity, and the Discovery of External Objects

In the *Treatise* Condillac uses the analysis of each sense the statue acquires to establish his view that "our senses by themselves give us no knowledge of external objects" (*Treatise*, p. 161); smell, hearing, and sight "give no idea of external objects" (*Treatise*, p. 162). In fact, Condillac goes so far as to claim with regard, say, to the sense of smell, initially the statue "believes himself to be and he can only believe himself to be the odors themselves" (*Treatise*, p. 162). How, then, do we come to acquire beliefs in external objects and realize that we can sense their qualities? His answer is, famously, that this is achieved via the sense of touch. First, it is the sense of touch that gives us knowledge of external objects (*Treatise*, p. 164), then touch "teaches" the other senses that they are perceiving objects that exist independently of them (*Treatise*, p. 165).

How does this happen? Through the sensation of solidity. By pressing one part of our body on another, we perceive that each part resists the other and that there are two parts to the body. Furthermore, "placing its hands on itself, the statue will only discover that it has a body when it distinguishes the different parts of that body and when it recognizes itself in each part to be the same sentient being" (*Treatise*, p. 233).

Touch gives rise to the experience of solidity which is both a sensation and an idea. When part of the body presses against another body and not part of itself, it leads us to believe in the existence of external objects. As Condillac puts it, the essence of this sensation of solidity is to represent at one and the same moment two things that exclude each other, ... it will perceive [solidity] as a state in which it finds two things that are mutually exclusive and as a result it will perceive it in these two things.

(*Treatise*, p. 233)

This is why solidity is both a sensation and an idea: it represents two objects excluding each other from the same space. There is no analogue of this with the sensations derived from the other senses.

It remains then to explain how the sense of touch teaches the other senses that the causes of their sensations are external objects. This is the subject of Part III, namely, "How touch teaches the other senses to judge external objects." We turn then to Part III, chapter 1, that deals with the sense of smell.

4.2 Touch and Smell

Once the statue has knowledge of its own body and that other objects exist independently of its body, the resources are in place for the instruction of the remaining senses. *Treatise* III. 1. 4 tells us:

The statue begins to suspect that odors come from bodies. Putting its hand, by chance, on the objects that it encounters, the statue grasps a flower which remains in its hand. It moves its arm aimlessly, now towards its face, now away: ... it repeats this experiment by design ... The statue confirms that it is in, or ceases to be in, a certain state, depending on whether it brings the flower close or holds it at a distance. Finally, it begins to suspect that the change of state is due to the flower.

(*Treatise*, pp. 267–268)

Just as the sensation of solidity allowed the statue to establish that other bodies exist, so the movement of the source of the smell to and from the nose allows the inference that the statue is not an odor but rather the flower that causes the odorous sensation. However, there is a crucial feature of the thought experiment that is not made explicit. Note the underlined clause "depending on whether it brings the flower close or holds it at a distance." How does the statue know that the hand is closer to or further from the nose? The answer seems obvious to us: through the sense of proprioception. Recall that at this point the statue lacks vision and, *ex hypothesi*, it does not yet have spatial awareness relative to the sense of smell. How then does it know that the hand holding the flower is distant? The answer must be through proprioception.

36   Peter R. Anstey

The final stage in the development of the statue's olfactory sense requires more experimentation until eventually "[t]he statue does not confine itself any longer to judging the odor as being in the flower, it senses it to be there" (p. 268). The culmination of the developmental process in the olfactory sense facilitated by touch is the attribution of a mind-independent quality of smell to the external object.

4.3   Touch, Vision, and Proprioception

An analogous account is given of how touch teaches vision to perceive depth. In the *Treatise*, Condillac adopts a central Berkelean claim that he had rejected in the *Essai*, namely, that the eye only perceives the very endpoint of rays of light and is not even aware that there are rays of light let alone their angles of incidence: "rays are to the eyes what these sticks were to its hands,"[36] it only perceives one end. So, the eyes need to be taught by the sense of touch.

> Either by chance or because of the pain caused by a light that is too bright, the statue puts its hand on its eyes: in that instant, colors disappear. It removes its hand and the colors are renewed. Thereafter, it ceases to consider colors to be its own states.
> (*Treatise* III. 3. 3, p. 275)

Very soon it begins to attribute colors to external objects. What about distance vision?

> Through curiosity or restlessness the statue places its hand in front of its eyes; it removes its hand and places it there again; and the surface that it sees is, as a result, more brightly lit or less so. From this it judges that the movement of its hand is the cause of these changes and, as <u>it knows that it moves it at a certain distance,</u> it suspects that this surface is not as close as it had thought.
> (*Treatise* III. 3. 7, p. 277)

"How," we might ask, does it know "that it moves it [the hand] at a certain distance"? Recall that this is the explanation of depth perception in vision, so the eye will be of no assistance here in explaining how the statue knows the distance moved. Again, we can see with hindsight that the answer is "because of proprioception."

Once we see the implicit role of proprioception in Condillac's thinking, we find it all over the place. Take for example *Treatise* III. 3. 10: "[i]n leading its hand successively from its eyes to the objects and conversely,

Condillac and the Molyneux Problem 37

the statue measures distances" (p. 278). Here, of course, it is not simply the proprioceptive knowledge of the location of the hand relative to the arm and shoulder, but also the proprioceptive knowledge of the location of the eyes.

Thus, Condillac's own explanations of the means by which touch teaches the other sense modalities contain an important explanatory gap, the sense of proprioception. It is only when this is added to his explanations that they start to become at all plausible. Should this observation be ruled out of court on the grounds of gross anachronism? Perhaps. However, it does provide an interesting case of the application of concepts from the contemporary psychology of perception to shed light on an early modern theory. Condillac and his generation lacked any understanding of the mechanisms humans have evolved to have to enable distance vision: stereopsis, motion parallax, vergence, perspective, and flicker. To be sure, there are hints in both Locke and Condillac that shading and reflection play a role in distance vision,[37] though these are not experimentally explored. Thus, given his scarce explanatory resources, it may be that Condillac's explanations are commendable for their time.

5 From Homogeneity to Heterogeneity?

According to Condillac, many assume that when we see, we have all the ideas that our sensations contain. But "we do not form ideas as soon as we see; we form ideas only insofar as we look in an orderly way" (*Treatise* III. 3. 6, p. 276). Our eyes must analyze, they need to move beyond merely "seeing" (*voir*) to begin to "look" (*regarder*).[38] This analysis by our eyes needs to follow an order: "to have an idea of the shape of that object... they must know how to direct themselves towards each of its parts, successively and in the order that they have among themselves" (*Treatise* III. 3. 6, p. 276).

Condillac's point can be nicely illustrated with a standard color-blind test. The red and green color-blind person cannot see the red numerals or shapes in the scattered green dots. However, after they are pointed out, they seem all too obvious. By analogy then, we are all initially "shape-blind"; we see only the plane surface variously speckled. It is only as we come to look with the aid of the sense of touch that we are able to perceive shapes.

Interestingly, however, Condillac does not endorse a radical Berkeley-style heterogeneity thesis. He now believes that the ideas produced by touch and vision are working together, and that after a complex array of sensory experiences involving both senses, even if tactile sensations are not present, the same ideas will appear. Here is how he puts it in Part III, Chapter 9:

We have proven that judgments link ideas of space, size, and shape to sensations of light and color. At first these judgments are occasioned by objects that act at the same time on vision and on touch; subsequently, they become so familiar that the statue repeats them even when the object makes an impression only on the eyes; and it forms the same ideas as if vision and touch continued to judge these objects together.

(*Treatise* III. 9. 1, p. 300)

So, rather than abandoning the homogeneity thesis, Condillac provides a far more sophisticated account in terms of homogeneity.

6 The Molyneux Problem and the Perception of Relief

We saw above that Condillac was not loath to bring empirical considerations to bear on the question of depth perception in vision. So, what of the powerful bas-relief argument from the *Essai*? How does he deal with that in the revamped treatment of the Molyneux Problem in the *Treatise*? This brings us to the final section of this chapter' on the *Treatise*'s treatment of the bas-relief argument.

Condillac addresses the question of the perception of relief in *Treatise* III, Chapter 3. Here the *volte face* is striking: "[t]he first time that it casts its gaze on a sphere, the impression that it receives represents only a flat circle mixed with shade and light" (*Treatise* III. 3. 11, p. 278). However, when it touches the object, "it learns to make the same judgments with vision that it made with touch, the object takes on in its eyes the relief that it has in its hands" (*Treatise*, p. 278). The statue then tries to judge the shape of another sphere: "[i]n the beginning no doubt it finds itself in some difficulty but touch removes the uncertainty" (*Treatise*, p. 278). It now begins to correlate different patterns of light and shade on the surface of the sphere with the tactile sensations of the three-dimensional object. This soon becomes habitual and

> so rapidly and confidently does it make this judgment and so thoroughly does it link the idea of this shape to a surface where light and shade are in a certain proportion, that finally it only sees each time what it said to itself so often it ought to see [that is, a sphere].
>
> (*Treatise*, p. 278)

Then, in paragraph 25, Condillac deals with the argument from the bas-relief. The paragraph is entitled, "Vision will contradict touch."

> For example, its eyes see convexity in a painted relief where its hand perceives only a flat surface. No doubt astonished by this new phenomenon, the statue does not know which of its two senses to believe: touch

detects the error in vain, since the eyes are accustomed to judging by themselves and no longer consult their teacher. Having learned from touch to see in one way, they can no longer learn to see differently.
(*Treatise* III. 3. 25, p. 283)

According to Condillac, through habituation, the perception of convexity in certain conditions of shade and light has become natural and irresistible. He then extends the bas-relief thought experiment:

If one arranged things so that among the objects that our statue would have occasion to touch, there were as many painted reliefs on flat surfaces as truly convex objects, the statue would have considerable difficulty in distinguishing by sight those that have convexity from those that do not. It would be mistaken so often that it would not dare to rely on its eyes; it would only believe touch thereafter.
(*Treatise*, p. 283)

To drive the point home, Condillac provides another thought experiment. When looking in a mirror the statue would see a great space beyond its reflection and would be astonished if it moved toward it only "to be stopped by a solid body" (*Treatise*, p. 283).

So there we have it: the bas-relief thought experiment is reinterpreted in the light of the new theory of sensory perception and the *volte face* is complete. Of course, Locke's general position still comes in for some critique: Condillac is not an uncritical Lockean acolyte.[39] But Condillac can now be grouped with Locke and Berkeley in their responses to the Molyneux Problem. The theory of perception in the *Treatise* completely and self-consciously supersedes that of the earlier *Essai*.

7   Afterword

While Condillac's views on the Molyneux Problem underwent no further changes, the story of the Problem in eighteenth-century optics did not end there. For in 1765 Leibniz's *New Essays on Human Understanding* was published and it contains a sustained discussion of the Problem and critique of Locke's position.[40] Then, in 1767, the most important optical textbook in eighteenth-century Europe was published. This was none other than a French translation of Robert Smith's *A Compleat System of Opticks* with considerable additions. Interestingly, some of those additions include the very lengthy notes on the Molyneux Problem and it is there that the writings of three philosophers are discussed: first, Jurin's original essay on the Molyneux Problem, now relegated from the main text to the notes; second, Diderot's *Letter on the Blind*; and third, Condillac's *Treatise on Sensations* which receives far and away the most attention.[41] Thus, Condillac's

40   Peter R. Anstey

revised position on the Problem in the *Treatise* was to receive a far wider circulation than he could ever have expected and the position of the *Essai* was completely superseded.

Notes

1 *Treatise*, in Condillac 1982, 1, p. 170 (all subsequent references to the *Treatise* are to the Philip translation in volume 1 of Condillac 1982). See also Condillac's "Memoire" to Gabriel Cramer, Condillac 1953, pp. 107–108.
2 The best and most thorough treatment of the Molyneux Problem in eighteenth-century France is Chottin 2014.
3 On July 7, 1688, Molyneux actually wrote to "the authors of the *Bibliothèque universelle*" where Locke's "Extrait" appeared, perhaps not knowing that Locke was the author. See Locke 1976–1989, 3, pp. 482–483.
4 Molyneux to Locke, March 2, 1693, Locke 1976–1989, 4, p. 651.
5 See Berkeley 1709, §127, pp. 150–151. See also Greene 1712, pp. 16–17.
6 This is not to say that Locke never utilized new discoveries relating to visual perception. He uses Mariotte's recent discovery of the blind spot against Malebranche's doctrine of the vision in God. See Locke 1823, p. 216.
7 Cheselden 1728.
8 Jurin 1738a. Jurin actually wrote the essay on the Molyneux Problem in 1733; see Robert Smith to Jurin October 18, 1733, Jurin 1996, p. 406.
9 See Jurin 1738a, p. 29; Diderot 2011, pp. 205–219. For Diderot and Saunderson, see Tunstall 2011, pp. 41–46, though Tunstall does not mention Jurin's precedent in associating Saunderson with the Molyneux Problem.
10 Jurin 1738b.
11 Jurin 1739.
12 See Jurin to Voltaire, February 1, 1740 and Voltaire to Jurin, 1741, in Jurin 2011, pp. 422–423 and 431.
13 Locke 1700, 2nd edition 1729.
14 Berkeley 1734 translated from Berkeley 1732.
15 Bouiller does not mention Berkeley's treatment of the Molyneux Problem; see Bouiller 1737, pp. 119–126.
16 See Degenaar 1996, pp. 46–48. Degenaar wrongly assumes that Bouiller addresses the Molyneux Problem in the first edition of 1728.
17 La Mettrie 1745, pp. 349–354. La Mettrie refers to the second, 1729, Coste edition of Locke's *Essay*.
18 See *Essai*, Condillac 2001, pp. 104, 108–109 (all subsequent references to the *Essai* are to the Aarsleff translation, Condillac 2001). Two reviews of the *Essai*, those in *Suite de la Clef* and *Journal des sçavans*, approve of Condillac's treatment of the Molyneux Problem, the latter claiming, "his reasons appear convincing" (May 1747, p. 265). For details, see Pariente and Pécharman 2014, pp. 50–52.
19 Aram Vartanian seems to overstate the evidence for Condillac having read La Mettrie on the Molyneux Problem. For example, one key piece of evidence, according to Vartanian, is that they both use the expression "j'ouvre ma fenêtre" (Vartanian 1983, p. 184), but Voltaire who uses "j'ouvre la fenêtre" (Voltaire 1738, p. 63) is just as likely to be Condillac's subliminal source.
20 See Diderot 2011, pp. 205–219.

Condillac and the Molyneux Problem   41

21 See Buffon 1749, pp. 318 (Diderot), 327 (Jurin), and 330 (Smith).
22 See *Essai*, p. 12; *Treatise on Systems*, Chapter 6, Condillac 1982, 1, pp. 33–39.
23 See *Essai*, p. 11; *Treatise*, p. 161.
24 *Essai*, I. 6. 4, p. 103. For further discussion, see Chottin 2014, pp. 189–200.
25 All underlining is added.
26 *Essai*, pp. 108–109.
27 See *Treatise* III. 3. 9, p. 283.
28 Bongie 1978, p. 89.
29 See Condillac 1980, pp. 203–204 and 85. *Les monades* was only attributed to Condillac in the twentieth century and not published until 1980; see Condillac 1980. For Condillac's reflections on the deaf and mute, see Marion Chottin's chapter in this volume.
30 See Condillac 1755, pp. 188–189; translated in *Treatise*, pp. 156–157.
31 *Treatise*, p. 170.
32 *Treatise* II. 11. 1, p. 213.
33 *Treatise* III. 5 and 6, pp. 290–295 and 165.
34 See *Treatise* II. 8. 7–8, p. 244; III. 3. 11–12, p. 278; III. 4. 3, p. 289.
35 *Treatise* III. 4, pp. 287–289.
36 See *Treatise* 3. 3. 2, p. 274; *Essai* 1. 6. 12, p. 106; Berkeley, *New Theory*, §2, pp. 1–2.
37 Locke, *Essay* II. ix. 8; Condillac, *Treatise* III. 3. 11, 25, pp. 278, 283.
38 On the distinction between seeing and looking, see *Treatise* III. 3. 6, p. 276.
39 See, for example, *Treatise* III. 4. 3, pp. 288–289. Condillac was particularly critical of Locke's claim that unconscious judgments only take place in visual perception and not the other sense modalities.
40 See Leibniz 1996, pp. 135–138.
41 See Smith 1767, pp. 90–102.

References

Berkeley, George (1709). *An Essay towards a New Theory of Vision*, 2nd edition, Dublin: Aaron Rhames.
Berkeley, George (1732). *Alciphron: or, the Minute Philosopher in Seven Dialogues*, vol. 2, 2nd edition, London: J. Tonson. (Contains *An Essay Towards a New Theory of Vision*.)
Berkeley, George (1734). *Essay sur une nouvelle théorie de la vision*, in *Alciphron, ou le petit philosophe*, vol. 2, The Hague: Benjamin Gibert (separate pagination).
Bongie, Laurence L. (1978). "A new Condillac letter and the genesis of the *Traité des sensations*," *Journal of the History of Philosophy*, 16, pp. 83–94.
Bouiller, David R. (1737). *Essai philosophique sur l'âme des bêtes*, vol. 2, 2nd edition, Amsterdam: François Changuion. 1st edition 1728.
Buffon, George-Louis Leclerc, comte de (1749). *Histoire naturalle, générale et particuliére*, vol. 3, Paris: N. P.
Cheselden, William (1728). "An account of some observations made by a young gentleman, who was born blind, or lost his sight so early, that he had no remembrance of ever having seen," *Philosophical Transactions*, 35(402), pp. 447–450.
Chottin, Marion (2014). *Le partage de l'empirisme: une histoire du problème de Molyneux aux xviie et xviiie siècles*, Paris: Honoré Champion.

Condillac, Etienne Bonnot de (1746). *Essai sur l'origine des connoissances humaines*, 2 vols, Amsterdam: Pierre Mortier.
Condillac, Etienne Bonnot de (1754). *Traité des sensations*, 2 vols, Paris: De Bure the Elder.
Condillac, Etienne Bonnot de (1755). *Traité des animaux*, Amsterdam: De Bure the Elder.
Condillac (1953). *Condillac: Lettres inédites à Gabriel Cramer*, Paris: Presses universitaires de France.
Condillac, Etienne Bonnot de (1980). *Les monades*, ed. Laurence L. Bongie, *Studies in Voltaire and the Eighteenth Century*, 187, Oxford: The Voltaire Foundation.
Condillac, Etienne Bonnot de (1982). *Philosophical Writings of Etienne Bonnot, Abbé de Condillac*, 2 vols, trans. Franklin Philip, New York: Psychology Press.
Condillac, Etienne Bonnot de (2001). *Essay on the Origin of Human Knowledge*, trans. Hans Aarsleff, Cambridge: Cambridge University Press. 1st French edition 1746.
Degenaar, Marjolein (1996). *Molyneux's Problem: Three Centuries of Discussion on the Perception of Forms*, Dordrecht: Kluwer.
Diderot, Denis (2011). "Letter on the blind for the use of those who can see," in Kate E. Tunstall, *Blindness and Enlightenment*, London: Continuum, pp. 171–219. 1st French edition 1749.
Greene, Robert (1712). *The Principles of Natural Philosophy*, Cambridge: Edmund Jeffery.
Jurin, James (1738a). "Dr. Jurin's solution of Mr. Molyneux's problem," in Robert Smith, *A Compleat System of Opticks in Four Books*, 2 vols, Cambridge: Printed for the Author, vol. 2, pp. 27–29 (2nd paginated section).
Jurin, James (1738b). "An essay upon distinct and indistinct vision," in Robert Smith, *A Compleat System of Opticks in Four Books*, 2 vols, Cambridge: Printed for the Author, vol. 2, pp. 115–171 (2nd paginated section).
Jurin, James (1739). *A Reply to Mr. Robins's Remarks on the Essay upon Distinct and Indistinct Vision*, London: W. Innys and R. Manby.
Jurin, James (1996). *The Correspondence of James Jurin (1684–1750)*, ed. Andrea Rusnock, Amsterdam: Rodopi.
La Mettrie, Julian d'Offroy de (1745). *Histoire naturelle de l'âme*, The Hague: Jean Neaulme.
Leibniz, G. W. (1996). *New Essays on Human Understanding*, trans. Peter Remnant and Jonathan Bennett, Cambridge: Cambridge University Press. 1st French edition 1765.
Locke, John (1688). Extrait d'un Livre Anglois qui n'est pas encore publié, intitulé Essai philosophique *concernant* l'entendement', *Bibliothèque universelle et historique*, 8, pp. 49–142.
Locke, John (1700). *Essai philosophique concernant l'entenement humain*, trans. Pierre Coste, Amsterdam: Henri Schelte. 2nd edition 1729.
Locke, John (1823). *An Examination of P. Malebranche*, in *Works of John Locke*, vol. 9, London: Tegg, pp. 211–255.
Locke, John (1975). *An Essay concerning Human Understanding*, ed. Peter H. Nidditch, Oxford: Clarendon Press. 1st edition 1690; 2nd edition 1694.

Locke, John (1976–1989). *The Correspondence of John Locke*, 8 vols, ed. Esmond S. de Beer, Oxford: Clarendon Press.
Pariente, Jean-Claude and Pécharman, Martine (2014). "Introduction" to *Essai sur l'origine des connaissances humaines*, Paris: Vrin, pp. 7–56.
Smith, Robert (1767). *Traité d'optique*, Paris: Durand.
Tunstall, Kate (2011). "Introduction" to *Blindness and the Enlightenment: An Essay. With a New Translation of Diderot's* Letter on the Blind *and La Mothe Le Vayer's "Of a Man Born Blind*," London: Continuum, pp. 1–142.
Vartanian, Aram (1983). "La Mettrie and Diderot revisited: an intertextual encounter," *Diderot Studies*, 21, pp. 155–197.
Voltaire (1738). *Elémens de la philosophie de Neuton*, Amsterdam N. P.

4 Reinventing Newtonianism
Hypotheses, Systems and Attraction in Condillac

Gianni Paganini

1 The Ban on Hypotheses and the Classic Enlightenment Narrative

The beliefs of philosophers of science underwent a profound shift after Newton. Most prominent were the fortunes and misfortunes of the method of hypotheses. Before Newton, this method assigned a major function to the construction of theoretical assumptions if they could explain phenomena. In the 1720s, this method fell into disfavor due to the success of Newton's physics (see Laudan 1981). From the methodological point of view, the most important factor that acted on this decline was Newton's deep commitment to having the empirical world serve not only as the ultimate arbiter but also as the sole basis for adopting a theory. He insisted on having specific phenomena decide each element of a theory, with the goal of limiting theorizing to inductive generalization derived from particular facts (see Smith 2002; Ducheyne 2013).

This stance is best summarized in Newton's fourth "Rule of reasoning," added to the third edition of the *Principia*, and in the *Scholium generale*, where he put the famous statement: "hypotheses non fingo" (Newton 1999a, II, 555 and 764). There Newton referred to the most controversial piece of his physics, the principle of attraction, which would imply an incomprehensible action at a distance between two bodies. He stressed that it was not useful to look for "hypothetical" explanations, "be they physical or metaphysical." Gravity and attraction must simply be accepted as phenomena, certainly ascertained, and exactly calculated. This "ban" on hypotheses constituted the foundation of experimental philosophy directed against Descartes's wrong "system" of whirls; at the same time, it informed the classic narrative of Enlightenment epistemology as a form of mathematized empiricism. While maintaining that gravity and attraction can be described through mathematical laws verified by experience, Newton rejected physical or metaphysical commitments to a supposed "force" of nature behind the experimental data. This supposition could not be but a "hypothesis," that is, a proposition not deduced from phenomena and assumed without any proof.

These assumptions defined the mainstream of the Anglo-French eighteenth-century science. Together, they framed also the most widespread Enlightenment self-representation. Already in the *Lettres philosophiques,* Voltaire contrasted Descartes's "esprit de système" to Newton's more experimental approach. The former would lead "from one supposition to another," with the result of bringing forth a "novel of physics" instead of real physics. Only Newton took the right way, even though "he despaired to ever find the real cause" of attraction (Voltaire 2010, XIV, 118; XV, 119 and 121). If we have a look at Voltaire's immense work, we realize that there is no entry on "hypothesis" in his *Dictionnaire philosophique* and that the *Eléments de la philosophie de Newton* completely neglect this topic. Silencing the opponents (Cartesians considered to be supporters of hypotheses) was for Voltaire the worst condemnation.

The quintessential Enlightenment text, the *Encyclopédie,* made this "ban" even more explicit. In the *Discours préliminaire,* D'Alembert made a case for rejecting hypotheses while praising Newton who put together empiricism and mathematical exactitude.

> Newton... finally appeared and gave philosophy a form which it seems bound to retain. This great genius saw that it was time to banish conjectures and vague hypotheses from physics, or at least to give them only for what they were worth, and that this science should be subject only to experiments and geometry.
> (Diderot and D'Alembert 1751, I, xxvi)

For D'Alembert, "physics is only limited to observations and calculations" (Diderot and D'Alembert 1751, I, xxxi). The ban on hypotheses is confirmed in the entry "Newtonianism or Newtonian Philosophy," where Newton's epistemology is presented as a

> method that consists in deducing one's reasonings and conclusions directly from phenomena, without any antecedent hypothesis, starting with simple principles, deducing the first laws of nature from a small number of chosen phenomena, and using these laws to explain the other effects.
> (Diderot and D'Alembert 1751, XI, 122)

2 The First Breach: Émilie Du Châtelet Re-Evaluation of Hypotheses

There were only a few exceptions to this mainstream epistemology and the narrative that it underpinned. In France, the most outstanding can be found in Chapter 4 of Émilie Du Châtelet's *Institutions de physique* (1740, republished with variants in 1742). This chapter contained the first major and self-contained study of the French Enlightenment that revaluated the heuristic function of hypotheses (Du Châtelet 1740, 74–89; 1742, 78–93). For the marquise, a hypothesis is supposed to "give reason," in the sense of explaining the "cause" of phenomena, albeit in a provisional way, waiting for a demonstration or an experimental confirmation. It is not a mere convention or simply a mathematical calculus without correspondence to physical reality:

> When certain things are used to explain what has been observed, and though the truth of what has been supposed is impossible to demonstrate, one is making a hypothesis. Thus, philosophers frame hypotheses to explain the phenomena, the cause of which cannot be discovered either by experiment or by demonstration.
> (Du Châtelet 1740, IV § 56: 80)

Du Châtelet outlined both a *methodology* and a *historical apology* of hypotheses. She explained historically why Newton had discredited hypotheses and at the same time showed how to rehabilitate them for the purpose of creating a new physics. First, she corrected the classic narrative of the Enlightenment. According to her, it is true that Descartes transformed hypotheses into "fictions," filling his books with "tales" and "dreams," and Newton reacted against this "abuse." However, his disciples went too far in the opposite direction, rejecting altogether the use of hypotheses. Du Châtelet argued instead that one should not entirely "banish" them (DC 1740, IV, § 54–55, 75). Even Newton "imagined hypotheses to be helpful to explain complex and difficult phenomena" (DC 1740, IV, § 71: 88–89). It is notable that her new narrative developed across the national and philosophical boundaries that divided European culture. These divisions had resulted in what Shank aptly called "the war of worlds," hinting at the struggle between the different "national" cosmologies of Cartesians, Leibnizians, and Newtonians (Shank 2008). In a balanced assessment of the respective merits, Du Châtelet showed instead that "good hypotheses were always made up by the greatest men such as Copernicus, Kepler, Huygens, Descartes, Leibniz, and Newton himself" (Du Châtelet 1740, IV, § 71, 89).

This new narrative is founded on an epistemology that, according to precise rules, sharply distinguishes between the "good" and the "bad" use of hypotheses. For Du Châtelet, methodology was not an end in itself; rather, she claimed that the notion of hypothesis allowed her to distinguish between two things: the *law of gravitation* based on mathematical deduction and experimental verification, on the one hand, and, on the other hand, the *hypothesis of a force of attraction*, which could be accepted only as a provisional explanation to be superseded by a more suitable theory in the progress of science. She hoped that this new theory would fit the requirements of both mechanistic physics and Leibnizian metaphysics, and above all the principle of sufficient reason.

As one can see in Chapter 16 of the *Institutions*, which is entirely dedicated to Newtonian attraction, Du Châtelet recognized the scientific merits of the mathematical law of gravitation that allowed the unification of celestial and terrestrial mechanics and explained the ebb and flow of tides, light effects, the cohesion of bodies, and chemical operations (Du Châtelet 1740, § 388, 317–320). Nevertheless, she refused to consider attraction (conceived of as an incomprehensible action at a distance) as a "true cause"; for her it remained a "phenomenon of which the cause is still sought" (Du Châtelet 1740, § 397, 332). In this discussion she gave hypotheses a central place. She presented the idea that an attracting force exists as a controversial hypothesis but also argued that explanations based on mechanical laws (that conceive of motion in terms of contact and impulse) would in their own right require a hypothesis on the existence of a fluid matter (Du Châtelet 1740, § 399, 333)—something of which there was no experimental proof yet. On this account, research remained still open and Du Châtelet stressed that, without formulating hypotheses, any scientific process would stop at a dead end. All this shows that in the *Institutions*, the heuristic function of hypotheses is strongly supported and goes hand in hand with the idea of science as a form of "inductive provisionalism"[1] that unfolds as a process in which one theory is replaced by a better one in a continuous attempt to approximate reality. Here science turns into a collaborative endeavor, but also a story of trials and errors, in which wrong or worse hypotheses are abandoned in favor of new and better ones.[2]

3 Condillac on Systems and Hypotheses in the *Traité des systèmes*

It is for their originality and Leibnizian leanings that Du Châtelet's epistemological views and reassessment of hypotheses never entered the mainstream of Enlightenment philosophy, to the extent that even her companion Voltaire did not accept them as true, as we have seen above. Despite this, there was another figure that challenged the dismissal of hypotheses in the French Enlightenment debate: Étienne Bonnot de Condillac. Although he was most probably inspired by the *Institutions* when writing his *Traité des systèmes* (1749), especially Chapter 12 "On Hypotheses" (see Condillac 1947–1951, I, 195–204), he never mentioned the marquise as his source. Yet we will show in what follows that some of Condillac's ideas are very close to Du Châtelet's in terms of both influence and reaction. If there was a reception, as it is most probable, it happened anyway *ad modum recipientis;* that is, Condillac reacted in his own way to the ideas he found in the work of Du Châtelet.

In many respects, Condillac shared central ideas of the mainstream narrative that opposed Descartes's "ingenious conjectures," and thus supported Newton's successful science. He described Descartes as "hiding in a corner of his study," working only with his imagination and "pretend[ing] to explain the world formation, body generation and all phenomena" by resorting to conjectures that gave him the illusion of "doing whatever he wanted." Therefore, he fell into the typical self-deception of a system builder. That was a big mistake, according to Condillac, as "such arbitrary hypotheses do not reveal any truth, on the contrary they delay the progress of the sciences and become very dangerous owing to the mistakes they lead them to adopt" (Condillac 1947–1951, I, 198a).[3] Referring implicitly to the *regulae philosophandi* of the *Principia,* Condillac described Newton's epistemology as more moderate than that of Descartes. "Instead of starting to build the world, Newton limited himself to observing it; [a] less nice project than that of Descartes, or rather a less daring but wiser one" (Condillac 1947–1951, I, 200a). Due to the self-restraint typical of empiricists, Newton narrowed the scope of his inquiry, as he did not "intend to divine or imagine the first principles of nature" (Condillac 1947–1951, I, 200a), thinking that our observations are not enough to "build a general system" of nature (Condillac 1947–1951, I, 197a).

These considerations reflect the mainstream Enlightenment narrative informed by the empiricist interpretation of Newton's method (see Charrak 2003). Condillac, however, broke away from this mainstream when re-evaluating and qualifying two notions that, after Descartes's "bad" example, had fallen into disrepute: the notions of system and hypothesis. The first lies at the heart of Condillac's *Traité* where different systems are understood to correspond to different underlying "principles." There are three types of systems. In "abstract systems," principles consist of "general or abstract maxims"; these constitute truisms that especially metaphysicians multiply without affording useful knowledge. In the *Traité,* Leibniz's system of monads features as the example *par excellence* of such "abstract systems" (Condillac 1947–1951, I, 151–164). The second type of system invents "abstract notions" and "imaginary suppositions" to "explain things that would be otherwise difficult to account for." However, these suppositions often seem to be no more than *ad hoc* explanations, while it would be better to "duly check experience and gather facts." The third and more fruitful kind of system ("true systems") starts from "facts" and resorts to "suppositions" as mere "suspicions" to be later ascertained by experience (Condillac 1947–1951, I, 124–127). For Condillac, only the third kind of system affords new and real knowledge since it monitors experience, collects facts, and adopts "principles" accounting for the "phenomena" at hand. Furthermore, Condillac emphasizes the difference between "abstract principles" (the polemical target of the *Traité*) that can never be "first" as they are only "an abridged expression of knowledge already acquired" and "hypotheses or suppositions." Unlike abstract notions, hypotheses "can also be principles, namely first truths that account for others" (Condillac 1947–1951, I, 195b).[4]

This is the spirit in which Condillac addresses the thorny issue of hypotheses. He accepts them with all the precautions dictated by his basic empiricism that prevents him from confusing hypotheses with facts (see Condillac 1947–1951, I, 124a). Together with the recovery of the notion of a system, which he defends against accusations made against the *esprit de système*, Condillac re-evaluates the role of hypotheses by offering a balanced assessment of their strengths and weaknesses. Concerning their strengths, the *Traité* is exceptional as it claims that hypotheses are "not only helpful but also necessary" (Condillac 1947–1951, I, 203b); they should not be "banned" (Condillac 1947–1951, I, 199b) from the sciences unless they are "gratuitous conjectures" like those of Descartes. This positive assessment, which is also developed in other chapters of the same work, distances Condillac from the mainstream narrative. In Chapter 16 ("On the usage of systems in physics"), Condillac again emphasizes the difference between hypotheses and facts (Condillac 1947–1951, I, 211b) from an empiricist point of view,[5] stating the impossibility of getting rid of any "conjectures," provided they can soon "be... confirmed by observation" (Condillac 1947–1951, I, 210b). In Chapter 14 ("When one can build systems upon principles that are ascertained by experience"), he is even more assertive, explaining that "hypotheses can be the ground of a system" when they are based on "a first fact well ascertained" (Condillac 1947–1951, I, 206b). In sum, Condillac refuses to "ban" hypotheses from science; he prefers qualifying them and distinguishing "good" hypotheses from the "gratuitous conjectures" of the Cartesian type (see Condillac 1947–1951, I, 198a–200b).

In providing this apt qualification, Condillac almost certainly followed Du Châtelet, as it is very unlikely that he could have ignored her *Institutions*.[6] Like her, Condillac refused the "ban" of hypotheses and argued instead for a judicious regulation of their use. The following passage looks like a response to Voltaire's silence and D'Alembert's condemnation:

Should we then ban all hypotheses from physics? Certainly not. Yet it would not be wise to adopt them without any discrimination and, in the first place, we must mistrust the most ingenious ones. In fact, what is only ingenious is not simple and the truth, for sure, is simple.
(Condillac 1947–1951, I, 199b–200a)

However, a detailed *methodology* for the "good" use of hypothetical knowledge is needed. The *Traité* contains four basic rules. First, all possible alternative explanations must be exhausted, which often happens in mathematics and seldom in physics. Second, according to the experimental method, apt means are needed to confirm or reject hypotheses (Condillac 1947–1951, I, 195b). Third, the explanations given for certain phenomena must agree with other experience-based explanations, so that the hypothesis under examination can account for all relevant facts without exception (Condillac 1947–1951, I, 203a–203b). Fourth, regarding the use of analogy in science, one must be cautious when operating with hypotheses that are suggested by analogy only, without being confirmed by any experimental data. Only verified hypotheses afford real evidence (Condillac 1947–1951, I, 202b–203a).

These rules laid out in the *Traité* are more concise than those presented in the *Institutions* and only partially coincide with them. However, both authors agree on the necessity to develop a methodology that distinguishes "good" hypotheses from "bad" conjectures. And what matters most is that both acknowledge the importance and utility of hypotheses, if appropriately regulated.

It is notable that this spectacular readmission of hypotheses to the scientific discourse involves not only an implicit dialogue with but also an explicit overcoming of Du Châtelet's positions. As can be seen from his arguments in the *Traité*, Condillac is even bolder than her. Du Châtelet compared hypotheses to the "scaffolding" of a building (Du Châtelet 1740, Avant-Propos viii, 9), which is usually removed when the construction is finished. Condillac reworks the architectonical metaphor to stress even more than Du Châtelet the importance of conjectures in the construction of science: "Suppositions are to a system what foundations are to a building. So it is not enough comparing them to machines used to construct a building" (Condillac 1947–1951, I, 199b). Hypotheses are no longer instrumental; they become foundational and, what is more, can also anticipate experience. Therefore, "we must not prohibit spirits gifted enough to go sometimes beyond experience from the use of hypotheses." Descartes's big mistake, Condillac argues, consisted in presenting his own philosophy of nature as "the true system of the world" and declaring it to be definitive, thus creating "obstacles to the progress of truth" (Condillac 1947–1951, I, 203b). He should instead have presented his system as a mere provisional hypothesis, taking care not to go against experimental data, which he unfortunately did (Condillac 1947–1951, I, 200a).

4   Hypotheses and Principles

The discussion on principles connects hypotheses to systems. In the *Traité des systèmes* the best example of a principle relevant to a system ("principles of Sciences") is provided by the principle of "gravity of the bodies," which accounts for many "phenomena." According to Condillac, this principle reflects the "first phenomenon" (Condillac 1947–1951, I, 200a) or the "first fact that is well ascertained" (Condillac 1947–1951, I, 206b). He refers to Newton as the best example of someone using principles fruitfully to establish limited but at the same time reliable systems:

> Newton did not set out to guess or imagine the first principles of nature. If he felt the usefulness of a system that explained everything, he was aware of all our inability in this regard. He observed and investigated whether among the phenomena there was one that could be considered as a principle, that is, as a first phenomenon suitable for explaining others.
> (Condillac 1947–1951, I, 200a)

Newton discovered "the first phenomenon" when observing planetary orbits and thinking that they could be explained by two different forces: one of projection and the other of attraction. This supposition, which was "neither gratuitous nor groundless," acted as a first principle in Newton's system, a system that thus turned out to be "more limited than that of nature, but as extensive as our knowledge can be" (Condillac 1947–1951, I, 200a).

In Chapter 14, where the case is made for "systems supported by experience," the author claims that "the foundation of a system" (meaning there it a "good" system) can also be afforded by a hypothesis as long as this is formulated following the rules above mentioned (Condillac 1947–1951, I, 206b). Condillac thus promotes hypotheses to the rank of "principles": "in the search for truth, hypotheses" or suppositions are not only means or suspicions; they can also be principles, that is, first truths that explain others. ...They are principles or first truths when confirmed by new observations that no longer allow for any doubt (Condillac 1947–1951, I, 195b). This is not the same as authorizing a mere supposition, since empirical confirmation is still needed: "we can create true systems only in cases where we have made enough observations to grasp the chain of phenomena" (Condillac 1947–1951, I, 207a).

Even if this rehabilitation of hypotheses is ultimately submitted to the check of experience, it challenges any staunch empiricist approach that distrusts systems as well as hypotheses. For according to Condillac, the scientist should accept "guesses" (another word meaning hypotheses), "as long as they take them for what they are." These conjectures have heuristic value because they may motivate further research and lead to discoveries. Newton set a good example of this practice as "analogy, observation and calculation" confirmed this new system of the world, so that gravity and attraction could attain the status of "principles" that ground fruitful, rather than unhelpfully abstract systems (Condillac 1947–1951, I, 220b).

All things considered, for Condillac, using hypotheses was neither paradoxical nor inconsistent. On the contrary, he insisted on the mutual synergy effects resulting from hypotheticism and empiricism. It is true that for him, too, experience remains the ultimate arbiter, as every "supposition" must be empirically validated. However, hypotheses can contribute to "the progress of physics" by generalizing inductive observations and providing wider explanations for a whole range of facts. Condillac presented in detail the requirements for this collaboration between theory and experience. Experience itself offers a model for the formulation of "good" hypotheses:

> Experience, making us see facts that are explained by other facts, offers us a model of how a hypothesis should account for all of them. Therefore, to ascertain the validity of a supposition, we need only to consider whether the explanations it provides for certain phenomena agree with those that experience gives for others; whether it explains them all, not one excepted; whether there are no observations that tend to disprove it. When all these requirements are gathered, there is no doubt that the hypothesis contributes to the progress of physics.
> (Condillac 1947–1951, I, 203a–203b)

5 Hypotheses and Attraction

Against this background, let us consider whether for Condillac attraction is a "phenomenon" (a "fact") or a "hypothesis." To answer this question, one should first recognize that the discussion of hypotheses cannot be understood if disconnected from the issue of attraction, and in particular if seen in isolation from the numerous objections that were raised against the latter in the triangular debate between Newton, Clarke, and Leibniz. There were many and substantial reasons related to the success of Newton's science that spoke in favor of attraction, even if there was the big "scandal" provoked by the idea of a force that can act remotely. As Koyré said, "the overwhelming success of Newtonian physics made it practically inevitable that its particular features became thought of as essential for the building of science as such" (Koyré 1965, 19).[7] Nevertheless, the impression always remained of an "occult" and ultimately irrational quality of matter related to the force of attraction. This is the reason why both Du Châtelet and Condillac neglected Newton's fourth rule of reasoning in order to make room for hypotheses in the construction of science.[8] While acknowledging Newton's best achievements in physics and astronomy, they faced what seemed to be a paradox: the principle of attraction and in particular the law of inverse-square were confirmed by experimental proofs, whereas the idea of a force acting remotely remained very difficult to understand.

Like Du Châtelet, Condillac did not see the debate on hypotheses as a mere controversy about methodology. There was a larger issue at stake: the question of what kind of status was to be conferred to the principle of attraction. Was it only an experimental fact, a phenomenon, or could it be a principle suitable for a physical explanation? And on what terms could such an explanation proceed?

Both Condillac and Du Châtelet conceived of attraction as "the first phenomenon of nature." The second, however, was much more critical than the first in presenting the force of attraction as a true and ultimate cause of gravity. Starting from the true metaphysical principles of Leibniz's philosophy of nature, which were ultimately based on the principle of sufficient reason, she claimed that attraction should be dismantled like an "enchanted castle" (Du Châtelet 1740, § 395, 328). She recommended looking for a mechanical explanation of attraction that saw it as an expression of impact or impulse rather than of action at a distance. She accepted Newton's theory only as a provisional conjecture that would sooner or later be replaced by a more appropriate explanation (Du Châtelet 1740, §397–399, 334). This point was made even stronger in the second edition of the *Institutions* (Du Châtelet 1742, § 397, 346).[9] Here the marquise argued that it was just a matter of time before a mechanical explanation would replace references to action at a distance with an account that details the motions of subtle fluids (Du Châtelet 1740, § 399, 334; cf. § 398, 332–333).[10] And yet, she admitted that the law of inverse-square could not be rejected, as it was constantly verified by experience.[11] She here relied on the Leibnizian notion of "well-grounded phenomenon." Du Châtelet applied this notion consistently in her *Institutions* to account for extension, active and passive forces; in doing so, she used the expression of "phénomène substantié" (Du Châtelet 1740, § 156, 170–171).

All in all, we can thus say that, in order to resolve what seemed to be a puzzle, Du Châtelet considered the force of attraction as a hypothesis, and it is for this reason that she engaged in a re-evaluation of the conjectural dimension of scientific thought. Du Châtelet reconceived of attraction as a provisional hypothesis ("l'hipothese de l'attraction"). Through this, she treated attraction as an explanation and not as a phenomenon mathematically and empirically ascertained, even though she admitted that this explanation might be replaced in the future by a new theory based on impulse. That could happen, she said, when all the properties of attraction would eventually be known, but from this, as she admitted, "we are very far" (Du Châtelet 1740, Avant-Propos vii). Therefore, also the Newtonian theory of attraction might be superseded by another clearer explanation in the progress of science.[12] The fact expressed by the mathematical law remains instead a well-ascertained phenomenon.

Condillac chose a similar dual approach to this complex issue. As we have seen, he did not only acknowledge gravity as the "first phenomenon," he also treated attraction as a hypothesis, and thus rehabilitated this heuristic tool that had been discredited after Newton's "ban." As he was not a Leibnizian, he could in principle have ignored many of those reservations that resulted from the marquise's commitment to the principle of sufficient reason. Yet he still set out to neutralize the objection, addressed by the Cartesians, of introducing "occult qualities" (as "no one has an idea of attraction"), by maintaining that Descartes' followers groundlessly think of "impulsion to be more intelligible" (Condillac 1947–1951, I, 200b–201a).[13] Furthermore, and here he closely followed Du Châtelet, Condillac treated references to an attracting force as a "hypothesis," while recognizing the "fact" that physical experiences of gravity confirm the mathematical law of the inverse-square. In this way, both philosophers exorcised the theoretical "scandal" of attraction and at the same time neutralized Newton's famous warnings about hypotheses.

The transition from the "first phenomenon" (Condillac 1947–1951, I, 200a) or the "first fact that is well ascertained" (Condillac 1947–1971, I, 206b) to the use of conjectures is clearly outlined in Chapter 16 "On the use of systems in physics" (Condillac 1947–1951, I, 210–212). The starting point is to observe the phenomena and to thus "climb up to those on which many others depend." In physics, "size" and "motion" are enough to account for the phenomena, without resorting to "force" as "this is the name of a thing of which we have no idea" (Condillac 1947–1951, I, 206b–207a). "Collecting the phenomena," says Condillac, "we will arrange them in an order in which the former account for the latter and we will see that they illuminate each other" (Condillac 1947–1951, I, 210a–210b).

The picture Condillac draws of Newton's scientific achievements is very close to a phenomenalist reading of the *Principia*. Condillac himself writes:

> Newton did not set out to guess or imagine the first principles of nature. Even while feeling the advantage of a system that could explain everything, he realized at the same time our inability in this regard. He observed and inquired if there was among phenomena, one that could be regarded as a principle, namely, that is, as a first phenomenon suited to explain the others.
> (Condillac 1947–1951, I, 200a)

Furthermore, the idea of "cautious" (as opposed to "ambitious") metaphysics that Condillac developed since the *Essay on the origin of human knowledge* pushes him to acknowledge the empirical limits of the human mind and to proceed accordingly. In fact, phenomenalism was a common result of this sort of approach. Scientists like Maupertuis also distinguished the "fact" of "attraction" and its "cause," stating that Newton focused on the former and did not take a side on the latter. The very Newtonian "style," as it was described by I. B. Cohen, "made it possible to put to one side, and to treat as an independent question, the problem of the cause of universal gravity and the matter of its action and transmission" (Cohen 1980, 16), thus allowing philosophers to focus on mathematical relations between phenomena instead.

What is particularly daring about Condillac's approach is that he sought to recover the notion of a "good" hypothesis, thus stressing the theoretical and heuristic function of theory. This move meant that he went against the vast majority of the *philosophes* and scientists of his time. As he says, "the light [shed by the phenomena] will foreshadow experiences to come; it will point them out to us and make us formulate conjectures that will often be confirmed by observation" (Condillac 1947–1951, I, 210b).

It is notable that in the first edition of the *Traité* (during his life two other editions were published, in 1769 and 1771), Condillac is very accurate about the status of hypotheses. Since it is usually neglected, this original text (subsequently modified) deserves to be quoted in its entirety. In fact, it is a major contribution to the epistemology of hypotheses during the French Enlightenment. Examining mathematics, astronomy, and physics in their growing complexity, Condillac summarizes the main claims of his apology for hypotheses:

The last case in which hypotheses can be made is in the hope of guessing the true cause of certain phenomena, and they are such to require more conditions.

If they were conceived only in a generic way and had no other advantage than that of being not proved to be impossible, it would be very rash to take them for the true principles of things. Even if they were perfectly conceived, that would not be enough yet; it would be necessary that, thanks to the explanations provided by them, all the phenomena were linked in a single system and that the generation of each one was sensibly developed. They would be less likely, in proportion to the greater number of effects that they did not justify.

Moreover, since it is reasonable not to guess, unless one has the means to recognize whether the truth has been found, one should not make hypotheses of that kind except in cases where experience can confirm or destroy them; they must be considered only conjectures as long as they are authorized by observations made with the utmost precision. Until then we have to fear that we will discover phenomena that falsify the imagined hypotheses and indicate other very different ones.

(Condillac 1947–1951, I, 202–203 variant)

In this passage, Condillac signals some critical points: the heuristic function of hypotheses, the crucial function of experimental verification, and the necessity that different hypotheses are combined in a consistent theory. Means of validation are to be found through experience, on the one hand, but also through the construction of a global theory, on the other. Moreover, the explanatory power of a hypothesis is taken to be necessarily required, but any given hypothesis also needs to connect to the other parts of theory. After Du Châtelet, Condillac was the only *philosophe* to claim that hypotheses can function as a "good" explanatory device in science.

6 Newton's System and the "Good" Use of Hypotheses

As already mentioned, in Condillac, there is a tight connection between the notions of system and hypothesis. This is particularly clear in the first edition of the *Traité des systèmes*, where he explicitly qualifies the "system of the world," be it Descartes's or Newton's, as a "hypothesis." When formulating his system of the world, Condillac writes, even Newton tried to "imagine a hypothesis rather than to grasp the true mechanism of the universe" (Condillac 1947–1951, I, 200 variant). By "hypothesis" Condillac did not mean the mathematical law of inverse-square that in the 1740s was already widely accepted, but only the explanation that stipulated a "real" physical force acting at a distance. Despite this caution, Condillac fairly acknowledged the "success" of Newtonian science over Cartesian physics. In the subsequent editions, the text displayed a more marked pro-Newtonian shift as Newton's and Descartes's systems were no longer on the same footing.

As a result of these reflections, the final part of Chapter 12 can be read as the strongest case for the rehabilitation of hypotheses that follows Du Châtelet's Chapter 4 of the *Institutions*.

> From all these reflections it appears that one can make good use of hypotheses differently depending on the different cases in which they are used.
>
> In the first place, they are not only useful, but also necessary when all assumptions can be exhausted and when there is a rule to recognize their validity. Mathematics offers examples.
>
> Second, one could not get rid of their help in astronomy; but we must limit their use to account for the apparent revolutions of the stars. Therefore, they begin to be less useful in astronomy than in mathematics.
>
> Third, hypotheses should not be refused when they can facilitate observations or make more evident truths documented by experience. Such are several hypotheses of physics if they are brought back to their proper value. Yet, the most perfect ones of which the physicist can avail himself are the hypotheses indicated by observation and which

give all phenomena similar explanations to those that experience offers in some cases.

(Condillac 1947–1951, I, 203b–204a)

All sciences, from mathematics to physics, draw advantages from the use of hypotheses, while their reliability decreases according to the complexity of the phenomena that they account for. Since we have no precise idea of the exact meaning of basic words such as "essence," "figure," and "force," we should limit our ambition to know in depth the structure of things. All this reinforces the hypothetical status of most of our explanatory knowledge (Condillac 1947–1951, I, 210a–210b).

7 After the *Traité*: The "Art of Reasoning" in the *Cours d'études*

Twenty-six years after the *Traité des systèmes*, in the *Cours d'études* (1775), written for the heir of the Bourbons-Parme, Condillac returned to the topic of scientific method and specifically the issue of hypotheses. One of the books of this single-authored encyclopedia, namely the treatise entitled *L'art de raisonner*, is entirely focused on Newton's scientific work, which here features as the best model of reasoning. Condillac argues that, in principle, knowledge should be based on evidence, provided either by reason or "sentiment" (meaning sensation). Despite this requirement, Condillac emphasizes "the strength of conjectures." They are supposed to lead "the path of truth," because it is "by them that all sciences and arts started," when evidence was not yet available (Condillac 1798: VIII, 232–240).

Condillac here explains that the art of conjecturing is useful at the beginning, but it needs to be controlled afterward. For instance, Condillac warns against the temptation of adopting some theories only because they most satisfy our desire for simplicity. He describes the shift from the circular to the elliptical model of the planetary motions. Kepler adopted the latter when abandoning the prejudices that favored the circle as the simplest geometrical figure. Newton then confirmed Kepler's insight with his theory of attracting forces that explained elliptical orbits. Through this example, Condillac sketches the dynamic evolution of science as a sequence of different hypotheses that are gradually replaced by better ones.[14]

Newton marks the peak of this progress and a long chapter on "Universal gravitation" focuses on him alone (Condillac 1798: VIII, 450–471).

To add more detail, we can remark that Condillac opens Book 4 (dedicated to "the means by which we try to make up for the lack of evidence") with a chapter entitled "Reflections on attraction." "Attraction exists, it cannot be doubted," he says here, but it is still a "mystery." Being neither "a primitive quality" nor "an essential quality" of matter, it is instead "a phenomenon and this is enough." We cannot establish whether the force of attraction is "the only cause of this phenomenon" as we "are ignorant of the way in which it acts." Instead of putting forth "vain speculations" on the nature of this force, Newton combined mathematical "reasoning" and "observation" to describe and calculate the physical events associated with it. Unfortunately, this kind of combination is not allowed when dealing with the microphysical level of matter, given that serious mistakes would result if Newtonian scientists advanced conjectures in that field (Condillac 1798: VIII, 222–223, 229–231). In particular, the way in which attraction acts "at a very little distance" seems to be peculiar and cannot be explained by the law of inverse-square. This is the reason why more investigations are required to explain this kind of phenomenon. Therefore, the way is open to formulating new hypotheses that could "push even further" the limits of our knowledge, if they can be confirmed by true experiments.

Considering that phenomena such as contact, fluidity, elasticity, hardness, softness, dissolution, fermentation, light, magnetism, and electricity do not abide by the general law of attraction, Condillac thought that the Newtonians displayed more imagination than reasoning in their attempts to generalize the laws of nature (Condillac 1798: VIII, 228). In those fields, "nothing is less uniform than the laws that attraction follows" (Condillac 1798: VIII, 224).

To conclude this point, we must bear in mind that Condillac's empiricism influences his methodological considerations and renders him cautious, even when asserting that theoretical conjectures are allowed: "Let us make up hypotheses as we love to do that; however, above all one should make experiences and maybe new discoveries will be made" (Condillac 1798: VIII, 230).

8 Conclusion: Reaching Across the Empiricism-Rationalism Divide

Is this epistemological caution still compatible with the hypotheticism displayed in Chapter 12 of the *Traité des systèmes*? A historical or developmental view of science should be able to avoid the excesses of ascribing either too much or too little explanatory power to theory. In fact, Condillac distinguished between the different stages of the process of scientific construction, and he was famous for drawing subtle and accurate distinctions.

Going further into detail to explain the developmental conception of scientific practice, Condillac stresses one particular feature: in the development of knowledge, we need to distinguish between the "perfect" system, which is an accomplished system, and the early efforts unfolding when this system is still in progress. It is true that in a "perfect system" hypotheses become superfluous and are superseded by "facts," but this is quite exceptional. Therefore, a historical or developmental view is needed because it makes it easier to understand the compatibility of empiricism with hypotheticism. According to the prescriptions of an ideal scientific model, the former is supposed to replace in the end the latter, but in real science this often does not happen, so both keep collaborating.

To conclude, in the history of philosophy, Condillac usually features as one of the most "moderate" Enlightenment thinkers, one who is very far from both Diderot's audacious metaphysics and Rousseau's political radicalism. In many respects, this conventional image requires robust corrections. For example, Condillac's political thought aimed at a radical reformation of the *Ancien Régime* and involved a complex re-formulation of Rousseau's idea of political covenant, which is anything but a moderate project (see Paganini 2007). We would call it nowadays radical liberalism, a program that would have been very audacious during Condillac's time. However, the fact that Condillac was not involved in the great production of the *Encyclopédie* only pushed him to write an entire encyclopedia himself: the *Cours d'études*. And although his idea of metaphysics was staunchly empiricist—[15]starting with the admission made in the *Essay* that we "only know how to reason on the basis of experience"—his epistemology was much bolder than that, as it also included rationalist aspects. Thus, he "freed" hypotheses from the Newtonian "ban" and distanced the notion of systems from the general distrust of the *philosophes*. In many ways, Condillac's efforts were anticipated by Du Châtelet, whom he did not acknowledge as he should have done, but Condillac himself fell into oblivion, too, just after the age of the *idéologues*. And yet both Condillac and Du Châtelet anticipated some important ideas of the "new philosophy of science" (meaning in particular the function of hypotheses, some kind of hypotheticism and fallibilism, holism, the idea of under-determination of theory by experience, etc.). But since both were ignored by posterity and no one knew of their pioneering contributions, their new views had to be (re)discovered later on. The least we can say is that history, including the history of epistemology, is not linear. Overcoming the divide between empiricism and rationalism and freeing hypotheses and systems from Newton's ban did not prevent either of them from being silenced, almost to this day.

Notes

1 With this expression, we pick up the label used by Ducheyne 2013: 230–234, to indicate the substance of Newton's method in his later period (1713–1726), when he resorted in the *Opticks* to hypotheses and conjectures, such as that of the corpuscular nature of light.
2 On the issue of hypotheses in Du Châtelet, see Paganini 2022a,b. For an update on research on the marquise, see Brown and Kölving 2022; Hagengruber 2022. On the generale debate on hypotheses during the Enlightenment, see Casini 2006.

60 Gianni Paganini

3 A similar picture is painted in Condillac 1775, XX, 338–339, where Cartesian physics is portrayed as a "novel." However, Condillac also acknowledged that the mechanization of the world offered "a first step toward truth," but added that "it would have been better to start by effects and then to come to causes, instead of starting by causes to come to effects" (1775, XX, 334).
4 *Traité*, p. 195b. In the *Dictionnaire des synonymes* (Condillac 1947–1951, III, 524b), *s.v.* "Suposition" Condillac subtly distinguishes between "supposition" and "hypothèse": "hypothesis is a supposition made for being the principle of a system."
5 Condillac writes: "a hypothesis becomes more and more uncertain as one finds out a great number of effects of which it does not give a reason, whereas a fact is always still certain and cannot stop being the principle of the phenomena it once accounted for" (Condillac 1947–1951, I, 211b).
6 As McNiven Hine (1979, 142) clearly pointed out, "Condillac was no doubt influenced by Mme Du Châtelet." See her perceptive, albeit too short, comparison between the two philosophers on the topic of hypotheses (1979, 142–144)
7 It is odd that neither Laudan nor Koyré considered Du Châtelet's theory of hypotheses. Koyré deals only with her translation of the *Principia*.
8 The fourth rule reads as follows: "*In experimental philosophy, propositions gathered from phenomena by induction should be considered either exactly or very nearly true notwithstanding any contrary hypotheses, until yet other phenomena make such propositions either more exact or liable to exceptions.* This rule should be followed so that arguments based on induction may not be nullified by hypotheses" (Newton 1999a, II, 555; trans. Newton 1999b, 796).
9 Du Châtelet here writes: "you should only look at it [attraction] as a phenomenon whose cause must be sought, and which cannot itself explain anything … attraction, when looked at as a property of matter, contradicts the principle of sufficient reason" (Du Châtelet 1742, § 397, 346).
10 This matter could be a fluid ether, as it is explained in Du Châtelet 1740, § 399, 333–334.
11 Du Châtelet admits that the law of attraction has a great explanatory power in many fields of physics (Du Châtelet 1740, § 388, 317). Cf. esp. § 163, p. 176: "we can stop at physical qualities, and make use of one or more phenomena, of which we do not know the mechanical reasons yet (whatever they may be), to explain another phenomenon, which depends on them." In the second edition, this part was omitted, with the result of softening this stronger liberalization of hypotheses.
12 This point is made stronger in the second edition: see Du Châtelet 1742, § 399, 334—"There will come a time when we will explain in detail the directions, the movements and the combinations of the fluids that operate the phenomena, which the Newtonians explain by attraction, and this is a research that all physicists should deal with."
13 Cf. Du Châtelet 1740, Avant Propos vii. Here she writes: "It seems to me, moreover, that it would be as unfair to the Cartesians to refuse to admit attraction as a hypothesis, as it is unreasonable to some Newtonians to want to make it a primitive property of matter… because to decide that the effects that the Newtonians attribute to attraction are not produced by impulse, one should know all the ways in which push can be employed, what is still a long way off. We are still in Physics, like that born blind Cheselden restored to sight."
14 This historical view of scientific thinking can be compared to similar reflections made by Du Châtelet 1740, § 57, 76.
15 On Condillac's empiricism see Paganini 1988, 1992.

References

Brown, A. and Kölving U., eds. (2022). *Émilie Du Châtelet. Son monde, ses travaux*. Ferney-Voltaire: Centre International d'Études du XVIIIe siècle.
Casini, P. (2006). *"Hypotheses non fingo": tra Newton e Kant*. Rome: Edizioni di storia e letteratura
Charrak, A. (2003). *Empirisme et métaphysique. L'Essai sur les origines des connaissances humaines de Condillac*. Paris: Vrin.
Cohen, I. B. (1980). *The Newtonian Revolution*. Cambridge: Cambridge University Press.
Condillac, Étienne Bonnot de (1798–1799). *Cours d'études* in *Œuvres complètes de Condillac*, 23 vols. Paris: chez Gratiot, Houel, Guillaume, Gide et Strasbourg, Levrault.
Condillac, Étienne Bonnot de (1947–1951). *Œuvres philosophiques*, edited by George Le Roy, 3 vols. Paris: PUF.
Diderot, D. and D'Alembert, F., eds. (1751–1772). *Encyclopédie ou Dictionnaire raisonné des sciences, des arts et des métiers*, 18 vols. Paris: Briasson, David, Le Breton, Durand.
Du Châtelet, É. (1740). *Institutions de physique*. Paris: chez Prault fils.
Du Châtelet, É. (1742). *Institutions physiques*. Amsterdam: Aux dépens de la Compagnie.
Ducheyne, S. (2013). *The "The Main Method of Natural Philosophy: I. Newton's Natural-Philosophical Methodology*. Dordrecht: Springer.
Hagengruber, R., ed. (2022). *Époque Émilienne*. Cham: Springer.
Koyré, A. (1965). *Newtonian Studies*. London: Chapman & Hall.
Laudan, L. (1981). *Science and Hypothesis. Historical Essays on Scentific Methodology*. Dordrecht: Springer.
McNiven Hine, E. (1979). *A Critical Study of Condillac's Traité des systems*.The Hague: M. Nijhoff.
Newton, I. (1999a). *Philosophiae naturalis principia mathematica*. The third edition (1726) with variant readings. Assembled and edited by Alexandre Koyré and I. Bernhard Cohen with the assistance of Anne Whitman, 2 vols. Cambridge, MA: Harvard University Press.
Newton, I. (1999b). *The Principia. Mathematical Principles of Natural Philosophy*. A New Translation by I. B. Cohen and A. Whitman, Berkeley-Los Angeles-London: University of California Press.
Paganini, G. (1988). "Signes, imagination et mémoire. De la psychologie de Wolff à l' 'Essai' de Condillac." *Revue des sciences philosophiques et théologiques*. 72: 287–300.
Paganini, G. (1992). 'Psychologie et physiologie de l'entendement chez Condillac'. *Dix-huitième siècle*. 24: 165–178.
Paganini, G. (2007). "Everything Must Be Redone: Condillac as Critic of Despotism and Defender of Toleration." In *Monarchisms in the Age of Enlightenment: Liberty, Patriotism and the Common Good*, edited by H. Blom, J. C. Laursen, and L. Simonutti, 144–161. Toronto-Buffalo-London: University of Toronto Press.
Paganini, G. (2022a). "Émilie Du Châtelet's Epistemology of Hypotheses." In *Époque Émilienne*, edited by R. Hagengruber, 21–56. Cham: Springer.

Paganini, G. (2022b). "Rehabilitating Hypotheses in the French Enlightenment." In *Émilie Du Châtelet. Son monde, ses travaux*, edited by A. Brown and U. Kölving, 327–358. Ferney-Voltaire: Centre International d'Études du XVIIIe siècle.
Shank, J. B. (2008). *The Newton Wars and the Beginning of the French Enlightenment*. Chicago, IL-London: The University of Chicago Press.
Smith, G. E. (2002). "The Methodology of the *Principia*." In *The Cambridge Companion to Newton*, 138–173 edited by I. B. Cohen and G. E. Smith. Cambridge: Cambridge UP.
Voltaire, F.-M. Arouet dit (2010). *Lettres philosophiques*, critical edition, edited by O. Ferret and A. McKenna. Paris: Classiques Garnier.

# 5 Languages of Action, Methodological Signs and Deafness
The Reception of Condillac by the Abbé de L'Épée—Or Was It the Other Way around?

Marion Chottin

1 Introduction

As a reminder, Charles-Michel de L'Épée (1712–1789) neither invented sign language—which initially appears in the same rudimentary form as vocal spoken languages as soon as two deaf people enter into a relationship— nor did he initiate the education of deaf people, the first historical traces of which go back to the eighth century (Rocheleau-Rouleau 1950, 347–348). In dealing with the possible reception of Condillac by L'Épée, it is therefore not a question of asking whether the philosophy of the former, and more generally the philosophy of the Enlightenment, inspired these two developments.

What L'Épée did from 1760 onward was to develop a new language, which he called "methodical signs." This language was based on the elementary sign language used by his pupils, and he added new gestures to it in order to model it on French grammar. He used this language as a means to establish an original form of education for deaf people: collective and democratic because it was free of charge. He himself added the phrase "Free teacher of the deaf and dumb" (as it was still inappropriately called at this time) after his name,[1] and intended above all to facilitate their spiritual and intellectual training by providing access to written culture. If there is a reception of Condillac by L'Épée, it is therefore most likely related to ideas that guided and accompanied the establishment of his original pedagogy. This is, moreover, what has been asserted (Branson and Miller 2002, 86; Markovits 2011, 179; Murgel 2016, 673b; Amann 2021, 101) but also denied (Presneau 1998, 101; Rée 1999, 148) both by the history of philosophy and by the history of deafness and Deaf Studies.[2] These disagreements are not only of a scholarly nature. It is a question of knowing whether the philosophies of the Enlightenment, in particular that of Condillac, to whom L'Épée seems theoretically closest, contributed to a form of education that was designed for deaf people, which, even if it

DOI: 10.4324/9781003334750-6

was far from being entirely satisfactory, laid the foundations for what deaf people today claim to be a collective and bilingual education. In short, the question is this: are we working today on the question of deafness within a framework that extended from, superseded or rather negated the Enlightenment? This chapter intends to offer a contribution to this debate.

2 The Abbé de L'Épée, a Reader of Condillac?

First of all, let us consider the theses common to both authors, formulated first by Condillac and then by L'Épée, which may thus indicate, as has often been suggested, a reception of the former by the latter.

2.1 The Twofold Naturalness of the "Language of Signs"

For the L'Épée, the "language of signs" is "natural" in a twofold sense:[3] (1) it demarcates a point of origin by constituting the first language of humanity; and (2) it is produced by nature, given that it arises through the spontaneous expression of needs and independently of any human intention (1774, 50). With this origin, the "language of signs" therefore counts as universal: it is "the natural and primordial language, the language of all countries and all nations" (54). But because other human beings, for the sake of expediency, have substituted voice for gesture, there is only "one people who speak it" (53): the deaf people and their relatives.

Now, this thesis of the twofold naturalness of sign language had in fact been formulated earlier by Condillac in his *Essai* from 1746—although here he did not mention the question of educating deaf people. According to Condillac, there is indeed a "language of action," made up of gestures and cries, which originates from nature. This language is also understood as a spontaneous expression of needs (2014, 196) and as forming "the germ of [all] languages" (298). While such a language of action, that is based on the sense of sight, excludes blind people, who cannot grasp what audible cries refer to, it is the same language that isolated deaf people seem to use when communicating with their hearing relatives. He suggests this point when speculating about ideas available to a young man—the "deaf man of Chartres"—before acquiring hearing at the age of 23: "[t]here is no doubt that he knew how to make known by gestures his main needs, and the things that could relieve them" (157).

The arguments Condillac provides for the twofold naturalness of the language of action are, on the one hand, grounded in the plausibility of the genesis of articulated languages that he thought initiated through the language of action. On the other hand, they are supported by the fact that the existence of such a language resolves what can be called "the aporia of reflection" (107): for the language of action allows Condillac to show how natural signs, that is, the effects of passions (for example the gestural and sound expressions of fear), could give human beings the opportunity to voluntarily create signs (by institution), but without having to create these signs for themselves—which would have presupposed reflection.

This last point underlines what nevertheless separates L'Épée from Condillac's account from 1746 on the question of the first language of humanity, which, for both, is also the language of the deaf people. (1) At no time in his *Letters*, or in the whole of his work, does L'Épée use the Condillaquian term "language of action." (2) Above all, L'Épée considers sign language to be mainly natural, whereas Condillac considers it to be *derived* from nature. Thus, for L'Épée, a need immediately generates the gestural sign of the object that can relieve it; so it generates not only the gesture itself but also its significatory function. For Condillac, the significatory function of gestures is comprehended only when the first human beings have "at last" accustomed themselves "to attach[ing] to the cries of the passions and to the various actions of the body, the perceptions that were expressed by them" (196). According to him, the human being has no innate linguistic ability. Nature only enables humans to provide for their needs and to associate them with a set of bodily manifestations.[4] For Condillac, as L'Épée writes, there are no signs given by nature "in the first place" (23). Instead, there is a genesis, or a transformation, of natural gestures and cries into signs when placed into an intersubjective context. This context does not simply constitute, like for L'Épée, the framework of gestural signification but acts as the motor of its genesis. For Condillac, it is for other people who are members of my species and are organized like me that the bodily effects of my needs can become signs, and vice versa. It is therefore through others, and the relevant experiences with them, that I learn to intentionally use my body to signify what I do not even need. (3) This difference between the two authors implies not only terminological differences but also semantic ones: whereas for L'Épée, the expression "natural signs" designates the gestures called forth by the things themselves under the influence of needs (32), in Condillac's *Essai*, this expression designates the effects of the passions that unwittingly have become signs in and through an intersubjective context (100). And whereas, in L'Épée's work, the term "arbitrary signs" designates words, oral or written, as well as gestures that bear no resemblance to their objects (33), in Condillac's work it designates signs "that we ourselves have chosen" (100)—whether or not their signifiers differ from those of natural signs. In this way, for L'Épée, the bodily expressions of fear voluntarily used as signs constitute natural signs, but for Condillac, they are institutional signs, or even arbitrary ones—given that they are derived from free will.

But do these theoretical differences mark one specific form of reception, one that involves critical appropriation? If this were the case, it would be a strange reception, however, as it would only retain from Condillac what others before him have already advanced, namely the claim that gestural language constitutes the origin of all languages. I agree with Presneau (44) who, among Condillac's predecessors in this field, cites Vitruvius, Warburton (wrongly, in my opinion)[5] and Vico, who, one might add, himself cites Plato, Jamblicus, the Stoics and Origen—thinkers who all regard the "language of signs" as the first of humanity. However, a second thesis of L'Épée on language seems to justify, more than the first, attributing to him a Condillaquian reception.

2.2 The Capacity of Gestures to Signify All Ideas, Including "the Most Metaphysical" Ideas

Employing gestures, L'Épée writes, is "similar to painting," which, as we know from Plutarch, "is a mute art"; for "the art of methodical signs is a language that speaks only to the eyes" (1776, 180–181). It nevertheless surpasses the art of painting, in that it is capable of "representing many more objects," even "the most metaphysical ideas" (181). As early as in the 1770s, the *Letters* of L'Épée set out to show that the language of deaf people, perfectible like all others, can be joined by new gestures, which, according to him, are capable of signifying not only articles (the hand to the hat for the masculine definite article, to the ear for the feminine) and all verbal tenses (the hand thrown once or several times behind the shoulder for the past tenses, and forward for the future) of the French language, but also abstract ideas:

> ... the word *believe*... recalls to our mind an idea which cannot be expressed by a single sign which gives it all its force. Then we write this word on the table and draw four lines from its center: on the first, we express the knowledge of the mind; on the second, the adherence of the heart; on the third, the outward profession of the word, and on the fourth, the deprivation of clear and evident sight.... From then on, we are back in the order of natural signs. The yes of the mind, the yes of the heart, the yes of the mouth, and the no of the eyes (which are executed in the blink of an eye), being joined to the signs which are general for all verbs, we have all that is necessary to render this one in all its parts. (1774, 25)

Now, and here I am playing devil's advocate—particularly as this argument in favor of L'Épée's reception of Condillac has never, to my knowledge, been produced: as early as 1746, Condillac maintained that gesture can signify absolutely everything. Through long quotations from Warburton, he points out that both the Jewish prophets from the Bible and the ancient Greeks, and then the Romans, when they invented the art of pantomime, signified by means of gestures everything that could be signified—from divine commandments to the most sophisticated plays (198-199).

Moreover, the method that de L'Épée uses to forge signs in analogy with nature "in [a] second instance" (33) is the same used by Condillac as early as 1746: it is analysis, which both thinkers conceive of as the practice of decomposing ideas. However, for L'Épée, signs come together to transmit a new idea, one that is of a complex nature—such as the act of believing, signified by means of a succession of gestures given by nature "in first [the] instance." In short, only for L'Epée, it is the case that analysis keeps ideas decomposed within the use of language.

2.3 A Very Uncertain Reception

In addition to the clues already encountered, three points render the thesis that Condillac's ideas were received by L'Épée suspicious and even erroneous in my opinion. First, until the early 1780s, at no time does L'Épée mention Condillac. He does not mention him in his four letters of the early 1770s, when, after a decade of practice, he was concerned with publicly proving his success. If he had drawn his method from the philosophy of Condillac, who had become a member of the Académie Française in 1768, would he not have had an interest in indicating this? Nor did he quote him in his book of 1776, when he sought to defend his method, against the assaults that his publicity had caused (1784, vi sq).

Second, when, in the early 1780s, L'Épée finally quotes Condillac, he does not mention this or that part of his philosophy: he quotes Condillac quoting *him*—and he does so on three occasions. The first can be found at the beginning of his first letter from around 1781 to Samuel Heinicke, who taught deaf people in Leipzig by trying to teach them to speak, thus following the example of Pereire (233)[6]. To refute Heinicke, who accused him of using simple "hieroglyphs" with the deaf people, L'Épée quoted the passage from the first volume of the *Cours d'étude* intended for the Prince of Parma, in which Condillac expressed his admiration (Condillac 1775, 11) for its pedagogy. Then, L'Épée mentions Condillac in the second letter to Heinicke—but this time, no longer to support the status of the famous use of methodical signs as a language in its own right, but to support the possibility that, by means of them, a universal education could be achieved (1784, 273). There is no reception here either: (1) contrary to what L'Épée maintains, Condillac never formulated the "desire" for such an education; (2) de L'Épée presents his methodical signs as the building blocks of a possibly universal language as early as in his letter of 1772. Finally, the "free teacher of the deaf and dumb" produced these lines from Condillac once again in his work from

1784, yet this time with the sole aim of promoting to future pedagogues the education of deaf people by means of his method (1784, 134). Therefore, after having read these lines from the "Grammaire," L'Épée did not modify his ideas or his pedagogy. He was content to take Condillac's judgment as a proof, intended for his detractors first and then for his successors.

Third, L'Épée himself describes the genesis of his method and there is no evidence of a specifically Condillaquian influence:

> ...but I had not forgotten, that in a conversation at the age of sixteen, with my Philosophy Tutor, who was an excellent Metaphysician, he had proved to me this incontestable principle, that there is no more natural connection between metaphysical ideas and articulated sounds, which strike our ears, than there is between these same ideas and characters traced in writing which strike our eyes.
>
> I remember very well that, as a good Philosopher, he drew the immediate conclusion *that it would be possible to instruct the Deaf and Dumb by characters traced in writing and always accompanied by sensitive signs, just as other men are instructed by words and gestures, which indicate their meaning* (I did not think at the time that Providence was laying the foundations of the work to which I was destined).
>
> (156–157, my emphasis)

If the arbitrariness of the sign makes the instruction of deaf people possible, it is because this arbitrariness makes the mediation of gesture necessary. Thus, people who are able to hear could only be taught signs because they were shown what they meant. It is therefore possible to educate deaf people by the same method. This idea runs through the entire work of L'Épée. While he was 16 years old when he learned it from his teacher Adrien Geffroy, Condillac himself was 14: so even indirectly, L'Épée could not have inherited these ideas from Condillac. However, Geffroy was a Jansenist, and therefore an Augustinian, and a Cartesian, and both Augustin and Descartes emphasized the ability of gestures to signify thought. Wouldn't L'Épée be a disciple of Augustine and Descartes?

3 Condillac's Anthropology: A Possible Foundation of the Pedagogy of the Abbé de L'Épée

3.1 *The Abbé de L'Épée's Approach to the Education of Deaf People Is neither Augustinian nor Cartesian*

According to Presneau (1998, 101), L'Épée is not a man of the Enlightenment. The instruction of deaf people by means of sign language has its roots in the fifth century and was revived in the seventeenth century under the impetus of Descartes and Jansenism. It is therefore only because the eighteenth century still bears the mark of Cornelius Jansen that it could produce this new form of education.

One could point out that neither Augustine nor even Descartes attributed to gestures the virtue of signifying all ideas as well as spoken languages.[7] However, to justify my disagreement with Presneau, it is more convincing to underline, first of all, that nowhere in his work does L'Épée mobilize the Cartesian thesis that sign gestures prove the presence of thought. Rather, as we shall soon see, what he emphasizes is the poverty of thought in deaf people deprived of education.

Moreover, because he follows Geffroy, who does not align with Arnauld and Nicole, L'Épée also departs from the seventeenth-century Port-Royalists: while for the authors of the *Logic* spoken words function as signs of thoughts and written words as signs of spoken words, Geffroy seems to believe that written words signify ideas as directly as sounds, thus according to the claims of L'Épée quoted above. These claims, which L'Épée inherited from Geffroy, played a decisive role in his pedagogy, perhaps even more so than the thesis of the arbitrariness of the sign. Because written characters can signify ideas without first referring to sounds, deaf people are able to learn to read and write (Amann 2021, 58 *sq*).[8]

Yet in his work, L'Épée also departs from Geffroy. We know from his notebooks that Geffroy sided with Descartes and his commitment to innate ideas against Locke and Gassendi[9] (Geffroy 1731–1733, 106[10]) and was therefore not in favor of their approach. Yet when teaching his deaf students, moving from the ideas of sense to those of "insensible things" is precisely what L'Épée did, thus demonstrating, contrary to what Bernard maintains (2012, 99), his empiricist leanings.[11] A metaphor, which is often used in his writings, also attests to this: thanks to *La véritable manière d'instruire les sourds et muets*,

[o]ne will see clearly how one must go about it in order to pass through the window what cannot enter through the door, that is to say, in order to enter the minds of the deaf and dumb, through the channel of their eyes, what cannot be introduced through the opening of their ears.

(iv–v)

Thus, according to him, knowledge comes through the senses and there is a hierarchy among them, with hearing (the "door") at its top followed by sight (the "window").

From Augustine to Locke, we progress in time and rejuvenate L'Épée's connection to previous thinkers. It is not, however, that he is in complete agreement with Locke. As early as in his letter of 1771, L'Épée wrote that deaf people deprived of education were little more than animals (1774, 11). Now, in Locke's view, although they do not and never will know the nature of sound, deaf people possess, in addition to the faculties of the mind, whose use is innate, the most instructive sense, namely sight. From this sense, they receive and form for themselves ideas, including the most abstract ones, thus formulating "mental propositions" (1975, 574) independently of the use of the slightest sign (Chottin 2018, 323–341). This is not the case with L'Épée.

3.2 The Anthropology of the Abbé de L'Épée

We find confirmation of the thesis that intelligence depends on language in all his work. According to L'Épée, instruction using methodical signs will not only provide deaf people with knowledge; in addition, it [will] "develop their intelligence" (1776, 179). For without education, they live almost like beasts, and with it, they become humanized. Hence it is necessary, according to him, to instruct them:

> [t]he interest that religion and humanity inspire in me for a truly unfortunate class of men similar to us, but reduced in some way to the condition of beasts, as long as we do not work to remove them from the thick darkness in which they are buried, imposes on me an indispensable obligation to come to their aid, as far as it is possible.
> (1784, iii–iv)

Uneducated deaf children are not entirely like animals, but share their condition: they suffer from a kind of metaphorical blindness, they have no access to light. They are, for L'Épée, the "eyeless" creatures of whom Leonardo da Vinci said that they were a kind of living dead (1987, 89).[12] For L'Épée, living like a beast thus seems to be equivalent to living not so much without expressing thought as without having thought. Indeed, he also describes deaf people as "some kind of automatons" (1774, 27).[13] However, he writes, "[t]hey are only like this because people do not cultivate in them the precious treasure they possess of a soul created in the image of God" (43). For L'Épée, uneducated deaf people have the outside appearance of a machine, imprisoning a thoughtless soul on the inside. Thus, according to L'Épée, ideas originate *through the senses*, but *from language*.

However, L'Épée insists on the identical nature of deaf and hearing people: far from having a different soul, which alone should be educated in order to humanize them, deaf people are exactly the same as other men. "The deaf and dumb are not of a different nature from ours," he writes, for example, in his work of 1776 (152). These are theses that were supported and, above all, substantiated by Condillac in his *Essai*.

3.3 A Condillaquian Support

According to Condillac's account of 1746, instituted signs, whether gestural or vocal, condition the genesis of specifically human operations of the mind (judgment and reflection in the first place) and thus distinguish humans from animals; this is because these signs tear up the moment of perception. Through such signs, I can freely summon ideas of objects, whether by means of my memory or my imagination, over which I thereby gain control (2014, 105). I can also fix my attention on them, and from there decompose and recompose my ideas, and thus reflect. Moreover, through arbitrary signs, I am enabled to have ideas, *i.e.*, to give my perceptions the status of representations (163): the gesture or the word signifies and simultaneously creates the idea because it reminds my mind of the impression of my soul and makes it the sign of what has produced it. This is how Condillac establishes that ideas originate from language rather than from the senses.

Thus, an isolated human being is inferior to a beast which possesses the natural signs proper to its species if it lives among its fellows (163). By contrast, a deaf human being who lives among hearing people is (somewhat) superior to animals because this human possesses a certain range of arbitrary signs—those relating to his needs—and, consequently, corresponding ideas. This explains Condillac's statement about the deaf man of Chartres, already quoted above. However, Condillac continues, "[n]ot having signs convenient enough to compare his most familiar ideas, he rarely formed judgments. It is even likely that, during the first twenty-three years of his life, he did not engage in a single process of reasoning" (158).

It is quite probable that it was L'Épée's practice as a teacher that enabled him to formulate, without having read Condillac, his theses on the nature of deaf people and human beings in general: like in hearing pupils whom he used to teach, he saw in his deaf pupils, who had poor ideas and underdeveloped faculties, a gradual progress. The paradox is that the work of Condillac that L'Épée cites as his evidence, the *Cours d'étude*, deploys an anthropology that is significantly different from, and much less similar to his own, than that of the *Essai*. Having given too much credit to language in the *Essai* and correcting this account in the *Traité des sensations* (1754), Condillac continues to argue in 1775 that human beings not only have ideas, but also reflect, judge and reason *without* language (1775, 37).[14]

An isolated man, like the deaf person deprived of a developed sign language, thus sees his humanity unfold, albeit imperfectly, through sensations and their transformations alone (73).[15] But because for Condillac, gestures still form the first language of humanity and signs remain fruitful for the development of ideas and faculties, the pedagogy of L'Épée can be perfectly integrated into this new framework of thought—to the point, it seems to me, of having partly constituted it, as will be shown in the next section.

4 Condillac as a Reader of the Abbé de L'Épée

4.1 The Distinction between Two Languages of Action

As we have seen, at the very beginning of the "Grammaire" in the first volume of the *Cours d'étude*, Condillac devotes a long note to the pedagogy of L'Épée. In it, he tells us that he has "been to his house," that he has "seen his pupils" and that the pedagogue has "informed him of his method" (1775, 12). The note in question is thus the result of an exchange between the two men, and Condillac's reflections on this exchange. Its purpose is to "do justice," writes Condillac, "to this generous citizen," who instructs the deaf in a more rigorous way than "our governesses and preceptors instruct people with hearing, since he gives his pupils "more exact and precise ideas than those commonly acquired with the aid of hearing" (11–12). We have seen why this is so: each sign of a simple idea resembles its object, and each sign of a complex idea, such as the act of believing, consists of the signs of the simple ideas that compose it. In this framework, no use of words is possible without the ideas they signify being attached to them. Above all, Condillac integrates L'Épée's concept of methodical signs into his own vocabulary: the latter "has made the language of action, a methodical art as simple as it is easy" (11). Condillac thus interprets L'Épée's invention as a transformation of what he has long called a "language of action"; this transformation, through art and into art, proves that this language can exist in an elaborate form, superior even to articulated languages.

The chapter in which this note is written is devoted to this concept of language of action, to which Condillac thus returns, almost 30 years after his first formulation. If L'Épée had read it, he would have seen that the philosopher did much more than pay tribute to his pedagogy. We must therefore speak of an authentic reception—a thesis that has already been supported by others in the following sense (Lane 1989, 68; Ehrsam 2012, 656): Condillac learned from L'Epée that gestures have the ability to signify all ideas. But, as we have seen, Condillac, as early as in the *Essai*, attributes this function to gestures. In my opinion, the Condillaquian reception of the pedagogy of L'Épée has a different focus: it lies in the distinction that Condillac draws between what he calls "two languages of action";[16] "the natural one," he writes, "whose signs are given by the conformation of the organs; and the artificial one, whose signs are given by analogy" (11).[17]

Languages of Action, Methodological Signs and Deafness 73

At this level, Condillac's two languages correspond exactly to those distinguished by L'Épée: the language of signs that human beings speak spontaneously, and the language, which is obtained by extending the first, by means of the addition of new signs. The expressions used by the two men are so similar that it seems more than probable that Condillac not only attended the classes of L'Épée but also read and was influenced by his letters. On the subject of the signs of the first language of action, Condillac writes: "[i]t is nature that has given them to us" (9)—an idea that does not appear in his *Essai*, as we have seen, but that, for his part, utilizes in his letters of the 1770s. Besides, Condillac emphasizes that he now says "artificial signs," not "arbitrary signs," because the latter are "chosen without reason and by caprice" (9). And L'Épée contrasts exactly his "methodical signs" with the "arbitrary" signs of vocal languages: "With purely arbitrary signs, he writes, we could never have made ourselves heard" (1774, 33). Moreover, Condillac twice uses this argument of the communicative impotence of signs chosen "without reason": "[t]hey would not be... heard" (9), he notes, and a little further on, on the subject of pantomimes, he adds: "[h]ow then did they manage to form this language little by little? Is it by imagining arbitrary signs? But they would not have been heard" (10). This is an argument that is absent from the *Essai*. Finally, as we have seen, Condillac, in order to qualify the methodical signs of L'Épée, uses the expression "methodical art"—which is also absent from his *Essai*, as is an idea central to his "Grammaire": the idea of language understood as an analytic method (2–3). And L'Épée describes the signs of his invention as "methodical art" as early as in his second letter (1774, 21). Could we not go so far as to argue that Condillac's identification of language and method, anchored in his new conceptualization of the language of action and formulated in the very passage where he cites the methodical art of L'Épée, is partly indebted to the latter's invention of methodical signs?

Certainly, in 1756, well before the first writings of L'Épée on the education of the deaf, Maupertuis had already conceived, without using the expression, the existence of two languages of action. He could thus be taken as the true source of Condillac's reconceptualization, which would turn L'Épée's methodical art of signs into a simple experimental confirmation (1756, 438). However, Condillac's "Grammaire" does not mention Maupertuis, nor does it use his terminology. It is therefore L'Épée who, in my opinion, constitutes his source of inspiration.

4.2 Introducing the Second Language of Action into the Genesis of Spoken Languages

Condillac's new distinction between two languages of action allows him to argue that "[w]e could... express all our thoughts with gestures, as we express them with words..." (1775, 9)—as if he were content to call the languages of the Jews, Greeks and Romans described in the *Essai* "languages of action," or as if he envisaged the creation of a complete sign language. Yet in this passage, he more likely wanted to insert the second language of action into the genesis of spoken languages, that is, give it a place between the first sign language and the development of articulated sounds. This means that, according to him, such a language was indeed used by human beings, before those who are capable of hearing developed, on the basis of its model, the spoken languages that we know (15–16).

Between 1746 and 1775, the art of pantomime changed its status in Condillac's writings: it was of course derived from the language of action, but nevertheless introduced as a new invention in the *Essai* (2014, 222), before figuring as a rediscovery of a forgotten language in the "Grammaire" (1775, 10). Introducing the second language of action into the genesis of spoken languages similarly shifted the status of de L'Épée's methodical signs. This shift did, of course, not occur in the specific form given by L'Épée and his pupils. But its status changed nonetheless from being an invention to being a kind of rediscovery. For L'Épée did not so much invent a new language as he rediscovered it—a language similar to the one used by all humans. Here a universal language is not to be made, it is to be exhumed, and this is what L'Épée did in his own way, without knowing it.

The introduction of the second language of action into the genesis of spoken languages allowed Condillac to do two things: first, to explain this genesis more precisely than he had done in the *Essai*. In the second chapter of the "Grammaire," he deploys a series of analogies between the second language of action and that of articulated sounds—analogies that enabled nothing less than the passage from one to the other (18–20). The second thing Condillac was able to do now was answer an implicit objection, which can be formulated as follows. If ideas and faculties are transformed sensations, how is it that in uneducated deaf people, such as the man of Chartres, they remain rudimentary and express very little? The reason for this is, he answers, that the transition from the first to the second language of action is articulated through a shift from space to time, like the transition from painting to articulating a gestural line (12). This is not the case for L'Épée, for whom the language of natural signs already has a temporal dimension (1774, 52), although he also compares this language to the art of painting. By contrast, for Condillac, only the second language of action is conceived as a temporal succession of articulated signs.

The idea of a simultaneous first language of action is made possible by the fact that the philosopher resorts, without quoting him, to Diderot's thesis that pre-language thought is another form of thought (2000, 111)—it is simultaneous by nature. And like Diderot, he adds that if we tend to deny this, it is precisely because our thoughts unfold in time. Reading these lines, while bearing in mind that this language of action is also the first language for the deaf people, helps to dispel some of the prejudices concerning sign languages that existed at the time, and still exist today. According to these prejudices, sign languages seem to be impoverished, yet this seems to be so only because they are different from spoken languages. As we speak of "ethnocentrism," we can thus speak of "validocentrism,"[18] or, more precisely, of "audicentrism":[19] an attitude that consists in judging the universe (notably a linguistic one) available to people with hearing as superior to others. Condillac here unwittingly reveals the origin of this attitude, showing that the disability attributed to deaf people in fact affects people with hearing: if, according to Condillac, deaf people express very few thoughts, it is not because they do not have any—as the account of the deaf man of Chartres might suggest—but because these are expressed in such a way that people without the ability to understand sign language cannot grasp.

It is nevertheless possible for a hearing person, and this is what Condillac argues here, to grasp the *existence* of such thoughts through reason and the use of analogy (1775, 13–14).

For him, all human beings of the past, be they deaf or hearing, spoke the first language of action; they were like painters who are better at discerning the qualities of a painting than lay persons, yet without having better eyes. For the people of the past grasped at once much more than a hearing person does today, when confronted with a human being whose language is unknown and who tries to signify something through the movements of her body. Thus, "we must not believe that for those familiar with [this language]" it "is as confusing as it would be for us" (15). Condillac even goes so far as to turn this opinion on its head by attributing the disability to those using vocalized languages:

> Our languages, on the contrary, make us drag ourselves painfully from idea to idea, and we seem to have difficulty to make heard all that we think. It even seems that these languages, which have become second nature to us, slow down the action of all our faculties.
>
> (14)

However, it is not Condillac's intention here to say that the languages of deaf people do not slow down thought and that deaf people are thus more intelligent than those with hearing. The distinction he draws in this passage is not between deaf and hearing people, but between two kinds of language common to all people: one unfolds in space and the other in time.

What Condillac writes here is therefore also true for the second language(s) of action, which are just as successive as the languages of articulated sounds, and thus should be just as slowing as spoken language.

However, the languages of time, whether gestural or vocal, remain for him superior to the languages of space (15–16) precisely because they decompose thought and thus allow it to be articulated. Finally, the second language of action is not intrinsically superior to spoken languages: thanks to the method of analysis, the latter can, according to Condillac, deliver ideas just as exact and precise as those enabled through the use of L'Épée's methodical signs.

5 Conclusion

Thanks to L'Épée, Condillac understood not so much that sign languages are in no way inferior to spoken languages—which is something he already knew—but that these languages constitute a form of elaborate language that was once used by all humans. Thus, in the account of 1775, Condillac argues much more radically that we have all once been users of sign language than he did in his account of 1746. To conceive of a second language of action, which also appeared before articulated languages, is not to make sign languages coarser. Identifying sign languages as natural languages rather means to include deaf and hearing people in the same community of language users—even if Condillac did not argue for this explicitly.

Accordingly, deaf people would still be a minority but the language they use would not be, by nature, but only historically, a minority language. Even if such a language had never existed, Condillac's idea would remain a beautiful possibility: even if hearing people, historically speaking, did not learn their language, as Condillac thinks, thanks to the use of a highly elaborate sign language, he suggests that deaf and hearing people could once again belong to the same linguistic community—it would suffice for hearing people to learn the sign language of their country.

Moreover, and again unlike L'Épée, whose ideas he thus pushed further, Condillac understood that there are languages of space and languages of time and that the former express another form of thought, which can nevertheless be translated into the terms of the latter. However, his mistake was similar to that of L'Épée, namely to believe that, in order to achieve the same degree of distinction, sign language had to adopt the successive form characteristic of spoken language. As current sign languages attest, spatial thinking is just as distinct as linear thinking.

At this point, we can better situate the relationship between the philosophies of the Enlightenment and the access deaf people gained to education by means of sign language. With Condillac the philosophy of the Enlightenment was influenced by such a pedagogy, and even by the deaf students themselves, such as Françoise Arnaud, Marguerite Augé, and Jean-Baptiste Premois (L'Épée 1774, iii), who actively participated in it (Rée 1999, 148).

Condillac's influence on the reception of L'Épée'pedagogy certainly led, in turn, to the official recognition and development of this pedagogy in the First Republic. However, L'Épée, a convinced empiricist, was a man of his time in the same way as Condillac. To advocate the importance of sign languages for all is therefore to defend an extension of traditional Enlightenment ideals.

Notes

1 If the expression "deaf-mute" is inappropriate, it is mainly because (1) with rare exceptions, the vocal cords of deaf people are perfectly functional; (2) even when they are deprived of oral language, they are not deprived of speech: they use a language, namely sign language.
2 The existence of a reception of Condillac by L'Épée was asserted as early as the nineteenth century (and perhaps even earlier), notably in the writings of Édouard Séguin (French pedagogue, 1812–1880; founder of the first school for intellectually impaired children) and in the context of his critique of the language of signs. To maintain the existence of such a reception then has the function of accusing the latter of the (alleged) materialism of the former (Rée 1999, 216).
3 I systematically translate the quotations, modernizing the spelling and typography.
4 See Waldow's chapter in this volume which discusses in more detail Condillac's account of the emergence of language and the transition from natural to artificial signs.
5 For Warburton, the first language of humanity was made up of vocal, but equivocal words, and was for this reason later accompanied by gestures. It should be noted that, without giving it the conceptual density that is characteristic of his disciple Condillac, he describes this first language as a "language of action" (Warburton 1744, 58–59).
6 Translated into french by J.-R. Armogathe, J.-M. Bai and F. Markovits (1986).
7 It is true that Augustine writes that gesture can signify more than visible objects—but then he mentions not this or that abstract idea but "sounds, tastes and the like" (1864–1873, 187–188). Quoted by Benvenuto (2009, 45). Descartes, for his part, writes: "but no beast has ever been so perfect, that it has used some sign to make other animals hear something which had no relation to its passions; and there is no man so imperfect, that he does not use it; so that those who are deaf and dumb, invent particular signs, by which they express their thoughts" (1996 t. IV, 575). The deaf people seem to be the most imperfect class of men here, that is, certainly, poorly endowed with abstract ideas.
8 I would point out that with this thesis of the decoupling of written signs from vocal signs (1774, 15), L'Épée also turned his back on Augustine, who also maintained that the latter were the reflections of the former, and consequently that the deaf people were incapable of learning to read and write (Benvenuto 2009, 44).
9 Rée is therefore wrong when he makes Geffroy a Lockean (1999, 216).
10 Translated in french and quoted by Firode (2005: 212).

11 It is true that L'Épée explicitly opposed those who embraced the principle that there is nothing in our minds which has not entered through our senses, but only those among them who did not endorse the idea of sensory supplementation (1774, 16–17).
12 Quoted by Weygand (2003, 44).
13 When, a little further on in this same letter (72), L'Épée describes those who make deaf people into automatons as "anti-deaf" and "anti-mute," he does not contradict himself, but targets thinkers, such as Le Bouvier-Desmortiers (1739–1827), who believe that the deaf people are definitively deprived of thoughts—which is obviously not his case (Amann 2021, 181).
14 From now on, signs are only required for reasoning conceived as a sequence (and not as a simultaneous seizure) of judgments. Thus, language still plays a decisive role in the genesis of the soul's operations, but it now conditions only one of form of reasoning.
15 I have thus erred in writing that Condillac "not grant the deaf man of Chartres any more in 1775 than he did in 1746" (2018, 340).
16 What I am trying to establish here, namely that there was in fact a reception of L'Épée by Condillac, is proposed as a simple hypothesis by Rosenfeld (2001, 101).
17 On the distinction between the *Essai* and the "Grammaire" regarding the first language of action, see Bertrand (2016).
18 See Gardien (2016), "Validocentrism corresponds to a collective and generally unconscious attitude that favours an understanding of situations and, more broadly, of the world based on the valid human as a reference, belittling and rejecting all other norms and values stemming from the diversity of bodies, and even denying the possibility of founding alternative bodily perspectives."
19 Audicentrism is sometimes identified with audism, conceived as the set of discriminations, based on the auditory norm, which affects deaf people (Humphries 1975).

References

Amann, F. (2021) *Sourds et muets. Entre savoir et fiction au tournant des Lumières* (1776–1815) (Paris: Classiques Garnier). DOI: 10.48611/isbn.978-2-406-11119-1. p.0383

Armogathe, J.-R., Bai, J.-M. and Markovits, F. (1986) "Controverse entre l'Abbé de l'Épée et Samuel Heinicke *(traduction)*," *Corpus*, 2: 87–115

Augustine (1864–1873) De Magistro, in Œuvres complètes de Saint-Augustin (Bar-le-Duc: Poujoulat et Raulx), t. 3

Benvenuto, A. (2009) *Qu'est-ce qu'un sourd? De la figure au sujet philosophique*, doctoral thesis, Université Paris 8

Bernard, Y. (2012) "Des différences au siècle des Lumières: la modernité des signes," in Y. Bernard and M. Kurtz eds., *L'héritage de l'abbé de l'Épée* (Chambéry: CNFEDS), 75–178

Bertrand, A. (2016) "Deux définitions du langage d'action, ou deux théories de l'esprit?," in A. Bertrand ed., *Condillac, philosophe du langage?* (Lyon: ENS Éditions). DOI: 10.4000/books.enseditions.7121

Branson, J. and Miller, D. (2002) *Damned for Their Difference: The Cultural Construction of Deaf People as Disabled* (Washington, DC: Gallaudet University Press). DOI: 10.1080/15017410510032244

Chottin, M. (2018) "Penser la surdité. L'histoire du sourd de Chartres et l'empirisme des Lumières," *Dix-huitième siècle* 50: 323–341. DOI: 10.3917/dhs.050.0323
Condillac, É. B. de (1775) *Cours d'étude pour l'instruction du Prince de Parme*, t. I (Parme: Imprimerie royale)
Condillac, É. B. de (2014) *Essai sur l'origine des connaissances humaines*, J.-C. Pariente and M. Pécharman eds. (Paris: Vrin)
Descartes, R. (1996) *Œuvres de Descartes*, Ch. Adam and P. Tannery eds. (Paris: C.N.R.S. and Vrin)
Diderot, D. (2000) *Lettre sur les sourds et les muets à l'usage de ceux qui entendent et qui parlent*, M. Hobson and S. Harvey eds. (Paris: Flammarion)
Ehrsam, R. (2012) "Représentation des sourds et muets et fonctions de la parole de Descartes à Kant," *Archives de Philosophie* 4: 643–667. DOI: 10.3917/aphi.754.0643
Firode, A. (2005) "Le cours de philosophie d'Adrien Geffroy," *Recherches sur Diderot et sur l'Encyclopédie* 38. DOI: http://journals.openedition.org/rde/309
Gardien, È. (2016) "De la liberté corporelle en situation: l'exemple de la résistance de personnes handicapées au validocentrisme," *Corps* 1(14): 105–114. DOI: 10.3917/corp1.014.0105
Geffroy, A. (1731–1733) *Cayers de philosophie dictés par Monsieur Geffroy professeur au collège Mazarin*, 4 vol., Bibliothèque municipale de Brive, "Metaphysica," vol. 2, Cote: P1-1-8
Humphries, T. (1975) *Audism: The Making of a Word*. Unpublished Essay
Lane, H. (1989) *When the Mind Hears: A History of the Deaf* (New York: Vintage).
L'Épée, Ch.-M. de (1774) *Institution des sourds et muets, Ou Recueil des exercices soutenus par les sourds et muets pendant les années 1771, 1772, 1773 et 1774* (Paris: Butard)
L'Épée, Ch.-M. de (1776) *Institution des sourds et muets, par la voie des signes méthodiques* (Paris: Nyon l'aîné)
L'Épée, Ch.-M. de (1784) *La véritable manière d'instruire les sourds et muets* (Paris: Nyon l'aîné)
Locke, J. (1975) *An Essay Concerning Human Understanding* (Oxford: Clarendon Press)
Markovits, F. (2011) "L'abbé de L'Épée : du verbe intérieur à la langue des signes," in *Le Décalogue sceptique. L'universel en question au temps des Lumières* (Paris: Hermann): 169–189
Maupertuis, P. L. M. de (1756) *Dissertation sur les différents moyens dont les hommes se sont servis pour exprimer leurs idées*, in *Œuvres de Mr. De Maupertuis*, vol. III (Lyon: Jean-Marie Bruyset)
Murgel, J. (2016) "Manualism, Philosophy and Models of," in G. Gertz and P. Boudreault eds., *The SAGE Deaf Studies Encyclopedia* (New-York: Sage Publications, vol. 1): 674–675. DOI: 10.4135/9781483346489.n210
Presneau, J.-R. (1998) *Signes et institutions des sourds. XVIIIe-XIXe siècle* (Paris: Champ Vallon)
Rée, J. (1999) *I See a Voice: Deafness, Language and the Senses. A Philosophical History* (London: Metropolitan Books)
Rocheleau-Rouleau, C. (1950) "Parler est chose facile vous croyez? Aperçu de l'histoire de l'instruction des sourds muets et de son application au Canada

français en marge de deux centenaires," *Revue d'histoire de l'Amérique française* 4(3): 345–374. DOI: 10.7202/801653ar

Rosenfeld, S. (2001) *A Revolution in Language: The Problem of Signs in Late Eighteenth-Century France* (Stanford, CA: Stanford University Press)

Vinci, L. de (1987) *Traité de la peinture*, A. Chastel ed. (Paris: Berger-Levrault)

Warburton, W. (1744) *Essai sur les hiéroglyphes des Égyptiens* (Paris: Hyppolite-Louis Guérin)

Weygand, Z. (2003) *Vivre sans voir. Les Aveugles dans la société française, du Moyen Âge au siècle de Louis Braille* (Paris: Créaphis)

Part II
Condillac's Reception in Nineteenth-Century France

6 Condillac Restored

The Paradox of Attention in Pierre Laromiguière's *Lessons on Philosophy* (1815)

Pierre Brouillet

1 Introduction: Condillac's Concept of Attention and Its Reception

Attention is a key concept in Condillac's theory of human knowledge. It is introduced in his first work, the *Essay on the Origin of Human Knowledge* (1746), where it works as a bond that enables the connection of ideas: "the connection of several ideas can have no other cause than the attention we have paid to them when they occur together" (Condillac, 2001, p. 32). As the first active operation of the mind, concerned with an intense and selective perception (Condillac, 2001, p. 21), attention also supports the development of other intellectual operations, as shown in sect. II, chap. III, entitled "How the connection of ideas, *formed by attention*, brings forth imagination, contemplation, and memory". In relation to this account of attention, the *Essay* describes reflection as "the power we have of directing our own attention" (Condillac, 2001, p. 44): it emerges as soon as our attention is at our disposal, thanks to the use of arbitrary signs (Condillac, 2001, p. 41). Moreover, scholars have stressed that in the *Essay* the principle of human knowledge lies in the connection of ideas[1] rather than perception or consciousness (Aarsleff, 1982, p. 29; Charrak, 2003, p. 39; Chottin, 2014, p. 1). The causal role of attention in fostering a connection between ideas thus turns attention into a crucial gnoseological concept, as it is tied to the very principle of knowledge. As Condillac wrote, "ideas are connected with signs and... this is the only way that ideas are connected together" (Condillac, 2001, p. 5); in fact, it is the only way that there are ideas at all. Condillac straightforwardly acknowledged this point and never said anything different in the *Essay*, so one wonders why scholars had to insist on defending this claim. I propose two hypothesis, one internal and the other external to Condillac's work, to explain this interpretive confusion. Both provide contrasting views on the ambiguous and dynamic function of the Condillaquian conception of attention.

DOI: 10.4324/9781003334750-8

1 The first hypothesis is that, paradoxically, the principle of the connection of ideas seems to be *derived* from the use of signs and, in that respect, does not seem to meet the requirements of being a principle (Charrak, 2003, p. 39). André Charrak addresses this apparent contradiction by distinguishing between "two forms of connection": a rudimentary one which bypasses the need for signs and which connects sensible impressions, and a fully fledged one which operates between ideas. However, insofar as the former does not, strictly speaking, connect *ideas*, it could be argued that attention functions as "the principle behind the connection of ideas" (Chottin, 2014, p. 6)[2] and, because of this, as the actual principle enabling knowledge. Indeed, attention offers the advantage that it counts as mysteriously underived: as Condillac wrote, the reason why the connection of ideas can be formed by attention "lies entirely in the nature of the soul and the body" (Condillac, 2001, p. 25), which makes this connection a "fundamental experience" (*ibid.*). Marion Chottin argues, however, that neither perceptions nor attention could be considered as *principles* because, for an empiricist thinker like Condillac, a principle has to be based on a "well-established fact" (Condillac, 1749/1992, p. 24; Chottin, 2014, p. 7). Yet we only experience composed impressions or ideas, and when we engage in reflection we use ideas that are connected to each other. As a result, it is not possible to establish a philosophical system based on the *empirical* finding that attention exists as an isolated phenomenon attached to an individual idea or impression. And even though one has to believe that perception and attention are chronologically prior to the connection of ideas, the latter must come first when considering the *logical* order of knowledge, because this connection is the first to be actually experienced as a well-established fact.

2 The second hypothesis on the reason why the connection of ideas was not unanimously recognized as the *Essay*'s foremost principle can be found in later assessments of his work by authors who argued that the *Essay* counts as a step toward, or as the first exposition of, more radical ideas exposed in the *Treatise on Sensations* (1754) and subsequent writings. In this book, sensation is established as the one original principle from which all other operations derive (Condillac, 1992, p. 279). Accepting or rejecting this principle, to which Condillac also referred as the principle of "transformed sensation" (*sensation transformée*), quickly separated his followers from the spiritualist thinkers who began classifying their adversaries as "sensualists" at the turn of the nineteenth century (see Daled, 2005). The main feature of spiritualism, in contrast with sensualism, can be presented as a concern with the ontological and epistemic superiority of mind over matter and of the soul over the senses. In this context, the point of contention was

that the new principle of "transformed sensation" seemed to imply that "the connecting power [of attention] is not an *activity* whatsoever" (Chottin, 2014, p. 4). And indeed, as André Charrak reminds us, "in his later works, [Condillac] meticulously denied that attention... is active and described it rather as a response to the outside circumstances" (Charrak, 2003, p. 52). What is at stake in the spiritualist refusal of the principle of "transformed sensation" is no less than the attempt to preserve an active power of the mind in the perceptual process—a power Condillac initially made part of his concept of attention, but that was abandoned through the role attributed to sensation. Among many others, Victor Cousin, the chief of the spiritualist eclectic school and a decisive figure in French nineteenth-century philosophy, provides a typical example of this reception. "The core of [Cousin's] argumentation consisted in distinguishing two moments in Condillac's philosophy", the allegedly reasonable and rationalist moment of the *Essay* and the *Treatise on Systems* (1749), and the regressive sensualist moment opened by the *Treatise on Sensations* (Antoine-Mahut, 2021, p. 273).

In light of these few remarks, I claim that Condillac's concept of attention crucially influenced the reception of Condillac's work and, more precisely, the early-nineteenth-century French metaphysical battle concerning the foundations of psychology. The historians of philosophy may regard these controversies as "family affairs" (Antoine-Mahut, 2013), insofar as they often revolve around identifying parental or rather father figures as the originators of lineages used to legitimate a certain school of thought, while condemning competing philosophical lineages. To be sure, these controversies involve philosophical arguments but also quarrels about how to interpret those parental figures, often resulting in intentional deformations of their doctrines. Accordingly, Condillac is a debated and controversial figure, as his own philosophical development made him

> both one of the main leading light of a condemnable philosophy, the eighteenth-century sensualism; and a figure that resists being reduced in this manner, because part of his philosophical project and achievements could, at least, be re-interpreted and taken up by the 'true' spiritualists or 'French philosophers'.
>
> (Antoine-Mahut, 2021, p. 271)

When analyzing such philosophical controversies, it is beneficial to select particularly polemical texts. Relevant materials include the first histories of philosophy as well as so-called lessons, i.e. orally delivered lectures that were then turned into written works. These lessons often contain animated debates unfolding among the students in the audience, thus providing a rich source of study. A further advantage of analyzing lessons is that they document how the authors of the past were reinterpreted in the teaching of the younger scholars and, thus, *in the context of their very transmission*. For this reason, working with lessons can help us to better understand the birth of some philosophical lineages and the genesis of their self-proclaimed characteristics.

My study will focus on the *Lessons on Philosophy* (1815) by Pierre Laromiguière (1756–1837). These lessons, first delivered orally in 1809–1811, were concerned with a broad approach to metaphysics and had such success after their first publication in 1815 that they were republished five times during the first half of the century (1820, 1823, 1828, 1833 and 1844). In this chapter, I will refer to the third edition of these lectures (1823), which is the one most often quoted and most accessible. In addition to meeting the inclusion criterion of being a polemical text concerned with the re-interpretation and transmission of Condillac's philosophy, this text meets two more requirements. First, as an editor of Condillac and the first chair of philosophy at La Sorbonne from 1809 to his death, Laromiguière devoted almost half his lessons between 1809 and 1811 to the critical re-elaboration of Condillac's system. Each of these lessons was said to be eloquent and met with great success and many questions from his audience; they were "meetings that gather[ed] all ages and all talents, students from the École Normale and first-class scholars" (Laromiguière, 1815/1823, p. 71). At the core of Laromiguière's arguments lies his critique of Condillac's concept of attention; in his new psychological theory, it plays the role of an active principle complementing sensibility. Through this focus, Laromiguière's lessons *offer an ideal opportunity for studying reception of Condillac's concept of attention.*

Second, because of his ambiguous relationship to Condillac, *Laromiguière holds a particularly interesting position in the controversy* between sensualist and spiritualist thinkers. Indeed, the nineteenth-century historiographer François Picavet regarded him as one of the "Idéologues" (Picavet, 1891)—a group of sensualist thinkers heavily influenced by Condillac, formed during the French Revolution. This group comprised, among others, the philosopher, economist and senator, Antoine Destutt de Tracy; the physician, philosopher and deputy, Pierre Jean Georges Cabanis; the historian and philosopher, Volney; and the philosopher and senator, Dominique Joseph Garat. Even if possible, it is probably vain to try and establish criteria that determine whether Laromiguière can be regarded as one of the Idéologues, insofar as they themselves did not use this term. Moreover, spiritualist historiographer Jean-Philibert Damiron, an advocate of the Cousinian school, conveniently classified Laromiguière as belonging to the "sensualist school", while also recognizing his spiritualist learnings. This classification was motivated by the fact that "we usually consider him as a disciple of Condillac" (Damiron, 1828, p. 65; see Barancy, 2019). By contrast, Victor Cousin, who confessed in 1833 that he decided to study philosophy the day he attended Laromiguière's class for the first time, recognized him as one of his three main mentors, together with the philosophers, Pierre-Paul Royer-Collard and Pierre Maine de Biran (Cousin, 1833, p. xxxiii). Even though Cousin established his own spiritualist school and heavily criticized his former teacher, his disagreement with Laromiguière indicates how important the reconstruction of Condillac's philosophy was, not only for both the sensualists and the spiritualists but also *among* the spiritualists themselves, as it marked intra-spiritualist differences.

This chapter aims to show that Laromiguière's "philosophy of attention" was indeed ambiguous in relation to the assessment and interpretation of Condillac's philosophy. For this reason, it served as a sharp weapon in the battle between the different philosophical camps as Laromiguière tried to fix Condillac's theory of knowledge to make it compatible with the spiritualist conception of the soul. I argue that Laromiguière tried to *restore* Condillac and, by doing so, may have influenced Cousin's own "family" history of philosophy. The word "restoring" has in fact two main meanings: (1) *protecting* something by returning it to an earlier better condition, and (2) *repairing* it using different materials while respecting its original manner. (This is what the Bourbon Restoration—which began in 1814, a year before Laromiguière's text was published—intended to do: to re-establish the full authority of the king on a basis that takes many revolutionary and imperial gains into account.) In this context, we also need to recognize that any rehabilitation, regardless of the authenticity it may attempt, is bound to achieve some kind of deformation, since it repairs something belonging to the past for it to be able to fit in the present. By describing and commenting on how Laromiguière presented Condillac as a member of the Cartesian spiritualist lineage, I will, on the one hand, show that he attempted to *protect* Condillac's philosophical legacy. By establishing a typology of Laromiguière's arguments against Condillac, I will, on the other hand, demonstrate that Laromiguière's amended version of Condillac's philosophy relies on spiritualist arguments. For the most part, these arguments draw on Cartesian views on the activity of the soul, but also, paradoxically enough, on an argument presented in Condillac's *Essay* of 1746 that was then abandoned: the idea that attention is a fundamentally active operation of the mind. Such a study clearly advocates for a less binary classificatory system of the history of French nineteenth-century philosophy. For Condillac and his reception make it clear that a philosophical system cannot be satisfactorily described as a manifestation of mere "sensualism" or "spiritualism" but must rather be seen as resulting from a spectrum of different influences and figures who, as part of engaging with the history of philosophical controversies, selectively chose and reinvented the characteristics of their various positions.

2 Protecting Condillac by Incorporating Him into a French Philosophical Lineage

According to Damiron's influential, yet biased, statement, Laromiguière was the first philosopher to undertake a critical analysis of Condillac, whose philosophy is claimed to have indisputably dominated in France until 1810 (Picavet, 1891, p. 523). Damiron mentions Laromiguière's "struggle to part with ideas to which he had devoted his primary faith and love" (Damiron, 1828, p. 77). Such statements tend to hide the fact that none of Condillac's disciples blindly accepted his system: the Idéologues praised him as a master of *methodological* unity. As a regular guest at the reunions of the Auteuil Society and associate member of the *Institut de France* in the 1800s, Laromiguière was close to the Idéologues. Like them, he found in Condillac's philosophy a new programmatic method, but he also identified some problems that required clarification and even correction. Laromiguière was no different from them in this respect and his criticism stemmed from what he considered to be his own Condillaquian commitments. To understand better how Laromiguière engaged in the construction of a philosophical lineage, it will be helpful to analyze how he introduced Condillac to his students.

2.1 A French Lineage: From Descartes to Condillac

In the "Discourse on the language of reason" delivered at the beginning of Laromiguière's first class, he declared that "only a French man of the eighteenth century, Condillac, could teach us what we do when we think and reason; just like a century before, only another French man, Descartes, could teach the whole of Europe how to think and reason" (Laromiguière, 1823, p. 18). By asserting a historical continuity, he implies that in the aftermath of the Revolution, there was a tradition on which proper modern French philosophy was built. Similarly, describing Condillac by insisting on his being a "French man" helps Laromiguière prevent others from associating Condillac with another country's philosophical tradition—for instance, the empiricist British tradition of Bacon and Locke.

This opening speech clearly aligns Condillac with Descartes' philosophy. It suggests that the Cartesian "revolution" of thought (Laromiguière, 1823, p. 19) had in fact two moments, as it credits the former with a discovery just as important as the latter's. In this respect, Laromiguière judges that "we owe [to Condillac] ideas that are truer than those that we could have received from the other philosophers on the matter of how thinking develops and on the nature of reasoning" (Laromiguière, 1823, p. 18). The hierarchy resulting from this discussion explicitly fits with the list of authors Laromiguière identifies as worthy of being taught and studied at La Sorbonne (Laromiguière, 1823, p. 70). In the establishment of this hierarchy, Laromiguière heavily committed to Condillac's philosophy in the year of 1809, a time when Condillac's major disciples, the Idéologues, were mostly in opposition to the Napoleonic government. As Condillac's name had become a bit suspect for this reason, Laromiguière thus had to cautiously specify the reasons why Condillac was France's last great metaphysician in order to protect his legacy. According to him, two particularly significant and pioneering ideas justify Condillac's distinguished status.

2.2 Condillac's Epistemological Superiority

The first of these ideas is tied to the requirement that "when studying the human mind, everything should be reduced to one unique principle that offers every phenomenon of reason and thought in an infinite variety of transmutations" (Laromiguière, 1823, p. 138). For Laromiguière, this discovery is analogous to that of introducing digits into arithmetic, the lever principle into mechanics and the resonance of the sounding body into music and acoustics. "Among all ancient and modern philosophers", he writes, Condillac was the only one who demonstrated the necessity of such a reduction in the philosophy of mind. Laromiguière mentions that Condillac embarked on this route as early as in his first work, the *Essay on the Origin of Human Knowledge* (1746), although he here "derived everything from perception or consciousness" (Laromiguière, 1823, p. 138). Although Condillac indeed explained his project in these terms in the "Introduction" to the *Essay* (Condillac, 2001, p. 35), that choice of words is crucial in allowing Laromiguière to conceal the differences between the *Essay* and his later works which, from the *Treatise on Sensations* onward, elaborate on the principle of "transformed sensation" (*sensation transformée*). Thus, Laromiguière implicitly suggests that the only difference between the *Essay* and the *Treatise* concerns the nature of this principle—first Condillac referred to perception, then to sensation. However, perception is not, as mentioned above, the actual logical principle of knowledge in the *Essay* but only a chronological starting point. In other words, Laromiguière concealed the fact that this principle was not at first conceived in relation to the mind's perceptual operations but in relation to the connection of ideas. If one follows Laromiguière's interpretation, the *Treatise*'s radical innovation would merely consist in the reformulation of an already sensualist thesis. We will come back to the reasons that might have motivated this simplification.

2.3 Attention as an Analytic Method: Drawing a Cartesian Lineage

Condillac's second innovative idea is that "the art of thinking depends on language", thus contrasting with the view, as Laromiguière warns, that "thinking depends on language" (Laromiguière, 1823, p. 20). While language is not needed for having thought, languages are "analytic methods" (Laromiguière, 1823, p. 23) that are indispensable for processes of reasoning, which constitute the art of decomposing thought. The first lesson of Laromiguière's course is entitled "On Method" and establishes another connection between Descartes and Condillac: the latter clarified that the former's "method" was nothing but analysis. Condillac redefined the analytic method as an operation that "merely consists in composing and decomposing our ideas to create new combinations and to discover, by this means, their mutual relations and the new ideas they can produce" (Condillac, 2001, p. 48). In Laromiguière's own formulation of Condillac's analysis, he specifically insisted on the role of attention in that process: analysis is

> a means to skillfully make up for a lack of strength, to reduce plurality to unity by reducing several ideas to one unique idea, and to embrace with one gaze what used to divide one's attention in so many ways.
> (Laromiguière, 1823, p. 59)

The need for method, and consequently Condillac's merit, thus results from the need to enhance our attention, a faculty that proves hard to use due to the epistemic weakness of the fallen man. In order to actually reason, it is "necessary to bring our attention back inside of us and to pay attention to thought" (Laromiguière, 1823, p. 57). Condillac's superiority as a philosopher therefore consisted in developing an analytic method based on the use of attention. Laromiguière symmetrically suggested that previous philosophers could not avoid their mistakes because they lacked attention (Laromiguière, 1823, p. 9), that is, the right kind of analytic spirit. As we will see presently, these observations about attention lead us to the heart of Laromiguière's critique of Condillac's system.

3 Assessing the Damage: Condillac's Concept of Attention and the Bounds of the Mind's Activity

In order to convince his audience that, despite his attentiveness, Condillac showed some kind of neglect, Laromiguière claimed that he spent long years meditating on the former's texts. He seemingly borrowed Descartes' language to motivate his attempt to fix Condillac's theory:

[Condillac's arguments] have been the subject of my meditations, not only for a few days but for several years. Their charming simplicity, an ordinary characteristic of truth, appealed to me and I went into some details that the author neglected; I took pleasure in developing what was only suggested; I sought to shed light on what could not be noticed at first, to affirm what seemed to lack support.

Pointless efforts! *The passage from sensation to attention has always been unfathomable to reasoning.*
(Laromiguière, 1823, pp. 140–141)

Strikingly, at this point, Laromiguière did not seem to focus on the *Essay*, but on the *Treatise on Sensations* and Condillac's later works, such as the *Logic*. One could object, as his students did, that the problematic "passage" that describes the transition from sensation to attention is not mentioned before the *Treatise*. Pointing to the evolution of Condillac's doctrine, however, does not fix the problem—at least not if one agrees with Laromiguière that the idea of a transformed sensation, conceived of as a "generating principle", was already present in his *Essay*. He wrote:

Since then, he substituted feeling and more generally sensation for these two words (perception and consciousness); but changing the words does not mean he changed the thing itself. The principle generating the other faculties remains the same: it is still the modification experienced when external objects cause a movement within the organs.
(Laromiguière, 1823, p. 138)

By reducing Condillac's philosophy to that formulated from 1754 onward, Laromiguière was able to criticize, at once, ideas from the *Essay* as well as those of his later works. Laromiguière first identified perception with sensation, even though for Condillac only the latter had the status of a principle, and then pointed to a flaw common to both. According to Laromiguière, the problem about moving from consciousness, perception or sensation to attention lies in the contradictory nature of the transition from the *passive capacity* to feel to the *active faculty* of being attentive. Yet Condillac himself explained in his *Logic* (1780) that attention and sensation do not have different natures:

the attention we pay to an object is therefore, as to the mind, *nothing but the sensation* which that object causes in us, a sensation which in some measure becomes exclusive; and this quality is the first we remark in the faculty of feeling.
(Condillac, 1992, pp. 601–602)

According to Laromiguière, Condillac's demonstration is logically flawed. "There is a gap and a break of continuity" (Laromiguière, 1823, p. 147) that needs to be fixed in order to rehabilitate Condillac. Neither perception nor sensation can be considered as having the same nature as attention. "Can passivity become activity?", Laromiguière asked, "can it *transform into* activity?" (Laromiguière, 1823, p. 104). This question could be termed "the paradox of Condillac's concept of attention" and to answer it means taking a philosophical position about the scope and limits of the mind's activity. Laromiguière and his students alternately debated many ostensible answers to this paradox and Laromiguière judged that all led to even more contradictions. Below I will establish a typology of these apparently unsatisfactory answers and discuss them in turn.

3.1 Assuming the Complete Passivity of the Mind: Is Condillac a Materialist Thinker?

The first answer to the paradox consists in regarding Condillac as a materialist thinker who did not believe in the spiritual activity of the soul; in that respect, the transformation from sensation to attention stands for nothing more than the passivity of the mind. In particular, Condillac's spiritualist opponents defended this interpretation. For instance, Damiron wrote in 1828 that "Condillac assumes that the soul is passive, and nothing but passive" (Damiron, 1828, p. 66). Thereupon, Laromiguière's ninth and tenth lectures set out to judge "whether Condillac's system promotes materialism", a question vividly debated by his students. In Laromiguière's opinion, Condillac decided too many times against materialism and in favor of the activity of mind for this hypothesis to be accurate. However, to show this, Laromiguière needed to draw on arguments that Condillac had put forward before he wrote the *Treatise on Sensations*. He quoted the *Treatise on Systems* (1749), which states "that the understanding is passive only as regards ideas that come directly from the senses, and that the others are all its product" (Condillac, 1992, p. 91). Laromiguière thereby refutes the materialist framework allegedly underpinning the doctrine of "transformed sensation" and justifies Condillac by aligning him with the spiritualist teaching program. In many regards, this statement is accurate, even if one takes into consideration the *Treatise* and the doctrine of "transformed sensation" formulated therein. Condillac's ontology, far from being materialist, is indeed spiritualist and dualist; however, one could respond that "the methodology undergirding his theory of the understanding is certainly not [dualist]: it has no need to assume a ghost in the machine" (Auroux, 1992, p. 163). By describing *operations* and *habits* of the soul, Condillac flatly denied the necessity of a system of *faculties* and initiated a shift away from the Cartesian subject of the *cogito*, for his theory of the understanding

Condillac Restored 93

does not allow one to "essentialize a subject": "the operator is within the operations, it is not a body separated from its operations" (Markovits-Pessel, 2018, p. 120). Such an interpretation appears to be a satisfactory contemporary answer to the aforementioned paradox of Condillac's concept of attention, as it questions the accuracy of the passive-active distinction in order to make sense of Condillac. However, as we shall see further, Laromiguière would probably not have accepted this answer, insofar as it requires us to portray Condillac as a critic of Cartesian metaphysics.

3.2 Assuming the Simultaneity of Sensation and Attention: Condillac as a Hyper-Spiritualist

The second answer to contemplate implies that passivity does not actually transform into activity because sensation and attention are the two sides of the same coin. On this account, the soul becomes active through attention as soon as it passively feels its very first sensation. According to André Charrak, who supports this interpretation, "describing all these operations as nothing but transformed sensation concretely means that they are nothing but transformed attention" (Charrak, 2003, p. 52). Laromiguière believed that this interpretation is the one Condillac truly aimed at, as he consistently stated it throughout his books. Hence his fictional summoning of Condillac to defend himself in his own words: "Sensation and attention are indeed two different words but not two different things; I highlighted this truth at the beginning of my book so to prevent your complaints about transforming passivity into activity when I transform sensation into attention" (Laromiguière, 1823, p. 149). However, according to Laromiguière, Condillac seems to be "overstating the activity of the mind by locating it not only in sensation but also in the very first sensation" (Laromiguière, 1823, p. 238). In a rhetorical *tour de force*, he concludes that "not only Condillac is not a materialist thinker", but also that he even "exaggerates spiritualism" (Laromiguière, 1823, p. 227) by endowing sensibility with an activity which only attention, an entirely different phenomenon, can have.

3.3 Assuming an Untamed, Involuntary Form of Attention: Is Attention an Act of the Will?

The last answer discussed in relation to the paradox of Condillac's concept of attention assumes that attention is at first passive and turns active when the mind becomes able to control it. In the *Essay*, the mastery of attention is made possible "as soon as the memory is formed, and the habit of the imagination is in our power" (Condillac, 2001, p. 41). Since "a single arbitrary sign is enough for a person to revive an idea by himself" (*ibid.*), reflection, conceived as "the power we have of directing our own attention" (Condillac, 2001, p. 44), can arise in its most primitive form. If this interpretation is taken seriously, however, a new obstacle appears: why should the first arbitrary sign of the soul be enough for it to become the master over its operations? Here the question on the moment when the soul *becomes active* only seems to be postponed as it is subtly replaced with the problem of *gaining mastery over* the soul's operations. Although a thorough discussion of activity in relation to the Condillaquian connection of ideas and his semiotic theory seems promising as a strategy that could successfully deal with the paradox, Laromiguière did not consider that this is how Condillac approaches the issue in the *Essay*. This is probably because acknowledging this would force him to admit that already here Condillac tacitly operated with a concept of involuntary activity, or a form of passive attention. However, it is not until the *Treatise on Sensations,* where Condillac regards the statue as both passive and active, that these notions are explicitly discussed: "it is active when it remembers a sensation, because it has in itself the cause that recalls it, that is, memory. It is passive at the moment it is experiencing a sensation, because the cause that produces that sensation is outside of it" (Condillac, 1992, p. 318). Consequently, one must distinguish between the statue's "passive attention" and its "active attention" (Condillac, 1992, p. 319). Laromiguière heuristically agreed that "sensation could be inseparably linked to an act of involuntary attention, in other words, to an instinctive reaction", but he firmly denied "that sensation is inseparable from a voluntary reaction, that is, from actual attention itself" (Laromiguière, 1823, p. 159). Dividing attention into two heterogeneous components does not, in fact, solve the paradoxical birth of activity. Even more so, this distinction leads to a conception of the will which implies a difference in nature between two forms of attention. Instead of calling both of these distinct phenomena by the name of "attention", Laromiguière reserved that term for the second. He thereby conceived of the original activity of the mind as an act of the will.

4 Repairing Condillac and Shaping a Cartesianized Condillacism: Attention and the Psychological Program of French Spiritualism

From Laromiguière's discussion of these three unsatisfactory solutions, we can draw some important conclusions. The arguments used to refute them tell us which characteristics of Condillac's philosophy a spiritualist teaching program would regard as unacceptable. They also reveal which aspects of Condillac's philosophy were considered worth keeping or singled out for correction, ignored or passed down, in the attempt to establish a psychological program for French nineteenth-century philosophy.

4.1 The Psychological Program of Early-Nineteenth-Century French Spiritualism

By "program" I do not mean that Laromiguière's system was unanimously accepted by his contemporaries—far from it (see Cousin and Biran, 1817, p. 6). Rather what I have in mind is that the idea of a new metaphysics grounded in psychology lies at the heart of Victor Cousin's philosophical ambitions. In this respect, Cousin, as he himself recognized, owed much to the teachings of Laromiguière, Royer-Collard and Maine de Biran. Thus, Cousin stated that Laromiguière introduced him "to the art of decomposing the thought", taught him how "to go from the most abstract and general ideas that we have today back to the most common sensations that originated them" and helped him understand "the interplay of the elementary and composed faculties that successively take part in the formation of ideas" (Cousin, 1833, p. xxxiii). The main lesson Cousin seems to have learned from Laromiguière is the use of the analytic method, which did not differ much—or at all—from Condillac's own. But, according to Cousin, it was Royer-Collard, the substitute teacher replacing Laromiguière at La Sorbonne from 1811 to 1814, who purportedly taught him how to leave the beaten track of Condillacism and explore the path of Scottish philosophy; he made it clearer than Laromiguière that sensation cannot be the source of every distinct law and principle governing the faculties (*ibid.*). Maine de Biran, finally, helped him identify the role of a voluntary activity in our knowledge and in each of our conscious states (*ibid.*). Through this narrative of a threefold influence, Cousin turned Laromiguière into someone who looks just like Condillac, while he attributed to Biran alone, as opposed to Laromiguière, the ability to fully appreciate the role of the will in the formation of ideas. Yet Cousin also seemed to be the first to have noticed the essentially voluntary aspect Laromiguière attributed to attention. When distancing himself from Laromiguière and beginning to set out his own philosophy, he summarized Laromiguière's psychology as a system where "everything is derived from sensibility and attention" (Cousin, 1833, p. 92). According to Cousin, some rational judgments involving the moral sentiments can neither be reduced to sensation nor to attention. Through this judgment, he suggested that his former teacher mistakenly explained all manifestations of the intellect through "*attention, that is, the will*, and the abstract, collective and vague word 'feeling'" (*ibid.*). At that time Cousin accused Laromiguière of not having recognized in full that the will is in fact the foundational principle of psychology, that is, something that is even prior to attention: through the inner experience of the Cartesian cogito, the subject says "I" and recognizes itself as a free will causing its own thought (see Cousin and Maine de Biran, 1817, pp. 76–77, 1829, pp. 143–146). Cousin was thus the first to notice that Laromiguière implicitly established a relationship between the will and attention, and even identified them with one another. Crucially, with regard to our subject, this restriction of attention to *voluntary* attention cannot be found in Condillac by any means.

Despite his criticism of Laromiguière's philosophy of attention, Cousin nonetheless made engagement with him a central part of his metaphysical investigation. As a member of the *Royal Council for Public Instruction* and a state councillor, Cousin tasked Laromiguière and Théodore Jouffroy, who was Laromiguière's eventual successor as the chair of philosophy at La Sorbonne in 1837, with the development of a new philosophical curriculum in 1832. This was the moment Cousin also became the director of the École Normale Supérieure. Jouffroy and Laromiguière, along with Jean-Jacques Séverin de Cardaillac—who was another substitute teacher at Laromiguière's chair from 1823 and an "independent and quite eclectic Laromiguierist" (Egger, 1881, p. 43)—also presided over the examination board for the *agrégation de philosophie*. The philosophical curriculum taught then at La Sorbonne found in Laromiguière's *Lessons* an instructive handbook that was certainly controversial, but nevertheless reliable enough to set the terms for the debate. Importantly, as the next section will show, a further effect of the version of Condillacism handed down through the spiritualist psychological program was that it now aligned well with the Cartesian tradition.

4.2 Reshaping Condillac's Concept of Attention in a Cartesian Manner

For Laromiguière, Condillac's overall mistake in fact consisted in misidentifying the moment he took to be the beginning of the activity of the soul. Condillac, on the one hand, failed to see that attention is the first activity of the soul instead of "the first [quality] we remark in the faculty of feeling" (Condillac, 1992, p. 602); he thereby endowed sensibility with an activity which it could not have. By not distinguishing between voluntary attention and an instinctive form of unconscious attention, he concealed, on the other hand, that there is a fundamental link between the activity of the mind and its acts of will. These two mistakes, and their corrections, constituted an opportunity for Laromiguière to break away from Condillac's legacy and meet Descartes' at the same time.

In Descartes' *Rules for the Direction of the Mind*, attention figured as "a structuring element of the primary *instrumentum* of knowledge, which is the 'clear and distinct idea'" (Santinelli, 2018, p. 51). According to Descartes, only attention could fulfill this role, as it articulates itself through understanding and will. Furthermore, as a product of an act of will and a condition for exercising judgment, Cartesian attention is conceived as a voluntary orientation of the subject of knowledge toward its object, an orientation which brings clearness and distinction to the representations of the mind. Contrary to what Laromiguière claimed, this account shows that the definition of attention he himself relied on is rather different from Condillac's and actually resembles more that of Descartes—or, at least, one that could be called Cartesian. Indeed, conceiving of the soul as possessing an irreducibly active part is a thought that found its first explicit expression in the writings of the Cartesian philosopher, Louis de la Forge, rather than in Descartes himself. For Descartes' work only contains various ambiguous views on the activity of the soul and the voluntary aspect marking attention. La Forge himself, who is not quoted by Laromiguière, put the matter like this:

> Descartes does not regard attention as an act of will, through which it wills, or at least agrees, that the same idea continues to be presented to the faculty of apperception, but rather as the disposition of the gland as well as its movements.
> (La Forge, in Descartes, 2018, p. 446)

A thorough study of Descartes' *Treatise on Man* and *The Passions of the Soul* indeed shows a less active dimension of the Cartesian concept of attention. When attention expresses itself in admiration, it does not seem "to be the product of a voluntary act anymore, but only a necessary consequence of a preceding affective state and a sort of mental reflex" (Barrier, 2017, p. 47). Despite their availability, both these texts by Descartes are remarkably absent from the philosophical references of early-nineteenth-century France. And it is likely that Laromiguière deliberately ignored them, since they did not fit with the spiritualist view that the soul is irreducibly active. In fact, these texts embarrassingly defended the third answer to Laromiguière's paradox that we discussed above: the hypothesis that attention can take an involuntary form.

4.3 Re-Establishing a Cartesianized Form of Condillac's Philosophy

Turning to other Cartesian texts which better underline Descartes' spiritualism, Laromiguière attributed to the concept of attention qualities mostly referred to in the *Rules for the Direction of the Mind*, thus focusing on a specific aspect of Descartes' philosophy: his method and criteria for evidence. Cousin was the first to edit Descartes' *Rules* in 1826, a text he considered to be Descartes' most important, or at least most complete, work; and his own views seem to follow and elaborate on Laromiguière's focus. This "Cousinian focalization" indeed "aimed at dispelling any doubt or indecision" about the possibility of truly appreciating Descartes' spiritualist arguments despite the persistent sensualism that misled Destutt de

Tracy, Joseph-Marie Degérando and, as now shown, "in some aspects, Laromiguière" (Antoine-Mahut, 2021, p. 299). Although Laromiguière's debt to Condillac is indeed undeniable, it is my hypothesis that his attempt to align Condillac's and Descartes' concepts of attention had an impact on Cousin's own project. According to this hypothesis, Cousin's relation to Laromiguière is consistent with what Delphine Antoine-Mahut already noticed with respect to the problem of innatism in Cousin's translation of Descartes' *Notae in Programma*: "whereas Laromiguière appeared concerned about taking into account the criticism of the Idéologues", "Cousin reintegrated what the Idéologues had excluded" (Antoine-Mahut, 2021, p. 29; see also Zijlstra, 2005, p. 94). Laromiguière's and Cousin's overall procedures were similar, but they had different starting points and arrived at different conclusions. In reference to Henri Gouhier's analysis of the mutual relations of Cartesianism and Augustinism in the seventeenth century in terms of "Cartesianized Augustinism" and "Augustinized Cartesianism" (Gouhier, 1978), I claim that Laromiguière proposed a Cartezianed Condillacism, while Cousin used Laromiguière's position to advance a moderately Condillacized Cartesianism. Laromiguierism can be considered a relatively modest position compared to the Cousinian School (Alfaric, 1929), which might explain why, today, Condillac is not included in the French philosophical canon and teaching programs. Despite this, the two spiritualist factions continued to maintain rather distinct relations to Condillac's philosophy.

Since Laromiguière intended to teach a revised version of Condillacism made compatible with Cartesian views on the will, one wonders why he needed to resort to Condillac's system at all. The reason is that prior to Condillac, the notion of attention had never been introduced in an explicit manner, nor had it been defined as part of a psychological system of the faculties. Laromiguière indeed held Condillac's analysis of the operations of the understanding in high esteem, to the point of entirely endorsing it once sensibility was removed from the system of the faculties. As mentioned above, Laromiguière thus supports the thesis of "transformed attention" rather than that of "transformed sensation". By so doing, he not only rendered Condillac more precise, but also turned his thought on its head. By denying that attention has a function in the transition from sensibility to the establishment of higher-order operations of the mind and by establishing at the same time that attention is the fundamental principle of intelligent thought, Laromiguière urged his readers to accept Condillac's system without its sensualist basis. In this way, he restored a strong spiritualist dualism and made it the foundation of psychology, while silently rehabilitating Condillac's arguments from the *Essay* of 1746. Here Condillac exposed views on attention and the activity of the soul that may not have been a perfect match with his own but nonetheless resembled them more than those formulated from 1754 onward. Paradoxically enough, it is because Laromiguière was taken to be "more Condillaquian than his renowned friends [the Idéologues] that Laromiguière could become popular, while their doctrines were fought from every direction" (Picavet, 1891, p. 523). From an ontological point of view, Laromiguière's philosophy accepts the existence of God and of an immortal spiritual soul; he might in that respect be more Condillaquian than them, who rejected such ideas. Moreover, Laromiguière might well deserve to be called Condillaquian due to the importance he attributed to the concept of attention in any kind of psychological investigation, provided, however, we acknowledge how modified and Cartesianized his Condillacism is. In a statement that is not without a sense of irony, Damiron almost seemed to notice Laromiguière's ambiguity concerning Condillac: "*This is not Condillacism as it is in Condillac*, in Destutt de Tracy or in Garat; but it is still Condillacism, for *there is a family resemblance*" (Damiron, 1828, p. 64).

5 Conclusion

By making the concept of attention central to psychology, Laromiguière paved the way for other French scientists who showed equal interest in this fundamental cognitive ability. One of them is the pioneer of French alienism, Jean-Étienne Esquirol. Having divided mental disorders into sensibility disorders, intelligence disorders and compulsive disorders, he maintained that all defects of intelligence "boil down to those of attention" (Esquirol, 1838, p. 20), thus treating the concept of attention as at the root of the emerging discipline of descriptive psychopathology. Incidentally, he then pointed out that Laromiguière had come to the same conclusion (*ibid.*), namely that attention is the root principle of an experimental philosophy grounded in psychology.

The notion of attention also became the subject of a study by Théodule Ribot (*The Psychology of Attention*, 1889), who is regarded as the founder of experimental psychology in France. In Henri Bergson's work, attention once again appeared as a component of the concept of intellectual effort and as a characteristic of the spiritual activity of the mind. It was also central to the philosophy of Maine de Biran.[3] Despite the diversity of the texts mentioned above—which cover as broad a territory as metaphysics, psychiatry and modern psychology—they are all testament to the persistent influence of Condillac's philosophy on nineteenth-century French philosophical debates. The scholarly tradition that continued Condillac's analysis of attention is, at least indirectly, part of his lineage, and, as we have seen, in the case of Laromiguière, this is explicitly so. Accordingly, the concept of attention seems worthy of further examination by historians of philosophy and science, as it often indicates diverging metaphysical commitments.

Notes

1 The title of the 1746 edition of the *Essay* is followed by the subtitle "A work in which everything about the human understanding is reduced to one single principle".
2 All quotations, except those from Condillac, are translated by myself.
3 See Devarieux's chapter in this volume for further discussion of the relation between Condillac and Maine de Biran.

References

Aarsleff, Hans. (1982) *From Locke to Saussure*. London: Athlone.
Alfaric, Prosper. (1929) *Laromiguière et son École*. Paris: Publications de la Faculté de Lettres de Strasbourg.
Antoine-Mahut, Delphine. (2013) 'Is the History of Philosophy a Family Affair? The Examples of Locke and Malebranche in the Cousinian School', in Laerke, Mogens, Smith, Justin E. H., Schliesser, Eric (eds.), *Philosophy and Its History: Aims and Methods in the Study of Early-Modern Philosophy*. Oxford: Oxford University Press, pp. 159–177.
Antoine-Mahut, Delphine. (2021) *L'autorité d'un canon philosophique. Le cas Descartes*. Paris: Vrin.
Auroux, Sylvain. (1992) 'Condillac, inventeur d'un nouveau matérialisme', *Dix-huitième Siècle*, 'Le matérialisme des Lumières', 24, 'Le matérialisme des Lumières', pp. 153–163.
Barancy, Félix. (2019) 'Politiques de l'éclectisme en situation de crise: Damiron promoteur d'une école philosophique', in Antoine-Mahut, Delphine, Whistler, Daniel (eds.), *Une arme philosophique: l'éclectisme de Victor Cousin*. Paris: Editions des Archives Contemporaines, pp. 81–92.
Barrier, Thibault. (2017) 'La capture de l'esprit: attention et admiration chez Descartes et Spinoza', *Les Études philosophiques*, 120, 'L'attention au XVIIe siècle: conceptions et usages', pp. 43–58.
Charrak, André. (2003) *Empirisme et métaphysique. L'Essai sur l'origine des connaissances humaines de Condillac*. Paris: Vrin.
Chottin, Marion. (2014) 'La liaison des idées chez Condillac: le langage au principe de l'empirisme', *Astérion*, 12, 'Le principe de la folie et de la raison. Association des idées et liaison des idées aux XVIIe et XVIIIe siècles'.
Condillac, Étienne Bonnot de. (1992) *Philosophical Writings*. 2 vol. Translated by Franklin Philip and Harlane Lane. London: Lawrence Erlbaum.
Condillac, Étienne Bonnot de. (2001) *Essay on the Origin of Human Knowledge*. Cambridge: Cambridge University Press.
Cousin, Victor. (1833) *Fragments Philosophiques*. 2nd edn. (1st edn. 1826). Paris: Ladrange.

Cousin, Victor, Maine de Biran, Pierre. (1817) *Examen des Leçons de philosophie de M. Laromiguière, ou Considérations sur le principe de la psychologie, sur la réalité de nos connaissances, et l'activité de l'âme.* Paris: Fournier.

Cousin, Victor, Maine de Biran, Pierre. (1829) *Leçons de philosophies de M. Laromiguière, jugées par M. Victor Cousin et M. Maine de Biran.* Paris: Rouen Frères and Johanneau.

Daled, Pierre-Frédéric. (2005) *Le matérialisme occulté et la genèse du « sensualisme ». Écrire l'histoire de la philosophie en France.* Paris: Vrin.

Damiron, Jean-Philibert. (1828) *Essai sur l'histoire de la philosophie en France au dix-neuvième siècle.* Paris: Ponthieu and Leipsig.

Descartes, René. (2018) *L'homme.* 1st edn. 1662. Paris: Flammarion.

Egger, Victor. (1881) *La parole intérieure: essai de psychologie descriptive.* Paris: Germer-Baillière.

Esquirol, Jean-Etienne. (1838) *Des maladies mentales considérées sous les rapports médical, hygiénique et médico-légal.* Paris: Baillière.

Gouhier, Henri. (1978) *Cartésianisme et augustinisme au XVIIe siècle.* Paris: Vrin.

Laromiguière, Pierre. (1823) *Leçons de philosophie.* 3rd edn. (1st edn. 1815–1816). Paris: Brunot-Labbé.

Markovits-Pessel, Francine. (2018) *La statue de Condillac. Les cinq sens en quête du moi.* Paris: Hermann.

Picavet, François. (1891) *Les idéologues. Essai sur l'histoire des idées scientifiques, philosophiques, religieuses, etc., en France depuis 1789.* Paris: Félix Alcan.

Santinelli, Cristina. (2018) 'Mos geometricus et attention après Descartes: Spinoza, Malebranche et la méthode de la philosophie', in Carbone, Raffaele, Jaquet, Chantal, Moreau, Pierre-François, (eds.), *Spinoza- Malebranche: À la croisée des interprétations.* Lyon: ENS Éditions, pp. 51–70.

Zijlstra, Christiaan Peter. (2005) *The Rebirth of Descartes: The Nineteenth-Century Reinstatement of Cartesian Metaphysics in France and Germany.* Groningen: University of Groningen.

7 Madness and Ideologist Philosophy of the Mind
Pinel and Condillac on the Dualism of Understanding and Will

Samuel Lézé

1 Introduction

The philosophy of Condillac constitutes a central reference for Philippe Pinel (1745–1826) at the end of the eighteenth century. The challenge was to develop clinical medicine and, more particularly, to shape a new medical specialisation dealing with mental alienation. However, these references to Condillac are interpreted by some as proof of a major intellectual *influence* of Condillac over Pinel, while others interpret them as merely being a rhetorical legitimising *strategy* on Pinel's part. What are the main arguments used by advocates of these two interpretations?

Let us first turn our attention to the advocates of the major intellectual influence thesis. In Pinel's famous medical treatises, the explicit references to Condillac or the "analytical method" lexicon easily serve to provide textual proof of this "influence" (Paradis, 1993). To finally endow medicine with the certainty which it has not previously attained in the study and therapeutic treatment of illnesses, Pinel declares that he is applying Condillac's analytical method to medicine, for it is the universal method of discovery in science. The importance of this methodological appropriation of Condillac by Pinel is worthy of note in, for example, the heading "Analysis" in the *Dictionnaire des sciences médicales*, written by the doctor Jean-Baptiste Nacquart (1780–1854). In it, Pinel is presented as "the famous doctor to whom this new doctrine is owed" (Nacquart, 1823: 19–20), and who, consequently, may subsequently write the entry "Analysis applied to medicine" in an autobiographical mode erasing any explicit reference to Condillac (Pinel, 1812: 23–30). It is interesting to note that even those who do not praise Pinel—the critics of the Ideologists in his day and age—can reinforce this interpretation. They maintain that Condillac is indeed Pinel's reference, but that this latter does not correctly apply the "analytical method" to medicine. His expository mode does not recompose the illnesses from the simplest elements; instead, he uses simple and complex illnesses to analyse the symptoms. Therefore, his practice is contrary to his declarations. And one should denounce Pinel's "misunderstanding" of the analytical method in the name of Condillac (Castel, 1798).

What about the partisans of the rhetorical legitimising *strategy* thesis? We often find the same extracts (as those used to support the other thesis) serving to validate Pinel's belonging to *Ideology* in both meanings of the term: the philosophical doctrine of the philosophical constellation of the salon d'Auteuil and the official philosophy of the new French Republic between the end of the Terror and Napoleon's First Empire (Albury, 1986). However, should it be concluded that "... clinical thinking only transposes, in the more laconic and often more confused vocabulary of practice, a conceptual configuration, of which Condillac disposes, freely, the discursive form" (Foucault, 1963: 133)? The case of another famous Ideologist scholar and friend of Pinel, Antoine Lavoisier (1743–1794), clearly shows the mere *transposition* of the discourse of analysis into his area of research: chemistry. The method of analysis is not so much the instrument of his discoveries as an expository mode for already known results. This is, thus, a legitimising strategy for the new chemistry (Bensaude-Vincent, 2010).

It is remarkable that these two types of study only deal with scholars' *positive declarations* regarding Condillac. They thus make them into a "commonplace" of analysis discourse about Ideologists, which is based on a shared *petitio principii*: since Condillac has authority, he has an intellectual influence and/or it is strategic to use him to reinforce the legitimacy of the Ideologists. However, the philosophical authority of an author depends less on his work and more on his critical reception and mediators (Antoine-Mahut and Lézé, 2018); they forge a "philosophical figure" reduced to a few features (Antoine-Mahut, 2021) representing the philosophical portrait of the author in question. To describe the mechanisms of the lasting recognition of Condillac as an inescapable philosophical figure, for the actors in France at the transition between eighteenth and nineteenth centuries, one must consider both the negative declarations and the laudatory discourse.

The accusation of materialism and the "sensualism" label constitute a ceremony of symbolic debasement, making Condillac the starting point for a series of discussions. Consequently, the challenge is to determine what in Condillac is "commonplace" in order to potentially adopt original philosophical positions within the philosophical constellation of the Ideologists (Mulsow, 2005). Thus, among the partisans, the philosopher Pierre Laromiguière (1756–1837) rehabilitates Condillac by seeking a Condillaquian response to the major criticism of the passivity of his philosophy of mind (see the contribution by Pierre Brouillet in this volume). Besides, the partisans never totally or dogmatically adhere to a closed *opus*. It is therefore possible to contrast not only the *Traité des sensations* with the *Essai sur l'origine des connaissances* but also the analytical method with

Condillac's own results. Thus, Pinel appropriates elements of Condillac's philosophy by discussing and testing them against his own medical experience, which provides him with particular cases with the potential to constitute pertinent objections. For Pinel, the problem to be solved is this: which dualism of understanding and will serves most appropriately as a foundation of a medical science of mental alienation?

The objective of this chapter is to analyse a medical reception of Condillac within a perspective of epistemological history. How does Pinel appropriate the method of analysis to shape a clinical judgement on mental alienation? In other words, how does he apply the analytical method? What is meant by "applying" a philosophy—in this case, that of Condillac—to medicine? Does he apply it correctly?

In this reception study, the entry "Manie, Vésanie, Aliénation mentale ou Dérangements des fonctions intellectuelles (Nosologie & Médecine pratique)" in the *Encyclopédie méthodique* (Pinel, 1808: 475–491) is, on the methodological plane, doubly interesting. On the one hand, it has the pedagogical function of transmitting stabilised knowledge within the framework of renewing the project of the *Encyclopédie* of Diderot and d'Alembert. The "methodical" order by discipline breaks with the alphabetical order. Contrary to what the initial project indicates, there is no re-edition but a re-writing of the entries (Schmitt, 2018). On the other hand, the components of this medical dictionary entry have the remarkable particularity of constituting a form of dialogue with Condillac. Pinel brings together four recurring arguments (from his first theses to the second edition of his treatise) from his writings on mental alienation. These arguments demonstrate both the borrowings and refusals of Pinel to such an extent that their examination enables us to better assess the rhetorical and epistemic function of Condillac in the work of Pinel.

2 The Analysis of Cognitive Symptoms

There are two dimensions to Condillac's psychology: a cognitive one (understanding) and an affective one (will). However, more often than not, the Ideologists isolate the psychology of understanding (that is, the intellectual faculties) from the affective dimension, which belongs to medicine. Although Condillac and a certain proportion of the Ideologists reject the term "psychology", doctors use it to qualify his empirical theory of human understanding. Similarly, Pinel bases his definition of mental alienation on these two dimensions. If the affective dimension deals with the passions, what is the status of will? Is it a cause or an effect of physiology? At the end of his *Traité des sensations*, Condillac specifies that when "I want" an object, it is not solely because of its moral qualities (the pleasant sensation) but also because it is a free object of my choice, of my reflection (Condillac,

1754). Pinel actually indicates the existence of a "sort of internal struggle" in some patients. This is a clinical criterion of the preservation of a portion of will and reflection in all cases of crises. Nevertheless, he does not address this problem of the psychological or physiological nature of will (Pinel, 1808: 476). He applies the epistemology of experience to the letter: what can be known is limited by what can be observed.

Thus, the first claim of Pinel states that Condillac's normal psychology is a clinical means for establishing a psychopathology by comparing the normal to the pathological. The epistemological premise of this argument comes from Condillac: analysis allows the passage from the known to the unknown. The unknown is not the observable symptom but the type of illness according to the impairments in the functions of understanding. The focus on the "functions" of understanding marks this position as Ideologist, although also doctors define illness as a lesion that impairs the functions of certain organs. Pinel adopts the medical language of "functions" without speaking of an organ behind the lesion of the functions of understanding. Rather, he shows that the variety of possible lesions of the functions of understanding (from sensations to judgements) can be used to identify distinct illnesses (Huneman, 2008).

For Pinel, the knowledge of the normal functions of understanding allows for the exact identification of the specific symptoms distinguishing different forms of mania. Consequently, the normal is a "term of comparison" for one to know the pathological. In this sense, he takes the opposite direction of the method prevailing at the end of the century, the famous "pathological method". For, in this latter method, the knowledge of normal functions is deduced from the alterations of the pathology. To legitimise this inversion, Pinel uses an explicit analogy with Condillac's *Traité des sensations*:

> It is [well-] known that Condillac, to better return, through analysis, to the origin of our knowledge, supposed an animated statue, & successively endowed it with the functions of smell, hearing, sight and touch, & this is how he managed to indicate the ideas which must be linked to diverse impressions. Similarly does it not import to the history of human understanding to be able to consider, in an isolated manner, the diverse functions, like attention, comparison, memory and reasoning, with the alterations to which these functions are susceptible.
> (Pinel, 1808: 475)

However, this analogy is formulated on the basis of a displacement and a reserve. On the one hand, Pinel displaces the interest in the analysis of the origin and development of the faculties or operations of understanding by a clinical description, isolating the "functions" so as to identify their activity or the scope of their activity. However, for Condillac, the history of the faculties of human understanding has a "developmental" meaning: the "origin" discovered through analysis is a principle which explains "generation". The term "history" means the empirical description of a cognitive genesis. For Pinel, it is a natural history: the empirical description is clinical (according to the cycle of an illness), nosographic (an illness in an ordered set) and static. The analytical method (the decomposition into "elements" to compare and discover the "relationships" between things) lies at the "base" of the descriptive method as asserted by Nacquart (1823: 19). The logical means—decomposition—has primacy over the genetic objective. Basically, the functions are "elements" of the mind which may or may not be altered according to the degrees of loss, to be assessed by the doctor. The symptom is an observable effect of this alteration. The symptom is also a simple or complex element in the identification of an illness, which always manifests as a mixed phenomenon. According to this psychological criterion, it is possible to pose a diagnosis and prognosis of a form of mental alienation.

However, Pinel contrasted his empirical research into the truths of activation and de-activation of the functions of understanding with the research "by the paths of abstraction" which he identifies in Condillac's works. Undoubtedly, Condillac's statue fiction is a didactic model of the analysis of the operations of understanding. But if the foundation of this analysis lies in nature, as Condillac claims, Pinel concludes that the method must, above all, consist in seeking an empirical order for the principle of clinical judgement. This empirical order implies relationships between principal and subordinate objects (Condillac, 1798a: 23). The mental alienation *genre* thus includes four *types* (Mania, Mania without delirium, Dementia and Idiocy), manifested according to diverse *forms*. The contribution of psychopathology is not the advancing of the knowledge of normal cognitive functions but the transformation of the very nature of Condillac's psychology by rendering it more concrete and conform to the complexity of the clinical experience. For Pinel, this basis makes it possible to deduce the prognosis and therapeutics most adapted to the specificities of the clinical case.

3   The Analysis of Affective Symptoms

The second argument does not restrict itself to explicitly formulating the distinction between cognitive and affective dimensions. On the one hand, a new element is defended: alienation is also based on affective symptoms. On the other hand, the affective dimension does not pertain to philosophy or psychology but to the medical jurisdiction. Indeed, for Pinel, the passions, such as deep sorrow, fear and terror, are the "determining causes" of mental alienation. A passion is a passing pathology which may take lasting root or return periodically. One condition for triggering a passion is the "profound sensitivity" of maniacs. In the manic crisis—or its synonym, fury, as Pinel reminds us—the model passion is anger.

The understanding of the patients is thus perturbed by another element pertaining to sensitivity: the acute "emotions" aroused by contingent? circumstances. The emotional aspect here is not treated in isolation from the moral aspect, for it is a violent "moral affection" illustrated by ambition, avarice, pride, bigotry, superstition, love, friendship or desire for reputation or conquests (Pinel, 1808: 477). The emotional aspect thus may serve to deduce the aetiology. The passion is the determining cause of the mental alienation in the sense that the circumstances of the sick person's environment upset his sensitivity. Moreover, the doctor, who is an element of the sick person's environment, should take care not to upset his patient.

This lesion of the will, caused by the emotional aspect of passions, is expressed in the affective symptoms of the patient's psychopathology, which are observable by the doctor. The interior can indeed be accessed through the exterior, that is, through a "physiognomy" of the sick person. This pathology of the disposition of the organs is, strictly speaking, the psychophysiology of the passions. The symptomatic expression of the face indicates the strength of the passion within the body and its effects on the whole of the body and understanding.

This argument presupposes the possibility of clearly detaching the method of analysis from its promoter, Condillac, and the results of his psychology:

> The analysis of the functions of human understanding has undoubtedly been much furthered by the works brought together by the ideologists. But there is another barely sketched analysis for which the support of medicine is necessary: that of moral affections, their nuances, their diverse degrees, their varied combinations.
> (Pinel, 1808: 478)

On the one hand, the analytical method should be expanded to cover the affective dimension so as to complete the history of understanding with a medical history of human passions. In other words, the passions do not pertain to psychology or ideology, but to medicine and, more widely, to "modern physiology". Pinel adopts the vitalist doctrine of the doctor Louis de Lacaze (1703–1765) of the Montpellier school, according to whom the passions have an effect on the "animal economy" (that is, the organic system). From this, he concludes that periodic mania has its primitive seat in the "epigastric region", the crisis being its radiation (Pinel, 1808: 481).

On the other hand, Pinel does not retain the Condillaquian analysis of the passions and will from the *Traité des sensations*. With the intention of describing, in Chapter 3, the "formation of [the] will" through sensations, Condillac distinguishes within reason, that is, within that mixture of understanding and will, several elements: (a) desire (that is, the action of the faculties on sensations) and passion (the "dominant desire"); (b) love and hatred of an object according to various degrees; and, finally, (c) the will which may become free thanks to reason. Passion results from understanding, which, basically, means that it is not very passive and physical. Consequently, Pinel seems to retain in his interpretation solely what Condillac explicitly states in §. 106 of the *Essai sur l'origine des connaissances humaines*:

> Moreover, to consider the mind in all its effects, it is not enough to have given an analysis of the operations of understanding, one should also have done that of the passions and noticed how all things combine and mingle into a single cause. The influence of the passions is so great that often, without them, understanding would have almost no execution, and that to have a mind, sometimes the passions are all that a man lacks. They are even absolutely necessary for certain talents. But an analysis of the passions would pertain to a work in which one would deal with the progress of our knowledge rather than one in which [one would deal with] their origin.
>
> (Condillac, 1798a)

There are at least four possible reasons for this truncated interpretation of Condillac. First, Condillac's psychology is outdated. Then, this is a result of borrowing from the medicine of his period. Next, Condillac values only one organ, the brain. Finally, Condillac, as seen in his psychology, reveals himself to be far less empirical than a doctor who must account for a greater diversity of experience. Thus, Condillac does not analyse the various passions to give them an order that might modify the state of a patient. The knowledge which he proposes cannot be applied. For Pinel, the analytical method should be applied to complex mixes of pathology, and the challenge is to show the variety of the possible combinations of the elements composing these mixes. More widely, Pinel does not accept that variety can result from "a single cause", such as the principle interlinking the ideas of the mind ("la liaison des idées") invoked by Condillac.

For Pinel, the model of the analysis of the passions is presented in the work of the English doctor Alexander Crichton (1763–1856). Moreover, Crichton also borrows the key term of the analytic method and finds himself in constant conversation with Condillac. His "history of the passions", at the end of his treatise, aims to offer knowledge applicable to affective

Madness and Ideologist Philosophy of the Mind 109

symptoms. Pinel thus indicates his interest in the physiological conditions of the will: "... he has subjected to a sort of analysis the principle of our actions, he has found their source in the primitive inclinations which derive from our organic structure" (Pinel, *ibid.*: 479).

The aim of this approach is to facilitate the explanation and recognition of a greater variety of possible clinical cases. Moreover, it is in this section, which is more medical than the first "psychological" one, that the developmental point of view makes a discreet return: indeed, there are specific ages of exposition to the "stormy passions" (p. 479). The interest of this incidental remark is to draw attention to the need to take into account the whole set of circumstances in the clinical judgement concerning mental alienation. To correctly judge a type of mental alienation requires revealing the *combinations* of symptoms, their *degree* (of severity) and the (individual) nuances at the intersection of cognitive psychopathology and the physiognomy of the passions. The form of the illness is a function of the circumstances which, in the life cycle of an individual, may trigger the crisis.

Even better, for Pinel, the empirical difference between the cognitive and affective dimensions is an epistemic condition for the clinical observation of the "intimate connections" (p. 478), and the "reciprocities and correspondences" between the two dimensions (p. 484). Consequently, the study of these "relationships" of the cognitive and affective dimensions implies the collaboration of two distinct disciplines: psychology and medicine. The distinction is empirically drawn for it implies two orders of phenomena: the physical and the moral. The social environment is at the confluence of these two orders since passions have both a physiological basis in the body and a moral basis in the individuals' *mores* and mental dimension. The body and the moral dimension form a physical environment which can make an impression on the patient. The effects of the passions on the mental (the psychology of the understanding) are thus both physiological and psychological. The moral dimension relates the individual mental and the collective mental. Here, physiology designates a physical dimension which is at the disposal of the organs, an "animal economy". If mania is a "nervous affection", it pertains to medicine. However, the foundation of the medicine of mental alienation is not the anatomic pathology of an "organic lesion" rendering mania incurable. Its reasoning is even inverted: since mania is sometimes curable with moral treatment, the illness does not result from an organic lesion or "congenital malformations of the brain or skull" (p. 479).

4 Fury: An Affective Symptom without Cognitive Symptoms

Pinel's third argument radicalises the separation between the cognitive and affective dimensions of the human mind. A clinical proof establishes this, for there exists a variety of mental alienation characterised by an "exclusive lesion of the functions of [the] will". The old form of the argument, in the first edition of Pinel's *Traité*, explicitly states the division of the mind:

> It is sufficient to say that the functions of the will are absolutely distinct from those of understanding, and that their seat, their causes, whatever they may be, in certain cases, their reciprocal dependence, have essential differences which cannot be ignored. Here, I limit myself to a proof taken from the exclusive lesion of the functions of the will. At Bicêtre, there was long before my eyes a maniac whose symptoms could appear to be a sort of enigma according to the ideas about lunatics given by Locke and Condillac.
> (Pinel, 1800: 81)

In the entry, Pinel returns twice to this important clinical fact. First, at its beginning where he places this case at the end of the section devoted to the analysis of the passions. He indicates three aspects which attract his clinical attention: the "internal disposition" (that is, "nervous") of this type of mania is only known through its effects and it resists cure; however, it is the least frequent of the various forms of mania. Consequently, the radical separation of will and understanding is a presupposition of the clinical example which was prepared by the generalities concerning the duality of mental alienation introducing the entry. Here, the "enigma" becomes a fact which is impossible to "reconcile", an empirical objection to the empirical principles. Thus, the formulation of the objection has an explicit bearing on the cognitive or intellectualist dimension embodied in Locke and Condillac:

> The particular character of the fits of these latter was to offer no disturbance, no disorder in their ideas, no extravagant flight of the imagination: these deranged [patients] answered the questions proposed most correctly and most accurately; but they were dominated by the most fiery fury and a blood-thirsty instinct, all the horror of which they themselves felt, but they would not have had the mastery to repress its atrocious impulse, without the obstacles of a severe reclusion. How can these facts be reconciled with the notions about madness given by Locke and Condillac which they maintain consist exclusively in a disposition allying naturally incompatible ideas and taking these allied ideas for a real truth?
> (Pinel, *ibid.*: 480)

The second time Pinel returns to the separation of will and understanding, he is concerned with the stabilisation of his nosology in the second part of his entry. He begins his work of distinction and classification with the first form of mania, a "mania without delirium". In this context, the name of Condillac disappears. Locke is the main target as well as the cognitive criterion of "delirium" as a specific characteristic of mania:

> One may have a just admiration for Locke, and yet agree that the notions which he gives on mania are very incomplete, when he regards it as inseparable from delirium. I myself, like this author, thought this when I resumed by research into this illness at Bicêtre, and I was not a little surprised to see several lunatics who at no time showed any lesion of the understanding and who were dominated by a force of instinct and fury, as if the faculties affected were alone injured.
> (Pinel, *Ibid.*: 484)

Embedding his approach in a discussion of Locke and Condillac is motivated by a commentary by Condillac about Locke in a passage evoking cases of madness in the *Essai sur l'origine de nos connaissances*. Pinel alludes to Chapter IX entitled "On the vices and advantages of imagination". Condillac comments on a concrete example of Locke concerning a reasonable man becoming mad because of a strong impression leading to a dangerous "linking" of incompatible ideas (§81). However, contrary to what Pinel asserts, this thesis on the origin of madness is not purely intellectual. It is, indeed, an "error", a cognitive effect of the unsettling of the faculty of imagination, a "delirium". Nevertheless, Condillac immediately distinguishes the effect from its physical cause, by recalling the determining role of the passions.

On the one hand, if madness is only a "degree of the imagination", this is because of the physical impression caused in the brain. Moreover, we all experience a "moment of madness" in our dreams. But on waking, this state does not last, for the impression made on the brain is not violent (§82). On the other hand, another example from Condillac, which Pinel does not retain, illustrates with a passion, the physical cause of the intensity of an *idée fixe*. The attachment to a phantasy, which Condillac calls "these fictions which are called *castles in Spain*", is caused by a slight impression made on the brain which may be neutralised through the principle of reality and the distraction of friends. But when the same idea is reinforced by sadness, it becomes lasting. It then is a pathological phenomenon: a melancholia. Here once again, the criterion of the texture of the brain, according to age, renders the reading of novels dangerous for children (§83).

Pinel rejects Condillac's analysis for at least three reasons. First, he argues that the origin of madness ("which, on the contrary, admits the exercise of all the operations") is only the unsettling of a single faculty (i.e. imagination) (§. 95) and a single organ (the brain). Next, he claims that the principle interlinking the ideas of the mind ("la liaison des idées") relies on an active cognitive cause (attention), which links "ideas of needs and those of the things related to them". Indeed, "the things only attract our attention through the relationship which they have to our temperament, our passions, our state, or, to say it all in one words, our needs" (§.28). Condillac cleverly associates the passions with the linking of ideas and the imagination (§. 105). But for Pinel passions have an active and ultimately "cognitive" dimension. The physical dimension only affects the degree and duration of madness. Finally, there is a determining clinical reason linked to the objection derived from empirical facts. Condillac indicates that examples of madness are "recognised by everyone". He indicates that there certainly exist deliria which are not called madness, but which should be included in the "same class", which "have their cause in the imagination" (§. 86). However, Pinel's clinical state cannot be recognised without clinical skulls. Outside the bout of fury, there is no discernible clue of madness. A new class of madness must thus be created. This pertains to another cause, one which is highly difficult to recognise for a clinician without training in the complete table of possible cases which are, in effect, only observable in an asylum. From the effects, Pinel ascends in his analysis not only to the faculties of understanding but also—and here he goes against Condillac—to the psychological and physiological functions.

5 A De-centred Psychophysiology

The fourth and final argument is presented as a summary of the ideal of exactitude of philosophy applied to medicine:

> One must hope that philosophical medicine will henceforth proscribe these vague and inexact expressions of, *images traced in the brain, unequal impulsion of the blood in different parts of this viscera, irregular movements of animal spirits, etc*, expressions which one still finds in the best works on human understanding, and which can no longer be in accord with the origin, the causes and the history of fits of mania.
> (Pinel, *Ibid.*: 482)

At first sight, the formula seems to be a mere commonplace, a perfect example of rhetoric transposing the scientific ideal of Condillac. Indeed, the analytical method is regarded not only as the discovery of a natural order but also as the expression of a new, ordered language, a nomenclature. And this language is then also treated as an analytical method. However, the content of this criticism first targets what Pinel calls the "jargon" of physiology. The target is clearly the mechanist explanation of the

Cartesians emphasising that the brain is the seat of the soul and centre of the human organism. This criticism closes the "analysis of the passions" section, which mainly consists in a defence and illustration of vitalist physiology emphasising the epigastric centre over the brain.

Nevertheless, the extract also presents itself as a free paraphrasing of Chapter IX "On the causes of sensitivity and memory" of *La logique*, which deals with physiology. Condillac criticises the "false hypotheses" of physiology which he himself had defended to explain the degrees and duration of madness in his *Essai sur l'origine des connaissances humaines*:

> Some represent the nerves as taut strings, capable of disturbance and vibration, and they believe [that they] have guessed the causes of sensitivity and memory. It is obvious that this supposition is quite imaginary.
> Others say the brain is a soft substance, in which animal spirits leave traces. These traces are preserved: the animal spirits pass and pass again; the animal is endowed with sentiment and memory. They have not noticed that, if the substance of the brain is soft enough to receive traces, it would not have sufficient consistency to preserve them; and they have not considered how impossible it is that an infinity of traces may subsist in a substance in which there is continual action and circulation.
> (Condillac, 1798a: 72–73)

The source of these "arbitrary" hypotheses is not observation but, according to Condillac, imagination. If ideas are not inscribed in the brain, where can they be located? Where is the memory of ideas? Condillac answer is "nowhere": they are neither in the soul nor in the body. The harpsichord metaphor is used to shed light on the thesis of the habit acquired by the brain. We know nothing of the mechanisms of the brain and it is mistaken to imagine these mechanisms. However, the brain is, indeed, "the principal organ", a "common centre", "the principal organ of the sentiment". The brain contracts habits. But through which physiological mechanism? Condillac does not wish to reply, so as not to risk a return descent into the errors of imagination. Thus, he goes no further than analogy: "It is not sufficient to judge the habits of the brain through the habits of each sense: one must content oneself with knowing that the same mechanism, whatever it may be, gives, preserves and reproduces ideas" (p. 88). In the end, physiology concentrates on the brain, but the brain is a "black box" which cannot be observed. This is a surprising way of excluding any possible progress in physiology. For Condillac, the substitute for imagination is reasoning through analogy. Instead of making hypotheses, one should find "homologies of structure". Thus, he writes:

Analogy authorises us to suppose that, in the organs which we cannot observe, something happens similar to what we observe in the others. I do not know by which mechanism my hand has enough flexibility and mobility to contract the habit of certain determinations of movement, and I suppose that all that can be found in the brain, and in the organs which, with it, are the seat of memory.

(Condillac, 1798a: 93)

Condillac willingly admits this in the conclusion to his chapter. One must accept this limit to our knowledge. The prime unobservable cause is unknowable. Yet to fix a limit also enables one to benefit from "the advantage to have rid of all arbitrary hypotheses that little knowledge which we have about one of the most obscure matters" (p. 94).

First, although Pinel may retain from this chapter Condillac's claim about the limits of classical physiology, he does not accept the epistemic consequence that Condillac infers concerning all progress in physiology. Pinel invokes not only the modern physiology of his time and its autonomy regarding psychology but also the medical jurisdiction of the passions. Then, although he retains Condillac's concern for exactitude and condemnation of the imagination of general and abstract hypotheses, it is in the name of observation and experience that he turns against Condillac, without discussing the evolution of his philosophy: he thus pits the Condillac of *La logique* against the Condillac of the *Essai sur l'origine des connaissances humaines*. More generally, he opposes Condillac's philosophy of experience, because for him a variety of experiences imposes a revision of the philosophy of experience in the name of the authority of clinical experiences. Finally, he rejects the principal physiological presupposition of Condillac, namely that the brain is the central organ.

Therefore, in the name of clinical experiences, Pinel rejects the very idea of the principle of a single centre, which he judges to be metaphysical, whether this centre be the body or the soul. The analytical method shows that everything is divisible. This divisibility of objects is the condition for the discovery of an order in diversity. But this diversity is not reducible to a single principle. This is why Pinel develops a psychophysiology. Mental alienation is based on an irreducible duality. Each dimension is also divided into diverse affective and cognitive functions. The intersecting of functions incessantly de-centres clinical observation. This de-centred psychophysiology does not only break with the classical physiology of the Cartesians; it also rejects the classical metaphysical idea of a substantial soul, the idea that there is a "... unique and indivisible seat or principle..." (Pinel, 1808: 476). The physiology of the passions and the thesis of Louis de Lacaze provide Pinel with the opportunity to object to the idea of a cerebral location of mental alienation. On the one hand, there exists no proof of an organic lesion on the anatomic-pathological plane. On the other hand, moral curability shows, by revealing the absurdity of the idea, that there exists no organic, by nature, incurable lesion of the brain.

6 Conclusion

Pinel's critical reception of Condillac shows how the relationship between metaphysics and medicine was reconfigured in early-nineteenth-century France. Pinel is undoubtedly the point of departure for a new medical specialisation: alienism. But he is also one of the major culminating points of a history of metaphysics which transforms the problem of the nature of ideas into an empirical epistemology of the origin of ideas. The questions of metaphysics become psychological, once the soul is subjected to experimental proof or once one strives to observe the phenomena of the soul (Antoine-Mahut, Winter, and Lézé, 2021). Basically, Pinel deals with Condillac like Condillac deals with Locke: by means of pursuing in greater depth the analysis of the experiences and functions of understanding and will. The challenge is the determination of the relationship between the two. Although clinical experience revises the philosophy of experience, it does not allow metaphysics to be rejected as a whole. It transforms metaphysics with a general method which depends upon it: the "method of analysis".

Very early on in his work, Pinel cites an extract from *La logique* which summarises, like a maxim, the principal instruction for all those who wish to analyse: "… observe in a successive order the qualities of an object, so as to give them in the mind the simultaneous order in which they exist" (Condillac, 1798b: 22). Pinel's object is illness. His objective is to organise illnesses into classifications according to the natural order of the symptoms: a "science of the characteristic signs of illnesses" (Pinel, 1812: 25). The specific challenge for this science is to show that madness is an illness, a knowable and curable object. The final result is a nomenclature (that is, nosology) for, in Condillac's scientific ideal, science is a language and every language is an analytical method. Nevertheless, like Condillac, Pinel defends an empirical metaphysics, since the authority of experience implies epistemological and ontological principles. It is thus possible to use Condillac as a basis to reconstruct the following reasoning of Pinel:

> The nosology of mental alienation establishes the possibility of a clinical judgement by crossing the cognitive psychology of Condillac (resulting from the analysis of the functions of understanding) with a new affective psychopathology. The return effect is to render Condillac's psychology

truly concrete, to spread his method of analysis to a medicine of the passions by completing its cognitive psychology with an affective psychology. Condillac's psychology of will is neither retained nor discussed. With regards to Condillac's cognitive psychology, the importance of the affective psychology innovation is constantly reinforced in the entry. On the one hand, Pinel invokes a possible form of "mania without delirium". Through this, he designates a mania manifesting an exclusive lesion of the will (that is, of the affective functions) without any lesion affecting the cognitive functions of understanding. This clinical objection demonstrates the limits of Condillac's intellectualist theory of madness. On the other hand, medicine may boast of being "philosophical" because of its exact terminology, which allows it to break with the classical physiological jargon of the Cartesians. But this implicit patronage of Condillac turns against himself since he continues to claim that the understanding has an anatomical seat (the brain). However, modern physiology, on the contrary, shows a focus of irradiation of the passions between the epigastrium and the brain. Pinel clearly derives from this the thesis of the physiological and psychological division of the various cognitive and affective functions. The classical metaphysics of substances is abstract and pessimistic. It does not take into account the concrete empirical variety which a natural order possesses. The curability of certain forms of mental alienation shows that they do not stem from a cognitive lesion of the brain.

In the end, this rhetorical formulation of the arguments of Pinel attests to an original medical reception of Condillac. This can be reduced neither to the thesis of "influence" nor to the thesis of the strategic or consensual use of "commonplaces". By showing how Condillac's philosophy was concretely put to the test by the first practitioners of mental alienation, this reception confers upon it a major social dimension. In this context, the reception of Condillac is critical. Condillac is a "philosophical figure" (Antoine-Mahut, 2021) since his philosophy is reconstructed in accordance with the clinical problems which Pinel proposes to solve. Consequently, even if the entry *genre*, by means of its didactic function, has a determining function in the legitimisation, transmission and reproduction of an element of knowledge, it is not a mere strategic and rhetorical transposition of Condillac's philosophy to already established knowledge. This rhetorical and strategic dimension is no less of a means to perfect and augment the medicine of his time.

On the one hand, Pinel establishes a hierarchy among the methods: the "particular" method of natural history is founded on the "general" method (or methodology) of analysis. On the other hand, he puts the results of Condillac's analysis to the test of facts. Thus, he detaches Condillac from his method. The knowledge of the past has been established by means of a method which he renders explicit neither in his entry nor in the rest of his work. Nevertheless, this method is the principle of selection and hierarchisation operated in the past of medicine and philosophy: the eclectic method. The epistemic authority of experience implies two axes: past experience and present experience. To account for experience implies combining and proportioning experience and the reasons which can account for it.

Consequently, the critical reception of Condillac is the sum of both the explicit and implicit borrowings of the Ideologists according to the eclectic method against a background of their tacit refusal of borrowings and their objections. And it is even a motor of reproduction of the school of the Ideologists like the innovations of its partisans, which veers very progressively away from Condillac's philosophy to re-conceive a duality of the physical and the moral (Lézé, 2020).

7 Acknowledgements

This study has been realised with the support of the LabEx COMOD, Université de Lyon (2017–2020) within the framework of the research programme: "The Battle for the Science of Man" (BATTMAN). My thanks to Delphine Antoine-Mahut, Pierre Brouillet and Anik Waldow for their remarks on the final version of this text. The English translation was provided by Nigel Briggs.

References

Albury, W. R. (1986). The order of ideas: Condillac's method of analysis as a political instrument in the French revolution. In: Schuster, J. A., Yeo, R. R. (eds) *The Politics and Rhetoric of Scientific Method*. Australasian Studies in History and Philosophy of Science, vol. 4. Dordrecht, Springer, 202–225.

Antoine-Mahut, D. (2021). Why do we need a concept of historiographical figures to do history of philosophy? *Academia Letters*. https://doi.org/10.20935/AL2150

Antoine-Mahut, D., & Lézé, S. (eds) (2018). *Les classiques à l'épreuve: Actualité de l'histoire de la philosophie*. Paris, Editions des Archives contemporaines.

Antoine-Mahut, D., Winter, M., & Lézé, S. (2021). Comment éveiller l'âme de Victor?. Le problème des idées innées de Descartes à Itard. *Revue d'histoire des sciences humaines*, 38(1), 69–87.

Bensaude-Vincent, B. (2010). Lavoisier lecteur de Condillac. *Dix-huitième siècle*, 42 (1), 473-489

Castel, L. (1798). *Analyse critique et impartiale de la nosographie philosophique de Ph. Pinel*, Paris, Imprimerie Lemaire.

Condillac, E. B. de (1754). *Traité des sensations*. Londres, Paris, De Bure l'aîné.

Condillac, E. B. de (1798a). *Essai sur l'origine des connaissances humaines.* Paris, Ch Houel, Imprimeur.
Condillac, E. B. de (1798b). *La logique ou les premiers développements de l'art de penser.* Paris, Ch Houel, Imprimeur.
Foucault, M. (1963) *Naissance de la Clinique,* Paris, Puf.
Huneman, P. (2008). Le projet aliéniste, la nosologie et la décomposition des fonctions mentales. In: Françoise Parot (ed), *Les fonctions en psychologie: Enjeux et débats.* Wavre: Mardaga, 49-66.
Lézé, S. (2020). Madness and spiritualist philosophy of mind: Maine de Biran and A. A. Royer-Collard on a 'true dualism'. *British Journal for the History of Philosophy,* 28(5), 885–902.
Mulsow, M. (2005). Zum Methodenprofil der Konstellationsforschung. In: Mulsow, M., Stamm, M. (eds) *Konstellationsforschung.* Frankfurt am Main, Suhrkamp, 74–97.
Nacquart, J. B. (1823). « Analyse », *Dictionnaire des sciences médicales.* Paris, Panckoucke, pp. 19–22.
Paradis, A. (1993). De Condillac à Pinel ou les fondements philosophiques du traitement moral. *Philosophiques,* 20(1), 69–112.
Pinel, P. (1800). *Traité médico-philosophique sur l'aliénation mentale ou la manie.* Paris, Richard, Caille & Ravier, An IX.
Pinel, P. (1808). « Manie, Vésanie, Aliénation mentale ou Dérangements des fonctions intellectuelles. (Nosologie & Médecine pratique) », (Félix Vicq-d'Azyr, ed.) *Encyclopédie méthodique de médecine,* Paris, Agasse, pp. 475–491.
Pinel, P. (1812). « Analyse appliquée à la médecine », *Dictionnaire des sciences médicales.* Paris, Panckoucke, pp. 23–30.
Schmitt, S. (2018). Inventaire des livraisons, des auteurs et du contenu de l'*Encyclopédie méthodique* (1782–1832). *Recherches sur Diderot et sur l'Encyclopédie,* 53, 207–270.

8 "The Only, the True French Metaphysician of the Eighteenth Century"

Condillac, Cousin and the "French School"

Delphine Antoine-Mahut

1 Introduction

The philosophical project of Victor Cousin (1792–1867)[1] is explicitly defined as "French." It manifests the intention of distinguishing itself from, on the one hand, a "British empiricism" rooting all knowledge in the senses while granting a minor role, if at all, to reflection. The figures of Bacon, Locke and Reid are repudiated while the benefit of the experimental approach is reinvested and successively applied to the study of nature and the mind. On the other hand, it also distinguishes itself from a "German idealism" which misunderstands the abilities of human reason and postulates ontology instead of arriving at it by means of reflection rooted in inner experience. Cousin targets Kant as well as his successors such as Fichte and Schelling. Given this, the sought "French philosophy" adopts the figurehead of a Descartes[2] as the psychologist promoting the epistemological virtues of both inner experience and a human reason of clearly circumscribed scope and limits.

The claim to a "French" identity of this eclectic spiritualism is also manifested in Franco-French demarcations, differentiating it from those other Spiritualists, labelled as "theologians"[3] and retrospectively designated as "anti-moderns" and "reactionaries" (Joseph De Maistre, 1753–1821; Louis De Bonald, 1754–1840; Félicité de Lammenais, 1782–1854; Pierre-Simon Ballanche, 1776–1847; or Louis Eugène Marie Bautain, 1796–1867). And, above all, in the aftermath of the epistemological, moral and political disaster of the French Revolution, the intent is to refute the dominant philosophy, the "sensualisms" of every type, reinvested by the Ideologists, such as Pierre Jean Georges Cabanis (1757–1808) and Antoine Destutt de Tracy (1754–1836), and their contemporary descendants, such as the famous physician François Broussais (1772–1838).

However, the place given by Cousin to the figure of Condillac in such a project seems eminently paradoxical. On the one hand, Condillac is designated as one of the main representatives of this specifically

DOI: 10.4324/9781003334750-10

eighteenth-century sensualism resulting from the regrettable acclimatisation, on French soil,[4] of seeds from across the English Channel. By distinguishing "two sorts of metaphysics"—one with the ambition "to pierce all the mysteries; the nature [and] the essence of beings, the most hidden causes," and the other which "knows how to contain itself within the limits traced for it"[5]—Condillac made Descartes into the main representative of the first sort and disqualified metaphysics as a whole. He can thus be swept aside in Cousin's global condemnation of the century of the Encyclopaedists: "Let us dare to speak the truth; the eighteenth century in France, so rich in great men, did not produce a single one in philosophy, if, at least, by philosophy we understand metaphysics" (Cousin, 1845, viii).[6]

Yet the most important point is not so much this metaphysical error as its practical consequences. Thus, Cousin does not hesitate to assert that, on the political and moral plane of its applications,[7] Condillac's metaphysics, systematised by a Helvetius nourished by the ideas of Hobbes and Spinoza, "necessarily" engendered "despotism" (Cousin, 1820, 31).

However, despite his severe criticism, Cousin recognises that in Condillac "the metaphysician dominates" (Cousin, 1829–1861, 29). What is more, he does not hesitate to present Condillac as "the only, the true French metaphysician of the eighteenth century" (Cousin, 1829–1866, 47–48). Alongside Anne Robert Jacques Turgot, "this universal and profound mind which penetrated all human knowledge, and which wrote the best piece of metaphysics published in that century, the author of the article *Existence* [in Diderot and d'Alembert's *Encyclopédie*]"; and in opposition to Diderot, "who was neither metaphysician, nor moralist, nor politician" (*Archives philosophiques*, 1817, in Cousin, 1826, 68), Condillac, as a metaphysician-psychologist, and thus as a philosopher, is likely to constitute a positive reference for the French philosophical school which Cousin presumes to lead.

We can thus identify a third network of demarcations among the actors sharing the concern to promote such a school. In this respect, the work of Jean Saphary (1797–1865) appears to be the most interesting. Like Cousin, Saphary criticises materialism, atheism and the influence of the Jesuits in the clergy. But this is only to better denounce the personification of philosophy teaching at the university by this very same Cousin. The main form of this conflict is the diffusion—first in the *lycée*, then at the Ecole Normale Supérieure where he lectures—of the philosophy of the editor of Condillac: Pierre Laromiguière (1756–1837).[8] His main weapon is the denouncing and correcting of the disastrous disfigurations of Condillac undertaken by Cousin:

> Venerated until now, Condillac is associated… with Mandeville and Collins, graciously flanked by Holbach and Lamétrie, and, for the effect

Condillac, Cousin, and the "French School" 121

of the tableau, followed by bloodthirsty hordes armed and unleashed by his perverse principles. One might believe one was seeing his disfigured statue presiding over the revolutionary saturnalia.... The name of Condillac, before which the darkness of philosophy seemed to have fled for ever, and with it so many abuses and prejudices, this name so great and so pure cannot be pronounced today without raising slanderous accusations. What a spirit of vertigo has thus blown on our century!

(Saphary, 1844, 33–35)

The paradoxical dimension of Cousin's relationship to Condillac can be clarified in the light of contemporary issues. Condillac *versus* Descartes is the filter which allows not only the establishment—by means of contrast of the outlines of this "State philosophy,"[9] also labelled "French"—but also the designation of oneself as the absolute monarch[10] of this philosophy. To rectify Cousin's philosophical interpretation of Condillac and, with it, the dominant historiography in its entirety is thus, at the same time, to propose another philosophy, another moral and political project and a master other than Cousin for the "French school": in this case, Pierre Laromiguière.[11]

So as to describe the decisive and complex role attributed to the figure of Condillac in the attempts to found a "French school"[12] of philosophy in the first half of the nineteenth century, I will distinguish five moments in the argumentation. Each is centred on a text exemplifying a phase of this same debate.

The first three moments correspond to successive phases of Cousin's own philosophy. By first focusing on two very rarely studied texts—his 1813 thesis in Latin and the 1820 *cours de morale*—and then his famous 1829 *Cours* and its reformulations in various editions, I will show how Cousin's work on the figure of Condillac can be described both as a reinvesting of the philosophical project of the Ideologists (in particular the link with Laromiguière) and as a demarcation, striving to recover the legacy of the Ideologists for his sole benefit. Depending on the period and the interlocutor, the emphasis is skilfully placed on one aspect or another. The fourth moment corresponds to the public and explicit criticism of Cousin's eclecticism by the "justification" of Laromiguière's Condillac in *L'École éclectique et l'école française* by Saphary (1844). The fifth and final moment is articulated around two texts: the one provided as an annex to his work by Saphary—the report by Joseph-Marie Degérando (1772–1842) concerning the papers received for the *appréciation de la philosophie de Laromiguière* competition; and the treatment of the reference to Condillac in the posthumous edition of the *Histoire comparée des systèmes de philosophie*, edited by Degérando's son in 1847.[13] The latter text is entirely devoted to the history of modern philosophy,[14] particularly the eighteenth century. This text is interesting in that it shows how a philosopher—often presented as

Cousin's inconsistent righthand man, nevertheless trained in Ideology and nourished by the criticisms of university eclecticism—mobilises a figure of Condillac, which is very close to Saphary's, to defend a spiritualism which is designated as both French and more inclusive than Cousin's.

By this means, we hope to convince our readers of the importance of the figure of Condillac in the laborious shaping of a "French philosophy" that attempts to unite an institutionally disfigured Cartesian legacy with a well-founded empiricist legacy.

2 The First Cousin and the First Condillac: Method and Application

The *Dissertatio philosophica de methodo sive de analysi, quam ad publicam disceptationem proponit ac doctoris gradum promovendus Victor Cousin, die julii decima nona* (The doctoral thesis in philosophy "on method or analysis," publicly defended by Victor Cousin, then a student at the Ecole normale and a graduate of the Faculté des Lettres, on 19 July 1813, from noon to two o'clock—Paris, Imprimerie de Fain, 1813) has never been translated or studied in its own right.[15] This might be because this text, of some 20 pages, is embarrassing. It is, indeed, a very academic and highly standardised exercise, presented at a time when the philosophy of Condillac is at the height of its glory and when Cousin is greatly influenced by the teaching of Pierre Laromiguière at the Faculté des Lettres of Paris.[16] Thus, we may be surprised by the difference in form and content between this first Cousin and the rhetorician who, at the summit of his later academic glory, attacks every possible form of sensualism, referring to Condillac in particular. In short, nourished by secondary literature focusing on this second Cousin, we might find it difficult to discover a meaning for what is, unquestionably, an eulogy of Condillac:

> If Condillac had not been snatched from us at the moment when he planned to write all his works again and to carry into the realm of philosophy that beautiful simplicity which he had shown in renewing, as it were, the elements of arithmetic and algebra, perhaps the vain quarrels and the darkness in which metaphysics is still shrouded today would have vanished, finally driven away and put to flight, by the torch of this new language which he had just forged.... Perhaps it will not seem out of place to praise Condillac so briefly, nor, principally in this out of season thesis, a thesis in which there is nothing that has not been drawn and taken from him... this man whose name and the name of method can in no way be disjoined.

This eulogy formalises at least three essential modalisations. First, Condillac did not write the work or works which Cousin and his contemporaries seek in their endeavour to put an end to the quarrels of metaphysics and enable its progress. Condillac merely endows his successors with "scattered and dispersed [as it were]" materials. As a result, the philosophers of Cousin's time are left "to gather together all the elements by uniting them in a single body," or to write that book "to discover new things." Second, what is worth retaining is not the totality of Condillac's philosophy but rather his method, which the rest of the thesis specifies as the method of analysis. From this point of view, Condillac is inscribed in the illustrious lineage of Bacon, Descartes, Malebranche and Locke, but by "augmenting" and "amplifying" its discoveries. Third, the as-yet-unwritten Condillac discourse on the method is specified as a particular ("as it were" in the quoted extract) application of the algebra and geometry of philosophy.

In detail, Cousin's philosophical reasoning, reconstructed from the materials provided by Condillac, comprises four phases. The first makes "self-evident" knowledge the model and basis of all our knowledge based on certainty. The second takes the famous example from the *Traité des Sensations*—the statue—to promote "a method of resolution" of the whole in its parts, followed by a return to unity directed by attention. The third explicitly reduces the operations of this method from four[17] to two, so as to redefine analysis as the "mixing" and "agreement" of the "method of decomposition" and the "synthetic method." The fourth and final phase defines the true meaning of philosophy as the seeking of how things are engendered, where they come from, or as the "science of relationships and principles" states, without examining in depth the link between these two characteristics *per se*. Finally, Cousin emphasises that this ordering will allow philosophers of the present to progress in metaphysics and thus also in morals, similar to how they progressed in the area of the sciences of nature.

This *Dissertatio philosophica...* thus appears to be a curious mixture. On the one hand, it is inscribed in the perfect continuity of the explicit project of the Ideologists, who considered metaphysics as a science of the methods to be applied to physics, the sciences of morals and the arts to perfect instruction, and who reasserted the value of the senses (the term retains its general meaning here) as the principle of knowledge. At the same time, this project is also promoted by Joseph-Marie Degérando. On the other hand, this text bears the clear and specific mark of the man who, in his teaching of Condillac, would rehabilitate attention, reduce the rules of the analytical method to two, and claim to commence with research into the origin of ideas rather than their nature: Pierre Laromiguière.[18] In other words, the *Dissertatio philosophica...* illustrates the ambiguity of those alternatively designated as the old Ideologists or the new spiritualists, and the particular aptitude of Condillac's philosophy to reconcile these paradoxes.

The "climacteric years"[19] which follow, in which Cousin becomes professor and fills the Sorbonne amphitheatres, witness the first inflexions. These are manifested in an exemplary fashion in the 1820 *cours de Philosophie morale*, which was never published as such by Cousin, but, as recently demonstrated by Renzo Ragghianti and Patrice Vermeren (2019, Introduction), promoted a new philosophy, one that drew on another new work on the figure of Condillac.

3 The *Cours* of 1820: Psychological Method and Experimental Philosophy

The 1820 *cours* reuses and accentuates two essential characteristics of the *Dissertatio philosophica…*: that is, on the one hand, the definition of philosophy "in its entirety" by its method and "the severity with which it follows it" (127);[20] and, on the other hand, the decisive importance of the "practical" or "applied" dimension of this same philosophy, that is, the passage from the "abstract" to the "concrete," "external things" or "real."[21]

However, Cousin significantly specifies these characteristics. Reason is identified as the active principle of these "mixed [forms] which are foreign to it," in which it recognises itself but as "disfigured" (241), and which manifests philosophy in the practical state. Observation becomes the method it implements, an observation which defines the spirit of modern philosophy. The historiography of modernity will thus be ruled by the question of knowing which philosopher has best used this method (90–91).

This is where we return to Condillac. In mid-eighteenth-century France, marked by what Cousin now designates as "sensualism," the man whose metaphysics is situated in the *Traité des sensations* becomes the origin of the morals and politics of self-esteem and interest later developed by Helvetius, Saint Lambert and the publicists. Condillac becomes the philosopher lacking a complete theory of the human mind because he finally absorbed free activity into sensitivity (99, 110 and 111). Condillac missed "man in his entirety," understood as a "free force, limited and modified by sensitivity and reason" or as consciousness and "coaction of these three unquestionable facts: reason, will and sensitivity" (170–171).

This figure of Condillac allows two new specifications of the type of observation and experimental philosophy envisaged by Cousin.[22] Observation is defined as both "all internal" or psychological (127), and as complex and obscure, because the subject observed is also the observing subject. Returning to the origin or principle by the psychological method is defined as "more philosophical" (113) when it starts out from the present or actual rather than simply postulating this origin. And this "adjourning,"[23] but not the negation of the knowledge of what rises above the limits of the actual, defines the truly experimental nature of the philosophy proposed, which is unlike a philosophy that would be, and only can be, transcendental (149–150).

Thus, in the 1820 *cours*, Cousin proposes nothing less than a *tour de force*. This consists in mobilising the analytical method of decomposition and composition promoted by Condillac and differently applied by his heirs to accede, at the price of a temporary adjourning, to ontological knowledge—a form of knowledge which Condillac defined most exactly as the renegade metaphysics which was being combatted.

The outlines of this second Cousin, born out of a close interaction with the Condillac of the *Traité des sensations*, become clear in the *Cours* of 1829 and its different editions.

4 The *Cours* of 1829: the Second Cousin and the Two Condillacs

Unlike the two previous texts, this *Cours* dealing with eighteenth-century sensualist philosophy was published. Its successive modifications in the subsequent editions consolidate an official doctrine in both the public and prescriptive sense. This is the bold and clear proclamation of "the true method" which has become the experimental method for "healthy psychology" and against "sensualism."

To this end, Cousin makes explicit the homology between this experimental psychological method and that which is recognised in physics or natural history. In each of these cases, the effect is observed to deduce the cause, rather than the cause being supposed to deduce the effect. No rigorous psychology can descend hypothetically from the origin of ideas to the ideas themselves; it must always progress from the ideas to their origin (8–9). Here, one must be attentive to the difference in formulation compared to the 1820 *cours*. For, here, the terms "cause," "ideas" and "origin" refer to an ontological dimension. They authorise, both upstream (after the "adjourning") and downstream (at the very moment of observation), the innatist theory. These terms attest to the resolute progression of Cousin, *cogito* in tow, towards that same abstract metaphysics which he claims to surpass when recovering the virtues of a well-understood Condillac.

Once more, this tension is particularly manifest in how he deals with Condillac. Cousin distinguishes two periods in Condillac's work: that of the *Essai sur l'origine des connaissances humaines* and that of the *Traité des sensations*.

For us, in this first period, in which Condillac, in a certain way, merely reproduces Locke, the most interesting point is the distinction Cousin draws between the spirit and the letter of the *Essai*. The more one progresses through the text, the more the distinction between the materials provided by sensations and the power working upon them (reflection) disappears. Yet this essential activity of the mind remains present beneath the surface. Thus, the first Condillac provides everything needed to found a healthy and true psychology. However, he already moves dangerously towards the *Traité des sensations*.

The *Traité des systèmes* is the turning point between the two Condillacs. Cousin emphasises how much Descartes is attacked and "openly sacrificed to Locke" (65) in this work; this makes the *Traité des systèmes* into a "manifesto of the school of Locke and pits the philosophy of the eighteenth century against the philosophy of the seventeenth century" (67). This intermediate Condillac is designated as abandoning experience and succumbing to abstraction. The Condillaquian principle of "the necessity of observation and experience" can now become "our arm against himself."

Condillac "is finally himself" (69) in the *Traité des sensations*; he makes abusive use of hypotheses in precisely the sense which he himself denounced in the *Traité des systèmes*; he dreams about a primitive human nature of man, because he does not know how to observe his current nature (73).[24] In short, Condillac "completely ignores the spirit of experimental philosophy" (51). Reflection, with which Locke saved the activity of the soul and what remained of it in the writing of the first Condillac, is here presented as but one of the numerous transformations (in the sense of effect) of the kind of sensation experienced by this fictitious and abstract man represented by the statue.

Here, Cousin contrasts, at length, the passivity, fatality and involuntary character of sensation on the one hand with the activity, liberty and voluntary character of ambition on the other. Cousin emphasises that sensation itself requires an active consciousness from within man. Finally, the previous distinction between the spirit and the letter of Condillac's doctrine, between his "admitted method" and what he really does, is intensified by a particular insistence on the disfigurations of Condillac by those who later claimed his lineage. This time, Cousin no longer refers to the body of the *Traité des sensations*, but to its appendix. For in this marginal text, Condillac recognises the existence of liberty, and, without a shadow of a doubt, he recognises it "sincerely." Nevertheless, his inheritors ignored this text, and a text which is not read, commented on, reinvested, applied... is, in effect, a text which does not exist. So, this appendix must be counted "for nothing" in the Condillac system, and the sensualists, particularly Helvetius and Saint Lambert, must take responsibility for this.

The 1829 *Cours* thus proposes a complex position on the philosophical and historiographical planes. In this work, Cousin recovers activity and liberty from the Condillac of the appendix. However, one can no longer take this Condillac into account because those who presently lay claim to his lineage have disfigured him to the extent of making him unrecognisable. The confrontation of this text with the *Dissertatio philosophica...* and the 1820 *Cours* does not allow us to talk of authentic reversals. However, it certainly attests to the crucial importance of the identification of the true philosophical lineage between the new French school and Condillac in the first decades of the nineteenth century.

The examination of the contributions of Saphary and Degérando will allow us to finish by describing two of the most interesting intertextualities on this point.

5   *L'École Éclectique et l'École Française* (1844). Saphary, the "True" Condillac and the "True" French School

L'École éclectique et l'école française (1844)[25] opens with a rebuttal in the form of an almost term by term response. In it, Saphary denounces Cousin's "scholarly staging," his invention of a "disfigured sensualism" and an "as fantastic as monstrous creation which exists only in the heads of its false interpreters" (p. VIII). In order to return to the true Descartes and the true Condillac, as well as correct Cousin's "false patronage" (xxiv), one must remember that the criticisms of Condillac by Cousin—in the spirit of system and a tendency to idealism and abstraction—are precisely those which make Cousin a disciple of Descartes. One should turn against academic eclecticism "the weapons [which it has] used against French philosophy!" (38–39).

The main effect of this reversal consists in promoting Laromiguière, over Cousin, to the rank of master of this French school. For he attributes to Laromiguière the honour of having attacked Condillac's system as being elaborated on a false basis—sensation, the passive principle of his nature—and having replaced it with an active principle—attention—to found a "philosophy of the sentiment" or "the philosophy of the heart." Laromiguière is the true contemporary disciple of the "French metaphysician," of the new and "true philosophy," the "totally practical" philosophy, articulating the rights of reason and the obligations of faith, the liberties of the country and the religion of our fathers (37, 45–46).

To "show both the *intimate thinking* of Condillac and the *secret thinking* of those who, with scholarly traps, have rendered necessary the rehabilitation of his memory," Saphary proposes a long "justification" (47–61, my emphasis). In several instances, he addresses him, without naming him, as that "serious philosopher" or "noble thinker" who all recognise as Cousin. As for the "gradually animated and illuminated" statue of the *Traité des sensations*, which we found as a conducting thread from the *Dissertatio philosophica...* to the 1829 *Cours*, Saphary plays the "personal reason" of Condillac against Cousin's impersonal reason. If "the most delicate reader can recognise himself and say: *De te fabula narratur*"—whereas the critic, upending the problem, makes a statue of the man (56)—this is because, in the work of Condillac, sentiment, not caricatured sensation, constitutes the true source of knowledge.

The second part of the volume is thus free to return to the content of the "true French philosophy," the "daughter of Locke, richly endowed by Condillac," "rectified," "enriched" and "perfected" by Laromiguière (72–74). Saphary compares "these two metaphysicians" on the decisive issues of the method and the origin of our ideas, so as to show what decisive corrections Laromiguière has made to the philosophy of Condillac, in order to perfect it.

First, Laromiguière has shown that Condillac moved away from the method which he had taught. For Condillac's analysis is only applied to the observations and not the reasoning. Consequently, Laromiguière has distinguished the *analysis of reasoning*, dealing with a single object, from *descriptive analysis*, dealing with the relationship between objects. Second, Condillac maintained a confusion between the sensation and the act of the mind characterising thought by talking of the *generation* or *transformation* of the one by the other. Laromiguière has shown that there is a mere relationship of succession between the two (93–94). Third, Laromiguière explains that, in principle, all the human soul's manners of acting are but attention. His greatest philosophical achievement is thus having returned to the soul its true activity and having replaced sensitivity by activity, designating the former as the ability to sense rather than as a faculty. Finally, between sensation and the interpretation of the acts of our peers, Laromiguière has placed the sentiment of our faculties and the moral sentiment. In so doing, he connects with the French tradition, parsing out Vauvenargues and Rousseau, Malebranche and Fenelon.

However, the most important point is how the issue of the origin of ideas is dealt with. Saphary returns to the objection of Cousin to Condillac and Laromiguière (as well as the publicists), according to which one cannot rule on the origin and the generation of ideas before establishing a "severe classification" of them (156). Saphary provides two types of answer, of different nature, to this objection. On the one hand, one may justify the method without actually justifying all its mistaken applications (169). But, on the other hand and above all (for on the first point, Cousin would not have disagreed), it is difficult to see how civil justice could be founded without recognising a justice anterior to civil societies: "one must therefore study man in man, before considering him in the citizen, subject or magistrate." The rational hypothesis of the state of nature and of a social pact is the rational origin of society. To found the new philosophy, it is thus necessary to return to the origin of ideas (173). A position which, this time, the later Cousin was not far from adopting.

Finally, Laromiguière has shown the decisive importance of liberty, understood as "power to want or not want after deliberation" (189). Thus, with him, metaphysics has become an analysis of sentiment, understanding and liberty—something which is very different from its Cousinian identification with psychology, which does not include the entire intellectual and moral life of man.

What is at stake in this struggle, mobilising large doses of the constructed figure of Condillac, is nothing less than the definition of the new metaphysics which is to command true morals and find a truly free State.

6   The *Rapport sur le Concours sur la Philosophie de Laromiguière* and the *Histoire comparée* (1847) by Degérando: Descartes and Condillac Reconciled

The Laromiguière philosophy competition report closes with the formulation of the wish that:

> the competitors show themselves more just in favour of the philosophers of the French school whose traces Laromiguière followed, by rectifying their errors; that they better note the misunderstandings to which the unfortunate use Condillac made of sensation gave rise; that they restitute their true character to the doctrines of the French school worthy of this name, by separating it from the grave deviations of the sectarians who usurped its language.
>
> (250)

However, before the competition is reopened, the report's author, Degérando, dies and he is replaced by Joseph Droz (1773–1850). In the new report (251–252), Droz, in his turn, also reminds us of the two essential reforms of Condillac's philosophy driven by Laromiguière: adding to sensation other sources of knowledge, so as to found morals not solely dictated by interest; and opposing passivity of sensation with activity of attention, so as to return to the bases of human dignity based on liberty. Droz underlines that it is, above all, this second point which leaves a "profound trace" upon those who, according to him, have held the "sceptre of philosophy."

The posthumous edition of the *Histoire comparée des systèmes de philosophie*, published by Degérando's son in 1847 (particularly Chapters XIX and XX), returns to the criteria for the identification of this new French eclectic philosophy, in the light of these debates. Here, once again, the figure of Condillac plays an essential role.

In a very Cartesian way, Degérando starts by reminding us that the "value of the word philosophy" derives from its applications, or resides in the concern to cultivate "useful truths" (234). But not all applications are of equal worth. On the philosophical plane, the only admissible ones are those rooted[26] in the science of prime truths, the study of man and his faculties, the art of methods and what teaches us how to live well. The other applications, which indeed proliferated in the eighteenth century, pertain to "a colour of opinion," a "personal conviction," "a certain turn of mind" (302) or even the passions (238). This produces an immediate effect: it enables Cartesianism to be found in that very century which, until then, had been said to have abandoned it. The continuity between the seventeenth and eighteenth centuries is thus re-established through highlighting these original "transplantations" of this Cartesian philosophy, in the theory of Beauty by the Jesuit father, Yves-Marie André, or in jurisprudence by Henri François d'Aguesseau. In the eighteenth century, Degérando rehabilitates a Cartesianism which one has every right to qualify as empirical, or at the very least, as an exemplar of this "philosophy of experience" which he intends to promote.

The second part of his argumentation more specifically concerns Condillac. The intent is to show that if the true French philosophical school combines Locke and Descartes, nobody achieved this combination better than Condillac. Degérando accentuates the extent of the Condillaquian disfiguration regarding Locke, in particular for "the very ones who re-established the true doctrine of Locke and have persevered in admitting the inexact idea which was given credit using that of Condillac" (318). He shows that this disfiguration comes from the "imagination" of a new term, "*sensualism*" (239 and 316, in italics in the text), as if Condillac's philosophy attributed the empire of man to the senses (317), and as if Condillac was confused with Helvetius, d'Alembert and Diderot. Degérando then refers to Laromiguière as the person who worked on rectifying this image. In short, Degérando uses certain arguments from Cousin and also their reversal by Saphary. Attempting to circumscribe, in the present, the kind of philosophy which France needs involves first correcting certain "vices of expression" with which Condillac, as it were, made a rod for his own back, as exemplified by his use of sensation for sentiment (323); and second, restoring to its place "the effort of the internal activity of the soul" (318).

In a final stage, this enables him to specify the difference between mere syncretism and true eclecticism.[27] The challenge is to found "another metaphysics," that is, a metaphysics distinct from both that of the "sensualists"—the abstract metaphysics so justly criticised by Condillac—and that which consists in juxtaposing them.

One final time, Degérando returns to Condillac. The initial contradiction lies in Condillac wishing, like Bacon and Locke, to provide observation and experience as guides to philosophy, and, like Descartes, to only conceive truth and method according to the type of purely speculative notions. This is why these two doctrines are not truly associated in his thoughts but rather juxtaposed to incessantly fight each other. In this sense, we are dealing with a syncretism rather than a true eclecticism. And this is what is commonly designated as the "paradoxes" of Condillac and explains, without justifying it, how it has been possible to alternately make him a materialist and an idealist. As for the true eclecticism, it should define a "true" or "healthy" metaphysics, that is, an "experimental metaphysics." Degérando reinvests Turgot's example (341–346), which attempts to embrace the primal philosophy not by dealing with ontology, but by dealing with the *existence of the "I"* (345–346). But this is Cousin as refracted and reconfigured in Saphary's criticisms.

7 Conclusion

In the philosophically laborious period in France that is the first part of the nineteenth century, the figure of Condillac plays a central role in the founding of a new metaphysics, which must distinguish itself from both that of the adversaries of Condillac and that of a Condillac often disfigured, even by his most zealous inheritors.

The paradoxical dimension of Condillac's philosophy, reinvested with different emphases, at different moments by the different actors of this period, is thus found in the empirical nature and the eminently practical vocation of this metaphysics, which must enable the founding of a new psychology, other morals and other politics. Yet this curious alliance of metaphysics and empiricism can only appear paradoxical to a mind convinced of the opposition between a metaphysics understood as *a priori* or pure (and, generally, Descartes is the figure who represents this type of metaphysics) and no metaphysics at all (which more or less means the rejection of any metaphysics).

Shedding light on the Cousin-Saphary-Degérando intertextuality thus reveals two essential effects of the laborious shaping of this metaphysics. On the one hand, the Descartes-Condillac-Cousin lineage was unquestionably considered as the origin of a national philosophy, characterised by its "spirit of method and analysis," for which "the sharpness, precision, clarity and perfect liaison are a need," and which, consequently, can adequately analyse the facts of consciousness. On the other side of the Rhine, it was even designated as "the French spirit *par excellence.*"[28] Yet, on the other hand, it was eminently contested in France, even within the spiritualist camp, because it masked a return to an unwanted abstract metaphysics, and because this exclusivity was manifested in abusive institutional power. From Saphary who wished "that, in philosophy as in geometry, there would be neither French, nor Scottish, nor German" (17, note 1); to Degérando who turned his focus from the Académie des Sciences Morales et Politiques to a place of international exchange, the Berlin Academy; from the starting point of Condillac, everything converges towards the rethinking of a French *philosophy* which would not be *French*, in the sense of its dominant institutional incarnation and which would shatter the philosophical dualisms and antagonisms structuring the official historiography of modernity.

Notes

1 In France, Cousin occupied numerous positions: the Chair in history of modern philosophy at the Sorbonne; director of the Ecole Normale, rue d'Ulm; State counsellor; Pair de France (peer); member of the Académie Française; director of the Académie des Sciences Morales et Politiques; Minister for Public Instruction; and president of the Agrégation jury charged with the nomination and inspection of teachers of philosophy throughout France. As such, he was the key actor in the process of institutionalising the philosophical canon which—in France and in continuity with what began a little earlier in Germany–would reach its apogee in the mid-nineteenth century.
2 On this point, see *L'autorité d'un canon philosophique. Le cas Descartes* (Antoine-Mahut, 2021) Chapters IX on Cousin, VIII on Destutt de Tracy and X on Renouvier, pp. 243–346; and "Figures de Descartes dans l'historiographie française au XIXe siècle" (Antoine-Mahut, 2022).
3 On the constitution and role of these labels, within the Cousin clan, see "Politiques de l'éclectisme en situation de crise" (Barancy, 2019).
4 According to Cousin, Voltaire is the principle figure who "turned the philosophy of the eighteenth century century against Cartesianism" (Cousin, 1845, viii–ix). Just think of the famous fourteenth letter of the *Lettres anglaises* (Voltaire, 1734) which opposes the Cartesian "novel of the soul" to its true "history" undertaken by Locke.
5 Condillac, 1746, pp. 59–60. Nigel Briggs's translation.
6 Existing studies focus on this "deliberate occultation… of which the work of Victor Cousin is undoubtedly the centre" (Bloch, 1979, 39 and Bloch, 1997, third part). This occultation process targets materialism in all its forms. See, in particular, Vermeren, 1996; Daled, 2006; Diderot, 2009 and Rey, 2015. On Helvetius, about whom Cousin wrote that he "contains in abridged [form] all the metaphysics of Condillac" (Cousin, 1820, 111), see "'Cette équitable distinction': Damiron lecteur d'Helvétius" (Moreau, 2022).
7 On the Condillacian method of analysis as political instrument of the French Revolution, see W.R. Albury, 1986.
8 In the *Essai analytique d'une métaphysique qui comprendrait les principes, la formation, la certitude de nos connaissances dans le plan de M. Laromiguière, dont on a résumé les leçons* (initially published in two volumes, in 1815–1818, republished in 1820, fourth edition in 1826), and which he dedicated to his master, Saphary successively examines the principle of our knowledge, its formation and certitude. On Laromiguière and Condillac, see the contribution by Pierre Brouillet, in this volume.
9 Saphary's complete expression is "a State philosophy which parodies the State religion" (quoted by Picavet, 1891, 563).
10 On this royalty metaphor, see "The empowered King of French Philosophy: Théodore Jouffroy (1792–1842)" (Antoine-Mahut, 2020a).
11 In this contribution, for reasons of space and clarity, I will leave to one side the complex and intersecting relationships between Cousin, Laromiguière, Maine

de Biran and Pierre Paul Royer-Collard (1773–1845). On Cousin and Maine de Biran, see "Maine de Biran's places in French Spiritualism: occultation, reduction and demarcation" (Antoine-Mahut, 2016); "L'éclectisme de Victor Cousin: une philosophie *française* sans *philosophie* française" (Antoine-Mahut, 2019b) and the contribution by Anne Devarieux in this volume. On Royer-Collard, see Cotten 1992 and 2007 and on Cousin and Scottish philosophy, see Etchegaray and Malherbe, 2007. On Royer-Collard, Cousin and Théodore Jouffroy, see Chignola, 2011. For a global presentation of Royer-Collard, see Doria, 2018, 119–156 for his philosophical thinking.

12 The expression is used on numerous occasions by both the Cousin clan and his adversaries. On the different possible meanings of the term "école" and what is meant by "Penser par école," see Orain and Marcel 2018.

13 On the complexity of Degérando, see Chappey, Christen and Moullier, 2014; on his relationship to empiricism, see Manzo, 2016; and on his comparatism, see Lézé, 2019. On the different uses of the figure of Descartes in the Cousin and Degérando historiographies, see Antoine-Mahut, 2020b.

14 The complete reference is *Histoire de la philosophie moderne, à partir de la renaissance des lettres jusqu'à la fin du XVIIIe siècle*. Paris: Ladrange, 4 vol., 1847.

15 I thank Jean-Pierre Cotten, a major specialist in this first Cousin, for providing me with the unpublished French translation of this work.

16 In the second preface to the *Fragments philosophiques* (Paris: Ladrange, 1833, xxxiii–xxxiv), Cousin designated the day when he first heard Laromiguière as the day which decided his whole life. For Laromiguière taught the philosophy of Locke and Condillac while intelligently modifying them on certain points, with a clarity and grace which, at least in appearance (undoubtedly the decisive point!), made the difficulties disappear, and with a charm and spiritual *bonhomie* which could not fail to persuade. On Cousin, Laromiguière and Maine de Biran, see Biran, 1817 and Cousin and Biran, 1829.

17 There were, of course, already four in the work of Descartes (evidence, analysis, synthesise and enumeration). But Cousin also found them in his present, and in the work of his interlocutors as influential as Cabanis. See, in particular, the four types of analysis (description, composition and decomposition, historical and deductive) contained in the *Coup d'œil sur les révolutions et sur les réformes de la médecine*, 1804. On the method of analysis of the Ideologists, see Clauzade, 1998.

18 See the contribution by Pierre Brouillet in this volume.

19 To use the expression of Paul Dubois, 1904, 39.

20 See also p. 133 and p. 150.

21 See, especially, p. 186. In this *cours*, Cousin envisages, in particular, the field of natural, civil and political law.

22 On this point, see Antoine-Mahut, 2019a.

23 On this adjourning of ontology, see Moreau, 2013.

24 On this point, see Antoine-Mahut, 2021, 276–277. Royer Collard is the source of the attribution to Condillac of a form of idealism, the principle of which was supposedly posited by Descartes.

25 The work opens with the following dedication: "To the memory of Laromiguière, my illustrious master and my true friend."

26 This is the sense of the image of the tree of philosophy proposed by Descartes in the Letter-preface to the *Principes de la philosophie*, in the French edition of 1647.

134 *Delphine Antoine-Mahut*

27 On the different meanings of this term and its criticisms in the nineteenth century, see Antoine-Mahut (forthcoming).
28 To use the expression of J. Willm in his "Essai sur la nationalité des philosophes," provided as an introduction to his translation of Friedrich Wilhelm Joseph Von Schelling's *Sur la philosophie de M. Cousin* in 1835 (our emphasis). Willm also qualifies the collaboration between Schelling and Cousin as that of the "successor to Kant and Fichte" and the "successor to Descartes and Condillac." For the preceding analyses, see, in particular, p. 37. On the analysis by Willm of this concept of nationality, see Bernard-Granger (forthcoming).

References

Albury, W.R. (1986). "The order of ideas: Condillac's method of analysis as a political instrument in the French revolution", in *The Politics and Rhetoric of Scientific Method*. Ed. J.A. Schuster and R.R. Yeo, Dordrecht/Boston, MA/Lancaster/Tokyo: D. Reidel Publishing Company, pp. 203–225.
Antoine-Mahut, D. (2016). "Maine de Biran's places in French Spiritualism: occultation, reduction and demarcation", in Edition and English Translation of Maine de Biran, *Rapport du physique et du moral chez l'homme*, with various Studies of Maine de Biran's Philosophy. Ed. D. Meacham and J. Spadola, London: Bloomsbury, pp. 33–46.
Antoine-Mahut, D. (2019a). "Experimental method in the spiritualist soul. The case of Victor Cousin", *Perspectives on Science*, 27(5), pp. 680–703.
Antoine-Mahut, D. (2019b). "L'éclectisme de Victor Cousin: une philosophie *française* sans *philosophie* française", in *Ad argumenta. Quaestio Special Issues*. Turnhout/Bari The Territories of Philosopy in Modern Historiography Ed. C. König-Pralong, M. Meliado and Z. Radeva, 1, pp. 149–168.
Antoine-Mahut, D. (2020a). "The empowered King of French Philosophy: Théodore Jouffroy (1792–1842)", *British Journal for the History of Philosophy*, 28(5), pp. 923–943.
Antoine-Mahut, D. (2020b). "Philosophizing with a historiographical figure. Descartes in Degérando's comparative history (1804 and 1847)", *British Journal for the History of Philosophy*, 28(3), pp. 533–552.
Antoine-Mahut, D. (2021). *L'autorité d'un canon philosophique. Le cas Descartes*. Paris: Vrin.
Antoine-Mahut, D. (2022). "Figures de Descartes dans l'historiographie française au XIXe siècle", *XVIIe Siècle*, 2022/3 (n°296), pp. 485–498.
Antoine-Mahut, D. (forthcoming). "Eclecticism and its discontents", in *The Oxford Handbook of French Philosophy*. Ed. M. Sinclair and D. Whistler, Oxford: Oxford University Press.
Barancy, F. (2019). "Politiques de l'éclectisme en situation de crise", in *Une arme philosophique: L'éclectisme de Victor Cousin*. Ed. D. Antoine-Mahut and D. Whistler, Paris: Editions des Archives Contemporaines, pp. 81–92.
Bernard-Granger, S. (forthcoming). "Universel philosophique et particularités nationales: Willm, entre Schelling et Cousin", *Schelling Studien*, 10. München, Kal Alber Freiburg
Biran (Maine de), Marie François Pierre Gontier de (1817). *Examen des Leçons de philosophie de M. Laromiguière, ou Considérations sur le principe de la*

psychologie, sur la réalité de nos connaissances, et l'activité de l'âme. Paris, chez Fournier, Libraire.
Bloch, O. (Ed.) (1979). *Images au XIXe siècle du matérialisme du XVIIIe siècle*. Paris: Desclée.
Bloch, O. (1997). *Matière à histoires*. Paris: Vrin.
Cabanis, P.J.G. (1804). *Coup d'œil sur les révolutions et sur les réformes de la médecine*. Paris: chez Crapart, Caille et Ravier.
Chappey, J.-L., Christen C. and Moullier, I. (Eds.) (2014). *J.-M. de Gérando (1772–1842). Connaître et réformer la société*. Rennes: PU de Rennes.
Chignola, S. (2011). "A Philosophy before Philosophy: Royer-Collard, Jouffroy, Cousin", *Rivista di Storia della Filosofia*, 66(3), pp. 471–504.
Clauzade, L. (1998). *L'idéologie ou la révolution de l'analyse*. Paris: Gallimard.
Condillac, Ét. Bonnot de (1746). *Essai sur l'origine des connaissances humaines*. Ed. J.-Cl. Pariente and M. Pécharman, Paris: Vrin, 2014, pp. 59–60.
Cotten, J.-P. (1992). *Autour de Victor Cousin. Une politique de la philosophie*. Paris: Belles Lettres.
Cotten, J.-P. (2007). "La rédécouverte de Reid par Royer-Collard: état des sources et des interprétations", in *Philosophie écossaise et philosophie française (1750–1850)*. Ed. E. Arosio and M. Malherbe, Paris: Vrin, pp. 53–74.
Cousin, V. (1813). Dissertatio philosophica de methodo sive de analysi, quam ad publicam disceptationem proponit ac doctoris gradum promovendus Victor Cousin, die julii decima nona (Doctoral thesis in philosophy 'on method or analysis', publicly defended by Victor Cousin, on 19 July 1813, from noon to two o'clock). Paris: Imprimerie de Fain.
Cousin, V. (1820). *Philosophie Morale*. S. Matton, R. Ragghianti and P. Vermeren Éd. Paris: Classiques Garnier, 2019.
Cousin, V. (1826). *Fragments Philosophiques*. Paris: Sautelet.
Cousin, V. (1829–1861). "Cours sur Locke", in *Philosophie de Locke*. 4th. Revised and expanded edition, 1861. Paris: Didier.
Cousin, V. (1829–1866). *Histoire de la philosophie du dix-huitième siècle*. Tome 2. "École *sensualiste. Locke*". Paris: Pichon et Didier. 5th. Revised and expanded edition, *Philosophie sensualiste au XVIIIe siècle*. 5th. Revised and expanded edition, Paris: Didier et Cie.
Cousin, V. (1833). *Fragments Philosophiques*. 2nd edition. Paris: Ladrange.
Cousin, V. (1845). *Fragments de philosophie cartésienne*. Paris: Charpentier.
Cousin, V. and Biran, M. Maine de (1829). *Leçons de philosophie de Laromiguière, jugées par M. Cousin et M. Maine de Biran*. Paris: chez les libraires-éditeurs Rouen Frères et Johanneau.
Daled, P.-F. (2006). *Le matérialisme occulté et la genèse du "sensualisme". Écrire l'histoire de la philosophie en France*. Paris: Vrin.
Daled, P.-F. (2009). "L'image de Denis Diderot dans l'historiographie philosophique française du début du XIXe siècle: un 'éclectique moderne'", *Diderot Studies*, 31, pp. 107–123.
Degérando, J.-M. (1847). *Histoire de la philosophie moderne, à partir de la renaissance des lettres jusqu'à la fin du XVIIIe siècle*. Paris: Ladrange, (4 vol.).
Doria, C. (2018). *Pierre-Paul Royer-Collard (1763–1845). Un philosophe entre deux révolutions*. Rennes: PU de Rennes.

Dubois, P. (1904). *Cousin, Jouffroy, Damiron. Souvenirs, avec une introduction par Adolphe Lair*. Paris: Perrin.

Etchegaray, C. (2007). "La réception de la philosophie écossaise chez Victor Cousin", in *Philosophie écossaise et philosophie française (1750–1850)*. Ed. E. Arosio and M. Malherbe, Paris: Vrin, pp. 95–114.

Lézé, S. (2019). "Contrôler le territoire philosophique à coups de canon: l'éclipse de 'l'histoire comparée' de Joseph-Marie de Gérando (1772–1842) à l'orée d'une juridiction de l'incomparable", in *Ad argumenta*. Quaestio Special Issues, Ed. C. Pralong-König, M. Meliado and Z. Radeva, 1, Turnhout: Brepols Publishers pp. 223–244.

Malherbe, M. (2007). "La réception de la philosophie écossaise chez le jeune Cousin (1815–1829)", in *Philosophie écossaise et philosophie française (1750–1850)*. Ed. E. Arosio and M. Malherbe, Paris: Vrin, pp. 115–136.

Manzo, S. (2016). "Historiographical approaches on experience and empiricism in the early nineteenth century: Degérando and Tennemann", *Perspectives on Science*, 27(5), pp. 655–672.

Moreau, P.-F. (2013). "'Ajourner l'ontologie'. Le cartésianisme relu par Victor Cousin", in *Qu'est-ce qu'être cartésien ?* Ed. D. Kolesnik-Antoine (Antoine-Mahut), Lyon: ENS Editions, pp. 521–530.

Moreau, P.-F. (2022). "'Cette équitable distinction': Damiron lecteur d'Helvétius", *Historia philosophica*, 20/2022, pp. 205–215.

Orain, P. and Marcel, J.-C. (Ed.) (2018, printemps). "Penser par écoles". *Revue des Sciences Humaines*, 1, 32.

Picavet, F. (1891). *Les Idéologues. Essai sur l'histoire des idées et des théories scientifiques, philosophiques, religieuses, etc. en France depuis 1789*. Paris: Félix Alcan.

Rey, L. (2015). "Les Lumières comme enjeu philosophique et politique: Pierre Leroux face à Victor Cousin", Dix-Huitième siècle, 2015/1, n°47, pp. 501–528.

Saphary, J. *Essai analytique d'une métaphysique qui comprendrait les principes, la formation, la certitude de nos connaissances dans le plan de M. Laromiguière, dont on a résumé les leçons* (initially published in two volumes, in 1815–1818, republished in 1820, 4th edition in 1827). Paris: Bruno-Labbe, Senef et Vincenot.

Saphary, J. (1844). *L'École éclectique et l'école française*. Paris: Joubert.

Vermeren, P. (1996). *Victor Cousin. Le jeu de la philosophie et de l'État*. Paris: l'Harmattan.

Voltaire, F.-M. A. (1734). *Lettres écrites de Londres sur les Anglais, et autres sujets*. Amsterdam: Chez Etienne Ledet, et compagnie.

Willm, J. (1835). "Essai sur la nationalité des philosophes". Provided as an introduction to his translation of *Jugement de M. de Schelling sur la philosophie de M. Cousin*. Paris et Strasbourg: F. G. Levrault.

9 Condillac's Puerile Reveries
The Reception of Condillac in Phrenology and in the Philosophy of Auguste Comte

Laurent Clauzade

1 Introduction

The history of Condillac's reception took a turn in the early years of the nineteenth century. Until then, the Ideology of Pierre-Jean-Georges Cabanis and Antoine Destutt de Tracy, which was arguably the official philosophy of the Revolution, had been conceived, even if not without some ambiguity, as an extension of the work of Condillac. But from the 1810s onwards, the new philosophical systems, namely the eclectic spiritualism of Victor Cousin and the positivism of Auguste Comte, thoroughly rejected Condillac's radical sensationalism. This reaction is mainly based on their rejection of both the genetic perspective and the reduction of the operations of the soul to sensation alone. In contrast to this philosophical programme, their systems prioritise a direct approach to intellectual and moral operations, either through an interior observation of the phenomena of consciousness, in the case of the Cousinians, or through sociological and biological investigation, in the case of Auguste Comte. The hostility towards the eighteenth century, which "saw in our intelligence only the action of the external senses", was typical of the period, as Comte points out at the beginning of his work, in one of the few passages where he acknowledges agreement with spiritualism:

> The well-founded objections to the ideology of Condillac and Helvetius alone give some justification to the influence of the existing psychology, which, moreover, merely popularises, by obscure and emphatic declamations, what physiologists such as Charles Bonnet, Cabanis and especially MM. Gall and Spurzheim, had long before put forward on this subject much more clearly and precisely.
> (Comte, 1875, IV, 648 / 1851–1854, IV, 221)

Even if this reaction against Condillac is common to this new generation of philosophers, their approaches are very different. What is specific about

DOI: 10.4324/9781003334750-11

the Comtean critique, to which this article is devoted, is that it first of all sets out a general socio-historical framework according to which Condillac is part of a critical and metaphysical movement that directly prepared the Revolution. This movement also provided the theoretical basis for the social reorganisation attempted by the Revolution, the evident failure of which led to a state of anarchy which only positivism could remedy. This is what Comte underlines in one of his last works when he mentions the revolutionary party, "the most noxious and the most belated of existing parties", which, as late as 1854, prevented the advent of a society organised according to the political principles of positive philosophy:

[The revolutionary party] alone denies the need of a spiritual reconstruction, which it feels itself incapable of giving; it bends its efforts to concentrate the aspirations of the people on the direct attainment of material reforms, and these reforms are principally destructive. Unacquainted with the more important advances made in the nineteenth century, it would solve the difficulties of the West with the religion of Voltaire, the philosophy of Condillac, the moral system of Helvetius and the political theory of Rousseau, rejecting Hume, Diderot, and Condorcet.
(Comte, 1875, IV, xx / 1851–1854, IV, xvi–vii)

This series presents Condillac as "the" philosopher: accordingly, he was discussed in a field that might, broadly speaking, be called "the theory of knowledge"; it includes questions relating to the philosophy of science and the conceptualisation of the mental faculties. Comte's characterisation explains why the social and historical context is of little importance in the case of Condillac. He is perceived as the author of transformed sensation and accused of having overestimated the importance of signs, while the other thinkers listed above are identified with the pursuit of strong moral or political issues: thus, Voltaire is associated with deism, Helvetius with the thesis of egoism and, secondarily, with that of the natural equality of minds, while Rousseau is associated with the "sophisms" of the social contract and the state of nature.

The above characterisation, however simplistic it may be, does in fact serve as a guide to Comtean criticism of eighteenth-century philosophy. A similar type of philosophical criticism can also be found in certain spiritualist analyses, for example in Victor Cousin's early lectures. Here too, the hostility to sensationalism often took the form of expressing slogans intended less to explain his philosophy than to justify antagonistic constructions.

This approach to eighteenth-century philosophy implies two points relevant to the present study. First of all, we learn little about Condillac's philosophy in Comte's reception, since it only very weakly adopts a style of philosophical debate based on a precise description of the texts. Second, since Condillac's theses are mainly understood through an alternative theory, they are often reformulated in terms quite different from his own.

However, the analysis of the references to Condillac in Comte's work as well as in Franz Joseph Gall's—whose main thesis on the issue of mental faculties Comte faithfully took up and integrated into his system—shows that Condillac was widely read at the time, and his theses, beyond the interpretation of the Ideologists, were known by his critics, even if not well understood. The impact of Condillac is not only revealed by the violence of the voices of his critics; it is also demonstrated by the fact that, anonymously or through the work of other authors, such as Charles-Georges Leroy or Henri de Blainville, certain theses with strong Condillaquian connotations were taken up by Auguste Comte. This chapter will discuss Comte's engagement with Condillac in relation to the following three themes: the thesis of transformed sensation, the method of analysis and the question of the language of calculation.

2 Phrenological Physiology and the Thesis of Transformed Sensation

Condillac is primarily regarded by Comte and Gall as the author of the thesis of transformed sensation. This thesis is taken to constitute the fundament of a psychological theory that directly competes with the psychophysiological conceptions of Gall's doctrine of the brain, which Comte endorsed. More precisely, the thesis of transformed sensation directly conflicts with four fundamental principles of phrenological physiology:

– The idea that the operations of the mind are generated from sensations goes against Gall's claim of the innateness of our fundamental faculties, which are organic functions with biologically fixed powers.
– The idea that all our cognitive and conative faculties derive from a single operation, namely sensation, is opposed to the phrenological idea of the irreducible plurality of the cerebral organs and of their functions.
– Condillac, as well as Locke, endorses an intellectualist approach—a kind of intellectualist psychology based on the epistemological analysis of the limits of the understanding; this psychology attributes a major role to the faculties of attention, memory, imagination, etc. Yet Gall considers these intellectual faculties as "abstractions". According to the Viennese physician, the *real* faculties must primarily determine behaviours and provide the basis for a differentialist approach, i.e. an approach capable of explaining the differences between individuals (see Young, 1970, 15, 21). In the same way, for Comte, Condillac's theory

is wrong in that it overestimates the importance of the intellect, while overlooking the dominance of the affective faculties.
– Finally, the thesis of transformed sensation gives by definition a determining role to sensations. By contrast, in Gall's doctrine, sense organs are conceived as systems that are anatomically and functionally submitted to the control of the cortical organs and fundamental faculties.

Against this background of opposing views, it is now possible to reconstruct the major questions discussed in Gall's and Comte's reception of Condillac's philosophy.

2.1 Gall

As regards Gall, one should not expect a "philosophical" type of analysis which characterises and criticises Condillac's theses respectfully; he is usually satisfied with a quotation that fails to fully characterise Condillac's position. Thus, Gall's polemical method consists in either summarily characterising the position of an author or providing a quotation from the targeted author that, without being contextualised, is relevant to his polemic. Moreover, to support his theses, Gall not only makes extensive use of long lists of authors but also accumulates those authors' analyses on the topic discussed in this context.

Thus, we find references to Condillac in three such types of lists and related series of analyses: lists that contain what Gall calls "philosophers", that is, all the thinkers who only took into account the abstract faculties (such as sensation, memory and imagination); lists that focus on what might be called the sensualist tradition; and lists relating to the analysis of more restricted themes. These lists correspond to the main points of disagreement just mentioned, and, as such, are more or less general in their scope.

Significantly, the example of the first type of list appears on the first few pages of Gall's second major work, *On the Functions of the Brain* (see Gall, 1835, I, 80). Here Condillac is included in a list of philosophers who claim that all faculties can be reduced to two fundamental ones: understanding and will, which are conceived in rather abstract terms, namely as capacities that either receive ideas or enable the mind to follow its inclinations. Aristotle, Bacon, Descartes, Hobbes, Locke, Bonnet, Condillac, Kant, Tracy and Laromiguière and their major claims are discussed on six pages. The inclusion of Condillac in this list amounts to a radical discrediting of his theory within the psycho-physiological framework of phrenology, for it makes him one of the representatives of the "philosophers" he describes in the most pejorative terms.

The second type of list is restricted to the representatives of the sensualist tradition. Condillac is here often associated with Locke and criticised

Condillac's Puerile Reveries 141

for adopting an uncompromising empiricist attitude: "M Broussais also adopts the axiom *Nihil est in intellectu quod non prius fuerit in sensu*; and adheres to the school of Locke, Condillac etc., etc." (Gall, 1835, II, 78). The same type of criticism is found in Comte, who blames Condillac for not having admitted "the indispensable restriction so well formulated by Leibniz", namely *"nisi intellectus ipse"*. Here again the reproach is redhibitory: this school, and Condillac in particular, ignored that the minds' faculties are dependent on an innately given structure of the brain.

Finally, the passages in which Condillac is mentioned for one of his signature theses are rather rare. The most significant statements can be found in the chapter dealing with touch. Although here Gall does not explicitly attribute to Condillac the authorship of the claim that touch is the most fundamental of all senses, he nevertheless suggests precisely this by referring to Condillac first:

Condillac derives from touch as from every other sense, attention, memory, judgment, imagination. He makes of it the corrector of all the other senses, the source of curiosity, of abstract ideas, and of all desires and passions. But he has invented so romantic a fable in relation to pain and pleasure, which he presents as the only motives of all the actions of man, that I cannot undertake the tedious task of correcting him.

(Gall, 1835, I, 115)

More generally, Gall criticises two claims in this chapter. First, Gall dismisses the claim that touch alone gives us knowledge of the external world by contrasting Locke and Tracy with Condillac (see Gall, 1835, I, 113–114). Second, by means of the human-animal comparison, he rejects the idea that touch is "the corrector of all the other senses"—an idea he relates to "Anaxagoras" (Gall, 1835, I, 119). All these refutations ultimately point in the same direction: for Gall, intellectual perfection depends on the internal structure of the brain but not on sensation.

Once again, Gall's analysis as a whole does not offer a comprehensive account of Condillac's philosophy: it is extremely laconic, and there is no attempt on his part to situate the French philosopher's work historically. Leaving aside those reservations, it is nevertheless undeniable that Condillac's thesis of transformed sensation drew Gall's attention and that he was aware of the need to refute it in order to establish his own theory of the faculties he took to be fundamental to the human mind.

2.2 Auguste Comte

The same cannot be said of Comte's critique, which is perfectly mastered from a philosophical point of view, and indeed carefully situates Condillac in the history of the different psychological schools. These schools, according to Comte, emerged as a result of a division introduced by Descartes. He assigned to metaphysics the study of the intellectual and moral phenomena, and to the physical sciences all other phenomena, whether inorganic or biological. In this context, Comte defines the French school of the eighteenth century by referring to Condillac. It is worth giving the quotation in full:

> The French school, which, in spite of appearances, was certainly the most systematic of all, feeling above all, according to the national genius, the need for clarity, attached itself to the only obvious principle it could see in such a subject, that is to say, to Aristotle's axiom, but without admitting the indispensable restriction so well formulated by Leibniz. Hence all the puerile reveries of Condillac and his successors about transformed sensation, in order to represent the various intellectual acts as ultimately identical; fantastic conceptions, which completely ignored all the primordial dispositions by which, not only the various animal organisms, but the various individuals of our species are so energetically distinguished from one another.
> (Comte, 1830–1842, III, L35, 789; my own translation)

According to Comte, the French school is the most systematic of all mainly because it rigorously obeys the imperative of unity is required by the metaphysical approach; it demands that the unity of the self has to correspond to the theological unity of the soul. The French school pushes this logic to its limits by using a twofold reduction to unity that manifests (1) in the "almost exclusive" study of intelligence and (2) the derivation of all intellectual acts from sensation. In doing so, it invites the criticism articulated by Gall, as it ignores the innate dispositions that determine behaviour, and thus misses the possibility of a differentialist approach.

Comte closes this passage by recalling the main idea of what Gall called his "philosophy of man":

> It is enough to refer to the refutation by which Gall and Spurzheim have introduced their labours and I would particularly point out the philosophical demonstration by which they have exhibited the conclusion that sensation, memory, imagination, and even judgment—all the scholastic faculties, in short—are not in fact fundamental and abstract faculties, but only different degrees or consecutive modes of the same phenomenon proper to each of the true elementary phrenological functions, and necessarily variable in different cases, with a proportionate activity.
> (Comte, 1858, 386–387 / 1830–1842, III, L35, 789–790)

The "philosophy of man" articulates the "fundamental faculties" (roughly the phrenological faculties) with attributes or modes that are relative and subordinate to these fundamental faculties. All "scholastic faculties" count as such modes: perception, recollection, memory, judgment, imagination, attention, etc. Through this re-arrangement, the "philosophy of man" considers as secondary psychological faculties which were the prime subject of Condillac's speculations, and of the French school in general. It thus expresses the irrelevance of Condillac's philosophy of transformed sensation, and justifies the radical change in the models used for the explanation of intellectual and moral phenomena in the early nineteenth century.

3 Animals

Beyond these profound differences, however, it is possible to identify some overlaps between Comte's and Condillac's views, when turning to the comparison between the intellectual and moral capacities of animals and humans. Like Gall, Comte was one of the thinkers who rejected the radical separation of humans and animals instituted by Descartes, which basically equated animals with machines devoid of a soul, a claim Comte describes as "the well-known automatic hypothesis of Descartes" (Comte, 1830–1842, III, L35, 787). From this point of view, Comte's analysis is very close in spirit, although not in detail, to the theory exposed in the *Traité des animaux* (Condillac, 1947–1951, I, 339–379), which was written by Condillac to oppose the Cartesian doctrine then defended by Georges-Louis Leclerc, comte de Buffon (see Condillac, 1947–1951, I, 339–341).

To be precise, in Comte, we find several conceptual tools introduced by Condillac for the analysis of the status of brutes, both in relation to their proximity to and difference from men. However, instead of identifying Condillac as the inventor of these conceptual tools, Comte credits other authors, such as the encyclopaedist Charles-Georges Leroy (1723–1789) and the biologist Henri-Marie Ducrotay de Blainville (1777–1850). In particular, Leroy's *Lettres sur les animaux* (Leroy, 1802), published in 1768, is one of the main sources of Comte—and also Gall—when debating the question of animal intelligence. This circumstance attests to the fact that a large part of the claims advanced during the Enlightenment, including those of Condillac, did not reach Comte directly, but through Leroy.

Two of these conceptual tools are particularly important. The first is the concept of *Ennui*. Comte writes that when "the social state is sufficiently advanced to make men feel a growing need to exercise their highest faculties", men, during a phase of physical inactivity, would experience a "remarkable state of irksome languor" (Comte, 1858, 518 / 1830–1842, IV, L51, 633); this state is called *Ennui*. It leads humans to exercise and strengthen their intellectual and moral faculties. By contrast, once an animal's physical needs have been satisfied, it experiences a state of mental and bodily torpor, a kind of non-productive lethargy. *Ennui* is thus a secondary, but permanent influence which affects and accelerates the speed of social evolution.

Undoubtedly, this analysis, which comes to Comte from Leroy who in turn received it from Helvétius (see Clauzade, 2012; Fedi, 2004), has its origin in Condillac. Indeed, in the *Traité des animaux*, Condillac mentions the same opposition between humans and animals, and he here also uses a psychological vocabulary of needs, desires and passions. Man's soul, he writes, is constantly kept awake by the multiplicity of desires, and "he continues to think and desire even at times when his body no longer demands anything" (Condillac, 1947–1951, I, 373). And he also adds that animals experience some kind of lethargy as soon as a physical good or evil has disappeared: "the activity of their souls is momentary; it ceases with the needs of the body, and is only renewed with them" (Condillac, 1947–1951, I, 373). In Comtean terms, this can be translated as follows: in most animals, their "functions are simply subservient to the demands of organic life" (Comte, 1875, I, 495 / 1851–1854, I, 612).

The second Condillaquian conceptual tool taken up by Comte, this time attributing it to Leroy and Blainville, concerns the difference between instinct and reason. The assertion that animals act only by instinct and in a fixed manner, without taking circumstances into account, is for Comte "a remnant of the automatic hypothesis of Descartes" (Comte, 1858, 386 / 1830–1842, III, L35, 787). However, according to him, Leroy has shown that the fixity of animal acts is purely illusory. Yet when dealing with these questions, Leroy unambiguously refers to Condillac: "As Abbé de Condillac says very well" the so-called fixity is explained by the identity of needs and by the fact that animals do not imitate each other (Leroy, 1802, 109–110; see Condillac, 1947–1951, I, 359). Leroy also mentions the Condillaquian distinction between the habitual self and the reflective self, and the idea that reflection necessarily presides over the birth of habits, which once formed take on the character of instinct in humans and in animals (Leroy, 1802, 223 and 289; see Condillac, 1947–1951, I, 362–363). A phrase that Comte claims to have borrowed from Blainville, but which could equally well be attributed to Condillac, expresses this distinction perfectly well: "instinct is fixed reason; reason is mobile instinct" (Comte, 1830–1842, III, L35, 788).

The above arguments—whether asserting a difference between humans and brutes through *Ennui*, or underlining that humans can act instinctively—assume the existence of a mechanism common to men and animals. Through this mechanism, human superiority can be explained as resulting from more developed faculties, that is, faculties that are superior because they are more developed than those of animals, but not from faculties that are radically different from them. In this respect, Comte's arguments align with the anti-Cartesian position introduced by Condillac, and it is surprising that he does not refer to it favourably.

4   Comte and Condillac on Analysis

The philosophy of science is another area where disagreements between Comte and Condillac show up. Condillac's theory of hypotheses provides Comte with the perfect occasion for a direct criticism of Condillac and his "strange" *Traité des systèmes*: "metaphysicians like Condillac", he argues, tried to handle the difficult question of hypotheses in physics without having established the encyclopaedic and historical basis provided by Comte's positive philosophy. To this explicitly expressed reproach another can be added. The Condillaquian theory of hypotheses is set out in a treatise that condemns philosophical systems (see Paganini's chapter in this volume). But there is no thinker more systematic than Comte, and Comte relies precisely on the system of the sciences—or what he calls the positive encyclopaedia—to settle the question of hypotheses.

It is difficult to enter into this debate in depth, since Comte's remarks about Condillac are very short and lacking in detail. In fact, on the issue of the heuristic role of analysis, the disagreement between Comte and Condillac is strongest and most consequential. One way of understanding Comte's conflicting attitude towards the idea of analysis is to consider the methodological differences dividing the inorganic and organic sciences, where the question of the relationship between simple and compound phenomena is addressed.

When Comte presents the sociological method in lesson 48—he was the first to conceive and build a science of the social, which he called "sociology"—he accepts the rule that "in every kind of study" there is the "obvious obligation to always proceed from the more known to the less [familiar]" (Comte, 1830–1842, IV, L48, 358/see 1858, 462–463). This is admittedly a very general rule, but it undoubtedly bears the stamp of Condillac. However, Comte adjusts this rule, demanding to consider whether the question under consideration deals with inorganic or organic phenomena, the latter category including social phenomena. In "inorganic philosophy" or in the study of the external world, it is appropriate to proceed from simple to compound phenomena, whereas in organic philosophy one proceeds from the compound to the simple. Comte signals that the procedure used in sociology runs counter to the "absolute and indefinite" dogma advocated by modern metaphysicians, which prescribes "to systematically proceed from the simple to the compound" (Comte, 1830–1842, IV, L48, 358/see 1858, 462–463).

One might think that Comte would return to the spirit of Condillac's doctrine by showing that both paths are possible, provided that they respect the obligation to proceed from the more known to the less familiar. Indeed, Condillac allowed for a double strategy of decomposition and composition, even if he treated analysis and the reduction to simple elements as explanatorily more valuable. However, it would be an error to interpret Comte's remark as a return to the Condillaquian rules. In the field of sociology and in the field of biology, the explanatory value lies in the synthesis, that is, in this kind of compound that determines a simple phenomenon, thereby giving it its meaning: in other words, the decomposition of a complex phenomenon or entity, which can be either a society or an organism, is not the method through which truth can be established. This is what Comtean holism consists of: it states that the collective is not only the starting point of analysis but also constitutes the relevant level at which understanding can be achieved.

In general, Comte's philosophy possesses a clear tendency to become increasingly assertive about this primacy of synthesis. For instance, this is what Comte says about biology in one of his last writings:

> In the normal state of Biology, we shall, indeed, examine carefully, as before, the special relations of functions of the organs. But these partial relations will no longer be isolated. Their study will begin and be carried out with a distinctly synthetic purpose; that of forming a clearer conception of the general relation between the Organism and its Environment; for this, and this only, is the ultimate goal at which the Science of Life aims. And not merely does this conception of the Whole mark the limit for investigations of detail, and supply the measure of their value. It should guide the course which they are to take; it should be their point of departure and their final aim. Otherwise, they will remain empirical, or degenerate into useless digression.
> (Comte, 1875, I, 519 [translation slightly modified]
> / 1851–1854, I, 642)

Thus, for Comte, it is necessary to remain committed to synthesis even when artificially decomposing a compound into its elements.

Comte's hostility to analysis and decomposition is not limited to his reflections on the organic sciences. At the end of the *Cours de philosophie positive*, Comte argues that there is "a happy fundamental agreement between sound philosophical contemplation and the spontaneous march of public reason" (Comte, 1830–1842, VI, L58, 705; our translation). It is therefore in all speculative fields that "sound philosophy" must take "the spontaneous wisdom of mankind" as its starting point, and confine itself to "generalising and systematising it, by extending it appropriately to abstract speculations" (Comte, 1858, 800 / 1830–1842, VI, L58, 706–707). Comte thus condemns and limits the analytic method in an extremely drastic way. He critiques "so-called modern psychology", which, according to him, employs a "chimerical and disturbing" mode of elementary analysis:

> The commonest facts are, as I have often said, the most important, in all orders of knowledge; and we have seen that the best instrumentalities of rational positivity are the systematized logical procedures given out by common sense. We see how modern psychology, setting out from the opposite point,—from the dogmatic formation of the first principles of human knowledge, and proceeding to analyse complex phenomena by the method which we now reject in the case of the simplest,—has never yet, with all its toil and perplexity, risen to the level of popular knowledge derived from general experience.
> (Comte, 1858, 800, / 1830–1842, VI, L58, 707–708)

It would be difficult to express any better Comte's refusal to accept analysis as the very methodological paradigm that Condillac significantly helped to establish, or his rejection of the genetic approach that this type of analysis promoted.

5   Mathematics and "The Language of Calculation"

The issue of language and the importance of signs also lie at the core of Comte's now explicit critique of Condillac's conception of the language of calculation. Comte's hostility to analysis was so pronounced at the end of his life that in the *Synthèse subjective*, which is in fact a *Treatise on Mathematical Philosophy*, the word "analysis" was banished from the mathematical vocabulary and replaced by the exclusive use of the term "algebra" (see Comte, 1856, 168–169 and 197–199).

Nevertheless, Comte has not always been so hostile to analysis and Condillac's idea that the progress of mathematics is due to the perfection of language, whether arithmetic or algebraic. In fact, there are two series of essays in the *Écrits de jeunesse* in which he unquestionably endorses the Condillaquian theses. These are "Essays on some points of philosophy of mathematics" (Comte, 1970, 491–505) and "Essays on the philosophy of mathematics" (Comte, 1970, 507–541). These essays were written in the years 1818–1820 in preparation for a treatise on mathematics that never was completed; they contain about 50 pages.

In these essays, Comte presents theories that were in fact inspired by Condillac. One of his general aims is "to accustom the pupils" to the idea that the perfection of algebraic language "accounts for the majority of the greatest discoveries made in mathematics" (Comte, 1970, 504), and that the mathematical transformations of equations used by this language "are nothing other than true transformations of grammar, absolutely analogous to the arrangements of words that one makes in Latin and in other languages" (Comte, 1970, 503). To support these claims, he compares ordinary language with arithmetic and algebraic language. One of the perfectly Condillaquian theses put forward here uses the following principle to explain the superiority of the algebraic over the arithmetical language: "It is easier to engage in general reasonings with general signs than with particular signs" (Comte, 1970, 519).

Yet these themes are not the only Condillaquian elements in Comte's reflections; they also include Condillac's definitional and argumentative framework. Thus, Comte's text discusses Clairaut's mathematical problem to illustrate the differences between languages (see Comte, 1970, 497; Condillac, 1948–1951, II, 458–462) as well as the definition of equations as comparisons that is also present in Condillac's discussion (see Comte, 1970, 509; Condillac, 1948–1951, II, 460). Comte even uses the term "analogy" in a perfectly Condillaquian sense to describe the relationship between signs and the ideas they represent (see Comte, 1970, 519–520; Condillac, 1948–1951, II, 470–471). And even when departing from Condillac, Comte still refers to *The Language of Calculation*, for example when he explains why he will not speak of the language of fingers, the language of stones or the language of names (see Comte, 1970, 496 and 513; Condillac, 1948–1951, II, 421–427, 457–462, and 471); or when he justifies that he will not engage with the fifth language projected by Condillac—the language of the "infinitesimal notation". To justify this decision, he mentions the algebraic reduction of the differential calculus operated by Lagrange in his *Theorie des fonctions analytiques* (see Comte, 1970, 513; Condillac, 1798, 478). Even the style of the Essays, which addresses the reader in a formal way, imitates Condillac's.

All of this shows that these early essays are unquestionably inspired by Condillac. And yet Condillac's influence ceases from 1821 onwards, when Comte's conceptual frame undergoes a radical change: an equation is now defined as a relation of equality between abstract functions; algebra is understood in terms of implicit and explicit functions (the concept of function is not present in Condillac); and the use of general signs is relegated to the background by understanding them in strictly instrumental terms.

As a result of this radical change, in 1830, Comte's "Philosophical Considerations on Mathematical Science" (the third lesson of the *Course*) condemns, without much transition, the Condillaquian approach:

> When we have seized the true general character of Mathematical Analysis, we easily see how perfect it is, in comparison with all other branches of our positive science. The perfection consists in the simplicity of the

ideas contemplated; and not, as Condillac and others have supposed, in the conciseness and generality of the signs used as instruments of reasoning. The signs are of admirable use to work out the ideas, when once obtained; but, in fact, all the great analytical conceptions were formed without any essential aid from the signs. Subjects which are by their nature inferior in simplicity and generality cannot be raised to logical perfection by any artifice of scientific language.

(Comte, 1858, 57 / 1830–1842, I, L3, 147–148)

Comte clearly disagrees with the thesis of *The Language of Calculation* on three points: first, for Comte the perfection of the science of calculation can be achieved due to the simplicity of the ideas considered; second, for him algebraic conceptions are formed without the help of algebraic signs; third, in view of the first two points, Comte also argues that, in general, the Condillaquian project of the perfection of the sciences through the progress of their languages must be abandoned. Throughout his work, Comte will remain faithful to these three points, and the only notable evolution will be an increasing hostility towards algebra.

Without going into further details that would lead us too far, we can say that Comte's growing hostility can mostly be explained by the fact that he saw in algebra a kind of metaphysics that lacked a defined object, developed in an unregulated way and claimed to preside over the encyclopaedia and to regulate all other sciences. This is the reason why he wanted to go back to Descartes and limit the use of the calculus to the field of geometry. Whatever the reasons for his hostility, Comte nevertheless seems to have preserved at least some of the Condillaquian spirit of 1819. It is perhaps because Comte did not completely get rid of the idea that algebra is a kind of grammar and can be studied like a language that he condemned it. If so, he would have condemned it for the sake of defending a type of research whose legitimacy or positivity, as one could also say, he took to be measurable by exerting reason and observing real phenomena, which in this concrete case would be geometric phenomena.

6 Conclusion

In conclusion, it is worth emphasising how important these objections to Condillac were, as they had an impact far beyond Comte's philosophy. Indeed, they informed the entire French positivist tradition. Comte's rejection of sensationalism partly explains why in France the philosophy of science has stayed away from fully embracing the empiricist tradition ranging from Mill's associationism to Mach's project of the analysis of sensations. From the point of view of Comtean orthodoxy, their approaches appear psychological and reductive. In the same way, the hostility towards the conception of language as a calculus and the kind of formalism expressed in the idea of the *Ideologues* according to which languages are "species of algebras" (Destutt de Tracy, 1817, 323) can to a large extent explain the French positivists' lack of interest in logicism and their hostility to the kind of logical positivism that would become popular in the twentieth century. In the context of French philosophy, Comtian positivism is certainly one of the elements that prevented the link between sensation, analysis and language from being renewed on the basis of the advances of logicism—a link that in his time Condillac was so keen to establish.

References

Clauzade, Laurent (2012). "L'ennui dans la philosophie comtienne : un héritage des Lumières?", in P. Goetschel (ed.) *L'ennui, Histoire d'un état d'âme (XIXe-XXe siècle)*. Paris: Publications de la Sorbonne, pp. 43–54.
Comte, Auguste (1830–1842). *Cours de philosophie positive*, 6 vols. Paris: Rouen, Bachelier, [reference to volume, lesson (L) and pages].
Comte, Auguste (1851–1854). *Système de politique positive*, 4 vols. Paris: Carilian-Goeury et V^{or} Dalmont, [reference to volume and pages].
Comte, Auguste (1856). *Synthèse subjective ou Système universel des conceptions propres à l'état normal de l'humanité*. Paris: chez l'auteur.
Comte, Auguste (1858). *The Positive Philosophy of Auguste Comte: Freely Translated and Condensed by Harriet Martineau*. New York: Calvin Blanchard [abbreviated reference to Comte 1858 and pages; if the translation given in the text is by Martineau, this reference appears first].
Comte, Auguste (1875–1877). *System of Positive Polity*, translated by J. H. Bridges, F. Harrison, E. S. Beesly, R. Congreve, and H. Dix-Hutton, 4 vols. London: Longmans and Green. [abbreviated reference to Comte 1875 volume and pages; if the translation given in the text comes from this edition, this reference appears first]
Comte, Auguste (1970). *Ecrits de jeunesse 1816–1828*, edited by Paulo E. Berrêdo de Carneiro and Pierre Arnaud. Paris, La Haye: Mouton/EPHE.
Condillac, Étienne Bonnot de (1798). *La langue des calculs*, in *Œuvres de Condillac*, t.23. Paris: Houel.
Condillac, Étienne Bonnot de (1947–1951). *Œuvres philosophiques*, edited by George Le Roy, 3 vols. Paris: PUF.
Destutt de Tracy, Antoine (1817). *Éléments d'Idéologie. Première partie. Idéologie proprement dite*. Paris: V^c Courcier.
Fedi, Laurent (2004). "Charles-Georges Leroy et la perfectibilité des animaux", in B. Binoche (ed.) *L'homme perfectible*. Seyssel: Champ Vallon, pp. 170–199.
Gall, François Joseph (1835). *On the Functions of the Brain and of Each of Its Parts with Observations on the Possibility of Determining the Instincts Propensities and Talents or the Moral and Intellectual Dispositions of Men and Animals by the Configuration of the Brain and Head*, 6 vols. Boston, MA: Marsh, Capen & Lyon.

Leroy, Charles-Georges (An X – 1802). *Lettres philosophiques sur l'intelligence et la perfectibilité des animaux, avec quelques lettres sur l'homme*. Paris: De Valade.

Young, Robert Maxwell (1990). *Mind, Brain and Adaptation in the Nineteenth Century: Cerebral Localisation and Its Biological Context from Gall to Ferrier*. 2nd ed. Oxford: Clarendon Press.

Part III
Condillac's Influence Beyond France

10 Between Debate and Reception
Formey Reads Condillac

Angela Ferraro

1 Introduction

The "Class of Speculative Philosophy" at the Berlin Academy was both the cradle and the expression of a Franco-German Enlightenment that resulted from several influences.[1] Recent research on the representatives of this movement and on the dynamics of the institution that welcomed them has shown that they were characterized not only by a shared stance vis-à-vis the German (Leibnizian and Wolffian) paradigm but also by different forms of appropriation of British (Lockean and Humean) thought and, of course, of French philosophy.[2] Given this variety and complexity, a single essay will hardly suffice to cover the reception of Condillac at the Berlin Academy in the second half of the eighteenth century in its entirety. It is thus indispensable to circumscribe the objective of the present chapter more clearly. It will focus essentially on the 1750s. This is not a purely opportunistic choice. In fact, the period in which Condillac is most discussed by the members of the Berlin Academy is the one immediately following his election to membership in this institution in 1749 and the publication of his major works.[3] Moreover, it is at just this moment that Condillac, even more so than Locke, embodies the main alternative to Leibniz in psychology, as Jean-Bernard Mérian's 1757 *Parallèle de deux principes de psychologie* (*A parallel exposition of two principles of psychology*, these being sensation for Condillac and representation for Leibniz) emblematically shows.[4]

In this text, Mérian portrays Condillac's thinking via its salient characteristics. He explains what it means to turn sensation into the general principle of our faculties with the help of a striking comparison: just as Descartes said, *give me matter and movement and I will make a world for you*, so Condillac said, *give me the faculty of sensing and I will make a human being for you*.[5] Mérian does not leave it at simply making the comparison, he supports it with the following argument. According to Condillac, "sensations are at the same time the material and the architect," and they "successively become all that we know of our soul": thus, "in a statue that gradually comes to life, we see all the faculties and all the operations of our intellect form from a single, identical principle."[6] The traits of this portrait become more precise thanks to the parallel announced in the title. Which thinkers prefer Condillac to Leibniz? Those who like clarity and shy away from risky speculations, in other words, "the circumspect speculators" and "observant philosophers."[7] What is the specificity of Condillac's theory compared to Leibniz's? It does not extend as far, but it goes deeper.[8] And what privilege does it enjoy over its competitor? It is not that it is any more demonstrable, but rather that it is more natural and more luminous: "the human mind recognizes itself in it, it thinks it is reading, or rather writing its own history: nature here seems to trace itself the path it is taking and the degrees by which it makes us go from insight to insight."[9]

For Mérian, Condillac is above all the author who managed to simplify Locke's philosophy and who, all in all, deserved the same kind of recognition that authors like Voltaire in his *Lettres philosophiques* (1733) and d'Alembert in the "Discours préliminaire" of the *Encyclopédie* (1751) accorded the English philosopher.[10] Mérian's view is thus situated within the perspective opened up by the programmatic publications of the French Enlightenment. One possibility—to be explored in future research—is to continue in that direction and detect further borrowings from Condillac in the writings of Mérian[11] or other authors who, like him, were well disposed toward the empiricist epistemological model, such as Maupertuis.[12] However, to focus my study even more, the question I would like to ask here is whether there is a member of the Berlin Academy who took up Condillac just as much but in a more nuanced way than Mérian. The author who allows us to answer this question in the affirmative is Jean Henri Samuel Formey. Formey—a protestant pastor, prolific author, and Maupertuis's successor (in 1748) as secretary of the Berlin Academy—is known especially for a work popularizing the thought of Christian Wolff, *La Belle Wolfienne* (1741–1753).[13] Despite a pronounced preference for the Leibnizian-Wolffian paradigm, he was also interested in other models of thought for reasons that have to do both with his intellectual curiosity and his cultural politics, that is, with his attempt to influence the debate in the republic of letters in his sense.

In this context, the first thing that comes to mind is his effort to contain the reception of Hume's work: assuming a very critical stance, he wrote reviews of the German translation in 1756 and 1758, and also the preface and notes for the French translation he had initiated.[14] Considering Condillac's empiricism less dangerous than Hume's "pyrrhonism," Formey approaches the former with more ambivalence than he does the latter. His attitude toward Condillac is highly complex and gives rise not only to disagreements and misunderstandings but also to expressions of mutual

Between Debate and Reception   157

respect and traces of productive exchange, for there is a correspondence between the two thinkers (its lacunary nature, at least in the presently available editions, notwithstanding). In addition to drawing on their letters, I examine the reviews Formey wrote of Condillac's major works for two of his journals (the *Bibliothèque impartiale* and the *Journal épistolaire*); I also take into account the papers he sold to the Encyclopédistes in 1747, after abandoning his own project of an encyclopedic dictionary,[15] and of course some of his *mémoires* for the Berlin Academy. I will proceed in three thematic steps, addressing, first, Formey's reception of the *Traité des systèmes*, then that of the *Essai sur l'origine des connaissances humaines* and the *Traité des sensations*, and finally that of the *Traité des animaux*. In keeping with the exploratory nature of this chapter, which is far from and does not aim to be exhaustive, I will conclude with a preliminary assessment.

2   Critique of the Critique of Systems

Among the works of Condillac reviewed by Formey, the *Traité des systèmes* certainly receives the most unfavorable treatment. From the very beginning, the tone of the account in the first issue of the *Bibliothèque impartiale* (1750) is very polemical.[16] The *Traité des systèmes* is presented as the work of a man of wit rather than of a philosopher, characterized by the neatness and order of its ideas, by the refinement and taste of its reflections, and by much stylistic elegance—traits that are capable to ensure the success of any book, including chimeric ones written by authors like Malebranche.[17] The first theoretical defect of Condillac's critique of systems that stands out to the reviewer is its excessive radicalness: Condillac is said to insist exclusively on the disadvantages of systems,[18] to present a caricature of the intentions of the systematic philosophers,[19] and to wrongly draw general conclusions from defects that only affect particular systems. Above all, he seems to be under the illusion that he could make do without abstract principles. In fact, even the systems he claims to advocate for—those founded on well-established facts—only become systems when the fact from which the other facts must draw their explanation is reduced to an abstract notion, which transforms it into a principle.[20] Therefore, Formey concludes, "whatever way the author turns, he'll never explain anything without a system, and he'll never build a system without abstractions."[21] This is a point on which he again insists, albeit less violently, when he writes his review of the *Traité des animaux* (1755),[22] where he does not let the fact that the second part of the book is entitled *Système des facultés des animaux* go uncommented.[23] In addition to being a surprise, given Condillac's aversion toward systems, such a title, for Formey, proves the impossibility of avoiding systems in presenting solid and sustained knowledge.[24]

158 *Angela Ferraro*

To come back to the review of the *Traité des systèmes*, Formey here also remarks that the cases Condillac chooses to study to support his thesis and accomplish his task were not the right examples: "All of what the author pleases to call system so that it can be said that he destroyed the systems is no more a system than the shabby inns of the Hero of La Mancha were castles."[25] Up to this point, according to Formey, the only philosopher to set out to develop a true system has been Wolff, an author Condillac neglects when he limits himself to two or three rather insignificant and, above all, ill-informed references.[26] But the greatest omission, according to Formey, is forgetting to address the case of geometry (insofar as it employs mathematics). Most interestingly, in the same review, Formey hints at the reasons (or, more simply, the bad faith) that prompted Condillac to omit any significant reference to the excesses of geometry:

> Why does the author not touch on geometry? It's the oldest of the systems and, in the eyes of many people, the only one. Was it not a magnificent field for him, to study its disadvantages and its advantages? But the author was afraid to get nothing out of it and to find it too hard a nut for him to crack.[27]

A criticism of the abstractions of geometry would necessarily challenge the positive paradigm Condillac presents and promotes, which is the Newtonian model.[28] That is why Formey says that the author of the *Traité des systèmes* would have broken a tooth on the hard nut of geometry and its (mis)use of mathematical abstractions.

In an earlier work, the *Recherches sur les éléments de la matière* (*Inquiry concerning the elements of matter*, 1747), Formey had already denounced this kind of misuse by defending instead a metaphysical approach to the essence of matter in keeping with the Leibnizian paradigm.[29] The most specific explanation for his polemic against Condillac's criticism of systems can undoubtedly be found in the opposition between Leibnizians and Newtonians within the Berlin Academy.[30] Yet there is another reason, less specific but no less crucial, which has to do with Formey's aversion to skepticism. While the road on which Condillac took his readers may be "strewn with flowers," it in fact opened up the "abyss of universal doubt." According to Condillac, the only path that would lead to truth is, by his own admission, impracticable because well-established facts, on which the only systems worthy of the name should rest, are few and far between. To my knowledge, there is no direct reply by Condillac to this attack. He was, however, the censor of a book published in 1753 by Louis de Beausobre (the *Dissertations philosophiques*) that echoes Formey's defense of abstract principles and thus renews the opposition to "the ingenious author of the *Traité des systèmes*" by claiming the right to contradict without violating the truth. In his response, Condillac adopts a rather sporting attitude:

> The author does me the honor of combating what I have said on abstract principles. I would perhaps be suspected of affectation if I praised him, and of injustice if I criticized him; I have found nothing in his work that could prevent its being printed.[31]

3   Virtues and Limits of the Analytic Path

Formey's approach to Condillac's theory of knowledge is more nuanced. We can identify at least two facets of his attitude toward it: the first is rather charitable, the other expresses reservation.

1   Let's begin with Formey's appreciation of individual aspects of Condillac's study of the operations of the mind, taking as our first proof the article "Erreur" from the fifth volume of the *Encyclopédie* (1755), which is based on Formey's papers:

> The mind resembles a man with a weak disposition who only relieves one sickness by falling into another; in place of abandoning its errors, it often only changes them. In order to deliver a man of weak constitution from his sicknesses, it would be necessary to give him a totally new disposition: to correct our mind of all these weaknesses, it would be necessary to give him new views, and without being mired in the details of his sicknesses, even to go back to their source and dry it up. We find this source in our habit of reasoning about things of which we have no idea, or for which we have only poorly determined ideas... What accustoms our mind to this inexactitude is the manner by which we learn to speak. We only reach the age of reason some time after having contracted the use of speech. If one excludes words destined to make our needs known, it is usually chance that occasions us to understand certain sounds rather than others and that has determined the ideas we have attached to them. By recalling our errors to the origin that I have just indicated, we enclose them in a single cause.[32]

This passage very much testifies to an authentic interest in Condillac's analysis of error in that it considers it to be exemplary and worthy of inclusion in an encyclopedic dictionary. In fact, Formey, as in a collage, faithfully takes up several passages from the *Essai sur l'origine des connaissances humaines* (1746): the nice comparison between error and disease, the explanation of the origin of error (from a lack of ideas or from badly defined ideas), and the identification of language as its ultimate cause.[33]

Formey also saw a source of inspiration in Condillac's psychology, no doubt intending to strike up a dialog. What draws his attention in the review of the *Traité des sensations*, published in the *Journal épistolaire* in 1755,[34] are two things: Condillac's definition of the self (as a collection of the sensations that the statue feels and that memory reminds it of) and his criticism of Pascal's conception.[35] From Formey's point of view, both (the definition and the criticism) have the merit of clearing the path for further reflections on the crucial question of identity and the distinction between the physical and moral self.[36] Condillac himself was well aware of the interlocutory impulse of the text, as his letter of August 2, 1755, published in Formey's *Souvenirs d'un citoyen* (*Recollections of a Citizen*, 1789), shows. On that occasion, he thanks Formey for his complementary remarks and congratulates him on his quality journalism:

> Your reflections on the *self* are very correct, very subtle, and very well developed. I would very much hope that journalists would do as you do, adding new light to the matters they discuss. The only thing missing from your praise for me, sir, are the critical observations you have made on a work whose defects cannot have escaped you.[37]

We do not, unfortunately, know whether the addressee seized on Condillac's invitation immediately in a response letter.

2 We do know, however, and this brings us to the second facet, that Formey did in fact have reservations concerning the *Traité des sensations*, which he expressed in a *mémoire* entitled *Principaux moyens employés pour découvrir l'origine du langage, des idées et des connaissances des hommes* (*The main means used to discover the origin of the language, ideas, and knowledge of human beings*, 1759).[38] Here, he questions the use of the fiction of the statue both in Condillac's and Charles Bonnet's works:[39]

> Man is not a statue and never finds himself in the situation of the statue represented in these works. He opens, simultaneously, eyes, ears, nostrils; he tastes, he touches at the same time; these impressions blend and intersect from the outset; they yield results that differ completely from those obtained from the state of an organized being that would begin with scenting and acquire use of the senses only one after the other. After that, accepting the supposition, it is quite gratuitous, I think, to have pleasure, desire, attention, memory arise in the soul immediately after the first kind of sensation, after some reiterated acts of the sense of smell. A soul housed in a body like ours,

Between Debate and Reception   161

if it only smelled a rose, a carnation, and only passed through the alternatives of these smells being substituted for one another, would be quite far, I believe, from exercising faculties properly so called; it would never go beyond the state of simple perception; its representations would be quite inferior to those of the snail or of the oyster; I would compare them at most to the end of a dream that is about to vanish and to be absorbed in a state of deep sleep.[40]

The author admits such "speculations" only to the extent that they can serve as a simple training for the mind. Any enthusiasm prompted by supposedly having made, thanks to them, real discoveries on "the natural and primitive state of the soul" must, by contrast, be rejected.[41]

We must suppose that Formey communicated his critical observations to Condillac even before he wrote this account. In fact, in his letter of September 20, 1755, once more collected in the *Souvenirs d'un citoyen*, Condillac defends himself, explaining again the development of the intellectual operations out of a single sense:

You have trouble believing that the development of a single sense could lead to intellectual operations. It seems to me, though, that the statue limited to the sense of smell is capable of attention; it has memory, it compares, it judges; it has all this with a single sense as it does with all five together. Adding the other senses to that of smell, we're not giving the statue its faculties, we are only giving its faculty a wider application. I think that, since the five senses make us capable of intellectual operations, each of them contributes to this and that, as a consequence, these operations would take place even if we were limited to the sense of smell; but you think that the concourse of the four senses, and above all of hearing, are necessary for this; I admit I do not see why.[42]

In a note to this letter, Formey returns to and affirms his reading: "Right now, I still see in all of this only a *petitio principii*. A human statue limited to the sense of smell does not seem to me to be superior to an oyster."[43]

As the rest of the account cited above shows, Formey does not agree that the analytic path taken with the supposition of the statue suffices to resolve all the questions that can be asked about the soul. Why? Because, against the manifest intention of those who have used the fiction of the statue, this path risks favoring materialism and mechanism. Moreover, it tells us nothing about the nature of the soul and its real distinction from the body.[44] Formey's disappointment with Condillac's method, though, was already manifest in his review of the *Traité des sensations* published in the *Bibliothèque impartiale* (1755).[45] There, he declares that the point of view from which Condillac's text appears truly novel relates to his claim that everything follows from sensation, because this claim affords a glimpse of the simplicity of the ways in which the author of nature acts. So the novelty does not in fact lie in the results of his analysis. Although Condillac may have break new ground in this domain and was original enough to go all the way, while his predecessors left it at merely announcing similar projects,[46] Formey argues that no analytic effort can reveal what the human being is and what substances are.[47] Closer to Wolff than to Locke, Formey tended to consider the problems of psychology to complement ontological, even theological principles. For this reason, he believed that the main source of our knowledge of the soul cannot derive from the inner and immediate perception of our faculties.

4 The Analogy between Human and Nonhuman Animals

Such perplexity about Condillac's achievements reappears in the first part of Formey's review of the *Traité des animaux*, published in the *Bibliothèque impartiale* in 1755.[48] There, he declares that the subject seems to him to have been exhausted, since any question that has already been discussed by better minds and on which no new experiments can be conducted cannot, by meditation alone, provide a satisfying or convincing opening: to realize it, it is enough to think about the fate of other issues like the relation between freedom and necessity, the union of body and soul, or the simplicity of the elements of matter. The same goes for the internal operations of animals: all the metaphysical speculations on this topic lead only to very hypothetical assertions because the object itself can never become any better known. Moreover, Formey would have preferred that Condillac's treatise be entitled *Of the soul of beasts* rather than *of animals* in general because, for him, this work is only concerned with the operations that make it possible to explain the impressions that objects make on beasts and the actions that follow from these impressions.[49] In his letter of February 25, 1756 (also published in the *Bibliothèque impartiale*),[50] Condillac responds to these remarks point by point. He notes that even if the subject he addresses is well-worn, it is not for all exhausted. Even if it were impossible to conduct new experiments, it remains possible to say new things on questions already discussed by better minds, since these minds, too, could have been victims of prejudice, which is "like a barrier that stops [even] the most vigorous athlete."[51] In fact, it seems that the same prejudice has always stumped observers: no one seems to have managed to untangle the operations of the soul in the use each animal makes of its senses; it was generally thought that they all, humans included, use them automatically.

Between Debate and Reception 163

The prejudice of assuming an automatism thus prevented the discovery of the true principle explicating the faculties of animals. It is therefore still possible to discuss the question in a satisfying and convincing way via the path of meditation.[52]

In this context, it is also interesting to see that Condillac provides further details on his use of analogy, by attributing to it demonstrative power much more explicitly than he did in the *Traité des animaux*:[53]

> I hope that you will not conclude that there were no discoveries left to be made by me, and that you will not regard my assertions as purely hypothetical. Analogy is their principle, and it proves them. For, sir, what reason do you have for believing you are not the only thinking being on earth? Why do you grant me the faculty of thinking? Is it because I resemble you in shape? No, undoubtedly. Is it because I speak, I write, and because you notice some coherence in my speech? What? If I didn't speak, if I didn't write, would you take me to be an automaton? Do the actions I share with beasts not outline for you in energetic characters the results of my thoughts? For me it would seem to be a contradiction to doubt the mental faculties of beasts and to positively assert that thinking is taking place in the individuals whose shape resembles our own. The assertions *all beasts think, all human being think* are both equally doubtful or proven.[54]

Moreover, Condillac goes on to say, although the facts have been the same since eternity, there can be new facts for us, namely those we have not noticed yet: it is possible that we have not yet observed everything there is to be observed in animals. This is proven by the way in which Cheselden's experiment served Condillac as a foundation of his treatises on sensation and on animals. As for the title, *Traité des animaux*, the author finds it perfectly suitable, especially given that the discussion in the second part of the book is on animals in general (even if the first part is more about the soul of beasts).[55]

This remark by Condillac on an inclusive definition of animality (a remark that once more pushes the limit the author had set for himself in his *Traité* with respect to defining the nature of animals)[56] is particularly interesting in that it seems to justify the fears Formey voices in the second part of his review of the *Traité des animaux*, published in the *Bibliothèque impartiale* in 1756. More than once, he intimates that Condillac establishes too much proximity between beasts and human beings.[57] Here are the main points of his argument: (A) Attributing to beasts the capacity for invention is suspicious and would authorize embarrassing conclusions. If beavers (to take an example of Condillac)[58] were able to depict their dwelling in their imagination before they started to build it, they would combine a host of ideas, which would go beyond what beavers are capable of. Moreover, assuming the presence of an inventive imagination in beasts would seem to conflict with the uniformity of their works. Thus, by wanting to prove too much, one would finally end up proving nothing.[59] (B) To explain instinct by habit and attribute it to reflection, as Condillac does, amounts to putting beasts above humans because their work always shows perfect regularity due to their instincts and for this reason considerably surpasses human attempts to produce similar works.[60] (C) Using the concepts of understanding and will to describe the faculties of beasts seems inappropriate: it spreads confusion and runs counter to the received notions of the philosophers who have gone furthest in examining these matters. Understanding and will, in fact, presuppose freedom and spirituality, whereas beasts never attain these higher-order faculties.[61]

5 Conclusion

This overview of a set of texts that at first sight seem heterogenous allows us to draw a number of conclusions. While one might initially be tempted to classify these sources as purely ancillary, it could be shown that there are several guiding threads as well as points of major interest. Formey's very attentive and original reading of Condillac delves into some crucial questions raised by the latter's works, questions that lie, more generally, at the heart of central debates in French-speaking circles at the beginning of the second half of the eighteenth century: the status of systems, the ambitions of psychology, and the definition of animals in relation to humans. Moreover, it could be shown that Formey's praise and criticism prompted an overall positive reaction from Condillac himself, pushing him to elaborate on some delicate points and elliptic passages in his works to which he would undoubtedly not have returned otherwise. Indeed, such elaboration seems to have required the kind of direct and immediate exchange we have looked at in this chapter. We may, moreover, suppose that Formey's early remarks, especially in connection with his journalistic work, not only contributed significantly to publicizing Condillac's thinking but also played a role in framing the debate, both with regard to the choice of subjects discussed and in the polarization of opinions.

What type of reception, then, takes shape in this corpus of texts that either contain references to Condillac or are even entirely devoted to examining his works? In Formey's case, I think, we are dealing with a reception biased by his Leibnizian (as we saw in relation to his critique of Condillac's critique of systems) and Wolffian orientation (his reservations about choosing the analytic path in the theory of knowledge) as well as by his apologetic concerns (notably concerning the proximity between human

Between Debate and Reception 165

and nonhuman animals). But the most interesting aspect, no doubt, is that Formey's reception has a dimension of interaction and debate that affected the author who was "received," as the more detailed discussion of certain theoretical points in Condillac's letters has shown. It is, finally, a reception that for Formey himself went beyond the occasional polemic. As a further piece of symbolic proof, it would suffice to recall that in the philosophy section of his *Conseils pour former une bibliothèque peu nombreuse mais choisie* (*Advice for assembling a small but select library*, 1756), the secretary of the Berlin Academy presents Condillac as a "distinguished writer" in metaphysics (alongside only Malebranche, Locke, Leibniz, and Hutcheson) and includes the *Traité des systèmes*, the *Essai sur l'origine des connaissances humaines*, and the *Traité des sensations* in his ideal catalog of philosophical works.[62]

Notes

1 The *Académie royale des sciences et des belles-lettres*, as it was called following the 1744 reform under Frederick II of Prussia, comprised four classes: experimental philosophy, mathematics, speculative philosophy, and belles-lettres. The presence of a class of speculative philosophy is worth pointing out, for the Berlin Academy was the only major academy to cover subjects in metaphysics, logic, ethics, and aesthetics; see Duchesneau et al., 2022.
2 On this subject, I'll only mention two collections: the special issue *La philosophie à l'Académie de Berlin au XVIIIe siècle* (Dumouchel and Leduc, 2015) and *The Berlin Academy in the reign of Frederick the Great: Philosophy and science* (Prunea-Bretonnet and Anstey, 2022).
3 The date of Condillac's election to the Academy is attested in two letters to Maupertuis from December 1749; see É. Bonnot de Condillac, *Œuvres philosophiques*, éd. par G. Le Roy, 3 vol., Paris, Presses Universitaires de France, 1947–1951), vol. II, p. 533. As for his works, the *Essai sur l'origine des connaissances humaines* (*Essay on the origin of human knowledge*) was published in 1746, the *Traité des systèmes* (*Treatise on systems*) in 1749, the *Traité des sensations* (*Treatise on sensations*) in 1754, and the *Traité des animaux* (*Treatise on animals*) in 1755. Condillac also participated, anonymously, in the 1746–1747 prize contest of the Berlin Academy with a text on monads; see Condillac, 1980 and Leduc, 2018.
4 Mérian, 1759; for the statement of the principles, see p. 376. For a biobibliographical profile of Mérian, a member of the Berlin Academy since 1750, see the entry on him in *The Bloomsbury Dictionary of Eighteenth-Century German Philosophers* (Klemme and Kuehn, 2016, pp. 529–531).
5 Mérian, 1759, p. 382. See R. Descartes, *The World*, Chapter 6: "For a while, then, allow your thought to wander beyond this world to view another, wholly new, world, which I call forth in imaginary spaces before it ... and let us suppose that the matter which God has created extends indefinitely far beyond in all directions... Let us ... conceive of it as a real, perfectly solid body, which uniformly fills the entire length, breadth, and depth of this great space in the midst of which we have brought our mind to rest... Let us add further that this matter may be divided into as many parts and shapes as we can imagine,

and that each of its parts can take on as many motions as we can conceive" (Descartes, 1998, pp. 21–23). See also É. Bonnot de Condillac, *Extrait raisonné du Traité des sensations*: "The main objective of this work is to show how all our knowledge and all our faculties come from the senses or, more exactly, from sensation . . . The entire system of the human is thus born from sensations: a complete system all of whose parts are linked and mutually support each other" (Condillac, 1947–1951, vol. I, pp. 323 and 325).
6 Mérian, 1759, p. 377. The paradigm, or thought experiment, of the statue plays a key role in the *Traité des sensations*, as Condillac explains in the "Plan" of the book: "we imagined a statue internally organized like ourselves, and animated by a mind deprived of every kind of idea. We further supposed that its marble exterior did not allow it the use of any of its senses, and we reserved for ourselves the freedom to open them at will to the different impressions they are susceptible of" (Condillac, 2014, 306).
7 Mérian, 1759, pp. 378–379.
8 Mérian, 1759, p. 381.
9 Mérian, 1759, p. 379.
10 See Voltaire, 1733, p. 98: "Such a Multitude of Reasoners having written the Romance of the Soul, a Sage at last arose, who gave, with an Air of the greatest Modesty, the History of it. Mr. Locke has display'd the human Soul, in the same Manner as an excellent Anatomist explains the Springs of the human Body." See also d'Alembert, 2009: "he [Locke] reduced metaphysics to what it really ought to be: the experimental physics of the soul—a very different kind of physics from that of bodies, not only in its object, but in its way of viewing that object. In the latter study we can, and often do, discover unknown phenomena. In the former, facts as ancient as the world exist equally in all men; so much the worse for whoever believes he is seeing something new."
11 For further details on this point, see Dumouchel, 2022.
12 This makes all the more sense in the case of Maupertuis, whose view of Leibniz's concept of the monad is quite indebted to what Condillac wrote on the subject (if not the text for the Academy prize, at least Chapter 8 of the *Traité des systèmes*). See Duchesneau, 2013, pp. 170–190.
13 For biographical details on Formey, see the entry on him in Klemme and Kuehn, 2016, pp. 225–227.
14 For further information on the reception of Hume in the Berlin Academy, see Laursen and Popkin, 1997, pp. 153–162.
15 On Formey's project of a philosophical dictionary and on the way the material he had collected was used in Diderot and d'Alembert's *Encyclopédie*, see Marcu, 1953.
16 Formey, 1750.
17 Formey, 1750, p. 19. This passage echoes the eighteenth-century cliché that Malebranche's philosophy is the result of an unhinged imagination.
18 Formey, 1750, p. 20.
19 Formey, 1750, p. 27.
20 Let's recall that Condillac takes on the great systems of the seventeenth century but at the same time holds on to a kind of systematicity. A system, according to him, is the disposition of the different parts of a science in an order in which they mutually support each other and in which the last is explained by the first. Those parts that account for the others are called principles. Condillac distinguishes between three types of principles corresponding to three types of systems: (1) abstract notions, which are necessary to organize our thoughts

(to classify ideas) but are not made to lead to particular knowledge; they correspond to abstract systems. (2) Suppositions we invent to explain things we cannot account for otherwise; they correspond to hypotheses. (3) Well-established facts, gathered from experience, which are the only principles of the sciences; they correspond to the true systems, those that deserve the name. See Condillac, 1947–1951, vol. I, pp. 121–124; 2014, pp. 1–5.
21 Formey, 1750, p. 21. We may add that in the text cited earlier, Mérian gives voice to a different opinion concerning the *Traité des systèmes*. His judgment sounds like a defense of the work, undoubtedly articulated in response to Formey's criticism: "No one had a better sense of the disadvantages of systems, as anyone will be convinced who reads his [Condillac's] excellent work on the matter. I'll thus take care not to reproach him, as others have done, for making a mistake he so well and so victoriously fought against, nor to believe that he hid systematic views under the modest appearance of simple observation" (Mérian, 1759, p. 389).
22 See Formey, 1756a. This review, to which I'll return in a moment, has two parts.
23 See Condillac, 1947–1951, vol. I.
24 See Formey, 1756a, p. 21.
25 Formey, 1750, p. 22.
26 Formey, 1750, pp. 24–26.
27 "Mais l'auteur craignait de n'y pas trouver son compte, et de briser ses dents contre la dureté de cette lime"; Formey, 1750, p. 30.
28 Just think of the example of a well-establish fact Condillac gives in defining true systems, namely the gravitation of bodies: there, he is certainly thinking of Newton. See Condillac, 1947–1951, vol. I, p. 122; 2014, p. 3.
29 Formey, 1747, pp. 20–30.
30 Formey's review is rooted in the context of the struggle waged between two philosophical and scientific factions at the Berlin Academy until the spirit of eclecticism begins to spread. In 1763, Nicolas de Béguelin, member of the Academy, could affirm that "the common fault of systems is that they show everything from a single point of view" and "that the best minds, without adopting the whole systems of the greatest men on the various branches of philosophy, take what to them seems solidly established in the most opposed sects" (Béguelin, 1771, pp. 345–346). But before then, that is to say in the 1740s and 1750s, Leibnizians and Wolffians on one side and Newtonians on the other clashed repeatedly, as a number of studies have shown, including Calinger, 1969.
31 Condillac, 1753.
32 Formey, 2013.
33 Condillac, *Essai sur l'origine des connaissances humaines*, pt. II, sect. II, ch. I, in Condillac, 1947–1951, vol. I, pp. 104–106; 2001, pp. 120–122.
34 Formey, 1755b.
35 Condillac, 1947–1951, pt. I, ch. VI, §3, pp. 239 and 239n1; 2014, pp. 200–201 and 201n17. Condillac here follows in the wake of Locke by defining the self of the statue as simultaneously consciousness of what it is and memory of what it has been. By way of contrast, he cites, in the note, Pascal's conception of the self that, in excluding everything superfluous, seems to him to be too demanding: "In Pascal's meaning, God alone can say 'I.'" To better contextualize this reference, see Carraud, 2010, pp. 70–84.
36 Formey, 1755b, p. 72.

168 *Angela Ferraro*

37 See Formey, 1789, vol. II, p. 291.
38 Formey, 1766.
39 The Swiss philosopher, too, uses the paradigm, or thought experiment, of the statue in his *Essai analytique sur les facultés de l'âme* (*Analytic essay on the faculties of the soul*, 1760). It is of interest to note that Formey, in a way, prefers his version: "The Rev. Abbé de Condillac was ahead of Mr. Bonnet, at least in publishing his work; but Mr. Bonnet was far ahead of the Rev. Abbé de Condillac; his procedure is so much more analytical; his definitions are more exact; and above all, the way one mental state leads to another, the way one faculty reduces to an act, [and] serves to excite the exercise of another, is defined with a precision that has no precedent" (Formey, 1766, p. 368).
40 Formey, 1766, p. 369.
41 Let's recall that Condillac took pains to defend the value and usefulness of his suppositions in the *Traité des sensations*: "While this system rests on suppositions, all the consequences drawn from them are attested by our experience" (Condillac, 1947–1951, vol. I, p. 325).
42 See Formey, 1789, vol. II, pp. 293–294.
43 Formey, 1789, vol. II, pp. 294n.
44 Formey, 1766, p. 369.
45 Formey, 1755a.
46 Formey, 1755a, p. 350.
47 Formey, 1755a, p. 343.
48 See Formey, 1755c.
49 Formey, Formey, 1755c, pp. 330–331.
50 See Condillac, 1756.
51 Condillac to Formey, February 25, 1756, in Condillac, 1947–1951, p. 539.
52 Condillac to Formey, February 25, 1756, in Condillac, 1947–1951, p. 540.
53 In a note, Condillac reproached Buffon for having asserted the inability of the analogy to prove that the faculty of thinking is common to all animals when "the opposite has evidently been proven" (Condillac, *Traité des animaux*, pt. II, ch. II, in Condillac 1947–1951, vol. I, p. 358n1).
54 Condillac to Formey, February 25, 1756, in Condillac, 1947–1951, p. 540.
55 Condillac to Formey, February 25, 1756, in Condillac, 1947–1951, p. 540.
56 See Condillac, *Traité des animaux*, preface: "In the second [part], I outline a system that I refrained from calling *Of the nature of animals*. I admit all my ignorance in this regard and content myself with observing the faculties of man according to what I sense and judging those of animals by analogy" (Condillac, 1947–1951, vol. I, p. 339). For further details about Condillac's conception of the human animal, see Waldow's chapter in this volume.
57 Formey, evidently, was not the only reader of the *Traité des animaux* to be worried by this, as, for instance, Joseph Adrien Lelarge de Lignac's polemical *Suite des lettres à un Américain* (*Continuation of the Letters to an American*, 1756) shows.
58 See Condillac, *Traité des animaux*, pt. II, ch. II, in Condillac, 1947–1951 vol. I, p. 358: "Beasts thus invent, if *invent* means the same thing as judging, comparing, discovering. They even invent if by that we understand picturing in advance what we will do. The beaver depicts the hut he wants to build; the bird, the nest he wants to construct. These animals would not build these works if the imagination did not provide them with their models."
59 Formey, 1756a, p. 23.
60 Formey, 1756a, p. 28.

61 Formey, 1756a, p. 35.
62 Formey, 1756b, p. 23.

References

Béguelin, N. (1771) "Conciliation des idées de Newton et de Leibniz sur l'espace et le vuide," in *Histoire de l'Académie royale des sciences et des belles-lettres, 1769*, Berlin: Chez Aude et Spener, pp. 344–360.
Calinger, R.S. (1969) "The Newtonian-Wolffian controversy (1740–1759)," *Journal of the History of Ideas* 30(3), pp. 319–330.
Carraud, V. (2010) *L'invention du moi*. Paris: Presses Universitaires de France, pp. 70–84.
Condillac, É. Bonnot de. (1753) "Approbation" in L. de Beausobre, *Dissertations philosophiques*.
Condillac, É. Bonnot de (1756) "Article X [Excerpt from a letter by Condillac to Formey]," *Bibliothèque impartiale* (mars-avril 1756), XIII-2, pp. 269–273.
Condillac, É. Bonnot de. (1947–1951) *Œuvres philosophiques*, Ed. G. Le Roy, 3 vols. Paris: Presses universitaires de France.
Condillac, É. Bonnot de. (1980) *Les monades*. Ed. L. L. Bongie. Oxford: The Voltaire Foundation.
Condillac, É. Bonnot de. (2001) *Essay on the origin of human knowledge*. Ed. and trans. Hans Aarsleff. Cambridge: Cambridge UP.
Condillac, É. Bonnot de. (2014) *The philosophical writings of Étienne Bonnot de Condillac*. Vol. 1. Trans. Franklin Philip and Harlan Lane. New York: Psychology Press.
d'Alembert, J. Le Rond. (2009) "Preliminary discourse." Trans. Richard N. Schwab and Walter E. Rex, in *The encyclopedia of Diderot & d'Alembert collaborative translation project*. Ann Arbor: Michigan Publishing, University of Michigan Library. http://hdl.handle.net/2027/spo.did2222.0001.083 (accessed September 11, 2022).
Descartes, R. (1998) *The world and other writings*. Trans. and Ed. Stephen Gaukroger. Cambridge: Cambridge University Press.
Duchesneau, F. (2013) "Critique et usage du concept de monade par Maupertuis," *Studia Leibnitiana* 45(2), pp. 170–190.
Duchesneau, F., D. Dumouchel, A. Ferraro, and C. Leduc (2022) "Introduction," in *Philosophie spéculative à l'Académie de Berlin: Mémoires 1745–1769*, Ed. F. Duchesneau, D. Dumouchel, A. Ferraro, and C. Leduc. Paris: Vrin, pp. 9–55.
Dumouchel, D. (2022) *Jean Bernard Mérian. Métaphysique et empirisme à l'Académie de Berlin*, in *Modernité et académies scientifiques européennes*. Ed. P. Girard, C. Leduc and M. Rioux-Beaulne. Paris: Classiques Garnier, pp. 101–126.
Dumouchel, D., and C. Leduc (eds.) (2015) « La philosophie à l'Académie de Berlin au XVIIIe siècle, » *Philosophiques* 42(1), PP. 7–130.
Formey, J.H.S. (1747) *Recherches sur les éléments de la matière*.
Formey, J.H.S. (1750) "Article II [Review of the *Traité des systèmes*]," *Bibliothèque impartiale*, janvier-février 1750, pp. 19–33.

Formey, J.H.S. (1755a) "Article III [Review of the *Traité des sensations*]," *Bibliothèque impartiale*, mai-juin 1755, XI-3, pp. 342–359.
Formey, J.H.S. (1755b) "Lettre V [Review of the *Traité des sensations*]," *Journal épistolaire* 1, part 1 (Berlin: Bordeaux, 1755), pp. 65–80.
Formey, J.H.S. (1755c) "Article II [Review of the *Traité des animaux*, part I]," *Bibliothèque impartiale*, novembre-décembre 1755, XII-3, pp. 329–346.
Formey, J.H.S. (1756a) "Article II [Review of the *Traité des animaux*, part II]," *Bibliothèque impartiale*, janvier-février 1756, XIII-1, pp. 21–36.
Formey, J.H.S. (1756b) *Conseils pour former une bibliothèque peu nombreuse mais choisie*. New corr. and exp. ed. Berlin: Haude and Spener.
Formey, J.H.S. (1766) "Réunion des principaux moyens employés pour découvrir l'origine du langage, des idées et des connaissances des hommes," *Histoire de l'Académie royale des sciences et des belles-lettres, année 1759*, Berlin: Chez Aude et Spener, pp. 367–377.
Formey, J.H.S. (1789) *Souvenirs d'un citoyen*. 2 vols. Berlin: La Garde.
Formey, J.H.S. (2013) "Error," trans. Gregory Bringman, in *The Encyclopedia of Diderot & d'Alembert Collaborative Translation Project*. Ann Arbor: Michigan Publishing, University of Michigan Library. http://hdl.handle.net/2027/spo.did2222.0002.683 (accessed September 11, 2022).
Klemme, H.F., and M. Kuehn (eds.) (2016) *The Bloomsbury dictionary of eighteenth-century German philosophers*. London: Bloomsbury.
Laursen, J.C., and R.H. Popkin (1997) "Hume in the Prussian Academy: Jean Bernard Mérian's *On the Phenomenalism of David Hume*," *Hume Studies*, 23(1), pp. 153–191.
Leduc, C. (2018) "Condillac et la critique d'un système: Le cas leibnizien," *Dialogue*, 57(4), pp. 767–789.
Marcu, E. (1953) "Un encyclopédiste oublié: Formey," *Revue d'Histoire littéraire de la France*, 53(3), pp. 296–305.
Mérian, J.-B. (1759) "Parallèle de deux principes de psychologie," *Histoire de l'Académie royale des sciences et des belles-lettres, année 1757*, Berlin, Chez Aude et Spener, pp. 375–391.
Prunea-Bretonnet, T., and P.R. Anstey (ed.) (2022) *The Berlin Academy in the reign of Frederick the Great: Philosophy and science, Oxford University Studies in the Enlightenment*, Oxford and Liverpool, Voltaire Foundation in association with Liverpool University Press, p. 11.
Voltaire (1733) *Letters concerning the English nation*. London: Davis.

11 Rethinking the Human Animal with Condillac and Herder

Anik Waldow

1 Introduction

Condillac agreed with Descartes that the capacity to use reason and language renders us uniquely human. In his famous language argument in the *Discourse on the Method*, Descartes states:

> Men born deaf and dumb, and thus deprived of speech-organs as much as the beasts or even more so, normally invent their own signs to make themselves understood by those who, being regularly in their company, have the time to learn their language. This shows not only that the beasts have less reason than men, but that they have no reason at all. For it patently requires very little reason to be able to speak.
> (AT VI 58, CSM I 140)[1]

Different from Descartes, however, Condillac did not think that reason is given simply because we have a soul—a claim which establishes that by nature there is a difference between soulless animals who lack reason and ensouled humans who have it;[2] nor did Condillac believe that we can have reasoned thoughts able to give us sophisticated knowledge regardless of whether we have language.[3] For Condillac the capacities to reason and use language depend on each other and require for their emergence a complex range of experiences that may or may not be present in one's life. Given that these experiences are contingent, Condillac foregrounds the possibility that we can fail to actualize ourselves as humans.[4] This happens when we fail to acquire mental capacities that non-human animals lack.

Condillac's position was long considered radical for the challenge it posed to the principal superiority of human beings *qua* natural endowment;[5] for, instead of focusing on innately given features (be they mental or physical), his account stressed the importance of experience for the acquisition of specifically human capacities.[6] He thus provoked speculations about the possibility that animals could potentially develop into creatures

DOI: 10.4324/9781003334750-14

with human-like abilities—provided they had the right kind of experiences. But also encouraged numerous attempts to reinforce the species border.[7]

This chapter looks at one such attempt by analyzing Johann Gottfried Herder's engagement with Condillac's proposal to conceive of humans in continuity with non-human animals. When speaking of Condillac's continuity thesis, I refer to two interrelated claims: (1) that human cognition is a more developed form of animal cognition and (2) that there is a temporal dimension that explains how human cognition could emerge out of a basic form of animal cognition. On the face of it, Herder rejected this thesis.[8] According to the account developed in his *Treatise on the Origin of Language* (1772), only humans can acquire language and reason because only humans are endowed with the right kind of reflective awareness (*Besonnenheit*) that, once affected by sensory experience, sets off a process through which language and reason emerge (*Philosophical Writings*, 128–131).[9] *Qua* natural reflective endowment, it is thus settled right from the start that even the most basic human capacities are different in kind from those animals possess.

In what follows, I will show that contrary to first appearance, Herder did not oppose Condillac's continuity thesis, but in fact transformed and enriched it. He did so by distinguishing between two kinds of developments: those that enabled the emergence of the human species and those that allow the individual members of this species to develop reason during their lifetime. Through this move, he was able to do two things at once: (1) align humans with the rest of nature, insofar as humans are taken to be just like other animals in that they develop species-specific features (i.e. having reason) by coping with environmental conditions dominating their lives,[10] and (2) uphold the claim that human cognition is unique, given that the process through which reason emerges ensures that it is an infinitely adjustable tool that is far more potent in its scope and complexity than animal instinct can ever be.

As we will see, Condillac himself already took important steps toward this naturalistic conception of human reason in his account of reflection. In his *Traité des animaux (1755, TdA* hereafter),[11] he argued that reflection is best characterized as a problem-solving capacity that responds to an animal's desires and needs. Against this backdrop, human reflection is then analyzed as a particularly complex variant of animal reflection.[12] What Herder added to this account is that he anchored the ability to engage in a reflective use of reason to the situational context in which humans find themselves. These contexts are historically shaped and culturally diverse, and as such can explain why human reason takes on different forms in different historical and cultural circumstances.

I will first outline central features of Condillac's continuity thesis by discussing the relevance of his claim that human development depends on contingent factors. In a second step, I will contrast Condillac's account with Herder's theory of the origin of human language. Herder here highlights that it is necessary for humans to acquire language and reason because of a specific kind of awareness that is naturally given to them. He thus conceived of the difference between humans and animals in terms of an innately given form of awareness that only humans possess, but animals lack. I show that, despite this attempt to fix the species border, Herder's engagement with Condillac endorses and even enriches his continuity thesis. He did so by distinguishing processes leading to the emergences of the human species from those that enable humans to cultivate a specific form of situated reason during their lifetime.

2   Condillac on Feral Children and Animal Cognition

Condillac took a great interest in the case of the Lithuanian boy—a child who was found in the forest in the second half of the seventeenth century. For him, this case empirically proved that uniquely human capacities are not innately given, but need to be developed through complex experiences.

Reflecting on the linguistic and cognitive limitations of the Lithuanian boy in the *Essay on the Origin of Human Knowledge* (1746), Condillac writes: "A child raised among bears" cannot be deprived "of the cries that are natural to each passion" (*Essay*, 1.4.2.25, 89). Yet Condillac notes that something fundamental is missing from the boys understanding:

> But how would [the child] suspect that [his cries] are suited to become signs of the sentiments he feels? If he lived among other people he would so often hear them utter cries similar to his own that sooner or later he would connect these cries with the sentiments they are intended to express.
>
> (*Essay*, 1.4.2.25, 89)

The question Condillac asks here concerns the ability to match the perception of a cry with the emotional state causing this cry. And he suggests that this matching requires two types of resemblance: (1) resemblance between the cries of oneself and those of others and (2) resemblance between the feelings that oneself and others experience when crying in a similar fashion.[13] The underlying idea thus seems to be that communication partners have to be sufficiently similar in order to render their expressions mutually comprehensible. If this condition is not met—as when members of different species interact with one another—their cries cannot be understood, lack meaning, and cannot function as signs:

> The bears cannot offer [the child] the same occasions; their roar does not have sufficient analogy with the human voice. In their own intercourse,

the animals probably connect their cries with the perceptions of which they are signs, but this is what this child did not know how to do.
(*Essay*, 1.4.2.25, 89)

In his discussion of the origin of human language, Condillac repeats the claim that the acquisition of language requires at least two members of the human species to interact with one another. He describes the situation of two children who meet for the first time and start expressing themselves by making sounds and gesturing toward desired objects (*Essay*, 2.1.1.2, 114). As part of this interaction, the children learn that sounds possess a signficatory function: they represent something that is not currently present, but that can be brought to mind when the sound in question allows the mind to form an idea of the thing signified. By becoming aware of this function, signs can be used for the organization of one's own and other people's thoughts and feelings—for instance when using a particular sound to trigger in oneself or others the association of certain ideas, or when articulating a cry to cause feelings of fear (*Essay*, 2.1.1.3, 115).

The first signs that Condillac's children discover are natural signs, which signify insofar as they make use of a pre-existing causal relation between the sign and the thing signified, as in the case of pain and the cries that express it. This is not the case for artificially established signs; they count as invented and arbitrary. Condillac states that inventing such signs becomes possible only after natural signs have been used for a while: "The natural cries served as a model for [the children] to make a new language" (*Essay*, 2.1.1.6, 116; also see 2.2.2.13 and 1.4.2.25).

Condillac is not entirely clear how exactly humans transition from the use of natural signs to the use of artificially established linguistic signs. He mentions that habit and practice play a role (*Essay* 2.11.6), and also notes that using signs in the attempt to recall past events trains the mind's reflective abilities: "[The children's] memory began to have some exercise; they gained command of their imagination, and little by little succeeded in doing by reflection what they had formerly done by instinct" (*Essay*, 2.1.1.3, 115).[14] Reflection, in turn, counts as a capacity that enables the mind to control its thoughts at will (*Essay*, 1.2.5.51, 42), and thus becomes crucial when learning to use signs intentionally for the purpose of communication.

To clarify how these different capacities interact to enable the emergence of language becomes particularly pressing when turning to Condillac's conception of reflection. For he frequently claims that reflection requires the use of linguistic signs (*Essay* 1.2.5.49, 41 & 1.4.2.27).[15] But if this were true, the early stages of the process through which the capacity for language arises could not involve reflection, even though this is exactly what Condillac says when interlinking the use of natural signs with the use of memory and reflection in his account of the two children (Essay, 2.1.1.3,

115; cf. Schwartz, 2019, 27–29). To make sense of this tension, it seems best to assume that for Condillac the capacity for reflection (and the way it interacts with memory) gradually takes shape when the mind becomes capable of taking control of its thoughts.[16]

Despite these difficulties, commentators generally agree that for Condillac having language requires that signs are created and used at will, which more or less means that it requires the establishment of artificial signs.[17] Before this stage, only some kind of proto-language— to which Condillac often refers as an innate language of action—is present.[18] This language, as he puts it in his *Logic* (1780), articulates itself spontaneously and without responding to the control of the will: "It is the natural and immediate effect of our make-up. It says all the time everything we feel" (*Logic*, 390). Animals, as Condillac's discussion of the Lithuanian boy has shown, are taken to possess a rudimentary understanding of natural signs when grasping the meaning of the cries of the members of their own species. They are thus taken to possess a rudimentary proto-language that is also in use during the early stages of human development, but which is then replaced by a "proper" language that comes into existence through the invention and use of linguistic signs.

That animals share important capacities with humans during the early stages of human development is also articulated in Condillac's *TdA*. He here argues that animals and humans are both capable of reflection and rely on it in the pursuit of pleasure and the avoidance of pain. However, the reflective capacities of non-human animals remain more basic. The reason for this is that animals have a more basic needs-desire structure that, on the top of being basic, also remains rather stable (*TdA*, 489–490). Through this stability, it is less urgent for animals to use reflection; for if reflection was once used to satisfy a specific need and this need then remained stable, the relevant course of action could simply be repeated, without using reflection again: "It is reflection that instruct us; and it will regulate our faculties, *until we have acquired a habit*" (*TdA*, 488, emphasis added). It is therefore due to the stability of an animal's needs that its actions count as habits governed by instinct:

> The time soon arrives when [animals] have done all that reflection has been able to teach them. All that remains is to repeat the same things every day: in the end, they must therefore have habits alone, they must be limited to instinct.
>
> (*TdA*, 489–490)

According to Condillac, the situation of humans is similar but more complex. Humans have more senses than other animals. And this means that their sensory experience is more varied, which in turn leads to a greater variety of desires and needs (*TdA*, 488 & 491). Moreover, human needs and desires keep changing, so more opportunities for the use of reflection arise, as no habit can be formed that could replace the reflective process used to devise a course of action suitable to satisfy them. A result of the frequent practice of reflection is that the capacity refines itself and becomes more varied and better adjusted to solving complex problems (*TdA*, 489–490).

Much more would need to be said about Condillac's account of reflection and its relation to instinct, but for reasons of space I will not be able to do so here.[19] Yet the preceding discussion has shown already that for Condillac animal and human reflection varies in complexity, but not in kind. For in both cases reflection is used to satisfy needs and desires created through species-specific bodily constitutions, which are determined through the number and quality of a species' sense organs. And it is only because Condillac thinks that humans have more sense organs that give way to more varied and changeable needs and desires that they have more opportunities to practice reflection. As a result, human reflection reaches a sophistication that animal reflection lacks.

Indeed, Condillac is clear that once linguistic signs have been invented, reflection turns into an operation with different features: endowed with language, humans can use signs to analyze and categorize their ideas so that they can understand them fully, which in turn enables them to develop a new type of knowledge, one that is theoretical rather than only practical (*TdS*, 252 & 307; *TdA*, 491).[20] Despite this, Condillac is clear that humans use reflection *before* they have linguistic signs (*TdS*, 251, TdS, 246; also see *TdS*, 259), and this means that they use a form of reflection that differs from animal reflection only by degree but not in kind.

If it is the case, however, that for Condillac animals and humans share important reflective capacities—and even a rudimentary understanding of natural signs—why is it, then, that only humans develop language while animals do not? Differently put, why, according to Condillac, do encounters with the members of one's own species only prompt humans to invent and use linguistic signs, while non-human animals do not respond in the same way? Finding an answer to this question leads us back to the relatively simple needs-desire structure of animals. In the *TdA*, Condillac repeats that animals have a proto-language of their own but also points out that they cannot use signs to communicate through spoken words (*parole*, *TdA*, 486). This proto-language allows the members of the same animal species to communicate shared needs and secure mutual advantage. In general, it holds that the more benefits the communication of such needs provides, the more advanced a species' language becomes (*TdA*, 484). Yet, as we have seen, for Condillac it is relatively easy to satisfy an animal's needs-desire structure. This suggests that Condillac's animals do not feel the need to engage in more elaborate forms of communication for which more than their rudimentary understanding of natural signs would be required.

Of course, if animals had a more complex needs-desire structure, the situation would be different. François Dagognet has therefore argued that it is the robustness of the animal's constitution that removes the pressure to develop a proper animal language (1987, 127, 129).

Without further discussing the potential of animals to develop a more sophisticated language here, we can say that, overall, Condillac is keen to stress important continuities between animal and human cognition. For him, animals and humans share key mental capacities during the early stages of human development. These include the capacity to understand natural signs as well as the capacity to reflect. But humans develop *further* than animals: for humans, comprehending natural signs is only a first step in a process that culminates in the institution and use of linguistic signs, through which the acquisition of theoretical knowledge becomes possible. The reason why humans develop further than animals is that their species-specific needs and desires push them toward a more varied use of reflection and, together with it, toward the invention of linguistic signs that accompanies the fortification of their more basic reflective powers. Yet, as the example of the Lithuanian boy has shown, for Condillac, even humans can fail to reach this more advanced developmental stage. This is the case when they fail to transition from the use of natural to the use of artificial signs and, as a result, never learn to engage in complex forms of reflection, analysis, and reasoning. When this happens, they fail to acquire the very capacities that are unique to their species, so one can say that they fail to actualize themselves as humans. That this possibility exists shows that for Condillac humans have to master for themselves, and as part of their individual development, a crucial transition: the transition from an animal-like cognitive state to a state that is unique to the human species. As we will see in the next section, it is precisely on this point that Herder disagrees.

3 Herder's Use of Condillac's Continuity Thesis

While Condillac's account stresses the contingent nature of human development, Herder foregrounds the necessity with which humans acquire linguistic capacities: "The human being as a human being can and must invent language" (*Philosophical Writings*, 96). As we have seen, the reason why for Condillac the acquisition of language can fail is that it requires social intercourse with others. Under normal circumstances it can of course be expected that the capacity for language will form, given that humans are born into society and thus have the right kind of experiences. But, for Condillac, the case of the Lithuanian boy shows that this need not be the case.

Herder relaxes the demand that specifies which kinds of experiences are needed to enable the process through which language emerges. For him, *any* kind of experience will activate the mind's naturally given capacity to name, classify, and distinguish its various sensations (*Philosophical Writings*, 128).[21] That some humans, such as the Lithuanian boy, lack language of course requires an explanation. But Herder could argue that in this particular case circumstances arose that compromised what must be thought of as an originally intact human nature that was once perfectly capable of developing language. That human nature has this feature is a consequence of having what Herder calls *Besonnenheit*; that is, a unique form of awareness that enables humans to reflectively relate to what passes in their minds:

> The human being demonstrates reflection when, out of the whole hovering dream of images which proceed before his senses, he can collect himself into a moment of alertness, freely dwell on a single image, pay it clear, more leisurely heed, and *separate off characteristic marks for the fact that this is that object and no other.*
> (Philosophical Writings, 87; emphasis mine)

While Condillac and Herder both claim that language is needed in order to develop higher-order rational capacities, there is a crucial aspect in which Herder's account differs. He argues that right from the start of their lives humans, and only humans, are reflectively aware of their sensations. Being endowed with this awareness then makes it possible to develop language, reason, and fullyfledged reflective capacities that enable humans to engage in the analysis of more complex theoretical and practical issues.[22] By contrast, for Condillac, animals and humans find themselves in the same position when they begin their cognitive development through the practice of basic perceptual capacities. A special type of awareness is not needed to start this process, and therefore it cannot be singled out as the condition which determines who is able to acquire language and other more sophisticated cognitive tools unique to the human species.

It has often been argued that Herder corrected a fundamental flaw in Condillac's argument.[23] Rousseau, for instance, pointed out that, on Condillac's account, it is not clear how humans can develop language.[24] His worry was that this development presupposes that humans already have what is said to emerge through the acquisition of language: the ability to reflect and reason. According to Charles Taylor, Herder successfully addressed this worry by treating reflective awareness as an innate endowment of the human mind (Taylor, 1999, 228). Through this move, Herder made it clear that "human reason and language" are "an integral part of our life form" (Taylor 1995, 91). Concretely, this means that reason "cannot be seen as forming a separate faculty, which is *simply added on to our animal nature*" (Taylor 1995, 91, emphasis added); instead, reason must be regarded as permeating and shaping every single aspect of human cognition.

Rethinking the Human Animal with Condillac and Herder 179

As a result, at no point in human development can humans be said to share with non-human animals their basic perceptual and sensory capacities.

Commentators like Martin Pécharman have pointed out that there are many options available to Condillac to respond to Rousseau's objection. He could, for instance, argue that the ability to use reason forms gradually as a result of having experiences that become more and more complex the more the mind advances in its development.[25] This, as we have seen above, is an interpretation that indeed makes sense considering the account of memory and reflection presented in the *Essay*. Moreover, Condillac agreed with Herder that with the use of linguistic signs human cognition acquires a structure that is fundamentally different from that which organizes animal cognition, so that he, too, believed that once language has emerged no sharing of perceptual capacities can take place. Despite this, it is correct to say that before this point has been reached, Condillac allows for such sharing. Herder rejects precisely this, as his concept of *Besonnenheit* rules out that animals and humans could ever participate in the same kind of cognition—not even during the earliest stages of human development.

To explicate this fundamental difference, Herder turns to the example of the ape—an animal he takes to be closest to the human being because of its relative lack of instincts. To compensate for this lack, the ape develops a range of sophisticated skills—skills that clearly show that its "power of thinking" is "close to the brink of reason" (*Ideas*, 117).[26] Yet despite all sophistication, the ape remains on "the meagre brink of imitation" (ibid.): although able to "process a thousand combinations of ideas of sense" (ibid.), the animal cannot give its ideas an order that was not already given in experience. The reason for this is that the ape lacks *Besonnenheit*: the kind of reflective awareness needed to start the process of naming through which humans learn to give their thoughts a linguistic structure. With this structure in place, humans learn to align their ideas in accordance with the principles of reason instead of simply associating them in the order of previously experienced events (*Philosophical Writings*, 130–131).

I will use the remainder of this section to argue that Herder did not so much deny Condillac's continuity thesis—as the example of the ape might suggest—but rather used it to develop a new perspective. This perspective embeds the human being in a system of nature marked by gradual change and development, but it does so *without* also suggesting, as Condillac did, that humans and animals progress in their development along a similar path. More specifically, Herder argued that long-term changes in the material conditions of life engendered changes in the cognitive make-up of the human species. Changes in nature thereby reconfigured the starting point from which each individual member of the human species henceforth embarked in their attempt to use reason for the mastery of their lives.

Herder's fascination with the concepts of gradation and change is particularly prominent in his *Ideas for a Philosophy of the History of Humanity* (1784-91). He here examines large-scale developments in the realm of nature to explain how the world as we know it has come into existence. He argues that vegetative processes in plants can be better understood if we assume that they have a drive for growth and generation (*Ideas*, 101),[27] and he takes it that the irritability and interdependencies of the functions of the animal body require us to stipulate that there are forces that work underneath nature's observable surface (*Ideas*, 100–101). For him, these forces do not abruptly overturn what exists, but alter and change prevalent structures through a change in the forces' direction and organization, thus establishing important continuities between higher and lower forms of life (*Ideas*, 82, 104, 407). To account for this aspect of nature, Herder speaks of a ladder of generation (*Stufenleiter*, *Ideas*, 168) that ascends from simple to complex organization (*Ideas*, 407).

Within this larger play of nature, Herder conceives of humans as having acquired their species-specific characteristics when the forces of nature changed once again, which enabled our ancestors to adopt an upright position (*Ideas*, 115). As a result of this change in posture, our ancestors' brains started to evolve: the upright position "gave the crown a beautiful position and direction" (*Ideas*, 130), providing the space for the growth of extra brain tissue so that the capacity for "refined thought formation" (*Ideas*, 131) could emerge. This account in principle describes how *Besonnenheit* could come into existence, the very feature that belongs to every member, and only the members, of the human species, and that rendered the emergence of reason possible. *Besonnenheit* formed when nature's forces pushed the members of our ancestor species (who were not yet humans) to assume an upright position and, as a result of this change, developed a uniquely complex brain structure.

Note that by drawing this large-scale picture of how nature evolved over time, Herder introduces a new perspective, which enables him to differentiate between two important points: (1) the evolutionary processes that made it possible for our species to acquire a unique cognitive structure and (2) the kind of development individual members of the human species undergo during their lifetime *as humans*. When turning to the large-scale evolutionary picture (1), he asks what changes in nature had to occur to make it possible for humans to distinguish themselves from other non-human species. The relevant change was that our ancestors stood up and acquired a special form of reflective awareness (*Besonnenheit*) that enabled the acquisition of language and reason. When thinking about (2), Herder takes it for granted that humans have *Besonnenheit* and concentrates on understanding better what happens when this unique feature of human cognition meets with differently situated environments that encompass natural as well as historically shaped circumstances. I will elaborate on this last point in the next section. What comes into focus here are the differences (and commonalities) *among humans*, rather than the differences (and commonalities) *between humans* and *animals*.

Distinguishing between two types of development (species-specific evolutionary developments, on the one hand, and individual human developments, on the other) has the advantage that it enabled Herder to accept Condillac's continuity theses, *while* recognizing the special status of humans *qua* natural endowment. This is possible because all Herder has to grant is that our ancestors, rather than humans themselves, once shared with animals important cognitive capacities and even engaged in similar developmental steps when practicing and refining these capacities. But this sharing ended once and for all when our ancestors stood up. For this event substantially altered the physiology of their brains and triggered the formation of a new specifically *human* cognitive structure. This cognitive structure remained in place, even after this event occurred, and, through this, enabled experiences that were substantially different from those our ancestors had had before this leap occurred.

4 Re-Locating the Human Animal

By introducing a perspective that recognizes the fact that the members of the human species start their cognitive development from a point different from that of any other species, Herder was able to shift his attention to a new question: the question of how to explain the many different variations that characterize expressions of reason across different times and places. Such variations, Herder argues, can be observed when paying close attention to locally situated and historically conditioned "manner[s] of thought" (*Philosophical Writings*, 247).[28] That such manners of thought exist in principle already follows from the fact that for Herder reason and language develop in unison; for if languages vary according to the time and place where they are spoken, the kind of reason that forms through the use of language must also vary. Herder expresses the tight connection between language and reason as follows:

> A people has no idea for which it has no word: the liveliest experience (Anschauung) remains an obscure feeling, until the soul finds a characteristic mark for it, and by means of a word incorporates it into the memory, the recollection, the understanding, indeed, finally into the understanding of mankind, into tradition: a pure reason, without language, on Earth, is a utopian land.
>
> (*Ideas*, 347)

Rejecting the idea that reason could be "pure" in the sense that it operates independently of the conditions through which it came into existence, Herder defines human reason as "an aggregate of observations and practices of the soul; a sum of the education of our species" (*Ideas*, 337).

Now, it is precisely through this historically shaped conception of reason that Herder was able to re-embed the human being in the macroscopic play of nature, as some further reflections on the relationship between instinct and reason will reveal. In the *Treatise*, Herder claims that one distinguishing feature of humans is that they are marked by a relative lack of instincts as well as a relative lack of highly specialized organs (*Philosophical Writings*, 127–128). Without these features, humans find themselves in a precarious situation: they are deprived of important tools that enable other animals to secure their survival; humans therefore count as *Mängelwesen* who can survive only if they acquire language and reason.

Although this argument straightforwardly acknowledges that human reason takes the place of animal instinct, Herder clarifies that reason is special. It enables humans to live anywhere on the planet by allowing them to adjust to the fact that their senses are underdetermined:

> The human being has no ... uniform and narrow sphere where only a single sort of work awaits him. ... His senses and organization are not sharpened for a single thing; he has senses for everything and hence naturally for each particular thing weaker and duller senses.
> (Philosophical Writings, 79)

Herder also repeatedly asserts that humans and animals differ in kind, not in degree: "The human species does not stand above the animal in *levels* of more or less, but in *kind*" (*Philosophical Writings*, 81). All this suggests that Herder was principally opposed to the idea that humans should be regarded as some kind of highly developed animal.

In the previous section, I have already pointed out that Herder has no problem acknowledging Condillac's continuity theses if the right kind of conceptual distinction is drawn: the distinction between developments enabling the emergence of the human species and developments forming part of the process through which individual humans acquire reason during their lifetime. A further overlap with Condillac comes into sight if we consider the function Herder assigns to human reason. Similar to Condillac, Herder thinks of reason as a problem-solving tool. It responds to the demands of a situated existence and thus enables humans to successfully manage challenges resulting from the fact that their lives unfold at a certain juncture in time and place. By making this point, Herder in principle places humans on a par with animals, who also strive to survive by adjusting to the demands of their environmental conditions. Yet in the case of animals, nature has given them instincts and highly specialized organs that enable them to manage their lives successfully, while in the case of humans, it is humans themselves who have to develop the tools fit for this task: they have to acquire reason to substitute for their relative lack of instincts and specialized organs (*Philosophical Writings*, 127–128).

When compared with instinct, reason is not only special because it must be formed by humans themselves and is not simply given by nature; it also stands out through its infinite adaptability. For Herder both points are related, as a closer look at some of his reflections in *This too a Philosophy of History for the Formation of Humanity* (1774) illustrates. When Egyptians started to cultivate their land, Herder here writes, they benefitted from the existence of the Nile (*Philosophical Writings*, 282). Yet because of the river's regular flooding, it became necessary for them to engage in sophisticated processes of measurement, reasoning, and calculation to anticipate the effects of the river's behavior. This in turn paved the way for the construction of dams, canals, and complex city structures. This example shows that it is through specific environmental conditions that humans learn to develop practices of reasoning that are specifically adapted to dealing with challenges that are particular to their sphere of life. Reason thus turns into an instrument that serves us well in an infinite variety of circumstances.

When turning to the description of ancient Greece, Herder makes the same point. He first diagnoses a relative lack of commercial skill among the Greeks, before explaining this lack through the conditions specific to their historical and geographic situation: "Egyptian *industry* and *civil administration* could not help them, because they had no Egypt and no Nile; *Phoenician* cleverness in trade could not help them because they had no *Lebanon* and no *India* behind them" (*Philosophical Writings*, 288). This example once again shows that, for Herder, it is the place and time defining the situation of differently situated peoples that matter to the way in which their reason forms and articulates itself. This is so because the natural and social conditions specific to their time and place jointly shape the emergence of reason. They thus determine how reason can express itself, given that it develops and fortifies itself when humans try to cope with the demands arising from their situation.

More generally, we can thus say that it is through the specific way in which Herder's concept of reason emerges and acquires its specific shape and form that it functions as an infinitely adjustable cognitive tool that is far more potent than animal instinct. It allows humans to live in highly variable conditions rather than in a limited biological niche that constitutes the habitat of an organism with highly specialized organs and instincts. This is possible because reason responds to the conditions it has to deal with, and it continues to do so when circumstances change. The fact that reason has this plasticity explains why humans can live anywhere on the planet and are not, like instinct-driven animals, confined to a rather limited climate zone. Despite this difference, human reason can still be identified as performing a function similar to animal instinct: it makes it possible for humans to survive in the conditions in which they find themselves by enabling them to deal with the challenges specific to their time and place.

Interestingly, it is not only in his later works that Herder understood reason through its adaptive function; he had already done so as early as in the *Treatise*. Herder here speaks of reason as a special "sense of the human soul," while conceiving of language as a "natural organ of the understanding" (*Philosophical Writings*, 97). This choice of words brings into focus the situation of the animal, which has specialized organs that allow it to successfully deal with the features of its environment. Humans use reason and language to achieve the same ends, only that the organ in question (reason) is infinitely more variable and, as such, is far more potent than an animal's naturally given instincts and bodily constitution can ever be.

Herder's commitment to this conception of reason shows that for him it was clear from very early on that humans are best comprehended if seen in relation to their sphere of life, just as much as non-human animals must be understood in relation to the environmental features that explain why they have highly adapted organs and instincts. This is an important parallel. It demonstrates that, despite all disagreement with Condillac, Herder continued to conceive of humans in analogy with animals insofar as for him both remain firmly integrated in the larger play of nature and the constraints arising from it. By so doing, he transformed Condillac's continuity thesis to encompass a naturalized conception of reason which presents it as an adaptable quasi-instinct, able to secure human survival in a multiplicity of conditions.

5 Conclusion

Different from Condillac, Herder was interested in distinguishing developments that made possible the emergence of the human species from developments that occurred after this had happened. While he took the former to be important for clarifying how humans could become cognitive creatures of a different kind, he concentrated on the latter to bring into focus the diversity and changeability of human reason. It is the combination of these two perspectives that transformed and enriched Condillac's developmental account of reason and related continuity thesis. It on the one hand confirmed Condillac's claim that reason must be developed and is not simply given, but on the other hand helpfully clarified that human individuals need not re-enact cognitive developmental steps that marked large-scale evolutionary processes. With this distinction in place, Herder was able to focus on an oft-overlooked aspect of human reason: its ability to form in

Rethinking the Human Animal with Condillac and Herder 185

communication with locally given environmental conditions. By highlighting this aspect, Herder not only challenged the traditional view that reason operates according to universal principles and independently of a given time and place; he was also able to re-align the human being with the rest of living nature. For what plants, animals, and humans have in common is that they need to develop features, strategies, and tools that enable them to thrive in environments specific to their existence; only in the human case these tools are more flexible.

Notes

1 "AT" refers to René Descartes (1964–1976), O*Euvres de Descartes*, 12 vols. (revised edition), edited by Charles Adam and Paul Tannery, followed by volume number and page number. "CSM" refers to René Descartes (1984–1991), *The Philosophical Writings of Descartes*, followed by volume and page number.
2 See for instance his claim that from earliest infancy we are capable of engaging in processes of reasoning (AT 7:438, CSM II 295). However, in the same context he also points out that we need to learn to use reason well (see Waldow 2017 and Chapter 1 in Waldow 2020). So, in Descartes, too, there is a developmental aspect that requires experience and training, even though he claims that there is a difference in nature between animals and humans. Thanks to Delphine Antoine-Mahut for having raised this point.
3 For Descartes, having thoughts is an essential attribute of the soul (AT VIIIA 25; CSM I 210–211). This means that not having language does not deprive humans of the ability to think. See Marin Chottin's chapter for further discussion of Condillac's reflections on the status of sign language for the purpose of forming and expressing thought.
4 See DeSouza 2012, and Pécharman forthcoming.
5 See for instance Ferraro's chapter in this volume where she discusses Formey's objection to the proximity that Condillac established between animals and humans.
6 While I do not deny that Condillac accepted that innate qualities are required for the development of language and reason, to my mind a focus on Condillac's innatism risks concealing the true nature of his methodological commitments. What Condillac wants to explain is why humans are cognitively special and, in order to do so, he adopts a temporally extended perspective that investigates how contingent circumstances impact on human life and, precisely through this, foster species-specific developments. See Waldow 2021 where I defend this claim in more detail. See Dunham 2019 for the claim that Condillac conceived of the mind as having an innate active power, also see Bertrand 2016 and Schwartz 1999.
7 See Aarsleff 1982, Forster 2018, Sloan 1976 and Zammito 2017.
8 See for instance Taylor 2016, Chapters 1 and 3.
9 I mainly rely on Forster's translation in *Philosophical Writings* (2002). For passages taken from works not contained in this volume I use my own.
10 Cf. Zuckert's conception of Herder's adaptive naturalism (2014, 2019).
11 I use my own translation for passages taken from the 1987 Vrin edition of the *Traité des animaux*. For the *Essay on the Origin of Human Knowledge* (1746) I use Aarsleff's translation in Condillac 2001, for the *Traité des Sensations*

186 *Anik Waldow*

(1754) and the *Logique* (1780) I use the Philip/Lane translation in Condillac 1982.
12 For more details see Waldow 2021.
13 Condillac thereby suggests that we understand others through an implicit argument from analogy; cf. Bertrand 2002, 140–142.
14 See Bertrand 2002, 2016, and Pécharman 2019.
15 In the *Logic* (1780, 2.2), Condillac suggests that first we only have sensations and then learn to organize them into ideas through the use of linguistic signs (Auroux 1992, Bertrand 2002, Kaitaro 2020, Schwartz 1999). But in the *Essay*, he at least sometimes seems to assume that humans have ideas even before they can use linguistic signs (Essay, 2.1.1.3, 115; see also Charrak 2003, 77). See Bertrand 2016, for a discussion of the changes through which Condillac's theory of the language of action went after the completion of the *Essay*. For passages that suggest that for Condillac reflection is required to organize sensations into ideas see *Essay* 1.4.2.18 & 25.
16 Also see Charrak 2003, 78–79, and Pécharman 1999, especially 99–103, for this progressivist reading.
17 See for instance Aarsleff 1982, 109, Bertrand 2002, 120–122, and Pécharman 1999, 97–98; also see Schwartz 1999, 45–46, for a discussion of Condillac's correspondence with Cramer in which he stresses that it is only through the use of artificial signs that freedom of thought can be established.
18 Bertrand therefore stresses: "La communication émotionnelle des bêtes n'est pas même qualifiée de « langage » et les capacités mentales des animaux sont limitées à l'imagination" (2016, 77). Also see Dessalles 2016.
19 It is for instance useful to distinguish between two types of human instincts: those that we have from the start of our lives and those we develop through habit, once we have the ability to reflect and determine a course of action beneficial to our needs, as Condillac argues in the *TdA* (see for instance 231–233, 293, 303 n. 34; henceforth *TdS*). In the *Essay*, Condillac also points out that reflection enables the mind to distance itself from its spontaneously arising thoughts and action impulses. As such, reflection can be used to distance oneself from existing habits of thought and action, for instance, for the purpose of changing or refining them; reflection is also instrumental in suppressing instinct. For a discussion of these more complex questions see Waldow 2021.
20 To clarify this point, Condillac added a footnote to the fourth part of the *TdS* when revising this work for the publication of his *Œuvres* (1798); see Kaitaro 2020.
21 This is not to say that Herder does not acknowledge the social function of language; he clearly states in the same context of the *Treatise* that every sign which, in and of itself, is "a *characteristic word* for me is a *communication word* for others" (*Philosophical Writings*, 97). See Forster for a discussion of Herder's social conception of human language, that nonetheless stresses the importance of "individuality in a person's language and meaning/thought" (2018, 71; also see 2018, 186).
22 See Gjesdal 2017, 108–110, for an emphasis on the developmental side of reflection in Herder; see Taylor 1995, 1999 and 2016 for the claim that according to Herder having reflective awareness is innate.
23 See Aarsleff 1982 and Pécharman forthcoming for a defense of Condillac against this objection.
24 See Rousseau's *Discourse on the Origin of Inequality* (1755). Herder repeats this worry, but also attacks Rousseau for having drawn the wrong conclusion:

"Condillac and Rousseau inevitably erred concerning the origin of language because they were so famously and variously mistaken about this difference since the former made animals into human beings, and the latter made human beings into animals" (*Philosophical Writings*, 77). For a good reconstruction of the various responses to "Rousseau's conundrum" see Lifschitz 2012, 78–87.
25 See Pécharman 1999, especially 99–103 and Charrak 2003, 78–79.
26 *Ideas* stands for Johann Gottfried Herder (1784–1791), *Ideas for a Philosophy of the History of Humanity*. Passages of this work are taken from Johann Gottfried Herder, (1985–) *Werke*, edited by Martin Bollacher et al., 10 vols, Frankfurt a. M.: Deutscher Klassiker Verlag. For passages taken form this work I use my own translation.
27 Herder himself puts this point as follows: "Each part, with its living forces, performs its task; and thus becomes visible in the general appearance the result of the forces that could reveal themselves only in precisely this, and no other composition. The active forces of nature, are all living, each in their own kind. Inside there must be something conformable to the effects outside ... That we have no name for this internal state of plants, or the powers still operating in them, is a defect of our language" (*Ideas*, 100–101).
28 Also see *Philosophical Writings*, 304–305, where Herder conceives of socially conditioned manners of thought as grounding the "loftiness and unearthly purity" (*Philosophical Writings*, 304–305) of Christian faith.

References

Aarsleff, Hans (1982). *From Locke to Saussure*. London: Athlone.
Auroux, Sylvain (1992). "Condillac, inventeur d'un nouveau matérialisme." *Dix-Huitième Siécle* 24: 153–163.
Bertrand, Aliènor (2002). "Le langage naturel, condition logique de l'institution des langues." In *Condillac: L'origine du langage*, edited by Aliènor Bertrand and Hans Aarsleff, 113–144. Paris: PUF.
Bertrand, Aliènor (2016). "Deux définitions du langage d'action, ou deux théories de l'esprit?" In *Condillac, philosophe du langage?*, edited by Aliènor Bertrand, 73–89. Lyon: ENS Éditions.
Charrak, André (2003). *Empiricisme et métaphysique*. Paris: Vrin.
Condillac, Étienne Bonnot de (1982). *Philosophical Writings of Étienne Bonnot de Condillac*, edited and translated by Franklin Philip and Harlan Lane, vol. 2. Hillsdale, NJ: Lawrence Erlbaum Associates.
Condillac, Étienne Bonnot de (1987). *Traité des animaux*, edited by François Dagognet. Paris: Vrin.
Condillac, Étienne Bonnot de (2001). *Essay on the Origin of Human Knowledge*, edited and translated by Hans Aarsleff. Cambridge: Cambridge University Press.
Dagognet, François (2004). *L'animal selon Condillac*. Paris: Vrin.
Descartes, René (1964–1976). *OEuvres de Descartes*, 12 vols. (revised edition), edited by Charles Adam and Paul Tannery. Paris: J. Vrin/CNRS.
Descartes, René (1984-1991). *The Philosophical Writings of Descartes*, 3 vols, translated by John Cottingham, Robert Stoothoff, Dugald Murdoch (and Anthony Kenny, vol. 3). Cambridge: Cambridge University Press.
DeSouza, Nigel (2012). "Language, Reason and Sociability: Herder's Critique of Rousseau." *Intellectual History Review* 22(2): 221–240.

Dessalles, Jean-Louis (2016). "Le proto-language: de quoi des hominidés parlaient-ils?" In *Condillac, philosophe du langage?*, edited by Aliènor Bertrand, 27–54. Lyon: ENS Éditions.
Dunham, Jeremy (2019). "Habits of Mind a Brand New Condillac." *Journal of Modern Philosophy* 1(1): 1–18.
Forster, Michael (2002). *Herder: Philosophical Writings*. Cambridge: Cambridge University Press.
Forster, Michael (2018). *Herder's Philosophy*. Oxford: Oxford University Press.
Gjesdal, Kristin (2017). *Herder's Hermeneutics: History, Poetry, Enlightenment*. Cambridge: Cambridge University Press.
Herder, Johann Gottfried (1985–). *Werke*, edited by Martin Bollacher et al., 10 vols. Frankfurt a. M.: Deutscher Klassiker Verlag.
Kaitaro, Timo (2020). *Language, Culture and Cognition from Descartes to Lewes*. Leiden: Brill.
Lifschitz, Avi (2012). *Language and Enlightenment: The Berlin Debates of the Eighteenth-Century*. Oxford: Oxford University Press.
Pécharman, Martine (1999). "Signification et langage dans l'*Essai* de Condillac." *Revue de Métaphysique et de Morale* 1: 81–103.
Pécharman, Martine (2019). "Avant-Propos." *Les Études philosophiques, Condillac après 1746* 1: 3–17.
Pécharman, Martine (forthcoming). "Les 'embarras' de la genèse du langage sont-ils insolubles? De Rousseau à Condillac (et non inverse)."
Rousseau, Jean-Jacques (1993). *Discourse on the Origins of Inequality, The Collected Writings of Rousseau*, vol. 3, edited by Roger Masters and Christopher Kelly. Hanover: University Press of New England.
Schwartz, Élisabeth (1999). "Les transformations de la sensation condillacienne: 'un opérateur secret.'" *Revue de Métaphysique et de Morale* 1: 27–51.
Schwartz, Élisabeth (2019). "Le status des signes et la presupposition mutuelle de la nature et de l'art dans le système de Condillac." *Les Études philosophiques, Condillac après 1746*, 1: 19–55.
Sloan, Phillip (1976). "The Buffon-Linnaeus Controversy." *Isis* 67(3): 356–375.
Taylor, Charles (1995). *Philosophical Arguments*. Cambridge, MA: Harvard University Press.
Taylor, Charles (1999). *Human Agency and Language*. Philosophical Papers 1. Cambridge: Cambridge University Press.
Taylor, Charles (2016). *The Language Animal: The Full Shape of the Human Linguistic Capacity*. Cambridge, MA: Harvard University Press.
Waldow, Anik (2017). "Activating the Mind: Descartes' Dreams and the Awakening of the Human Animal Machine." *Philosophy and Phenomenological Research* 94(2): 299–325.
Waldow, Anik (2020). *Experience Embodied: Early Modern Accounts of the Human Place in Nature*. New York: Oxford University Press.
Waldow, Anik (2021). "Condillac on Being Human: Language and Reflection Reconsidered." *European Journal of Philosophy* 29(2): 504–519.

Zammito, John (2017). "Herder between Remarius and Tetens: The Problem of an Animal-Human Boundary." In *Herder: Philosophy and Anthropology*, edited by Anik Waldow and Nigel DeSouza, 127–146. Oxford: Oxford University Press.
Zuckert, Rachel (2014). "Herder and Philosophical Naturalism." *Herder Jahrbuch* 12(1): 125–144.
Zuckert, Rachel (2019). *Herder's Naturalist Aesthetics*. Cambridge: Cambridge University Press.

12 The Reception of Condillac in Argentina

From the Nineteenth-Century Professors of *idéologie* to José Ingenieros

Silvia Manzo

1 Introduction

In the 1910s, the Italo-Argentinian polymath José Ingenieros wrote one of the first accounts of the history of Argentinian philosophy.[1] Describing the general situation of philosophy within the context of emancipation of the South American Spanish colonies during the first half of the nineteenth century, Ingenieros stated:

> From the beginning, the French influence in Spain and in America took two different directions. The one—more or less compatible with traditional doctrines—corresponded to the philosophy of the seventeenth century, in which Descartes was the predominant figure; the other—clearly antagonistic [to the first]—corresponded to the philosophy of the eighteenth century and was represented by the Encyclopedists and Condillac, finishing at the end of the century in the ideological school of Cabanis and Destutt de Tracy. The conservative spirits—forced to renew their philosophy—were inclined towards the Cartesians; the liberal spirits—adjusted to the thriving rhythm of the Revolution—were oriented towards the Encyclopedists.
>
> (Ingenieros 1918a, 84)[2]

In this account, Condillac is portrayed as the main representative of the "philosophical liberalism" that influenced the renewal of the philosophical teaching during the first half of the nineteenth century. Such a narrative, which is strongly biased by Ingenieros's sympathy for positivism, has however some failures and deserves a reappraisal. First, we will explore the reception of Condillac in the teaching of philosophy in Buenos Aires between 1819 and 1842. During these years, known in the scholarly literature as the period of the *idéologues*, Juan Crisóstomo Lafinur, Juan Manuel Fernández de Agüero, Luis José de la Peña, and Diego Alcorta were highly inspired by French philosophical trends. The presence of Condillac in their lectures

DOI: 10.4324/9781003334750-15

and writings was mediated by the interpretations of other authors: Antoine Destutt de Tracy, Pierre Jean Cabanis, and Pierre Laromiguière. Second, we will point out how Ingenieros's narrative of the nineteenth-century reception of Condillac was conditioned by his own political, philosophical, and personal agenda. In each case, we can identify different receptions that must be interpreted not only in light of the philosophical concerns of the authors that made them but also in light of the wider cultural and politic context in which they emerged. In the first half of the nineteenth century, Condillac was received as a philosopher who integrated the new philosophical canon that would replace the Scholastic canon that had been imposed by the colonial regime. In the early twentieth century, in turn, Ingenieros inserted Condillac into a narrative that, starting with Bacon and Locke, culminated in positivism, a current that, in his view, offered the best framework to make Argentina shine in the concert of civilized nations.

2 Condillac in Ingenieros' narrative

In the specific case of the nascent Argentina, Ingenieros described the French Enlightenment as a source of philosophical (Étienne Bonnot de Condillac), political (Jean-Jacques Rousseau), and economic (François Quesnay) liberalism that was essential for building a new cultural and political era. Condillac's *Traité des Sensations* (1754) was, according to Ingenieros, "assimilated from second-hand [sources]" to the universities of Córdoba (Argentina), Chuquisaca (Bolivia), México, Bogotá, and Lima, despite the inquisitorial prohibition; and it is said to be the work referred to by "all those who wanted to emancipate education" from "Spanish Scholasticism." Indeed, he claimed that most intellectuals in the "philosophical and psychological" field followed that work. On his account, Pierre Jean Georges Cabanis and Antoine Destutt de Tracy were mediators who transformed Condillac's sensualism and increased its circulation. While Cabanis gave to sensualism "a very broad physiological and naturalistic basis," Destutt developed its consequences "in the domain of the so-called moral sciences" (Ingenieros 1918a, 159–160; 385–387). Ingenieros provided a similar genealogy in psychiatry, a field in which he himself was engaged. He traced a historical line of influence that began with Condillac and Locke, continued with the "naturalist psychology" of the *idéologues*, and culminated in Philippe Pinel and Jean-Étienne Dominique Esquirol, who "had revolutionized" mental pathology (Ingenieros 1920b, 12).

Ingenieros's perspective is, of course, biased by his own philosophical, political, and personal agenda. He wrote these historiographical narratives during a period when positivism and anti-positivism competed with one another to become the dominant influence in Argentinian philosophy. Between 1890 and 1910, positivism was the hegemonic philosophical current in Argentina, mainly under the influence of Auguste Comte and Hebert

Spencer. However, since the 1900s, an anti-positivist reaction began. This reaction manifested through diverse philosophical currents at different stages. First, in the 1910s, Kant's philosophy was adopted as a good alternative to positivism (Dotti 1992, 149–154). Second, between the late 1910s and the 1930s, spiritualist philosophies, such as those of Benedetto Croce and Henri Bergson, gradually rose to prominence, alongside Neo-Kantianism and Dilthey's philosophy, among others (Torchia Estrada 1967).[3]

Ingenieros studied medicine at the University of Buenos Aires. Until 1911 he served as a state expert dedicated to psychiatry, legal medicine, and sociology, endorsing a positivist, determinist, and social Darwinist perspective (Plotkin 2016). Despite being persistent, his endorsement of positivism was not monolithic or seamless. Indeed, his philosophy departs from positivism by going beyond it. In 1914, he stated that philosophy should be scientific, that is, "a system of hypothesis based on the most general laws, demonstrated by the particular sciences, addressed to explain the problems that exceed the current or possible experience." This philosophy is therefore "a true metaphysics of experience" (Ingenieros 1914, 410). Some years later, in 1918, he takes the same line but talks instead of "a metaphysics of the un-experiential" (Ingenieros 1918b, 133–149; Terán 1986, 48–91) in so far as it addresses problems that are not given in experience.

Given the importance of experience in Ingenieros's philosophy, we can understand why Condillac is so relevant to him and is identified as a follower of the path initiated by Bacon and consolidated by Locke. Inductive experimental method, empiricism, and sensualism are seen as components of the process that permitted the advancement of science. In contrast, Ingenieros found in Cartesianism a wrong way anchored in innatism and a sterile method that did not draw on observation and experiment. For that reason, for Ingenieros, Cartesianism was closer to Scholasticism than to scientific progress. Critical attitudes toward Cartesianism were also common in the nineteenth century, albeit for a variety of reasons. On the one hand, sympathizers of Late Scholaticism used to reject Descartes for not being Scholastic. On the other hand, advocates of sensualism and Newtonian science believed that Cartesianism represented the past and was as traditional as Scholasticism (Chiaramonte 2007, 54–58).

Ingenieros maintains a persistently staunch anti-Scholastic stance and believes that colonial education was deficient because of its Scholastic setting (Ingenieros 1918a, 25–78). He acknowledges, however, attempts at improvement made by the first chancellor (*cancelario*) of the Real Colegio de San Carlos, the Argentinian theologian and lawyer Juan Baltasar Maciel (1727–1788). Maciel (or Maziel) wrote proposals for higher studies that were heterodox compared to the common practice of Spanish academic institutions in his time. Concerning philosophy, he advised that it should not be mandatory to teach a determined system. Especially in "physics" (natural philosophy), Aristotle's principles might be left to give place to other systems like Descartes's, Gassendi's, or Newton's. Despite this flexibility, Maciel added that in case Aristotle's system was preferred, it should be taught according to Aquinas' interpretation. Besides, he proposed discontinuing the use of the Thomistic manual of the French Dominican Antoine Goudin (1639–1695), *Philosophia juxta inconcussa tutissimaque divi Thomae dogmata* (1671), to teach logic and metaphysics. Maciel recommended replacing the Thomistic approach with an "eclectic" one,[4] which, in his view, entailed that in matters not dependent on scriptural revelation, professors were free to choose the method and the stance they judge to be the best.

Maciel's innovative proposals were, however, quite ineffectual. Although the free teaching of modern physical systems was permitted, authorities of the Viceroyalty rejected the advice to abandon Goudin's manual, because they were afraid of the negative consequences that this would have on the course of theology (Gutiérrez 1868, 255; Chiaramonte 2007, 49–53; 124–127; Torchia Estrada 2012). As Ingenieros rightly notes, even though members of the young clergy of Buenos Aires were often politically revolutionary, anti-Spanish in spirit, and interested in introducing the systems of modern physics, they were not in a position to teach them because of a lack of learning (Ingenieros 1918a, 121–126). What finally occurred was that the systems of Descartes or Newton were vaguely mentioned and inserted into a Scholastic framework, which resulted in a quite incoherent philosophical course (Chiaramonte 2007, 58–65). Interestingly, Ingenieros judges that the "modest liberality" (*discreta liberalidad*) of Maciel did not dare to embrace the philosophy of Condillac and the Encyclopedists, because they engaged in extreme positions that orthodox authorities would see as heretical. In fact, Maciel was forced to exile in 1786 (Ingenieros 1918a, 116–120; cf. Gutiérrez 1868, 63, 255).

As an intellectual, Ingenieros intervened in the public sphere, advocating for the democratization and modernization of the country. He was both witness and agent of the transition that Argentina underwent since the end of the 1880s. The new sociocultural structure that was being consolidated at that time, governed by a Republican government with oligarchic characteristics, gave way to a political order transitioning to a democratic republic. When looking at the last 100 years and the very beginnings of the independent nation, Ingenieros allied Condillac's philosophy with political and economic liberalism. In so doing, he interpreted the philosophical past in binary terms, confronting the Spanish Scholastic and theological legacy with the French philosophy of Condillac, the Enlightenment, and the *idéologues*. He thus legitimized the modernization that he advocated for, claiming that it must be seen as the natural result of a "national evolution" that started in the nineteenth century with independence from Spain.

Ingenieros' historical narrative of the French influence on nineteenth-century Argentina is correct, in particular with respect to two points. First, after the independence of Spain in 1816, the long dominance of Late Scholasticism over the colonial educational system began to weaken. Second, it is also true that prominent political figures such as Gregorio Funes (1749–1829) and Manuel Belgrano (1770–1820), among others, resorted to Condillac to modify the curricula, specially following his logic. Reforms were proposed to several disciplines, such as mathematics, law, medicine, and philosophy (Ghirardi 2004; Carozzi 2011, 190–194, 318–322; Cornejo and Santilli 2013; Di Pasquale 2015). Condillac's corpus was read in French or in the Spanish translations of *Logique*, *Le Commerce et le Gouvernement*, *La langue des calculs*, and *Cours d'études pour l'instruction du Prince de Parme* (Jimenez García 1990; Weinberg 1997).

In philosophy, the first significant renewal took place in Buenos Aires between 1819 and 1842 and was inspired by the French Enlightenment and, above all, by the *idéologie*, a philosophical movement developed in France between the late eighteenth century and the first decades of the nineteenth century (Varela Domínguez de Ghioldi 1938; Zamudio Silva 1940; Di Pasquale 2012). As critical disciples of Condillac, the *idéologues* were inspired by his method of analysis to study the formation, expression, and combination of ideas. The name *idéologie* was coined by Destutt de Tracy, who conceived it as a "science of ideas," while Cabanis provided the physiological basis for this inquiry. By means of the study of ideas, the *idéologues* intended to deal with psychologic, linguistic, logic, epistemic, ethical, and political issues of the human life. Most of them were close to the political ideals of the French Revolution, while some contemporaries often associated them with materialism (Staum 1980, 3–14).[5]

The only university during the colonial period in the territory now comprising Argentina was the University of Córdoba, founded in 1613, 700 kilometers away from Buenos Aires. In Buenos Aires, the most important academic institution was the Real Colegio de San Carlos, a college of higher education founded in 1773. Both academic institutions were dominated by Late Scholasticism since their foundation. After the declaration of independence from Spain, the Real Colegio de San Carlos quickly underwent reforms. Under the government of Martín de Pueyrredón (1816–1819), the college was turned into the Colegio de la Unión del Sud in 1818. In 1819, Juan Crisóstomo Lafinur was appointed to the chair of philosophy. Lafinur's course fully adopted the perspective of the *idéologie*, which entailed a radical renewal (Gutiérrez 1868, 45–50). As we have noted, during the first decade of the nineteenth century, proposals for renewing the curriculum through the introduction of Condillac's logic circulated in Buenos Aires (Chiaramonte 2007, 74–77). However, it was only with the arrival of Lafinur that Condillac's logic began to be taught as a replacement of Scholastic logic. Along with that, Lafinur introduced topics that were completely absent in the precedent syllabus, such as the application of the method of analysis in the formation, expression, and combination of ideas, and in the physiological explanation of perception. This choice was soon questioned by conservative authorities. As a result, Lafinur gave up his chair the following year and was finally forced into exile in Chile in 1822 (Gallo 2014).

However, the teachings of the *idéologie* resumed in 1822, under the protection of Bernardino Rivadavia (1780–1845), minister of the governor Martín Rodríguez (1771–1845). Rivadavia, a great enthusiast of the *idéologie* who was well acquainted with Tracy, introduced several important cultural reforms. In 1823, the chair of "Ideología" was created as part of the recently founded University of Buenos Aires, to which the Colegio de la Union Sud was annexed in the same year (under the name "Colegio de Ciencias Morales").[6] The chair was successively held by Juan Manuel Fernández de Agüero (1822–1827), Luis José de la Peña (1827), and Diego Alcorta (1827–1842) (Zamudio Silva 1940; cf. Ingenieros 1918a, 316).[7] In the following sections, we will analyze the reception of Condillac by Lafinur and these three professors. We will focus on their account of method, the origin of ideas and mental faculties, and their narratives of the main early modern philosophical currents of thought.

3 Lafinur's Course and the Introduction of Condillac's Logic

Juan Crisóstomo Lafinur (1797–1824) was born in San Luis, Argentina. Although he studied philosophy and completed his arts degree at the University of Córdoba, he did not pursue the study of theology because he was expelled from the university. It has been suggested that his interest and knowledge of French philosophy was initiated when he met the French soldier Jean Joseph Dauxion Lavaisse, who was the director of the military academy under the auspices of Manuel Belgrano. We know his philosophical ideas from brief polemical writings and, above all, from a transcript of notes by one of his students, published posthumously without his review (Varela Domínguez de Ghioldi 1938; Korn 1940, 143–148; Zamudio 1940; Ingenieros 1918a, 388–394). Juan María Gutiérrez, who transcribed these lessons, remarks that Lafinur read Condillac, Locke, Tracy, and Cabanis (among others), even if only superficially (Lafinur 2015, 69).

Part of Lafinur's *Curso filosófico* (2015) provides a summary of some passages from Tracy's *Logique* (1805). It begins with a very brief preface that offers a tight synthesis of the history of philosophy from the Chaldeans to Newton. In this review, the figure of Condillac does not appear. René Descartes and Galileo are celebrated as those who shook "with more happiness the yoke of Aristotle" (Lafinur 2015, 57–60). The systematic part of the course reviews the most common topics of the *idéologie* and mentions some of the canonical philosophers. The most prominent figure is the "immortal [John] Locke" (Lafinur 2015, 81, 86, 88, 115 and 140). Yet, far from contrasting Locke's empiricism with Cartesianism, Lafinur comprehends Francis Bacon and Descartes as the two co-founders of a new era. Thus, for him, it is the combination of the legacies of both figures that provided the *idéologie* with its foundation, as it unites the claim that ideas are mental "facts" (Bacon) with the conception of the Cartesian *cogito* as "the first fact (...) from which they all derive" (Lafinur 2015, 93).

The fundamental importance that Lafinur gives to the *cogito* and the articulation it has when seen in connection with Bacon and Descartes draws on Tracy's *Logique*. For Tracy, Bacon and Descartes do not oppose each other; instead, all the useful elements of Bacon's logic unfold in the *Discours de la méthode* (1637). However, for Tracy, Descartes is better than Bacon because he was able to reduce the method of research to four rules, to establish that research must begin with the intellectual faculties, and to state that the first certainty we can have is *je pense, donc je suis* (Tracy 1805, 109–111; Head 1985, 25–44).

This assessment of Bacon and Descartes is very different from Condillac's. In the *Essai sur l'origine des connoissances humaines* (1746), Condillac places these authors in different categories both with respect to their methods and the principles that underlie their respective theories of the origin of ideas. Pointing out that Bacon knew better than anyone else the causes of our mistakes, Condillac regrets that the Cartesians "borrowed nothing" from his method (Condillac 2001, 216). Indeed, Bacon and Locke knew well how to apply the Peripatetic principle that "all our knowledge comes from the senses"; yet the Cartesians and Descartes himself despised it, and instead of using it only adopted the errors of the Peripatetics (Condillac 2001, 6). Interestingly, this narrative establishes an *association* between Cartesianism and Scholasticism:

> The scholastics and the Cartesians knew neither the origin nor the generation of our knowledge, for the good reason that the principle of innate ideas and the vague notion of the understanding, on which their thinking was based, have no connection with this discovery.
> (Condillac 2001, 214)

Following Tracy, Lafinur claims that the most secure basis of practicing logic—which he also calls the "art of reasoning"—can be found in the *idéologie* or "science of examining ideas." From this point onward, he paraphrases Tracy's *Logique* pointing out that Condillac's way of understanding the ideas figuring in processes of reasoning as some kind of mathematical calculus is not enough to determine whether judgments are certain. According to Tracy, resorting to the *cogito*—the "first fact" [*premier fait*]—cannot be left out, since the certainty of ideas derives from the more fundamental certainty of the *cogito* (Tracy 1805, 180–195; Lafinur 2015, 104–109; also cf. 152–156).

The stricture that Lafinur places on Condillac's method does not prevent him from arguing that the method of analysis is indeed able to explain the origin of ideas and mental faculties (Lafinur 2015, 62–63; 88–89; 93–98; cf. Condillac 1982 *Logic*, 601–602). He also fully agrees with Condillac's claim that faculties are "transformed sensation." After explaining the generation of ideas by the famous example of the statue, Condillac concludes: "The principle determining the development of [mental] faculties is simple; sensations themselves contain it(...) Judgment, reflection, desires, passions, and so forth are only sensation itself differently transformed" (Condillac 1982 *Treatise*, 307).

In the same way, Lafinur claims: "If attention, comparison, and judgment are nothing but transformed sensation, therefore they are nothing more than decomposed sensation or sensation successively considered from different points of view" (Lafinur 2015, 89).

According to Condillac, the analytic method seeks to alternate the composition and decomposition of ideas "to create new combinations and to discover, by this means, their mutual relations and the new ideas they can produce" (Condillac 2001, 48; cf. Condillac, 1982, *Logic* 574, 577). This method unites a progressive and regressive process in the sense that it aims "to return to the origin of our ideas, follow their generation, and compare them in terms of all their possible relations" (Condillac 2001, 49; cf. Charrak 2003, 21–22).

4 Condillac as an Intermediary between Locke and Tracy in Agüero's Lectures

Juan Manuel Fernández de Agüero (1772–1840) was born in Spain, studied in Buenos Aires at the Colegio, and was ordained a Catholic priest in Chile. He taught Scholastic philosophy at the Colegio between 1805 and 1807. However, he later became interested in the *idéologie*, drawing mainly on Tracy and, to a lesser extent, on Cabanis. His appointment as the chair of *idéologie* was supported by Rivadavia, which permitted him to keep this position despite the opposition of conservative factions, until he was forced to resign in 1827. The publication of his manual *Principios de Ideología* (1824–1826) was financed with public funds (Ingenieros 1918a, 413–419; Zamudio Silva 1940; Di Pasquale 2011).

Agüero's manual is deeply concerned with the reform of the philosophical curriculum. He admits that he follows Tracy, but also states his disagreement with him, especially regarding his conception of logic.

Concerning the physiological content of his lessons, which deal with the functioning of the brain and the sense organs of perception, voluntary and involuntary motions, and the formation of several kinds of ideas and feelings, he follows Cabanis very closely (Agüero 1940 I, 159–160; 239–240). In this context, Condillac appears as an intermediary between Locke and Tracy. Ingenieros rightly notes that Agüero was not "a strict disciple of Condillac, much less of Descartes, whom he knows thoroughly and comments on with sagacity. On certain issues he departs from the second and refutes him, following the *idéologues*" (1918a, 416).

In Agüero we find both an antagonistic and a unifying reading of seventeenth-century philosophers. The antagonistic reading agrees with Condillac's distinction between two philosophical currents regarding the origin of ideas. Agüero celebrates as a "triumph of the *idéologie*" that it is no longer required to remember what "innatism" and "archetypism" consisted of. He gives an account of the main differences between Descartes's and Locke's accounts of the origin of ideas, and aligns Locke and Aristotle, on the one hand, and Descartes, Malebranche, and Plato, on the other (Agüero 1940 I, 135, 146).

Like in Lafinur, his unifying reading of seventeenth-century philosophy draws on Tracy. Bacon, Descartes, and Locke are portrayed as pioneers of a development through which abstract metaphysics was set aside and philosophy took precedence over religion. Bacon is celebrated as the "restorer," who challenged Scholasticism and opened up new possibilities that enabled the discovery of the secrets of nature through factual observation. Descartes provided the *cogito*, the first "fact" that constitutes the beginning of all human sciences (Agüero 1940 II, 11–12; 62).

Drawing on Cabanis (and without mentioning him),[8] Agüero criticizes Condillac for having reduced the origin of ideas to sensation. According to Agüero, "external sensation" is not enough to explain the origin of *all* ideas (1940 II, 50–53; cf. Cabanis 1802 I, 106–118). He argues that moral ideas are sometimes partially or exclusively caused by the "internal impressions" of the bodily organs. For example, the viscera of the lower belly can cause feelings of joy, sadness, or madness. In a similar way, animal instincts, like the maternal instinct, "must refer to internal impressions, that necessarily emanate from vital functions" (1940 II, 61–63; cf. Cabanis 1802 1, 130–138). Despite this criticism, Agüero remarks that Condillac's analytic method is essential, because it establishes a link between moral ideas and the different internal organs (1940 II, 52–53).

Condillac himself foresaw such criticisms by acknowledging that moral ideas do not *seem* to derive from the senses, at least for those philosophers "who deny that our knowledge comes from sensation." To this objection he replies that morality consists "uniquely in the conformity of our actions with laws." Actions are "visible," so they do fall under the domain of sense perception. The same goes for laws "because they are conventions that men have made" (Condillac 1982 *Logic*, 598). Concerning instincts, he explicitly confronts the Cartesian view that animals are automata. Condillac claims that instinct is "an imagination which in the presence of an object revives the perceptions that are immediately connected with it and which by that means guides all kinds of animals without the assistance of reflection." Both human beings and animals are endowed with instincts, so that "[t]he similarity between animals and us proves that they have a soul; and the difference between us proves that it is inferior to ours" (Condillac 2001, 39). In *Traité des animaux* (1755), he explains that human and non-human animals have the natural instinct to satisfy the basic needs and desires oriented to self-preservation, by which they acquire practical knowledge. Humans have, in addition, a further capacity to develop theoretical knowledge for which linguistic signs are required. This difference between human and non-human animals is due to the fact that human body has more senses and more complex sense organs than other animals, and therefore humans encounter more needs in their life experience, which stimulate more complex reflection in order to find solutions that satisfy the needs (Condillac 1982 *A Treatise of the Sensations*, 512–513; *Logic*, 681; 1755 ch. 5; Dunham 2019; Waldow 2021 and this volume).

In short, in Agüero's lectures, Condillac is seen through the lens of Tracy and Cabanis. Condillac's main achievement consists in his method, and his main failure is expressed in the claim that all ideas can be reduced to sensation. And even though Agüero agrees with Condillac's contrast between Descartes and Locke regarding the origin of ideas, he follows Tracy's idea of a confluence of Descartes' *cogito* and the method of Locke and Bacon.

5 De la Peña's Conjunction of Condillac with Larromiguiére

Luis José de la Peña (1796–1871) was born in Buenos Aires. He studied at the Colegio and attended courses of philosophy and theology at the University of Córdoba, where he received his doctorate. Ordained a priest, he resigned as soon as he could. We know his philosophical ideas from the transcriptions of the lectures he taught at the Colegio in 1827 (De la Peña 2006; Jalif de Bertranou 2006).

De la Peña agrees with Condillac's reflections on the method of analysis and his demand to study the process through which ideas and mental faculties come into existence. He acknowledges Condillac, Tracy, and Laromiguière as admirable guides but also remarks that he will not follow them blindly. One important disagreement with Condillac concerns the limits of the study of the human mind. Condillac explicitly excludes the investigation of the "essence" or "nature" of the human mind from philosophy, advocating a non-essentialist examination of mental operations and their effects, an approach which was later adopted by Tracy and Cabanis (Gusdorf 1974, 175–176; 281–283; 194–195):

> We must never forget that our first aim is the study of the human mind [*esprit humain*], not to discover its nature, but to know its operations, to observe how artfully they interact, and how we ought to conduct them in order to acquire all the knowledge of which we are capable.
> (Condillac 2001, 5)

Moreover, he even argues that it would be useless to inquire into the nature of our thoughts, since we would immediately discover that we have no means of conducting such an inquiry (Condillac 2001, 11).

By contrast, De la Peña's lectures draw on Laromiguière's approach and are explicitly focused on the "nature," "effects," and "procedures" of mental faculties (Laromiguière 1815, 57; De la Peña 2006). Concerning the nature of mind, De la Peña also followed Laromiguière, as he avoids contrasting Descartes and the empiricists. However, unlike Condillac, he does not align Descartes with the Scholastics, but does quite the opposite. He treats Descartes as a pioneer who "annihilated forever the vegetative and sensitive souls so beloved by the Scholastics" (De la Peña 2006, 105). In addition, De la Peña claims that Locke and Condillac were Descartes's successors (and not Bacon's). According to this narrative, Descartes's conception of mind and mental faculties provided Locke with an ideal theoretical framework through which he could introduce the analysis of ideas as a key method that Condillac later perfected (De la Peña 2006, 107–111).

Condillac's greatest achievement, in De la Peña's view, was that he was the first philosopher to argue that the study of the mind could proceed by a single principle, when trying to explain the origin of all mental faculties. As Condillac states:

> It is evident that my design is to reduce everything that pertains to the human understanding [*entendement*] to a single principle, and that this principle shall be neither a vague proposition, nor an abstract maxim, nor a gratuitous supposition, but a firm fact of experience whose consequences will all be confirmed by new acts of experience.
> (Condillac 2001, 5)[9]

De la Peña observes that before Condillac, philosophers confused causes with effects and faculties with ideas. Condillac corrected this flaw.

He followed Locke in postulating that all ideas derive from sensation and then argued that it is through sensation alone that mental faculties arise.[10] While De la Peña agreed with Laromiguière that Condillac was right in postulating that there is just one single principle that lies at the origin of all mental faculties, he thought he was wrong in claiming that sensation is that principle (De la Peña 2006, 86–90; 104).

De la Peña's explicitly comments on Condillac's *Logique*, Part 1, Chapter 7. He claims that sensation is not a necessary and sufficient condition for knowledge. Against this, he argues that for knowledge to arise all that is necessary is "the activity of mind." This criticism of Condillac is deeply indebted to Laromiguière (Laromiguière 1815, 74–183) and his focus on the notion of attention. Following Laromiguière, De la Peña argues that the unity of mental faculties is possible because attention is their common principle.[11] For in attention we employ for the first time the active capacity of our mind. It therefore follows that attention is the "first faculty" to which "all others owe their existence and origin" (De la Peña 2006, 110–111; Laromiguière 1815, 356).

This concept of attention contrasts with Condillac's. For him, it is true that attention is original in the sense "that we notice [it] in the faculty of having sensations"; however, he rejects that the other faculties are reducible to it. Sensation comes first and attention is only one particular kind of sensation. When considering the body, attention is the action by which a bodily organ directs itself to an object. The sensation that we experience here presents the object as if it existed alone and without all other things around it. Hence, for the mind, attention is "the sensation that that object engenders in us—sensation that becomes in some sense exclusive" (Condillac 1982 *Logic*, 601–602). Against this view, De la Peña argues that sensation and attention are two entirely different states in the body and mind. Sensation consists in a passive reception of the impression of an object. Attention, by contrast, is active, in the sense that the mind has a "reaction" to an object perceived by sensation. De la Peña criticizes Condillac for confusing the mind's activity with its passivity (De la Peña 2006, 103).

Condillac offers a quite different view of the activity and passivity of mind. According to him, "a being is active or passive depending on whether the cause of the effect produced is in it or outside of it" (Condillac 1982 *Treatise on sensations*, 334). In this regard, the sense of touch plays an important role. The statue is entirely passive with respect to the impressions made by smell, hearing, vision, and taste, if they are separately considered. But when these senses are united by touch—by which the statue discovers the existence of the external world—the statue becomes active, for now "it has the means to seek the impressions that objects make on it or to avoid them" (Condillac 1982 *Treatise on sensations*, 510–511). Hence, when sensations are sought by the subject, they are active; when they are not sought, they are passive.[12] With respect to the origin of ideas, De la Peña offers groupings already seen in Agüero. Descartes and Locke appear as the early modern representatives of the two "main doctrines" that have divided philosophers since Antiquity. Thus, De la Peña draws a connection between ancient and early modern philosophers: Plato-Descartes, on the one hand, and Aristotle-Locke, on the other. In his opinion, both doctrines are wrong and "so opposed to each other that they have no point of contact" (De la Peña 2006, 125, 138). Moreover, according to him, empiricism was as wrong as sensualism, a statement which shows that his approval of the *idéologie* was not so strong as to lead him to embrace all the tenets of Condillac's philosophy. Laromiguière's influence led De la Peña much closer to eclectic spiritualism than sensualism.

An important remark is in order here. De la Peña's lectures were ignored by the historiography until a few decades ago (Jalif de Bertranou 2006). Ingenieros apparently was unaware of De la Peña's course and of his sympathy for eclectic spiritualism. For that reason, he could not observe that in the context of the first half of the nineteenth century De la Peña's course was seen as a kind of alternative middle term between Encyclopedy-Condillac and Scholasticism.

6   Alcorta's Course: Condillac in the Convergence of Philosophy and Medicine

Born in Buenos Aires, Diego Alcorta (1801–1842) was a physician at the University of Buenos Aires and a professor of philosophy. In his youth he attended Lafinur's philosophy course. At the medical school he was a student of Francisco Cosme Argerich (1787–1846), who continued the approach of his father, Cosme Mariano Argerich (1758–1820), a highly influential figure of medical education in Argentina. Argerich father endorsed Condillac's philosophy and was well acquainted with Pinel's and Cabanis's work (Ingenieros 1920b, 114, 155; Stagnaro 1990, 57).

Alcorta's commitment to the *idéologie* manifested in both areas relevant to his intellectual career. His doctoral thesis "Disertación sobre la manía aguda" ("Dissertation on Acute Mania," 1827) operates with a sensualist psychology that was influenced by some of the most important French "alienists" (psychiatrists) of his time: the psychiatric research of Pinel, who applied Condillac's method of analysis to the study and classification of mental illness in his *Traité médico-philosophique sur l'aliénation mentale* (1801);[13] and Esquirol who was well known for his treatise *Les Passions considérées comme causes, symptômes et moyens curatifs de l'aliénation mentale* (1805) (Alcorta 1990, 61; Stagnaro 1990, 58–59; Di Pasquale 2014; Greif 2019).

Condillac's influence is evident in relation to a number of topics discussed in the transcripts of Alcorta's philosophy lectures, which were held at the Colegio, *Lecciones de filosofía* (Alcorta 2000). At the very beginning of these lectures, he states his endorsement of Condillac's philosophy. Alcorta follows Condillac's definition of metaphysics as the study of "human thought" (Alcorta 2000, 33). Through this definition, Condillac intends to do away with the idea that metaphysics must solve mysteries and discover the nature, essence, and most hidden causes of all things. For Condillac, metaphysics is "unconcerned about what must lie beyond its grasp" (Condillac 2001, 3).

Different from others, Alcorta is not interested in pointing out an antagonism between philosophical currents regarding the origin of ideas. Nonetheless, he notes the existence of two distinct and not mutually exclusive methods: the analytic method promoted by Bacon, Locke, Condillac, and Bonnett, and the synthetic method supported by Descartes and Malebranche. In keeping with Condillac's and Pinel's approach, he claims that the analytic method is fundamentally important for discovery, while the synthetic method is better suited to organizing or exposing knowledge. However, Alcorta follows Condillac, when stating that both methods can be combined and be useful as teaching methods. However, one must decide on which occasion which method is better suited than the other (Alcorta 2000, 54; 84–88; 184–185; 192).

For Condillac the analytic method is the only means to acquire knowledge. And although synthesis is the "exact opposite of analysis," it would "be absurd to suppose that these two procedures are mutually exclusive," since synthesis also includes decomposition as well as composition (Condillac 2001, 49; 1982 *Logic*, 560–561). The difference between them lies in this:

> Analysis always begins well and synthesis always begins badly. The former, without pretending to order, has order naturally because it is the method of nature; the latter, which is unacquainted with the natural order, because it is the method of philosophers, pretends to much order only to weary the mind without enlightening it.
> (Condillac 1982 *Logic*, 660)

Concerning the origin of ideas, Alcorta agrees with the Condillacian account, but adds to it the physiological perspective of Cabanis. The influence of Cabanis is most evident in his physiological explanation of the sense organs of the "physical man," which is a discussion that is absent in Condillac's writings. In addition, Alcorta shares Cabanis' vitalist approach, which leads him to maintain that the senses are not only governed by "mechanical laws" but also by "vital laws" (Alcorta 2000, 34–46).

Cabanis thinks that the Condillacian transformation of sensation cannot be explained in purely mechanical terms and must be complemented with a vitalistic physiology that accounts for the activity inherent in sensation (Staum 1980, 197–198).

As for the description of different mental faculties, Alcorta more or less follows Condillac's approach in the *Essai* and *Logique* (Alcorta 2001, 50–57; Condillac 2001, 19–70; 1982 *Logic*, part I, ch. 7–8). Regarding the classification of ideas, he almost literally reproduces passages from the *Course for the Prince of Parma* (Alcorta 2000, 60–62; Condillac 1982 *Course*, Art. 1). In response to the question of whether the senses are a source of error, Alcorta states that he follows Condillac, "who has perfectly clarified this ideological question." When perception is clear and distinct, the senses do not deceive us. The error consists in judging on the basis of "vague ideas." And he adds: "There is (Condillac repeats) no error, confusion or darkness in what happens inside us nor in the relationship we have to the external object" (Alcorta 2000, 47–50). Indeed, for Alcorta, Condillac rightly criticizes "the Cartesians and the Malebranchists" for blaming the senses. They repeat so often that the senses are nothing but sources of error and illusion that we end up considering them as obstacles to the acquisition of knowledge. By contrast, the senses are sources of truth *and* error. The important point is to precisely distinguish truth from error. Nothing is clearer and more distinct than perceptions derived from particular sensations. For this reason, "we must distinguish three things in our sensations: (1) The perception we have. (2) The reference we give it to something outside ourselves. (3) The judgment that what we refer to things really belong to them." Alcorta draws on Condillac's example to illustrate this claim:

> If for instance I see a square building from the distance, it will appear round. In that case, is there any obscurity or confusion in the idea of roundness or in the reference I give it? No, but I judge this building to be round, and that is where the error lies.
> (Condillac 2001, 16; cf. Alcorta, 2000, 48)

Moreover, on certain occasions, the senses themselves help us correct "momentary errors."

Arguing that the error is not sensitive but judicative, Alcorta concludes in full agreement with Condillac: "In certain cases the final judgment is false, and hence the error is born; therefore, the senses are but the occasional cause of all errors as well as of all truths that we know" (Alcorta 2000, 48). This statement clearly echoes Condillac's claim that "our senses are only the occasional cause of our knowledge." For him this is so because, in so far as mind is "distinct and different from body, the latter can only be the occasional cause of what it seems to produce in the former."

He thereby distinguishes sensation—an act of mind—from impression, an operation of the sense organs (Condillac 2001, 13). The faculty of sensation belongs to the mind, and it is "occasioned" by stimuli affecting the sense organs. Condillac's dualism is evident in the *Course*, where he says:

> Sensations are in something different from any bodily thing, that is, they are in a substance where there is something other than movement. It is what we call soul or mind or spiritual substance. The more we reflect on the properties of this substance, the more convinced we will be that it is completely different from the body.
> (Condillac 1982, art. IV)[14]

Alcorta shares Condillac's dualist approach and notes that the "mysterious union" between our sense organs and the thinking principle can be explained by the analytic method (Alcorta 2000, 42–43).

7 Conclusion: Condillac's Double Reception

This brief study of the "*idéologie* period" of the Colegio shows that Condillac's ideas, as they were expressed in the *Essai, Traité des Sensations, Logique* and *Cours* were widely circulated in the classrooms between 1819 and 1842. In the case of Lafinur, Agüero, and De la Peña, it seems that Condillac's philosophy was not read first-hand. They interpreted and criticized him through the prism of other philosophies: the rational *idéologie* of Destutt de Tracy (in Lafinur and Agüero), the physiological *idéologie* of Cabanis (in Agüero), and the eclectic spiritualism of Pierre Laromiguière (in De la Peña). In this way, Condillac was not the most outstanding figure for the professors of Buenos Aires, but only a philosopher of certain relevance, someone with whom they agreed only in part and whom they criticized. Alcorta's case is different. His direct knowledge of Condillac is evident in his long and frequent paraphrases of various works. Here, Condillac is undoubtedly Alcorta's main influence (Groussac 1918, 26–31). The fact that Alcorta adds Cabanis' physiological and vitalist perspective to Condillac's own should not be taken as a criticism but as an attempt to complete Condillac's sensualist principles. That Alcorta aligns Condillac and Cabanis is, of course, a consequence of his medical education.

The four professors of the Colegio placed Condillac in the pantheon of early modern philosophers in their attempt to replace the old Scholastic canon established during the colonial period. In so far as Condillac's logic opened the door to a new approach to inquiry that was not enclosed in the rigid hylomorphic metaphysics and syllogistic logic of the Scholastic canon, one can say that for these professors his philosophy had an emancipatory potential: it permitted them to search for those philosophical subject matters that really interested them. This interest embraced not only Condillac's explanation of the formation, expression, and composition of ideas and mental faculties but also many ethical, political, and even theological matters. Moreover, in so far as Condillac's followers, the *idéologues*, were defenders of the revolutionary ideas that circulated in the first decades of the postcolonial period, Condillac's philosophy also endowed them with an emancipatory political connotation.

Despite divergences and criticisms, they accepted—to a different extent—Condillac's central ideas on analytic method and the explanation of the origin of ideas and mental faculties. The professors also pointed to an antagonism between Condillac and Cartesianism regarding the origin of ideas (Lafinur, Agüero, and De la Peña) and method (Alcorta). However, Lafinur and Agüero—drawing on Tracy—unified Bacon's and Descartes' legacies, which were seen as antecedent to Condillac's philosophy. Laromiguière continued this unifying interpretation—albeit for different reasons—and so did De la Peña, who focused on the origin of mental faculties.

The discussion in this chapter has thus shown that Ingenieros's early twentieth-century narrative of the reception of Condillac in the "*idéologie* period" was wrong in two important points. First, his claim that Condillac was the most important philosopher in the reception of French philosophy in Buenos Aires during this period in some respect overestimates the true place of Condillac in the philosophical canon. On the one hand, it is true that the professors of *idéologie* agreed that the method of Condillac was best suited to philosophy and science and should replace the Scholastic logic that was taught at the time in the Colegio. Condillac was thereby considered the leading figure of logic and method. However, on the other hand, regarding the other specific philosophical question here analyzed—the origin of ideas—Bacon, Locke, Descartes, Tracy, Cabanis, and Laromiguiére were seen as equally central figures as Condillac, while their doctrines were critically addressed. In this sense, these philosophers *along with Condillac* constitute an alternative philosophical canon in the attempt to replace the Scholastic one, whose main figures were Aristotle, Aquinas, and Suárez. Second, Ingenieros's claim that the reception of European philosophy took "two antagonistic directions"—the Cartesian and the Condillacian—is exaggerated as well. For it overemphasizes the antagonism between both currents of thought, given that there were several attempts to unify them. As we have shown, the reason why Ingenieros exaggerated the importance of Condillac and his antagonism to Cartesianism is related to his strong scientistic convictions that fueled his intellectual and political agenda.

Ingenieros defended the existence of what he called a "historical homology" (*homología histórica*), that is, a parallel between the series of major events unfolding in Europe and Argentina, and other young nations (Ingenieros 1920a, 19; Degiovanni 2019, 79–81). He believed that ideas inform and support historical facts, and that Argentinian ideas replicate—with some delay—ideological schemes from Spain or France. According to this homology, European ideas become gradually integrated into the Argentinian mentality, which receives them, but at the same time adds its own mark. For this historic-ideological parallelism to work, it is required that nations be part of the same civilization so that the particularity of each can integrate into the universal pattern that links and transcends them all.

From such a perspective, Ingenieros argues that in the historical period, extending from the mid-seventeenth to the mid-nineteenth century, one observes a historical homology between France and Argentina consisting in a sequence of conservatism, revolution, and restoration. This sequence must not be seen as if each moment of the cycle were completely uniform. Although one political force and ideological system prevailed at each moment, there were others competing with it. In France this cycle manifested at the level of ideas and politics as follows: Cartesianism/*ancient régime*; Encyclopedy (including Condillac's philosophy) and *idéologie*/political revolution; Cousinian school (return to Cartesianism)/monarchic restoration. In turn, there was a similar historical sequence in Argentina: the conservative moment belongs to the Spanish colonial dominion in which Scholasticism dominated the academic life; the revolutionary moment corresponded to the independentist movement which coincided with the Encyclopedy, Condillac, and the *idéologie*; finally, the political regime of Juan Manuel de Rosas (1793–1877), known as the "Restorer of laws," belongs to the restoration stage and coincides with the return to Scholasticism.

Each country, claims Ingenieros, "restored" what it had previously experienced: "while the eclectics [i.e. the Cousinian school]—after the Bourbon restoration—returned France to the predominance of the Cartesian tradition, in Argentina the Jesuits were called in to restore the Spanish-colonial Scholasticism." Although Ingenieros's narrative places Cartesianism and Scholasticism in the conservative side of the cycle, Ingenieros admits that "Descartes was not Suárez" (Ingenieros 1918a, 433). That is, historical homology does not entail historical identity. One can infer from Ingenieros' account that the value of different philosophies is relative and must be weighed in their historical, cultural, and political context. Perhaps he would agree, for example, that, on the one hand, Descartes and his followers could be considered revolutionary as compared to medieval Scholasticism in the French context, but, on the other hand, they would be considered as conservatives when compared to empiricism and sensualism.

Ingenieros believes that throughout history, cultural hegemony was never anchored in the same nation, but was ever changing. With great confidence, he states that his time is the time of America, whose young civilizations are in a position to give "new senses," new approaches to philosophical problems. In North America, he tells us, the philosophy of the United States stands out already; in South America, Argentinian philosophical thinking is in the ascendency (Ingenieros 1914, 261–264; Galfione 2015). It is noteworthy that this optimistic announcement suggests something else than the mere replication and integration of Europe into America. This prospect of the new cultural hegemony located on American soil seems to entail that European ideas are not merely replicated but rather transformed and re-signified by the new languages spoken by the culturally most outstanding younger nations.

All of this reveals two different receptions of Condillac's philosophy in Argentina. The reception by the professors of *idéologie*, in the nineteenth century, was related to the desire to establish a new philosophical canon that superseded the Scholastic inheritance and aligned with the rational and physiological approach of the *ideologists* during the early decades of the independent nation. Despite the opposition they faced, they won the battle and managed to abolish the Scholastic canon. Indeed, in most Argentinian public universities, Scholasticism has not constituted the basis of the philosophy curriculum since this change. However, in some universities, especially under the military regime that extended between 1976 and 1983, Thomism occasionally recuperated part of the hegemony it had.

The reception by Ingenieros, in the early twentieth century, added to the nineteenth-century reception the insertion of Condillac into a genealogy that begins with Francis Bacon and ends in positivism and so expanded the canon in which Condillac takes part. This *terminus ad quem* of this canon marked the agenda that should inform the modernization of Argentina during his time, under the auspices of the latest advancements of science. Since the 1920s or 1930s the positivist canon was replaced by others, first by spiritualist philosophies and later by Neokantianism. It was always European philosophy that remained the main star of the philosophical canon taught in Argentina. Ingenieros thought that Argentina was going to be an *avant-garde* focus irradiating intellectual and scientific progress from South America to the rest of the world. However, his dream—which was the dream of many of his generation—did not come true.

Notes

1 For a survey of the intellectual career of Ingenieros, see Plotkin (2021).
2 All translations of Spanish texts are mine.
3 For a short survey of the wider intellectual and political context, see Halperin Donghi 2015, 19–65.
4 In talking of the "eclectic sect" he refers to Potamon of Alexandria (death in the year 14 of the Christian era) (Chiaramonte 2007: 126; Torchia Estrada 2012).
5 This brief description of the *idéologie* does not intend to consider the historical context nor the many complexities and varieties within this movement. Picavet (1891) and Gusdorf (1974) provide a wider survey.

6 Given that the institution changed its name three times across of the period studied in this chapter, hereafter, I will refer to it simply as the Colegio.
7 Ingenieros does not mention De la Peña. His work remained almost unknown for a long time until, in 2006, his philosophy lessons were published.
8 For a survey of Cabanis and his criticism of Condillac, see Gusdorf (1974, 293–300).
9 I have lightly modified the English translation.
10 As we have seen above, Condillac invoked the Peripatetics and Bacon as antecedents of Locke.
11 On Laromiguière's notion of attention and its differences with Condillac, see Pierre Broulliet's chapter in this book.
12 For an interesting new reading of the activity and passivity of the mind in Condillac's *corpus* which connects him with vitalist materialism, see Dunham (2019).
13 On Pinel and Condillac, see Samuel Léze's chapter in this book.
14 For different interpretations concerning dualism and materialism in Condillac, see Aroux (1992), Bardout (2017), and Dunham (2019).

References

Alcorta, D. (1990). *Disertación sobre la manía aguda*. In: Stagnaro, J.C. op. cit., 60–83.
Alcorta, D. (2000). *Lecciones de Filosofía*. Prologado por Paul Groussac. Introducción por Santiago Kovadloff. Buenos Aires: Fondo Nacional de las Artes.
Auroux, S. (1992). "Condillac, inventeur d'un nouveau matérialisme." *Dix-huitième Siècle* 24: 153–163.
Bardout, J.-Ch. (2017). "Le corps du moi. Remarques sur le *Traité des sensations*." *Les Études philosophiques* 123: 531–554.
Cabanis, J. G. (1802). *Rapports du physique et du morale de l'homme*, vol. 1. Paris: Crapelett.
Carozzi, S. (2011). *Las filosofías de la revolución. Mariano Moreno y los jacobinos rioplatenses en la prensa de Mayo (1810–1815)*. Buenos Aires: Prometeo.
Charrak, A. (2003). *Empirisme et métaphysique: l'Essai sur l'origine des connaissances humaines de Condillac*. Paris: Vrin.
Chiaramonte, J. C. (2007). *La Ilustración en el Río de la Plata: Cultura eclesiástica y cultura laica durante el Virreinato*. Buenos Aires: Sudamericana.
Condillac, É. B. de (1982). *Philosophical Writings*. Volume 1. Translated by Franklin Philip and Harlane Lane. Sussex: Lawrence Erlbaum
Condillac, É. B. de (2001). *Essay on the Origin of Human Knowledge*. Cambridge: Cambridge University Press.
Condillac, É. B. de (2012). *Philosophical Writings*. Volume 2. Translated by Franklin Philip. New York: Routledge. First ed. (1987) Mahwah, NJ: Lawrence Erlbaum.
Cornejo, J. N., and Santilli, H. (2013). "La influencia de Condillac en la enseñanza de las ciencias en la Ciudad de Buenos Aires (1810–1830)." *Historia de la educación-anuario* 14: 21–42.
De la Peña, L. J. (2006). *Lecciones de filosofía*. Prólogo de Clara Alicia Jalif de Bertranou. Mendoza: Qellqasqa; Ediciones Biblioteca Digital UNCuyo. https://bdigital.uncu.edu.ar/5735.

Degiovanni, F. (2019). "Un breviario de moral cívica: José Ingenieros y La evolución de las ideas argentinas." In: *La Argentina como problema: Temas, visiones y pasiones del siglo XX*, edited by C. Altamirano and A. Gorelik, 69–83. Buenos Aires: Siglo XXI.
Di Pasquale, M. (2011). "La recepción de la *Idéologie* en la Universidad de Buenos Aires: el caso de Juan Manuel Fernández de Agüero (1821–1827)." *Prismas* 15: 63–86.
Di Pasquale, M. (2012). "La recepción de la *Idéologie* y su impacto en la educación médica porteña, 1821–1840." *Revista de Historia de la Medicina y Epistemología Médica* 4: 1–20.
Di Pasquale, M. (2014). "Diego Alcorta y la difusión de saberes médicos en Buenos Aires, 1821–1842." *Dynamis* 34: 125–146.
Di Pasquale, M. (2015). "Vitalismo, idéologie y fisiología en Buenos Aires. La polémica entre Cosme Argerich y Crisóstomo Lafinur en El Americano, 1819." *Revista de Ciencias de la Salud* 13: 13–28.
Dotti, J. (1992). *La letra gótica: Recepción de Kant en Argentina, desde el Romanticismo hasta el treinta*. Buenos Aires: Facultad de Filosofía y Letras, UBA.
Dunham, J. (2019). "Habits of Mind a Brand New Condillac." *Journal of Modern Philosophy* 1: 1–18.
Fernández de Agüero, J. M. (1940). *Principios de ideología elemental, abstractiva y oratoria*. Edited by J. R. Zamudio Silva. Buenos Aires: Universidad de Buenos Aires.
Galfione, M. C. (2015). "Filosofía y literatura en el Centenario: caminos con dirección inversa." *Andamios* 12: 11–31.
Gallo, K. (2014). "El exilio forzado de un *idéologue* rioplatense. El pensamiento republicano de Lafinur y sus traumas." *Estudios de Teoría Literaria-Revista digital: artes, letras y humanidades* 3: 187–200.
Ghirardi, O. A. (2004). "La lógica en Alberdi." *Cuadernos de Historia* (Academia Nacional de Derecho y Ciencias Sociales de Córdoba, Instituto de Historia del Derecho y de las Ideas Políticas "Roberto I. Peña") 15–24.
Greif, E. A. (2019). "Edición de la *Disertación sobre la manía aguda* (1827) del médico Diego Alcorta." *História, Ciências, Saúde—Manguinhos, Río de Janeiro* 26: 1027–1037.
Groussac, P. (2000). "El Dr. Don Diego Alcorta." In: *Lecciones de Filosofía*, D. Alcorta, 13–32, op. cit. First ed. Groussac, P. (1918). *Estudios De Historia Argentina*. Buenos Aires: Jesús Menéndez.
Gusdorf, G. (1974). *Introduction aux sciences humaines. Essai critique sur leurs origins et leur développement*, Nouvelle edition. Paris: Les Éditions Ophrys.
Gutiérrez, J. M. (1868). *Noticias históricas sobre el oríjen [sic] y desarrollo de la enseñanza superior en Buenos Aires [...]*. Buenos Aires: Imprenta del Siglo de J. M. Cantillo.
Halperin Donghi, T. (2015). *Las tormentas del mundo en el Río de la Plata. Cómo pensaron su época los intelectuales del siglo XX*, Buenos Aires: Siglo XXI.
Head, B. (1985). *Ideology and social science: Destutt de Tracy and French Liberalism*. Dordrecht: M. Nijhoff.
Ingenieros, J. (1914). "Direcciones de la cultura filosófica argentina." *Revista de la Universidad de Buenos Aires* 27: 261–300; 372–412.

Ingenieros, J. (1918a). *La evolución de las ideas argentinas*, vol. 1. Buenos Aires: Rosso.
Ingenieros, J. (1918b). *Proposiciones relativas al porvenir de la filosofía*. Buenos Aires: Rosso.
Ingenieros, J. (1920a). *La evolución de las ideas argentinas*, vol. 2. Buenos Aires: Rosso.
Ingenieros, J. (1920b). *La locura en Argentina*. Buenos Aires: Compañía editorial limitada.
Jalif de Bertranou, C. (2006). "Prólogo." In: De la Peña, L. J., *Lecciones de filosofía*, 15–48, op. cit.
Jiménez García, A. (1990). "Las traducciones de Condillac y el desarrollo del sensismo en España." In: *Actas del VI Seminario de Historia de la Filosofía Española e Iberoamericana: Salamanca, del 26 al 30 de septiembre de 1988*, edited by A. Heredia Soriano, 253–281. Salamanca: Ediciones Universidad de Salamanca.
Korn, A. (1940). *Las influencias filosóficas en nuestra evolución nacional*. In: A. Korn, *Obras*, vol. 3. La Plata: Universidad Nacional de La Plata.
Lafinur, J. C. (2015). *Curso filosófico*. Edición facsimilar. Estudio preliminar por Pablo Vialatte. Buenos Aires: Biblioteca Nacional.
Laromiguière, P. (1815). *Leçons de philosophie, ou essai sur les facultés de l'ame*, vol. 1. Paris: Brunot-Labbe.
Picavet, F. (1891). *Les idéologues: Essai sur l'histoire des idées et des théories scientifiques, philosophiques, religieuses etc. en France depuis 1789*. Paris: Alcan.
Plotkin, M. (2016). "José Ingenieros, *El Hombre Mediocre*, and Social Integration in Turn-of-the-20th-Century Argentina." In: *Oxford Research Encyclopedia of Latin American History*. https://oxfordre.com/latinamericanhistory/view/10.1093/acrefore/9780199366439.001.0001/acrefore-9780199366439-e-346, last accessed 5 April 2021.
Plotkin, M. (2021). *José Ingenieros. El hombre que lo quería todo*. Buenos Aires: Edhasa.
Stagnaro, J. C. (1990). "Diego Alcorta y la manía aguda: preliminares de la psiquiatría en la Argentina." *Vertex, Revista Argentina de Psiquiatría* 1: 57–63.
Staum, M. S. (1980). *Cabanis: Enlightenment and Medical Philosophy in the French Revolution*. Princeton, NJ: Princeton University Press.
Terán, O. (1986). *José Ingenieros: Pensar la nación. Antología de textos*. Buenos Aires: Alianza.
Torchia Estrada, J. C. (1967). "Tres pensadores en la vida intelectual Argentina: Ingenieros, Korn, Romero." *Journal of Inter-American Studies* 9: 248–272.
Torchia Estrada, J. C. (2012). "Juan Baltasar Maziel y su contribución a la enseñanza de la filosofía en el Río de la Plata." *Cuyo. Anuario de filosofía argentina y americana* 28: 193–228.
Tracy, D. de (1805). *Elements d'idéologie. Troisième Partie. Logique*. Paris: Courcier.
Varela Domínguez de Ghioldi, D. (1938). *Filosofía Argentina. Los Ideólogos*. Buenos Aires: La Vanguardia.
Waldow, A. (2021). "Condillac on Being Human: Language and Reflection Reconsidered." *European Journal of Philosophy* 2: 504–519.

Weinberg, G. (1997). *Ilustración y educación superior en Hispanoamérica siglo XVIII*. Buenos Aires: Academia Nacional de Educación.
Zamudio Silva, J. (1940). *Juan Manuel Fernández de Agüero. Primer profesor de filosofía de la Universidad de Buenos Aires*. Buenos Aires: Universidad de Buenos Aires, Facultad de Filosofía y Letras, Instituto de Filosofía.

Part IV
Contemporary Receptions

13 Time, Order and the Concept of a Human Interior
Paths towards Condillac

Christopher Goodey

1 Introduction

Psychology is one historical subset of a broader enquiry with a much longer past than its own existence as a formal discipline: namely what are the questions that people ask each other, about each other? And, in a more peculiarly modern way of putting it, how do the individual's abilities relate to their goals and eventual destinies? The positing and study of a human nature and the very possibility of such a thing as "human sciences" form one historically specific phase in the framing of such questions. I examine here how the 100 years leading up to Condillac dealt with such matters, and finish with an account of how they relate to his work on psychology and education.

I see the influences on Condillac in the century prior to his flourishing not as the historian of philosophy might see them, as a matter of doctrine and belief to be debated at some more or less explicit level, but rather as what the philosopher of history might term that era's "absolute presuppositions,"[1] that is to say, things about which it would not occur to contemporaries to ask questions in the first place. The nature and very existence of "abilities" might be counted among them. Condillac was the receptor of a whole set of presuppositions about human interiority, scarcely perceptible to himself. They had religious sources, and as such, they are necessary to his role as a participant in the more or less seamless transition from an expressly religious to a quasi-secular psychologistic framing of human interiority, a transition that was both a de- and a re-sacralization. My question then is, what is it that would enable us to position Condillac along the uninterrupted historical course that runs from a Christian interiority to a psychological one?

The period from roughly 1650 to 1750 was crucial to the early modern transition from a spatial ordering of the universe to a temporal one. "The temporalizing of the Chain of Being" was already noted by Arthur Lovejoy 80 years ago.[2] Since then, there has been little detailed investigation as to the what and the how of this transition. And in any case Lovejoy himself saw temporalization as a breaking up of the Chain rather than (as I would argue) its continuation in modern human-science forms.

My chief example here is the concept of development,[3] whose history has to do with the history of religious thought, and, in one and the same respect, with the history of psychology as a scientific discipline. In today's developmental psychology, the newly born human creature finds itself positioned at point zero of a timeline. At the other end of this timeline is a goal: namely the future adult in whom ideal types of emotional maturity, normal intelligence and moral competence indicative of a "human nature" are embodied. Moreover, the timeline exhibits set stages leading towards this goal: precise dates when the developer should stop doing this and start doing that.

The conceptual origins of development can be located within relatively recent recorded history. It coincides with the start of monotheism. The developmental idea imputes to human individuals a permanent interiority, described by linear time, structured by stages and tending towards a uniform final goal. And then from the sixteenth century onwards, a further item is added: that is, an obsessive anxiety about the *causes* of one's interior status and interior condition. Originally this referred to divine causes, but the obsession continues today over genetic causes. The very transfer of this determinism from the divine to the biological is itself just one event in the longer history of the relationship between human interiority and time.

It is the interdependence of that handful of principles, and not any one of them taken separately, that reveals the historicity of the developmental idea. For our purposes here, however, I will initially lay them out one by one.

First of all, time. "Development" is only one of the possible ways of conceptualizing a deeper-lying metaphysic, that of *change*. Change does not have to be developmental. It could be, and once was, seen otherwise: as cyclical, or arc-shaped, or as an unfolding of some already existing potentiality. These other ways of representing change can still be found in various present-day cultures, as well as in certain corners of the life sciences. Pagan contemporaries of the first Christian intellectuals had seen human time as cyclical, modelling it on exterior events such as the return of the planets. By contrast, the second-century church father Irenaeus insisted that the human being's time on earth has a linear trajectory, aimed at a successful "recapitulation" of Adam's failed one (this term is familiar in modern psychology too).[4] Augustine would subsequently oppose pagan cyclical notions, replacing them with the idea of time as an irreversible arrow; for him, time had no objective existence other than as the linear "distention" of *homo interior*, by which he meant its inevitable deviation from the goal of being with God.[5]

Time, Order and the Concept of a Human Interior 217

The second historically derived principle is that of interiority itself, premised on the division between an exterior and an interior human being. This interiority is a permanent and (directly or indirectly) observable entity. In pre-monotheistic contexts, interiority was a temporary visitation or possession: intermittent, revocable and hypothesized rather than observed. The notion of interiority brought with it corresponding and more divisive forms of status, in which a permanence of certain absolute conditions lay in some human individuals and not in others.

Third is structure. Early medieval writers proposed six ages of man (sometimes seven, sometimes four), which gave the human timeline a fixed structure marked off by stages. These stages became increasingly determinate in the early modern era. They came with sharp debate about the mechanisms by which God's gift of grace arrives inside the human individual, i.e. not the natural grace due to everyone but the kind of grace that was additionally necessary if you were to be saved. Crucial to these debates was an unsureness about whether this saving grace arrives gradually or on a single occasion and instantaneously. Gradualism won out, but only by incorporating a certain *stadial* determinism, a quasi-mechanistic account of interior change through stages. The mechanism exists within the individual soul or mind, but it is also ultimately dependent on pre-natal determination by external forces (whether divine or biological). An inner life is fixed by the chronological appropriateness of predictable periods.

As for the goal itself, this end-point was initially redemption, the means to salvation. Redemption gave access to a realm which Christian iconography represents spatially, above the earth, but which we have come to speak of not so much as the "above life" but as the afterlife. This situating of heavenly perfection in the dimension of time would be the eventual access point for the idea of earthly perfectibility through progress. And transition, not transformation, is the right word here: the philosophy of the eighteenth century did not undergo an abrupt abandonment of faith for an atheism which did not yet exist in any ready-made form.

Finally comes that anxiety about causes, added to the picture only later. The primary explanatory framework of medieval psychology and medicine was a theory of signs, but in the early modern era it gave way to one based on origins instead. During the sixteenth century, the model of a structured interior growth over linear time was being reinforced by a personal anxiety about one's final salvation or damnation. This fixed attention on what had happened at or before the beginning of one's personal timeline. People were desperate to know exactly how that bifurcation in human destinies had come about. The sixteenth-century's revival of Augustine had brought to light his previously esoteric ideas on the so-called predestination of souls. The elect were that small minority of humans whom God had chosen to be saved, as distinct from the mass of reprobates who remain

218 *Christopher Goodey*

damned and who can do nothing by themselves to change their destiny. God had determined which individuals were in which category, either before the beginning of time or no later than the moment of birth.

2   How the Elect Started to Become the Normal

This template of a permanent interiority structured by linear time and oriented towards a uniform goal went on to accommodate two major conceptual events. The first event was what I call "the normalization of the elect," by which I mean the expansion of the seventeenth century's elect minority into the normal majority of the mid-nineteenth century and thereafter. This involved a shift in the principal descriptors of interiority from religious to psychological, while simultaneously maintaining the necessity for an absolute distinction between two fundamental human groups, marked by presence and absence. The notion of personal change transitioned from the acquisition of saving grace and faith, to a supposedly secular acquisition of things like maturity and intelligence.

The reason why this was a mere transition rather than a transformation is that grace and intelligence are comparable, even similar entities. They are both what I have elsewhere defined, in sociological terms, as "modal" concepts.[6] By this I mean that both are general headings that group together interior characteristics whose definition is limitlessly variable because they are impalpable. They are modal in the sense that they channel these characteristics aspirationally towards the seemingly palpable personal status which those headings denote.

As regards the *absence* of status, just as the elect would become the (normal) majority, the previous reprobate majority would reduce to a pathological and abnormal minority. In the emerging view of writers such as Leibniz, Hell became an interior suffering of the soul alone rather than of the body (*pace* Voltaire Leibniz thought earthquakes were a minor test of God's justice in comparison with this suffering of souls in Hell and the sheer numbers of them).[7] This was the precondition for the interior status of reprobates to resurface as that of the "idiots" and "imbeciles" in nineteenth-century medical terminology, whom we now term "developmentally delayed."

To understand the normalization of the elect, we need to discard the assumption that development is a natural kind and to think instead about both the elect and, subsequently, the normal in terms of how they express the idea of individual human change over linear time. Predestination raised one particularly important debate, whose opposing sides transcended the formal schism between Roman and Protestant churches. On one side were those who saw God mainly as all-powerful: so powerful that he does not need to have excuses made for him, for example, when he preordains the

Time, Order and the Concept of a Human Interior 219

majority of people to Hell without their being able to do anything about it. On the other side were those who saw mainly an all-loving God who therefore did have to be defended against the accusation of harshness. Their defence consisted in claiming that God does not directly condemn reprobates to Hell, he merely knows in advance that they are going to resist his offer of saving grace.

It is important to grasp that both sides were predestinarian. It is simply that the first group—Calvinists, Jansenists and others—saw no problem in telling everyone all about God's severity, whereas the second group—(Catholic) Molinists and Jesuits, (Protestant) Arminians—thought that if there was public denial of any role for human agency, the reprobate masses might see no point in good behaviour. True, this second group did try to allocate a secondary place to free will, but a mountain of contemporary texts shows us how fragile this effort was. In the end, the idea that you could be rewarded for your efforts in this life was a *veritas vulgaris*, i.e. not really veritas at all, merely a pabulum for mass consumption; blind predestination remained the *veritas arcana*, the esoteric but harsh truth which theologians and preachers alone were tough enough to handle.

This dispute ran in close parallel with another one, between single and double predestination. According to double predestinarians, election and reprobation were opposite and equal: God determines both who is saved and who is damned. However, most theologians were single predestinarians; that God has determined salvation for some but Hell for the rest is merely a secondary consequence of this. Both single and double predestination shared one important assumption. Reprobation, whose cause lay outside of time, marked every human being without exception at birth. It was just that God had revoked the reprobate status of a small handful of individuals by pardoning their innate sin, while everyone else's souls remained stuck in their original condition.

This meant not only that they were damned but also, by the same token, that temporal descriptors did not apply to them. Their interior condition—though they could scarcely be said to possess any kind of interiority at all—was static. They simply did not change. The elect did. They changed precisely in being pulled by God's gift of faith out of their initially reprobate status. However, their election was confirmed on this earth only by degrees, by determinate stages in a determinate order: regeneration (the call to a new life), then justification (excusal from the reprobate condition) and then sanctification (the permanent guarantee of the first two).

Nevertheless, the possibility of human agency within this largely determinate system refused to go away. Many Calvinists of that period and at least one Jansenist fellow-traveller, Blaise Pascal, divided man's status not into a rigid binary of the saved and the damned, but implicitly into three. Pascal identifies people who have found God and attempt to serve him;

people who have not found God and have never searched for him; and people who have not found God but who persevere in searching for him.[8] And broadly, it was this last category that would expand in numbers over the course of the eighteenth century to become a notional majority. The sense that you yourself belonged in that fragile but hopeful category was instrumental in turning the elect into the normal, through the religious notion of "perseverance." For example, it played a huge role in the schooling of children.

This third category was an outcome of single predestination. When an eighteenth-century writer expressly rejects predestination, they are often only rejecting double predestination. Single predestination effectively opened the door for people to become searchers and hopers, and thus—albeit only later in the century—for imputing a degree of genuine agency to the majority of individuals. As for reprobation, emerging developmentalist concepts would simply omit it from their explanatory frameworks; it was neglected (and then channelled into the asylums) rather than repudiated.

For the century between Pascal and Rousseau, a distinction must be drawn between doctrine, belief and presupposition. The concept of a predestined election certainly had an abundance of doctrinaires and believers, but above all it had presupposers. It had anxious presupposers like Pascal and Leibniz. It had discreet presupposers like Malebranche. It had presupposers who tried to negotiate its terms, like Pierre Nicole. And it had writers who, despite their reputation for abandoning the whole farrago for a more modern psychology, never quite managed to free themselves of its implications; for example, Locke, Montesquieu and Rousseau.

In Pascal's case, an awareness of time as linear was intrinsic to his thought. To take just one example, he insists that grace, once it has arrived, must nevertheless continually involve movement. Forward movement is the essential function of resistance to the Devil. Jansenists believed even the elect could lapse, even after sanctification. Pascal shares this anxiety. He searches for a "counterweight," *un contrepoids*, that will push back against the Devil's continuing advances.[9] Within the individual, grace acts as the continuous forward process of "eradicating error."

This counter-movement is not itself a subjective ability or act of free will. Nevertheless, it exists within the human subject as a kind of externally implanted causal mechanism in its own right—a sort of a heart pacemaker for the soul. It exists at least in those to whom election is imputed. This counter-movement does not have the ultimate power to direct itself, because it is subordinate to the master mechanism of the external divine will; it is unfree, but also maintains some distance from the latter. Remembering here that Pascal seems to have intended to make "Order" his opening header for the *Pensées*, we can say that he saw *forward movement* as the essential operation of *order* within the human interior.

Election had to carry some sort of guarantee. Even if there were only a hypothetical possibility that everyone might lapse, there would have been no point in the Creation and no role for a Christian redeemer. So if even the sanctification of the elect cannot actually confirm their salvation, then its location must lie elsewhere because there must be a guarantee. For Pascal this elsewhere was whatever constituted resistance or opposition to lapse. He describes its trajectory as *"itus et reditus"*: three steps forward, two steps back—though often (with his typical existential anxiety) the other way around.[10]

Malebranche rarely mentions the predestination disputes. But the cause of this reluctance may have partly been the pacificism of the Oratorian Order to which he belonged; he wanted to avoid the bitterness of the previous generation's debates. Nevertheless, when Malebranche mentions interior change, he assumes that his readers know whose interior he is talking about, and it clearly indicates an exclusive group. Malebranche was not stuck in the Augustinian mud. He played a major role, alongside Pierre Bayle, in the merger between nature and grace, which would one day help to bring grace down to earth and to resacralize it for modern psychology as a set of normal natural abilities. However, this did not mean that he had abandoned the underlying presupposition, derived ultimately from those Augustinian roots, that there must always be a fundamental divide between two basic human groups defined by their interior status and characteristics or the lack thereof.

Notions of interior change, which by definition cannot apply to the non-elect individual who is "hardened" and thus unchangeable, are evident in Malebranche's special interest in children. It is "necessary to the formation of the foetus" that some sort of communication occurs between the mother's material brain and the child's material brain.[11] It means, he says, that no child can be born innocent. The initial communication occurs via the mother's concupiscent body; innocence would imply that the communication had somehow been "suspended," an event that could only have occurred with the immaculately conceived Jesus.

This inevitability of the parental sexual act makes all children to be born reprobate. Children, he says here, are "in a state of disorder," so that God, "who loves Order"—and Order is the supreme principle for Malebranche—"hates the child." The fleshly communication between mother and child "has to be excused [*justifié*], in order to remove God's conduct from all reproach." The onus in this explanation therefore lies on what must occur in the child's interior later to show that despite God's "hatred," the child has been chosen. The change occurs "in spite of themselves," that is to say, in spite of having arrived on earth via a carnal relationship. Change can only occur in such a way as to prove God's conformity with Order: and that way lies over time. Such passages can only be understood if we know that it is the elect child alone whom he is talking about.

John Locke is a further example. On the single occasion where he confronts predestination directly, he does not repudiate it. He merely claims to be unable to know about it with any certainty.[12] In the *Essay Concerning Human Understanding*, we see that the fundamental division between elect and reprobate gives way to an apparently different one, between what he calls "the moral man," capable of acquiring reason empirically, and those he calls "idiots," unable to do so. This could be mistaken for a modern-type psychological categorization. Yet much of the shift from that earlier, religious binary to the later one is merely terminological. Locke had grown up in a strict Calvinist household. The descriptive characteristics he applies to idiots are drawn almost verbatim from the writings of earlier Calvinist preachers referring to reprobation. Idiots and reprobates, he says, belong to one and the same category of human being: the category of those who are "totally determined."[13]

As for Montesquieu, when he attacked predestination, he was attacking the doctrine, the "dogma" as he calls it, but not exactly the underlying belief. His point was that if you believe your fate in the afterlife is arbitrary, this will lead to mental "laziness": this leaves you vulnerable, if not to the Devil, then at least to arbitrary political despotism.[14] However, in writings not subject to the censors, he considers election to be a possibility: it is a "rare" instance of God depriving us of our freedom. "Those who are predestined are saved. But it does not follow that all those who are not predestined, are damned."[15] There is a strong echo of single predestination here.

Montesquieu seems not to have attempted to apply his concept of law-governed natural causation to the ordinary psychological realm, and so it is not clear how such an attempt would have fit with that older Augustinian principle which selects certain people out of the ranks of the *massa damnata*. The section of Montesquieu's *Pensées* where predestination features is entitled "Doubts." But his doubts are clearly less about election as such than about where election might stand in the wider order of things. The saved are now a mere subset within a larger set, namely the set of all things which are determined. And so now, to be elect means to belong to a natural order: that is to say, the more general order of the naturally determined. In other words, he supplies a framework into which biological causes might one day enter.

Then we have Rousseau, brought up in Calvinist Geneva. In his *Confessions* he recalls his anxiety as a young man about whether he was saved or not.[16] *Julie* features an explicit repudiation of predestinarian doctrine, albeit ventriloquized through the character of Wolmar.[17] But there are also some slightly more ambiguous references. When elsewhere Rousseau rejects predestination on the grounds that a loving God would not condemn his own creatures to Hell, this sentimental explanation remains the same one that had motivated single predestinarians.[18]

The big difference now is the new, accommodating relationship between grace and nature, and the increase in the number of people on the favoured side of the intra-human divide. Rousseau has not discarded the underlying requirement for such a divide. The most pertinent example occurs in *Emile*. Here, he describes the ideal education, derived from nature, that would constitute what he calls *l'homme abstrait*.[19] However, this abstraction is no longer a scholastic-type universal: in the very same text we find him announcing that there are exceptions. There are the poor, for example. They do not need education, since it is irrelevant to their social role. Likewise very young children, he says, are "born stupid," akin to "imbeciles."[20] As human beings, they are incomplete. And so, as with Locke, the strict intra-human division implicit in election and reprobation is sustained, even as its descriptors become those of universal man in nature rather than in the realm of grace.

As a divisive presupposition behind the descriptive template, whatever was said about grace in the seventeenth century was re-said about nature in the eighteenth century. Nature—human nature in its "interior" aspect, and its various subdivisions and categories—is (to adapt Clausewitz's famous formula) the continuation of grace by other means. In the history of ideas and especially of psychological ideas, a repudiation is rarely a wholesale abandonment.

Finally, on this issue of the normalization of the elect, the concept of election somehow survived the birth of biological determinism, to which it had in any case contributed. The important author here is David Hartley. His work on the association of ideas, *Observations on Man, His Frame, His Duty, and His Expectations*, was published within three years of Condillac's *Essai sur l'origine des connaissances humaines* and is often cited by historians of psychology in a similar context to Condillac as an approach to the discipline that was not only empirical but also, if not fully materialist, certainly accessible to physiological and sensationalist explanations. And although Hartley spends a lot of effort sketching the possibility for a sort of neuroscience, he nevertheless still sees the physiological factors as secondary to the larger framework of first causes, that is, divine ones. What after all are those "expectations" of the book's subtitle, other than those of an afterlife?

These first causes appear in his conclusion, where he distinguishes the chosen, such as himself, from the reprobate mass. These latter are by now defined socially: a feral mob, whose threatening behaviour represents the social chaos believed to be a sign of Christ's imminent return to earth. Hartley's theory of a physiological causation of psychological events is a supplement to this deeper-rooted anxiety (which in this text verges on hysteria). Moreover, his accommodation between the two types of cause, divine and biological, unites two things which predestination theory had previously held largely separate—one being God's determination of souls or minds, the other the determination of events in the physical realm, in this case physiological ones.

3 The Beginnings of a Developmental Theory

The second major event in our conceptual history was the emergence of an actual developmental *theory*. This was drawn from existing theories of physical growth. Unlike (say) the association of ideas, it was not a concerted intellectual project. Nevertheless, most of the texts mentioned below were published around the same time and were accessible to contemporaries. It gives us some indication as to how the mind sciences took their modern, albeit historically contingent form: a process in which Condillac would play a major role.

Physical growth, in the decades around 1700, had three possible explanations: epigenesis, spontaneous generation, and preformation. In epigenesis, the living creature grows by gradual differentiation from initially undifferentiated matter supplied by parents; change is therefore smoothly continuous. In spontaneous generation, life can spring from non-living matter; for example, flies and maggots are generated directly from excrement. Preformation opposed both of these theories on religious grounds. In 1669 the Dutch experimental biologist Jan Swammerdam had first observed the preformed stages of caterpillar and chrysalis inside the butterfly. Spontaneous generation was surely atheistic because it seemed to operate by mere chance, whereas a world ruled by God had to have order; he made the same accusation against epigenesis, whose unproblematic gradualism lacked any sense of the structured order appropriate to a divine Creator. Swammerdam's own discovery of preformation in biological nature was itself, he tried to suggest, the actual historical fulfilment of the opening of the seven seals predicted in Book of Revelation.[21]

Swammerdam was endorsed by Malebranche, whose own experiments with tulip bulbs revealed the presence of the tulip flower inside them. But Malebranche, unlike his Dutch predecessor, also gave preformation an outline theoretical framework. That was because he was interested above all in the metaphysics of change and only secondarily in its biological expression. If, as Malebranche believed, nature has general laws, this must surely include general laws of growth. Malebranche wondered how such laws might operate in the case of the human being. His answer was that all our physical "parts" pre-exist; they have all been in place since the Creation, but simply "boxed up" (*emboîtés*). So, these parts simply need to "unfold."[22] The word here is *se développer*, although the emphasis is as much on their initial state as on their goal, so that the sense communicated is equally close to that of *se dérouler*, which he does not use here.

Malebranche's sense of "unfolding" created a window of opportunity in which an analogy might be drawn from bodily to psychological change. And the burglar who climbed in through this window was Leibniz. In his *Theodicy* he explicitly cites preformation in order to propose that in all of us, "those souls which one day shall be human souls ... have been in our progenitors as far back as Adam."[23] Leibniz stated here, moreover, that it was exactly this very analogy that formed the ultimate "confirmation of my system of pre-established harmony" between body and soul. That harmony, he said, is established pre-natally within what he calls the human "seed." The individual's interior changes already lie within their biological inheritance.

It is true that here the word "soul" signifies merely the sensitive or animal soul, that aspect of interiority which has direct contact with the material world through sensation and perception. However, in his later treatments of the same topic, Leibniz writes also about the developmental unfolding of the rational soul—its divine, immaterial aspect. And here, unlike his scholastic predecessors, he confines possession of the rational soul only to the elect, to those who are "predestined for happiness"[24] (this at a time not long before the word "happiness" was starting to acquire its utilitarian resonances).

It is Leibniz also who completes the levelling out of the path of linear time. He places a plank across its last remaining crevasse, the one between life and death. All that happens at death, he says, is that the soul, having unfolded in this life, is infinitesimally folded up, *enveloppée* or *pliée*, before unfolding once again (*se développer*) in the afterlife.[25] The line of interiority thus remains unbroken, even at this crucial point. So the ultimate problem in the linear concept of human interiority, previously expressed as "What exactly happens to the soul at death?" gets explained here in semi-naturalistic terms rather than in terms of the miraculous. For example, according to Leibniz, soul and mind are subject to the same kind of rules in both places. In heaven, as on earth, there is still room for things like penitence and justice, and room also for further cognitive development.

Once the theory of preformation was applied to the soul and the mind, it was bound to displace the theory of innate ideas. Innatism was compatible with preformationism inasmuch as it suggested that we are born with something already pre-programmed. Leibniz, for example, championed both theories. When anti-innatism began to get the upper hand (as in Condillac), this was partly because innatism was ceding its former historical importance to theories, developmentalism among them, that privileged a pre-existing temporal *structure* of the mind over the *content* of ideas as such. Thus a *tabula* of some sort or other remained.

Leibniz's adaptation of bodily preformation to psychology was taken further by Charles Bonnet, the entomologist who discovered the preformed stages of insect growth. The devout Bonnet finally made explicit the close relationship between developmental stages in psychology and the staged acquisition of saving grace. In his *Essai de psychologie*, searching for a way to describe this new discipline "psychology," he defines it as "the Economy of Grace"—a phrase taken from St Paul.[26] But whereas in that biblical text "economy" referred to a dispensation, Bonnet uses it to mean something more like distribution. Following hints in Leibniz, he says that God's allocation of saving grace may perhaps be proportional to the value or interior status of each human individual. We could even say that this sense of proportionality exhibits the beginnings of the statistical outlook that would one day be applied to cognitive and affective norms.

This whole proto-theoretical wave, emerging partly from the first Jansenists and some of their Calvinist contemporaries, partly from Leibniz, and partly from Bonnet, seems to culminate in *Emile*. Rousseau's story is certainly saturated with the developmental idea, but also, now and suddenly, with the word itself: the body, the senses, intelligence, the passions, conscience, knowledge—all these things, he says, "develop." Even the very principle of development itself "develops." It is the second most important word in *Emile*, precisely because it is the principle that describes the first and most important concept, which is "Order." *Emile*, the text, therefore begins to look like the fulcrum of the whole historical transition from the religious to the pseudo-secular as described above, while Emile, the character, as he heads towards his developmental goal, is also unfolding *from* something, from a causal origin located in a divinely ordered nature.

4 What Relationship Does Condillac's Work Bear to the Presuppositions about Time and Interiority Discussed Above?

In the *discours préliminaire* to his book on education (as elsewhere), Rousseau attacks existing notions of pedagogical order. These scholastic-derived notions presupposed the ordered relationship to each other of ready-formed "systems," i.e. "general principles of knowledge." This was a static representation, inasmuch as any temporal aspect would have to consist here, says Condillac, in the absurd assumption that human reason arrives instantaneously. Knowledge is ordered, he says, "in the opposite way" (*dans un ordre contraire*): namely a gradual build-up of "observations" within the individual.[27] Moreover, this is no mere reversal from top-down to bottom-up: it is also an order that proceeds over time. He notes how order runs "from the known to the unknown" and "from knowledge to new knowledge," just as his famous statue acquires sense and faculties incrementally, not all of a sudden.

Condillac acknowledges this temporality in theoretical terms that are considerably firmer than those of Locke. He will not start, he says, with "definitions, axioms, and principles"; he will start instead by "observing the lessons which nature gives us" rather than confronting the pupil with "systems of general knowledge" whose relationship to each other is conceived statically. By contrast, he asks, in what order do things appear to us? "What is this order? Nature herself indicates it: it is the order in which she offers her objects" to creatures who are ignorant of them.[28] There is no age at which one might understand the general principles of a sphere of knowledge if one has not made the observations which lead to those principles. The individual's age of reason is thus that age when one has observed, and consequently, "reason will come in good time if we teach the children to make observations."[29] And the whole business of making observations is temporal.

There are points of difference between Condillac and Rousseau. First, whereas Rousseau's theory of stages was implicitly a preformationist one, Condillac was an epigenist in terms of his psychology, not a preformationist: that is to say, the temporal order that marks the human interior is a more or less smoothly *gradual* one, in the sense that it is not split into discrete stages. True, he has absorbed the vocabulary of "development." But unlike Rousseau, who applies that term to everything that moves, Condillac's usages are relatively infrequent and largely abstract. Occasionally in the *Essai sur l'origine* he writes how specific psychological operations themselves "develop," using the reflexive form of the verb; and in the *Traité des sensations*, he notes that we all have the "germ" of certain perceptive abilities, though only in some of us are they "developed" to the full extent by their habitual interaction with bodily growth. Nevertheless, it is not development as such but above all the sense operations that are important to "*la science des vérités sensibles,*"[30] represented as they often are in temporal terms (*changements, instants,* etc.). It is just that these latter necessarily presuppose a global category (as, for example, in "the development of children's faculties")[31].

Development thus belongs in Condillac's work with reason, intelligence and progress, i.e. it is one of the vaguer, loftier concepts. These certainly form a "natural theology" that "raises us towards God," yet they are by no means the chief object of Condillac's research. They are simply a reminder that his thought does indeed have a metaphysics, in spite of his own claims to the contrary, and that it consists in assuming the temporal character of a law-governed interior universe. It provides a framework within which the discrete psychological entities that *are* of interest to him can be located.

With effectively the first words he ever committed to publication, Condillac resorts to a statement of first principles (as one tends to do on such occasions): "Whether we raise ourselves, to speak metaphorically, into the heavens or descend into the abyss, we do not go beyond ourselves; and we never perceive anything but our own thought."[32] Interpreted retrospectively, this might be taken to mean that we have an urge to know the thought of others but cannot obtain it. Interpreted in the spirit of that era, however, the inference would have been that there is someone who does know our thoughts, and if not oneself, it is obviously the Almighty. (That is what Malebranche had meant when he said roughly the same thing, even if Hume, who echoed him, was already meaning it sceptically.) Moreover, an additional inference is possible: both (a) it is only *our own* thinking that we perceive and (b) it is our own *thinking* that we perceive. Interiority has other aspects than *pensée*. These aspects are equally important and equally unknowable, such as one's status with God. In short, the fact that we can perceive our own thinking contrasts with the fact that we cannot perceive our own afterlife status. God's "foreknowledge" is of both.

Condillac scarcely mentions salvation thereafter. Why here? Was he just starting out with a mere gesture, one that would preserve him against trouble with the ecclesiastical authorities? But if this is not the case—and on the reasonable assumption that his religious faith was genuine—might we not go to the opposite extreme and see this opening sentence as the premise without which the rest of the book could not have followed?

After all, there is a necessary connection between the two parts of the above sentence. Taken together, they echo the introspective anxiety from which the epistemological turn in modern philosophy derived. The prospect of heaven and hell is intrinsic to the assertion that we cannot get outside our own thoughts. The question "How can knowledge be certain" had once meant, primarily: how can one have certain knowledge that one possesses saving grace? Certainty or uncertainty of this kind may have been what had motivated Locke's *Essay*, which (it must always be remembered) was conceived as the mere preliminary to a Lockean natural theology. Of course Condillac comes several decades later and we cannot necessarily assume that his motivation was an anxiety about election. But we surely know what his motivation was *not*. It was not, absurdly but temptingly, that he could already see what a positive twenty-first century science of psychology would look like and that he had decided to blaze a trail towards it.

If Condillac displays little further interest in salvation, it may have been because he simply wanted to ensure that his readers focus on the topic under discussion. Any digression into eschatology might have provoked heated debate, and this would have hindered the task of establishing the kind of certainty that might come from an exact detailed knowledge of the order which the mind follows. Such a digression would, in itself, constitute a disorder. In that same first paragraph Condillac implies that the order of thoughts, one after the other, over time, is what the mind substantively

Time, Order and the Concept of a Human Interior 229

is: a replacement version of the scholastic "essence of man." The philosopher's task, he says, is to unfold the thoughts, in parallel as they themselves unfold: *C'est cet ordre de pensées qu'il faut développer, si nous voulons connaître les idées que nous avons des choses.*

So is this what he means by having spoken "metaphorically," as he says, in that opening sentence? Whatever is expressed in spatial terms (*les cieux, les abîmes*) is metaphor, whereas the reality of the human interior is the sequence of thoughts over time. It is in this sense that if one wanted to play a game called "Who was the first modern psychologist?" Condillac might be one of the answers. But it is impossible to play this game simply by ignoring and ejecting religion from it.

5   Conclusion

The history of the mind sciences constitutes a method for external monitoring of the disciplines themselves. The interest of historians in a Condillac who seems to tend towards the present, without an equal interest in the range of possibilities concerning what came before him, imputes a certain positivity to the mind sciences as they now stand. The result is a circularity. To neglect the prior religious contexts is thereby to obscure the historical fact that the modern psychological science towards which Condillac is heading is itself a contingent extension of the Christian outlook. If he was a proto-d'Holbachian and proto-Helvetian, it is possible that he was also, in ways which I admit are less obvious, a post-Pascalian and a post-Malebranchian. This raises one last question. Without that prior context, would the very substance—the formative categories—of today's human sciences and therefore of the abilities of all of us be what they are now?

Notes

1 R. G. Collingwood, *An Essay on Metaphysics* (Oxford: Clarendon Press, 2014 [1940]).
2 Arthur Lovejoy, *The Great Chain of Being: A Study of the History of an Idea* (New York: Harper & Row, 2005 [1936], Chapter 9.
3 For a detailed treatment, see Christopher Goodey, *Development: The History of a Psychological Concept* (Cambridge: Cambridge University Press, 2021).
4 St Irenaeus of Lyons, *Against Heresies* (Sterling Heights: Ex Fontibus, 2010), Book 4.
5 Augustine of Hippo, *Confessions* 11.27.
6 C. F. Goodey, *A History of Intelligence and "Intellectual Disability": The Shaping of Psychology in Early Modern Europe* (Abingdon: Routledge, 2011).
7 Gottfried Wilhelm Leibniz, *Theodicy: Essays on the Goodness of God, the Freedom of Man and the Origins of Evil*, translated by E.M. Huggard (London: Routledge, 1951), p. 125.

8 Hélène Bouchilloux, *Pascal: La force de la raison* (Paris: Vrin, 2004), p. 113.
9 Blaise Pascal, *Pensées*, texte établi par Louis Lafuma (Paris: Editions du Seuil, 1962), p. 418.
10 Pascal, *Pensées*, 771.
11 Nicolas Malebranche, *De la recherche de la vérité, esclaircissement* 8, in *Œuvres complètes* (Paris: Vrin, 1962), vol. 3, p. 77.
12 E.S. de Beer (ed.), *The Correspondence of John Locke* (Oxford: Clarendon, 1979), vol. 4, p. 625.
13 John Locke, *An Essay Concerning Human Understanding* (Oxford: Clarendon, 1975), p. 265.
14 Montesquieu, *L'esprit des lois*, 2.5 ; 25.9–10, in *Œuvres complètes* (Le Seuil, 1964).
15 Montesquieu, *Pensées*, i.945.
16 Jean-Jacques Rousseau, *The Confessions* (Ware: Wordsworth, 1996), p. 236.
17 Rousseau, *Julie, or the new Héloïse*, letter 7.
18 Rousseau, Letter to Beaumont, in *Letters Written from the Mountain, and Related Writings*, (eds) Christopher Kelly and Eve Grace (Hanover, NH: Dartmouth College Press, 2012), pp. 29, 204.
19 Rousseau, *Emile, ou de l'éducation* (Paris: Flammarion, 1966), pp. 33, 42.
20 Rousseau, *Emile*, p. 37.
21 Jan Swammerdam, *Bybel der Natuure sive Historia Insectorum* (Leiden: Herman Severinus, 1737), p. 28.
22 Malebranche, *Entretiens sur la métaphysique et sur la religion*, in *Œuvres*, vol. 12, pp. 228–229, 252–253.
23 Leibniz, *Theodicy*, p. 274.
24 Leibniz, *Monadology*, para. 61.
25 Leibniz, *Système nouveau de la nature*, in (ed.) Paul Janet, *Œuvres philosophiques de Leibniz* (Paris: Alcan, 1900), vol. 1, p. 639.
26 Charles Bonnet, *Essai de psychologie, ou considérations sur les opérations de l'âme*, in *Œuvres*, vol. 8, p. 112.
27 *Cours d'étude, pour l'instruction des jeunes gens* (Paris: Dufart, 1794–1795 [an 3]), vol. 1, p. 5.
28 Ibid., p. 25.
29 Ibid., p. 7.
30 Ibid., vol. 6, *L'art de raisonner*, p. 6ff.
31 Ibid., vol. 5, *La logique, ou les premiers développements de l'art de penser*, p. 13. Note the temporal twist given to the title of the standard logic of the era, Antoine Arnauld and Pierre Nicole's *La logique, ou l'art de penser*.
32 Condillac, *Essai sur l'origine des connaissances humaines*, p. 11. (I have used Aarsleff's tranlation in Condillac 2001.)

References

Augustine of Hippo, *Confessions* (New York: Penguin Random House, 2008).
Bonnet, Charles, *Œuvres d'histoire naturelle et de philosophie* (Neuchâtel: Samuel Fauche, 1779–1783).
Bouchilloux, Hélène, *Pascal: La force de la raison* (Paris: Vrin, 2004).
Collingwood, R. G, *An Essay on Metaphysics* (Oxford: Clarendon Press, 2014 [1940]).
Condillac, Etienne Bonnot de, *Cours d'étude, pour l'instruction des jeunes gens* (Paris: Dufart, [1794–1795]).

Condillac, Etienne Bonnot de, *Essai sur l'origine des connaissances humaines* (Paris: Vrin, 2014).
Condillac, Etienne Bonnot de, *Essay on the Origin of Human Knowledge*, edited by Hans Aarsleff (Cambridge: Cambridge University Press, 2001).
Goodey, Christopher, *Development: The History of a Psychological Concept* (Cambridge: Cambridge University Press, 2021).
Goodey, C. F., *A History of Intelligence and "Intellectual Disability:" The Shaping of Psychology in Early Modern Europe* (Abingdon: Routledge, 2011).
Hartley, David, *Observations on Man, His Frame, His Duty, and His Expectations* (London: Thomas Tegg, 1834 [1749]).
Irenaeus of Lyons, *Against Heresies* (Sterling Heights: Ex Fontibus, 2010).
Leibniz, Gottfried Wilhelm, *Œuvres philosophiques de Leibniz* (Paris: Alcan, 1900).
Leibniz, Gottfried Wilhelm, *Theodicy: Essays on the Goodness of God, the Freedom of Man and the Origins of Evil*, translated by E.M. Huggard (London: Routledge, 1951).
Leibniz, Gottfried Wilhelm (ed. Emile Boutroux), *La monadologie* (Paris: LGF, 1991).
Locke, John, *An Essay Concerning Human Understanding* (Oxford: Clarendon, 1975).
Locke, John (ed. E.S. de Beer), *The Correspondence of John Locke* (Oxford: Clarendon, 1979).
Lovejoy, Arthur, *The Great Chain of Being: A Study of the History of an Idea* (New York: Harper & Row, 2005 [1936]).
Malebranche, Nicolas (ed. André Robinet), *Œuvres complètes* (Paris: Vrin, 1962).
Montesquieu, *Œuvres complètes* (Paris: Le Seuil, 1964).
Pascal, Blaise (ed. Louis Lafuma), *Pensées* (Paris: Editions du Seuil, 1962).
Rousseau, Jean-Jacques, *The Confessions* (Ware: Wordsworth, 1996).
Rousseau, Jean-Jacques, *Emile, ou de l'éducation* (Paris: Flammarion, 1966).
Rousseau, Jean-Jacques, *Julie, or the new Héloïse* (Hanover, NH: Dartmouth College Press, 1997).
Rousseau, Jean-Jacques (ed. Christopher Kelly and Eve Grace), *Letters Written from the Mountain, and Related Writings* (Hanover, NH: Dartmouth College Press, 2012).
Swammerdam, Jan, *Bybel der Natuure sive Historia Insectorum* (Leiden: Herman Severinus, 1737).

14 Representations of the Body and Self-Knowledge

Condillac's *Treatise on Sensations* and Contemporary Naturalistic Psychology

Aliènor Bertrand

1 Introduction

While nascent psychiatry, in the person of Pinel, recognised Condillac's philosophy as its primary reference,[1] contemporary psychology does not acknowledge any debt to it. However, reading the *Treatise*[2] reveals a certain number of propositions which bear strange resemblance to contemporary naturalistic theses: the assertion that there exists a non-discursive thought which makes it possible to explain animal action, the distinction between "sentience"— that is to say, sentiment—and reflection, and the link between the capacity to locate in space and the representative faculty. It is true that Condillac does not yet define himself as a "naturalist" in 1754, the use of this term being confined to Buffon's Cartesian philosophy, which Condillac criticises, or to mechanistic materialism, the presuppositions of which he challenges:

> Naturalism, s.m
> Mistake made by ones who believe that blind and necessary nature is the principle of all.
> Naturalist, s.m
> One who professes naturalism. But it is more usually said of those philosophers who study natural history and who have written on the productions of nature, such as metals, minerals, vegetables and animals, etc.[3]

The *Treatise* is undeniably a decisive stage on a journey that will lead Condillac to state that "logic is learned from nature itself." We will seek to define hereafter the features of that "logical naturalism." In response to Locke and Berkeley, Condillac maintains that the capacity to produce representations of one's own body is a condition of explicit reflective knowledge. Like contemporary naturalists, Condillac attempts to explain the origin of human knowledge—the knowledge of the self is only a part of it—on the basis of forms of thought shared with animals.

DOI: 10.4324/9781003334750-18

Representations of the Body and Self-Knowledge 233

The *Treatise* constitutes a spectacular departure from Locke and expounds an original philosophy of consciousness and self-consciousness. Although I know there are other readings of the *Treatise*[4] and I am well aware of the many problems related to the ontology of the mind, I will set out to highlight the correspondence between Condillac's analysis and contemporary naturalistic theories. Putting to one side Condillac's principle of the sentiment-based logical "generation" of faculties, which is alien to post-Darwinism, I will consider the different forms of self-knowledge identified by Condillac as conditions for the emergence of self-consciousness. Through this, I will obtain the criteria thereof. By cross-referencing and translating two languages, two eras and two traditions, I will establish the common arguments Condillac and contemporary naturalists used to develop parallel theses: first, the thesis that only human beings have self-consciousness; second, that humans share elementary relations to the self with animals; and, third, that representations of one's own body are essential to self-consciousness formation.

In the first part, I will strive to justify this comparison between contemporary naturalism and Condillac's philosophy on a general level. I will do this not by defending a systematic comparative method between the history of philosophy and contemporary philosophy but by pointing out significant and remarkable points of convergence. I will then endeavour to show how far this comparison may be extended by developing three main aspects of the problems raised by self-consciousness: theory of memory, function of representations of one's own body and imitation. Our purpose is to re-evaluate the *Treatise* by showing that the central role given by Condillac to "sentiment," which contemporary philosophers of perception have long considered to be an epistemological prejudice, should now be put on the agenda of naturalistic philosophers of the mind.

2 Does It Make Sense to Compare the *Treatise on Sensations* with Contemporary Naturalism?

Although this chapter does not seek to answer the objection that the proposed interpretation simply conforms to an intellectual fashion,[5] it is useful to provide further justification for the proposed angle. The *Treatise* is indeed often treated as a text much closer to Husserl's phenomenology than to naturalism: Condillac has a reputation for being a philosopher of consciousness, a successor of Locke, while contemporary naturalism is known to have struck consciousness off the list of problems worthy of interest.

However, the upheavals that the philosophy of the mind has recently encountered oblige historians of philosophy to revise this view. It is true to say that today consciousness has become one of the principal focal points of the "naturalists."[6] It is not that the "functionalist" philosophy of perception has been renounced when a preponderant role was given to *qualia*; rather, the new awareness of the natural conditions of human self-consciousness has profoundly changed the way in which consciousness is understood.

Philosophers in the Anglo-American tradition have long dealt with self-consciousness by reasoning *a priori* on its conditions of possibility, according to a philosophy of language approach. Following Wittgenstein,[7] they have considered all propositions of subjective self-attribution to be invalid. They have defined a general problem—they call it the "problem of transition"—in the following terms: if self-knowledge implies that true thoughts can be formed as "I psi that P," where "psi" refers to a propositional attitude, "P" to its content and "I" to the person thinking this thought, on what conditions can the content "P" of a propositional attitude justify being attributed in the first person?

A large number of naturalists now reject this way of addressing the problem of self-consciousness and refute the argument of Wittgenstein, who asserts that propositions of subjective self-attribution are invalid.[8] Wittgenstein's argument, which was picked up on and developed by Shoemaker under the name of the "immunity of the subject to the error through misidentification,"[9] amounts to stating that the "I" as "subject" is not susceptible to false recognition and that propositions of subjective self-attribution are tautologies. In recent publications, naturalists not only reject the argument with an *a priori* metaphysical-type analysis justifying the conditions of subjective self-attribution, but they also highlight the actual conditions which enable a subject to think in order to act. With this shift, the problem is no longer that of the relations of the judgement by which the subject attributes to himself a thought with this occurrent thought; the problem is that of the role of self-attribution in practical reasoning with regard to the functional properties of action.[10] Argumentation is backed up by the study of the psychology of action seen from an etiological perspective, with regard to the evolution of organisms and human development.

It is worth noting that a number of conceptual distinctions established recently by naturalists overlap with the divisions drawn up by Condillac. Nonetheless, these distinctions enjoy opposite reputations in terms of technical difficulty. Indeed, the contemporary distinctions come across as jargon to the layman, while those of Condillac are expounded in a language so familiar to a French speaker that we may not notice them. However, as we will show later on, there is no need to dwell on the stylistic difference since, to take one example, the contemporary concept of "metacognition" is considerably closer to the elementary forms of self-knowledge set out in the analysis of action in Condillac's *Treatise* than the difference in lexis might suggest.

In more general terms, we should stress that the *Treatise* constitutes a profound departure from the type of "philosophy of language" which is practised by Condillac in the *Essay*, and that this departure can be compared to the internal upheaval in contemporary philosophy of the mind that we mentioned earlier. In the *Essay*, Condillac makes reflection depend on language capacities,[11] as if a person's grammar were enough to explain explicit self-consciousness. However, in *Treatise* and later in *Treatise on Animals*, he links reflection with action and grants animals reflective capacities that they were denied in the *Essay*.[12] These texts mark a decisive break with Locke, and constitute a crucial step down the path towards naturalism. Unlike Locke, Condillac no longer identifies consciousness with self-consciousness.[13] Self-consciousness is based on multiple mental capacities being exercised together, the most important of which is likely to be the production of representations of one's own body. Though contemporary philosophy of the mind often refers to Locke[14] on that topic, it never refers to Condillac for essential reasons. The truth is that reference to Locke is made as much out of reverence as it is to serve as a foil;[15] referring to Condillac would be less rhetorical and more to the point.

As a philosopher of consciousness, Condillac distinguishes himself by a sharp distinction between consciousness and self-consciousness. He also opposes memory and reflective capacities. In his *Treatise*, he dissociates, in an unprecedented fashion, simple consciousness (in which some contemporary philosophers might recognise "sentience") from self-consciousness.[16] Moreover, while the statue is then described as being "conscious of its internal states," in that it feels them, it nonetheless does not form concepts, nor is it capable of having a representation of its own mind. The consciousness of internal modifications is not equivalent to a consciousness "of the self."

We should stress that the genesis of faculties in the statue mental experiment is not considered by contemporary naturalism as a "logical generation." Let's take it this way: the "logical generation" establishes for Condillac the series of criteria necessary for self-knowledge. As such, Condillac's analytical method is superior to the "plain and historical method" of Locke:[17] far from drawing up an inventory of faculties or pretending to describe the mind as it presents itself, Condillac's method divides up what is given by experience into elementary components. Starting with the fact of self-knowledge and the phenomenon of consciousness, the method breaks them down, showing how divided elements are related to each other. The value of Condillac's analysis lies in the rigorous nature of this decomposition, which does not take the easy option of using consciousness directly to explain self-knowledge. All the more, beyond Condillac's self-interpretation of the human mind's genesis, the fiction could also be construed as a paradigm, both speculative and heuristic, to help scientists understand the evolution from early stages of consciousness to self-consciousness. As a matter of fact, Condillac draws a link between children's mental development and the conclusions drawn from his statue mental experiment.

236 *Aliènor Bertrand*

In any case, it is worth noting that a number of general theses are common to both Condillac and contemporary naturalism:

- first, the thesis of the existence of thought without concepts;
- second, the thesis of reflectivity without language to support the idea of a "rationality" in animal behaviour, without stating that animals possess our scope for conceptual manipulation, our self-consciousness, our will, etc.;
- third, the need to distinguish between different modes of perception, including, at the very least, the perception of features ("traits"), the perception of objects (through categorisation and conceptualisation) and the perception of actions.

There thus appears a remarkable point of convergence between Condillac's philosophy and contemporary naturalistic psychology: the discovery that reflexivity contributes to self-knowledge only in so far as it mobilises representations of one's own acting body. In order to demonstrate that, we have chosen to develop three more specific points:

- the description of the means by which memory conditions self-consciousness;
- the role of representations of one's own body in reflectivity;
- the role of physical imitation in the acquisition of concepts allowing self-knowledge as knowledge of a mind.

3 Memory, Reflection, Imitation: Representations of the Body as a Condition for Self-knowledge

3.1 *Memory*

Memory is the elementary operation which would appear to be the most indispensable to self-knowledge. However, like in contemporary philosophy, there is not one single definition of memory in Condillac's thought; nor does he confuse memory with reflective capacities more than contemporary philosophers do.

Like a great many philosophers active 250 years later, Condillac takes Locke's definition of the person as a starting point. In the *Essay*, Condillac's first work, he takes Locke's concept of reminiscence as his own, and in so doing ensures the unity of the "self" and guarantees the possibility of a reflection on "oneself."[18] One difference from Locke can be noted, in that Condillac does not refer to the abstract distinction between substance, soul and person.[19] He chooses instead to produce a grammatical analysis of the "subject" and to make reflective capacities directly dependent on language.[20] However, even though reflection depends on language, it is just as closely conditioned by reminiscence; as with Locke, it is the continuity produced by reminiscence, which ultimately ensures the unity of the person in the *Essay*.[21]

The *Treatise* revolutionises Locke's legacy. In this text, the role Condillac attributes to memory pre-empts the theses advanced by contemporary naturalists on the same subject. This is hardly surprising, since the two analyses stem from deep meditations on Locke's theory. But the fact that they are so close to one another is nevertheless noteworthy: in a sense, the solutions proposed by Condillac foreshadow those of on-going research. Let us remind ourselves briefly of the two major objections levelled today at Locke's theory of memory by the majority of philosophers of the mind, be they involved in the project of "naturalisation of intentionality" or not.[22]

The first objection shows that memorial continuity produced by reminiscence does not provide a sufficient ground for personal identity.[23] The second reveals the existence of a circle that could lead one to presuppose the self[24] in itself. All the paths that are explored to counter these objections have a common feature: they assert the necessity of ordering relations between the different forms of recollection, so as to constitute a unique memory chain which enables transitive relations. Working on that basis, different strategies and solutions have been envisaged to reply to the second objection regarding the circle. Some contemporary solutions could be criticised for falling short of Locke's distinctions, for example when personal identity is reduced to a purely artefactual relationship[25] or to a form of substantial unity.[26] However, the naturalistic strategy preserves what is interesting about Locke's conceptual invention while at the same time correcting it. This strategy involves sufficiently multiplying the constitutive strata of self-identity, more finely than Locke's notion of memory enables it to be done, and turns the approach to the problem on its head. Thus the identity of the person appears less as being composed of the abstract possibility of going through a continuous, ordered memory chain, and more as being constituted of a capacity to act with a "coherence of its own," bringing into play not just a "memory in action" but a reflectivity of a different order.[27] The naturalistic strategy is confirmed in a number of works on psychopathology and identity disorders,[28] as well as in the psychology of action and neurophysiology.[29]

On a philosophical level, the naturalistic solution has many assets of its own: it substantiates the intuitive view that memory is the most indispensable element of personality without identifying reflexivity and memory, and it allows a distinction to be drawn between the self as itself and the capacity to know oneself explicitly as such, which requires, as the expression goes, a "theory of the mind."

The role that Condillac reserves for memory in his *Treatise* comes near to the naturalistic solution. In this text, Condillac drops Locke's vocabulary of reminiscence and initial conception of the person based entirely on language. Condillac defines different sorts of memory, not one of which corresponds to reminiscence; he distinguishes between an elementary memory which is involuntary and dynamic[30] and a memory which is controlled but still commanded by current events,[31] and he sets these first two types of memory apart from the discursive memory that allows orientation in a wider timeframe. The definition of this third type of memory, introduced in the *Essay*, appears unchanged in the *Treatise*,[32] and beyond. It emphasises the link between language and voluntary memory.

Condillac thus considers that knowledge of the self must be divided into distinct strata; he does not confuse memory continuity with personal identity, nor with reflective identity. As it is described in the *Treatise*, memory is a dynamic operation, of which the two most basic types have a kind of reflexivity always in phase with current events. Reduced to smell, the statue has a self, which can be defined, at every instant: "This is its personality. If it could say 'I,' it would say it every instant of its duration, and each time its 'I' would include every moment it remembered."[33]

The elementary activity of the self does not, therefore, involve any form of representation of the self, or any knowledge of the self as a mind. However, this activity allows the formation of a sort of implicit but functional "personality": "Its 'I' is only the collection of sensations it experiences, and of those that its memory recalls. In short, it is at once the consciousness of what it is and the memory of what it was."[34]

The personality of the statue confined to smell does not rest on an explicit self-consciousness but on a process whereby present sensations are linked to past sensations. It requires a basic memory, the reduced performance of which is not comparable to memory enabled by the use of speech: basic memory does not permit voluntary recollections nor, therefore, voluntary access to the self.

The analysis proposed in the *Treatise* provides the same asset as the contemporary naturalistic perspective: not identifying memory with the reflectivity involved in knowledge of oneself as a mind, and highlighting a "proto-subjective function" of the self that cannot be reduced to knowledge of oneself as a mind. In either case, the refinement of the theory of memory once again gives rise to a new necessity: to produce mediations between the elementary operations of memory and discursive self-knowledge of oneself. From this point of view, too, there is a remarkable degree of proximity between the *Treatise* and contemporary naturalistic philosophy: Condillac attributes to the representation of one's own body (which is enabled by the use of reflection linked to action) a decisive role in the genesis of an explicit self-consciousness. Let's now compare the theory of reflectivity found in contemporary naturalistic philosophy with Condillac's.

3.2 Reflectivity

Naturalistic philosophers state that there are reflective functional structures which give sense to propositions of subjective self-attribution.[35] Let us note, first of all, that while these structures are linked to action, they are distinct from both the mere capacity to act and the capacity to represent one's own mind. Reflectivity is not the general condition of action, since it is easy to show with ethological data that not all actions presuppose reflectivity;[36] reflectivity is neither "theoretical" knowledge of what a mind can do in the sense of being a capacity for "metarepresentations," nor does it give us a "theory of the mind." Naturalistic philosophers call "metacognition" the type of implicit self-knowledge which is involved in the monitoring and control that a mind has over its own mental states. Metacognition is thus opposed to metarepresentation, which is the conceptual knowledge that a mind has of its own mental states.[37]

Is reflectivity specifically human, or can it be found in animals, that is in beings deprived of language? It has long been accepted that the necessary condition for a subject to arrive at reflective consciousness lies in the aptitude to form metarepresentations concerning the thought content of "simple" representations.[38] In other words, it has long been held that the access to concepts of the type "I had that thought" was necessary to establish the existence of any reflective capacity. It has been supposed that the ability to refer to the self, independently of any context, was a necessary condition of all reflectivity, which is certainly an excessive condition. Moreover, some recent studies show that animals, apparently incapable of metarepresentations, are capable of resolving metacognitive problems and thus display "reflectivity."[39] Ethological research tends to show that metacognition does not depend on metarepresentations, while, however, any metarepresentative capacity necessarily presupposes metacognitive capacities. In this sense, reflectivity appears as a necessary but not sufficient condition of "self-consciousness" and does not necessarily suppose "theoretical" knowledge of what a mind in general is.

Procedural reflectivity involved in metacognition is only a property which allows one to evaluate one's mental states, to review them and to modify them in order to act. It presupposes a faculty to carry out "mental actions" that is to say, to perform actions which, like all actions, are caused by desires and beliefs, but "whose intentional content is to obtain a new mental property, using for that purpose means which are themselves mental."[40] Controlled attention is a prime example of "mental action," controlled memory provides another example and deliberate modification of preferences provides a third example. Any animal capable of controlled attention thereby possesses reflective capacities.

This is the thesis found in the *Treatise* and the *Treatise on Animals*, and some of the reasons why it is supported today are identical to those given

240 *Aliènor Bertrand*

by Condillac. Having reflected on the difficulties that he experienced in the *Essay* to explain how speech is born from communication through actions, Condillac introduced a new step between involuntary communication of emotions and the use of instituted signs. Unlike what he had first maintained, he admitted that reflection independent of the use of instituted signs conditioned spoken language. To describe this reflection, he later used a distinction which he included in the corrected edition of *Treatise* by contrasting the non-theoretical mode of self-knowledge with the theoretical knowledge enabled by speech:

> But one must distinguish, as I did above, between theoretical knowledge and practical knowledge. It is for the former that we need a form of language, because it consists of a sequence of distinct ideas, and consequently, signs have been needed to classify them in an orderly manner and to determine them.
>
> ...These judgments which it does not notice are the instincts which guide it, and the habits of action which it has contracted according to these judgments, are what I understand by *practical knowledge*. While I am obliged to develop these judgments in order to make them known I am not claiming that it develops them itself. It cannot do so, since in having no language, it lacks the means to conduct an analysis.[41]

According to Condillac, self-knowledge related to action is practical knowledge, or, in other words, an implicit knowledge which "regulates our actions without our being able to notice it." This does not mean that we are talking about unconscious and automatic learning, since, on the contrary, practical knowledge is the result of judgements. What is implicit here is that we do not know "how practical knowledge makes us act"; we do not know how it regulates our actions, since they are no equivalent of "a theoretical knowledge of our own mind."

The existence of implicit mental operations, as some think, is not an inconceivable phenomenon for a "philosopher of consciousness," or even for a philosopher who, like Condillac, sets out to show that all our faculties are generated on the basis of sensations. However, the *Treatise*, one might think, is aimed at understanding, making explicit and analysing those implicit functions that allow us to act without realising what we are doing. Condillac heralds this in the opening lines of his work:

> To notice what we are learning, we must already know something. We must experience some ideas in order to observe that we experience ideas that we once lacked. This reflective memory, which now makes it so evident when we go from one bit of knowledge to another, cannot work

its way back to original knowledge; on the contrary, it presupposes that knowledge, and this is the origin of our propensity to believe that we were born with it.[42]

What is valid for perception is equally valid for knowledge and action, but also for self-knowledge. Condillac persistently makes explicit the mental operations which are at work while the mind is not capable of noticing them.[43] Before proceeding any further, an item of vocabulary needs to be clarified. Condillac does not use the term "reflectivity" to describe the implicit self-knowledge that an organism endowed with certain natural abilities uses in order to act. But he considers this implicit "knowledge" of the self as the product of "reflection" and gives new meaning to this concept in the *Treatise*. Reflection is a mode of thought linked to action: it is linked to tactile capacities which enable location in space.[44] It is characterised by a deliberate mode of attention, which is quite distinct from elementary attention. While elementary attention only allows one to isolate sensorial traits, reflective attention enables one to represent spatial units and to define characteristics to be attributed to them. It enables one to categorise objects and to relatively pre-empt the effects of one's actions in the world.[45]

By enabling these representations, reflection becomes a condition of controlled action. It generates "practical knowledge," including "practical" knowledge of one's self. This "practical" knowledge of the self presupposes the mental manipulation of representations of the body in action and the possibility of reviewing its judgements and beliefs in order to act. Condillac does not, therefore, identify this practical knowledge either with the capacity to represent minds as minds—or to possess a general "theory" of the mind—or with self-knowledge made possible through discursivity. However, this practical knowledge entails a mode of self-knowledge which is quite distinct from mere consciousness and considerably more complex than what is involved in mere memory.

We are now able to take a further step towards connecting the *Treatise* with recent developments in naturalistic philosophy. As it is defined in this work, reflection produces "mental actions" which are similar to those performed by the metacognitive reflectivity of contemporary naturalism, since they allow for the evaluation and revision of beliefs in order to act; reflection makes it possible to explain the formation of a link between intentions to act and representations of the acting body. Such a link, now called a "cognitive loop," is nowadays put forward as the principle for explaining "pre-theoretical" self-knowledge.

"Practical" self-knowledge, as defined by Condillac, is thus not a "theory of the mind" applied to one's self at all, but rather a representation of one's self as agent or acting body, which is something quite different. It could be said that it brings into play an "imaginative representation" of agency rather than a (conceptual) "theory of the mind."

How then does one make the transition from practical self-knowledge to "theoretical" self-knowledge? How does the disposal of concepts of mind, intention and desire enabled by language dovetail with "practical" knowledge?

Condillac sees an intermediary stage between "practical" self-knowledge and theoretical knowledge; this stage involves a random use of representations of action to judge the actions of the other (s).[46] Practical knowledge of oneself is then extended to others by way of a spontaneous expansion: the intentions and beliefs that allow one's own actions to be controlled are deemed to be the cause of all action. The perception of the actions of others is achieved by attributing to them by analogy representations of actions of oneself. However, this attribution by analogy is flawed in two ways:

1 it applies in the same way to both actions, which are actually intentional and those which are not, as well as to even to simple natural movements;
2 it confuses the effect of the actions on oneself with the intentions that cause them.

All this happens as if the "loop," which first links the intentions to act with the perception of actions, were extended to include the intentions of others as if they were linked to my own body: indeed, other people's intentions to act are therefore linked to their own actions, but on the basis of the effect that they have on me.

> The statue believes that everything acting on it does so by design. The statue feels at every instant how dependent it is on everything that surrounds it. If objects often respond to its wishes, they also controvert its projects almost as often: they make it unhappy or give it only a portion of the happiness that it desires. Persuaded that it does nothing without having the intention to do it, the statue believes that it sees a plan wherever it discovers some action. In truth, it can only judge such things according to what it perceives in itself; and it would require many observations indeed to guide its judgments better. The statue thinks then that what is pleasing to it has its pleasure as a goal and what is offensive has as a goal to offend it.[47]

If a closer look is taken, this stage is marked by a maximum extension of the "practical" concepts based on the givens of perception. What is missing here is a "theoretical" concept of mind, which alone is likely to enable intentions and beliefs to be correctly attributed. The other does not appear to me as an agent endowed with a mind of his own, absolutely irreducible to me, but as an agent directly causing certain effects on my body and my environment. It is on the basis of the perception of the actions of the other on myself that the representation of action is formed, and not on the basis of a link between the perception of his action and "his mind." The perception of actions, including those of the other, remains ego-centred.

However, in spite of its imperfections, this intermediary stage conditions the theoretical knowledge of oneself and the other as a "mind." As it happens, a number of contemporary naturalistic philosophers share this conviction: they state that representations of the actions of others are found in children and are used randomly before they can be used discriminatingly; and they also believe that having the ability to understand the intentions of other minds and to achieve knowledge of oneself as a mind constitutes a decisive stage. For a third and final time, we have to admit that there exists a striking parallel between the solution envisaged by Condillac and the path being traced today by naturalistic psychology.

3.3 Simulation, Language of Action and Knowledge of the Self as Mind

The *Treatise* does not in itself allow us to understand Condillac's conception of the knowledge of oneself and other(s) as minds, because it sets out to study the faculties of an "isolated" man, *mettant en abyme*, through reading, a logical situation of interlocution.[48] In order to retrace the passage from "practical" knowledge of oneself and other(s) to theoretical knowledge, we must go back to Condillac's *Grammar* and *Logic*.[49] The extent to which Condillac's thinking has changed on that subject since the *Essay* is striking.

In the *Essay*, Condillac describes the existence of a language of action which enables the existence of an immediate and non-reflected communication between human beings, independently of language.[50] This spontaneous communication rests on innate properties of the mind linked to the existence of "natural signs" constituted by emotions.[51] As instituted signs are progressively acquired, the elementary modes of communication become the object of hypotheses and reasoning.[52] Knowledge of oneself and of others as "minds" are thus the results of observations and deductions; this knowledge consists of a "theory" of the mind which can be applied to oneself and to others. The development of this theory is made possible by the spontaneous use of communication through emotions: through mutual imitation, human beings succeed in representing the mind of others as being analogous to their own. In the scenario set out in the *Essay*, knowledge of the self and the other is directly dependent on the acquisition of spoken language. The *Treatise* contradicts the thesis that language and language alone enable the acquisition of the concepts of belief, desire and intention,[53] at least as practical concepts. Unlike the former text, the *Treatise* shows that the use of such concepts is involved in voluntary action and affirms the existence of implicit self-knowledge linked to action. As we have seen, this implicit self-knowledge is not enough to form representations of the mind "in general" or independent of any context; however, "practical" knowledge of oneself must nevertheless be considered an indispensable intermediary stage in the acquisition of a concept of mind.

The opposition between the *Treatise* and *Essay* foreshadows the debate now taking place among naturalistic philosophers regarding the modes of acquisition which allow knowledge of the self as a mind. This debate divides the proponents of a theoretical "theory" of mind from those who consider that simulation is at the heart of the acquisition processes through which a concept of mind forms. Indeed, unlike the advocates of the "theoretical" theory of the mind, Condillac does not believe that the manipulation of concepts depends on a mental module that immediately becomes operational; on the contrary, the *Essay* stresses the gradual and acquired nature of the use of these concepts and, moreover, the *Treatise* does nothing to change this essential thesis. Yet what is comparable here is the way in which the link between the acquisition of concepts of mind and action is dealt with. Like advocates of the "theoretical" theory of the mind, Condillac starts by admitting that concepts of mind are applied directly to the analysis of elementary communication through the effect of reasoning based on information gathered during imitation.[54] He maintains at first that the application of these concepts is made directly to actions, be they "my own" or not.

Later, however, Condillac considers that he has read too much into the reasoning and that he has not succeeded in sufficiently explaining how this reasoning applies.[55,56] This is exactly the kind of objection levelled at proponents of a "theoretical" theory of the mind by the advocates of simulation theory. In order to overcome this difficulty, the *Treatise* introduces the idea of "practical" self-knowledge linked to action, which will provide support for constructing concepts which allow for conceiving of the activity of the mind. In the *Grammar* and *Logic*, Condillac asserts that the language of action is the instrument used to construct mental concepts: the language of action is thus defined as an analytical method of action and not just as the vehicle for communication through emotions.[57] Therefore, imitation is not an empirical research tool enabling signs of action to be established and used in the most appropriate way, but a method by which the individual distinguishes himself/herself from others and constructs the knowledge that he/she has of himself/herself.[58]

In the latter part of his work, Condillac's position can be compared to that of the advocates of the "executive theory of mentalisation," who assert that acquiring a sense of the self depends on relating the non-conceptual contents of action to the concepts which allow us to conceive of the mind, called "mental concepts" for short. The "executive theory of mentalization" assumes that the knowledge of each individual of his own mental states is conditioned by the procedural reflectivity at work in action. As we have seen, procedural reflectivity is the process which enables one to apprehend oneself as an agent independently of the use of concepts that enable one to represent one's own mind. The proponents of the "executive theory of mentalization" challenge the idea of a direct application of mental concepts to the analysis of actions and assert, on the contrary, that it is procedural reflectivity which conditions the representation of oneself as mind and the representation of the mind of the other(s).

In his theory of the language of action, Condillac says the same: he highlights the antecedence of "practical" knowledge of oneself over "theoretical" knowledge, and he shows that the latter is the condition of the former.[59] Yet he goes further than that: he maintains that the use of concepts of intentions, desires and beliefs stems from the *explicitation* of the reflection at work in the execution of actions. He sees the language of action as the method of *explicitation* enabling the division of thought at work in action. The language of action transforms practical self-knowledge into explicit knowledge through the manipulation of signs of action. It presupposes the recognition, in oneself and the other, of internal states having a defined behavioural meaning. However, the "explicit" self-knowledge implemented in the language of action and characterised by the intentional use of signs of action remains in a way "practical" knowledge, since it is limited by its use in defined circumstances;[60] but, even though it is not yet theoretical knowledge, it is the most immediate condition of the possibility of this knowledge, for in practical knowledge the first concepts of mind are applied to something other than emotional communication. "Practical" self-knowledge, that is the totality of judgements implemented in order to act and communicate, is thus at the centre of the process by which knowledge of the self as a mind is developed.

In other words, to put this in contemporary terms, the reflectivity at work when the body acts and communicates is a constituent part of the "theory of mind" that is constructed through imitation. This is sufficient for us to see in Condillac a forerunner of a form of "executive theory of mentalisation."

Thus, self-knowledge does not appear in the *Treatise* as a pure phenomenon of consciousness, but, furthermore, it is essentially conditioned by representations of the body in action. In marked contrast to Locke, Condillac dissociates self-consciousness from consciousness, and shows that the relationship with one's own body is a constituent part of knowledge of the self as "mind." The body is not joined to the soul in a relationship of ownership based on theology, but it is at the core of the processes which command the knowledge of the mind by itself. Much more so than Locke, Condillac ought to be the reference of those who seek to "naturalise" self-knowledge. In so doing, one must resolve not to be daunted by the role that this Enlightenment philosopher nonetheless attributes to consciousness.

In conclusion, I will show that re-assessing Condillac's work does not necessarily involve establishing a radical critical distance from his conception of consciousness. In this way, rather than downplaying the place of consciousness in Condillac's philosophy, I will end by putting forward several arguments which plead in favour of a reading that embraces this consciousness. I do this both because, right from the *Treatise*, consciousness is a capacity to feel or to feel oneself in action and not an abstract consciousness, and because contemporary naturalistic philosophy itself ascribes a notable role to the "consciousness to act" and not only to "representations" of the body in action.

In the process which leads to self-knowledge, a preponderant role is today attributed to consciousness on two different levels: first, because consciousness allows one to apprehend oneself in action by providing an elementary experience of oneself, and second, because it offers a "donation" of all the elements which will be used to conceptualise mental states. These two levels are clearly not unrelated to one another, but a distinction must be drawn between them. As for the first level, we have reviewed the reasons why consciousness to act should be considered as a first apprehension of oneself in a non-conceptual mode. This does not mean that all the mechanisms enabling one to act are conscious. Quite the reverse. The experience of action cannot be dissociated from the "consciousness" of being in action. The consciousness of "being in action" is indeed not just a consciousness of wanting or "believing," which could be exclusively internal, nor a sensitive consciousness produced by sensations of the body in action, but it is precisely where the two come together, and it is in this respect that it is a constituent part of the experience of action.[61] The concordance between the executive and the perceptive cannot be reduced to the simple addition of execution and volition; it can operate only by a common reference to the acting body. Yet this common reference is not the only common denominator of calculations necessary for action to be realised, as if it were a pure frame of reference or a set of abstract coordinates. Thanks to continuing modifications of sensations, this common reference is experienced in a direct apprehension of oneself.

On the second level, we have seen that the consciousness to act is the result of multiple mechanisms allowing action to be controlled. Numerous recent studies have interpreted pathologies marked by intermittences or deficiencies of self-consciousness, particularly schizophrenia, by highlighting the deficiency of one or other of the underlying reflective processes which command action.[62] Even though this was not the precise purpose of these studies, they show the extent to which the "consciousness to act" is correlated with the mechanisms which command action. Thus, they accord to "pretheoretical consciousness" of the self an epistemic value which philosophers of perception refuse to accord to *qualia* or sensations.

However, "consciousness to act" plays a much more important role when it is related to the acquisition of the concepts which allow the mind to be conceived of; it actually finds itself at the interface between "mental" concepts and the objects of application of these concepts. "Consciousness to act" provides a non-conceptual given to which mental concepts apply with few ambiguities in defined contexts, since it "expresses" the totality of operations of the mind that enable action.

If we look more closely, there is nothing all that surprising about Condillac making consciousness of one's own body, as an acting body, the essential condition of consciousness of the self as a mind. Starting with the *Essay*, he set out to show how language has come about; to this end, he has consistently pursued the elementary modes of knowledge and communication that have conditioned the use of speech. As an Enlightenment philosopher, he could have chosen a more radical materialist position, granting consciousness an epiphenomenal role. If the statue in *Treatise* is not a machine, if it is first and foremost "the scent of a rose," it is not because Condillac is making some obscure sacrifice to the manes of Locke and Descartes. It is because the solution to the enigma of the origin of language presupposes acceptance of a form of self-consciousness and the other preconditions of language. This elementary self-consciousness, which gives meaning to the imitation of the other and enables progress in the language of action, is "consciousness to act," of which sensations are an essential component.

Let us finish by highlighting a paradox: what allowed Condillac to sense the fundamental role of representations of action in self-knowledge is the very thing which has for so long comprised a barrier to reading his work, i.e. the preponderance of sentiment in all the solutions that he proposes to the problems of the theory of knowledge. His *Treatise* has long been viewed as a prime example of a victim of the epistemological prejudice of philosophies of consciousness. Condillac is not content to describe sensations as the source or one of the sources of knowledge. He makes them the principle of all knowledge, and claims to explain the possibility of representations on the basis of sensations. Such a claim is probably open to criticism, as contemporary philosophers of perception have persistently pointed out: sensations do not account for all perceptive mechanisms and are probably not the origin of representations. However, Condillac's singular undertaking had at least one extremely positive aspect, far from being insignificant, which can be considered a discovery: it bound psychology in with the body and shed light on, long before the latest research, how much is owed by self-knowledge as a mind endowed with desire, intention and belief to the disposal of representations of the body in action. That this undertaking achieved what it did is due to the attention that it paid to "sensations" and not just to "perceptive information" or even to the primary qualities of the body in Locke's philosophy, the vocabulary and grounds of which it challenges in part.

Notes

1 Pinel, 1800; Riese, 1968; Paradis, 1993. See also Samuel Lézé in this volume.
2 The abbreviations *Essay* and *Sensations* refer respectively to *Essay on the Origin of Human Knowledge* and *Treatise on Sensations*.
3 Condillac (1947–1951) III. *Dictionnaire des synonymes*, p. 398. Condillac's works will be quoted in Georges Le Roy's edition, *OP* in an abbreviated form. Where an English translation still exists, it will be indicated in a footnote. In this paper, the most frequently used translation is Franklin Philip's, Condillac, 2014. But *Essay on the Origin of Human Knowledge* will be quoted in Hans Aarsleff's translation, Condillac, 2001.
4 It is worth mentioning Derrida, 1980 and Anne Devarieux in this volume, without forgetting the more literary or historically approaches to the *Treatise on Sensations*: see also Markovits, 2018.
5 Trying to define Condillac's naturalism is not an absolutely new undertaking. See Schaupp, 1891, and, to a lesser extent, Dewaule, 1891. Although our view is quite different, these earlier works provide arguments to our current reading of *Treatise on Sensations*.
6 Among the impressive number of publications on this subject, see more particularly, Dennett, 1992; Lycan, 1995; Chalmers, 1997; Seager, 1999; Catalano, 2000; Rowlands, 2001; Bennett and Hacker, 2003. It is also worth mentioning the website of the electronic journal *Psyche*, organ of The *Association for the Scientific Study of Consciousness*, http://psyche.cs.monash.edu.au
7 See Wittgenstein, 1958.
8 For further details of this debate, and particularly the refutation of the different classical solutions of the "transition problem" and the problem's resumption based on a functional study of action, see Proust, 2000, 2003.
9 Shoemaker, 1968, 1984; Evans, 1982; Peacoke, 1999.
10 One issue of *Consciousness and Cognition*, number 12 (2003) is entirely devoted to this question. It collects the proceedings of the Max Planck Institute Symposium, "Self and Action," which took place in October 2002.
11 *Essay*,I, II, ch. V.
12 Condillac (1947–1951), *Traité des animaux*, II, ch. 5, OP. vol. 1, p. 363 ; *Essay, I, II, 4, § 43*.
13 This thesis, which also serves as a starting point for contemporary naturalistic philosophers, boils down to stating that it is impossible to deduce the existence of self-consciousness from the mere existence of any current thought; a thought may be analysed in terms of "it thinks," in other words, in the third person, without involving any self-knowledge from oneself as subject. Condillac stresses this point when he writes that the statue is "the scent of rose" or that it "is entirely the impression which is made on its organs," without being able to say "I" at the very first moment it exists. *Sensations*, I, 1.

Representations of the Body and Self-Knowledge   249

14 The polemic engaged in by Paul Ricœur against Derek Parfit perfectly illustrates this link with Locke; see Parfit, 1984; Ricœur, 1990 .
15 Locke is frequently used to condemn the confusion between consciousness and self-consciousness, or the inadequacy of the memory theory as a foundation for self-consciousness.
16 "If we present it with a rose, to us it will be a statue that smells a rose; but to itself, it will be the smell itself of this flower," *Sensations*, I, 1, § 2.
17 Locke, 1975, Introduction, p. 44.
18 *Essay*, I, sect. 2, ch.1, § 15.
19 Locke, 1975, pp. 331–348.
20 *Essay*, II, sect. I, ch. 8 et ch. 9.
21 "It follows that consciousness not only give us knowledge of ours perceptions, but furthermore, if those perceptions are repeated, it often makes us aware that we had them before and makes us recognize them as belonging to us or as affecting a being that is constantly the same 'self' despite their variety and succession. Seen in relation to these new effects, consciousness is a new operation which is at our service every instant and is the foundation of experience," *Essay, I. 2., 1, §15.*
22 These objections mainly extend the first criticism addressed to Locke in the English language by Joseph Butler and Thomas Reid, Butler, 1736; Reid, 1785, pp. 333–334.
23 Shoemaker and Swinburne, 1984, pp. 67–132.
24 Shomaker, 1970.
25 Dennett, 1991.
26 Gallagher, 2000.
27 Proust, 1996.
28 Schizophrenia and autism are the most frequently studied pathologies in this perspective. Proust and Grivois, 1998; Campbell Schizophrenia, 1999; Stephen and Graham, 2000.
29 Jeannerod, 1994.
30 *Sensations*, I, 2, § 6.
31 *Sensations*, II, 11.
32 Condillac, *1947–1951, De l'Art de penser,* OP. vol. 2, p.733.
33 *Sensations*, I, 6, § 1.
34 *Sensations*, I, 6, § 3.
35 The specification and the description of these structures became the focus of many debates, which are partly set out in Roessler and Eilan, 2003.
36 Gallistel, 1990.
37 Guttenplan,1994; Sperber, 2000.
38 The study of links between metacognition and representation was the purpose of the seminar *Action, Perception, Intention, Consciousness* 2004–2005, supervised by Joëlle Proust, Elisabeth Pacherie and Jérôme Dokic, in the Institut Jean Nicod (Paris). See also Joëlle Proust, 2003.
39 Therefore, dolphins and monkeys, which are apparently unable to form metarepresentations, display abilities to solve relatively complex metacognitive problems; Smith, Hields, and Washburn, 2003.
40 Proust, p. 183.
41 *Sensations*, IV, pp. 512–513.
42 *Sensations, The Plan of This Work*, p. 305.
43 Drawing general implications from this idea, see Derrida, 1980.
44 *Sensations*, II, 8.

250 *Aliènor Bertrand*

45 *Sensations*, III & IV.
46 *Sensations*, IV, 5.
47 *Sensations*, IV, 4, p. 533.
48 *Sensations*, IV.
49 Condillac (1947–1951), *OP.* vol. 1 *Grammaire*, I, ch. 1, pp. 428–431 ; *OP.* vol. 2, *La Logique*, II, ch. 2, pp. 396–398.
50 *Essay*, II, sect. I, ch. 1.
51 *Essay*, I, II, ch.4, §35.
52 "Their memory began to have some exercise; they gained command to their imagination, and little by little they succeeded in doing by reflection what they had formerly done only by instinct." *Essay*, II, sect.1, 4, § 3; see also, *Essai*, II, I, X, §105.
53 *Sensations*, IV, II, §2.
54 *Essay*, I, II, ch. 6, § 58.
55 *Essay*, I, sect. 2 , 1, §3. Let us compare to "But if this man had not noticed what his body does in such cases, he would not have learned to recognise desire in the movements of another. He would therefore not understand the meaning of the movements made in front of him: he would therefore not be able to make similar movements on purpose to make himself be understood." Condillac (1947–1951), *OP. vol. 1, Grammaire*, I, ch.1, p. 429.
56 The modification of the definition of institutional signs, qualified in the *Grammar* as artificial signs and no longer as arbitrary signs, aims to resolve part of this difficulty. Condillac (1947–1951), *OP. vol. 1, Grammaire*, I , ch. 1, p. 429.
57 Condillac (1947–1951), *OP. vol. 2, La logique*.
58 Condillac (1947–1951), *OP. vol. 1, Traité des animaux*, II, 3, pp. 358–359.
59 "The decomposition of a thought presupposes the existence of that thought; and it would be absurd to say that I only begin to judge and reason when I begin to be able to represent successively what I know when I judge and when I reason." Condillac (1947–1951), *OP. vol. 1, Grammaire*, I, ch.3, *OP*, p. 436.
60 "These ideas will only be decomposed insofar as circumstances will determine to point out, one after the other, the movements which are the natural signs of them." Condillac (1947–1951), *OP. vol. 1, Grammaire*, I, ch. 7, *OP*, p. 444.
61 Grivois and Proust 1998, p. 18.
62 Grivois and Proust 1998, p. 19.

References

Bennett, M. R., & Hacker, P. M. S. (2003). *Philosophical Foundations of Neuroscience*. Oxford: Blackwell.
Block, N., Flanagan, O., & Güzeldere, G. (Eds.) (1997). *The Nature of Consciousness: Philosophical Debates*. Cambridge, MA: The MIT Press.
Butler, J. (1736). *Dissertation I: Of personal identity*. In The Analogy of Religion, Natural and Revealed. London: printed for James, John and Paul Knapton, pp. 300–309.
Campbell, J. (1999). "Schizophrenia, The Space of Reasons and Thinking as a Motor Process," *The Monist* 82(4), 609–625.
Catalano, J. S. (2000). *Thinking Matter: Consciousness from Aristotle to Putnam and Sartre*. London: Routledge.

Representations of the Body and Self-Knowledge 251

Chalmers, D. J. (1997). *The Conscious Mind: In Search of a Fundamental Theory.* Oxford: Oxford University Press.
Condillac, É. Bonnot de (1947–1951). *Œuvres philosophiques*, Ed. G. Le Roy, 3 vols. Paris: Presses Universitaires de France.
Condillac, É. Bonnot de. (2001). *Essay on the Origin of Human Knowledge.* Ed. and trans. Hans Aarsleff. Cambridge: Cambridge UP.
Condillac, É. Bonnot de. (2014). *The Philosophical Writings of Étienne Bonnot de Condillac.* Trans. Franklin Philip and Harlan Lane. New York: Psychology Press.
Dennett, D. C. (1991). *Consciousness Explained.* Boston, MA: Little Brown.
Derrida, J. (1980). *The Archeology of the Frivolous: Reading Condillac.* Lincoln: University of Nebraska Press.
Dewaule, L. (1891). *Condillac et la psychologie anglaise contemporaine.* Paris: Alcan.
Evans, G. (1982). *The Varieties of Reference.* Oxford: Oxford University Press.
Gallagher, S. (2000). "Self-reference and Schizophrenia," in D. Zahavi (ed.), *Exploring the Self.* Amsterdam: John Benjamin, pp. 203–239.
Gallistel, R. C. (1990). *The Organization of Learning.* Cambridge, MA: MIT Press.
Grivois, H., & Proust, J. (1998). *Subjectivité et conscience d'agir dans la psychose. Approches cognitive et clinique.* Paris: Puf.
Guttenplan, S. (1994). *A Companion to the Philosophy of Mind.* Oxford: Blackwell.
Jeannerod, M. (1994). "The Representing Brain. Neural Correlates of Motor Intention and Imagery." *Behavioral and Brain Sciences* 17, 187–245.
Locke, J. (1975). *An Essay Concerning Human Understanding.* Oxford: Clarendon Press.
Lycan, W. G. (1995). *Consciousness.* Cambridge, MA: Bradford Books/MIT Press.
Markovits, F. (2018). *La statue de Condillac: les cinq sens en quête de moi.* Paris: Hermann.
Paradis, A. (1993). "De Condillac à Pinel ou les fondements philosophiques du traitement moral." *Philosophiques, Revue de la société philosophique du Québec*, vol. XX, N°1, Spring 1993, pp. 69–112.
Peacoke, C. (1999). *Being Known.* Oxford: Oxford University Press.
Pinel, P. (1800). *Traité médico-philosophique* sur l'aliénation mentale. Paris: Richard, Caille et Ravier.
Proust, J. (1996)."Identité personnelle et pathologie de l'action," in Joseph, I. et Proust, J. *La folie dans la place*, Paris: Éditions de l'École des hautes études en sciences sociales, pp. 155–176.
Proust, J. (2000). "Les conditions de la connaissance de soi." *Philosophiques* 27/1, Printemps 2000, pp. 161–186.
Proust, J. (2003). "Thinking of Oneself as the Same." *Consciousness and Cognition* 12, 495–509.
Proust, J. (2003). "Does Metacognition Necessarily Involve Metarepresentation?," *Behavioral and Brain Sciences* 26, 352–352. Cambridge University Press.
Reid, T. (1785). "Of Mr Locke's Account of Our Personal Identity," in *Essays on the Intellectual Powers of Man*, Essay III, chapter 6, Edinburgh: printed for John Bell, and G.G.J. & J. Robinson, London, pp. 333–334.

Riese, W. (1968). "La méthode analytique de Condillac et ses rapports avec l'œuvre de Philippe Pinel." *Revue Philosophique de la France et de l'étranger* 158, 321–336.
Ricœur, P. (1990). *Soi-même comme un autre*. Paris: Seuil.
Roessler, J., & Eilan, N. (Eds.) (2003). *Agency and Self-awareness*. Oxford: Clarendon Press.
Rowlands, M. (2001). *The Nature of Consciousness*. Cambridge: Cambridge University Press.
Schaupp, Z. (1925). *The Naturalism of Condillac*. Lincoln: University of Nebraska Press.
Seager, W. (1999). *Theories of Consciousness*. London: Routledge.
Shoemaker, S. (1968). "Self-Reference and Self-awareness." *Journal of Philosophy*, 65, 555–567.
Shoemaker, S. (1970). "Persons and Their Past." *American Philosophical Quaterly* 7(4), also in *Identity, Cause and Mind*. Cambridge, 19–47.
Shoemaker, S., & Swinburne, R. (1984). *Personal Identity*. Oxford: Blackwell.
Smith, J. D., Hields, W. E., & Washburn, D. A. (2003). "The Comparative Psychology of Uncertainty Monitiring and Metacognition." *Behaviour and Brain Sciences*, 26, 03.
Sperber, D. (Ed.) (2000). *Metarepresentations. A Multidisciplinary Perspective*. Oxford: Oxford University Press.
Stephen, G. L., & Graham, G. (2000). *When Self-consciousness Breaks*. Cambridge, MA: MIT Press.
Wittgenstein, L. (1958). *The Blue and Brown Books*, R. Rhees ed. Oxford: Blackwell.

15 Reductions and Radicalisation of Reductions

Condillac, Michel Henry and Maine de Biran

Anne Devarieux

1 Introduction

In this chapter I will examine two important moments in the French reception of Condillac: the influence of his *Traité des sensations* (1754) on Maine de Biran's *Mémoire sur la décomposition de la pensée* (1805), and the resumption of that influence in Michel Henry's phenomenology of life as exposed in *Incarnation* (2000). The role of Maine de Biran in Henry's phenomenology is already known.[1] However, how he integrates Condillac's sensualism into his material phenomenology is a question to be addressed. I claim that Henry's Condillacism is built on Biran's legacy. Whenever Henry wants to pay tribute to Maine de Biran's unprecedented discovery of the very Being of the ego, he underlines the essential role played in this discovery by Biran's criticism of Condillac.[2]

Although Destutt de Tracy led Biran to derive the "sentiment of effort" from the simple "sensation of movement," Condillac's role should not be underestimated, especially with regard to his analysis of the statue's knowledge of its own body and external bodies (Chapter V of *A Treatise on Sensations*). This analysis allowed Biran to specify the meaning of the "continuously resistant inner extension" (Biran passim), the second term of the primitive inner relation, the first being the so-called "hyperorganic" force.[3]

These two moments in the French reception of Condillac should be understood as a story of reduction in two meanings: first, in the sense of the properly phenomenological method of a Husserlian epoche of the natural attitude, leading to the "reconduction" of the world-region to the consciousness-region; second, as a reduction to the simplest elements, which, in the banal sense, is a reconduction to, or even a reduction of, with the underlying question: who emerges augmented, if not transformed, from this philosophical-chemical operation, from this reduction to the elementary?

DOI: 10.4324/9781003334750-19

2 The Condillaquian Reduction

2.1 Questioning the Condillaquian Requisits

For this purpose... we farther supposed that its marble exterior did not allow it the use of any of its senses, and we reserved for ourselves the freedom to open the mat will to the different impressions they are susceptible of.
(*A Treatise on Sensations*, p. 170)[4]

In these lines, Condillac tells the reader the purpose of his work: to trace the development and transformation of our faculties, the principle of which is none other than sensation (*A Treatise on Sensations*, p. 171).

Biran tells us that he sought with no success the word of the "enigma" of transformed sensation (*Mémoire sur la decomposition de la pensée*, p. 342).[5] In fact, Condillac's method, far from being a real analysis or decomposition of thought, is, according to him, an abstract construction. "Abstract" because, instead of analysing sensations, Condillac first eliminates their distinctive characteristics in order to retain an abstract element (devoid of any reality) which he calls "sensation," and then describes the different aspects that sensation takes on, that is, if it is exclusive, or coexists with another, or reproduces itself in the absence of its object. By giving these transformations known names, without worrying about whether he is diverting them from their true meaning, Condillac builds a coherent, logical system, but one without any common measure with which we are familiar. Condillac is paradoxically the victim of "l'esprit de système." In the *Traité des* sensations, he denies the duality based on intimate sense that he recognised, according to Biran, in his first work—*An Essay on the Origin of Human Knowledge* (Part 1, Sect. I, Ch. I, §5)—where he distinguished between the operations and the materials of our knowledge.[6] In the *Traité* he admits only one class of passive and homogeneous modes (Biran, *Mémoire sur la décomposition de la pensée*, p. 344).

But what does the term "sensation" mean? According to Biran, this abstract term "derives either from an adjective or from the participle of an action verb" (*Mémoire*, pp. 57–58). In the first case, it designates a permanent attribute of the self, but in the second it stands for an action produced by its constitutive force. In the first case, it contains the idea of a subject participating in each of its modes; in the other, it contains the idea of a force inseparable from its acts. Now, if sensation is the fundamental and permanent attribute of thought, how can it be said to be transformed, if it remains identical within all its variable modifications? And if it does not enclose any precise idea of the "self [le moi]" (*Mémoire*, p. 342)—by dismissing the idea of force Condillac dismisses the idea of personal insight or immediate apperception—the term "sensation" only represents an abstract

Reductions and Radicalisation of Reductions   255

modification of its subject of inherence and can become the logical subject of various propositions, without having in itself any kind of reality.

In short, if "sensation" is taken as a whole (affective and intuitive), Condillac's decomposition cannot be said to be a true one; for in order to be so it would need to be the "resolution of a complex mode or idea into its simple elements," and not a "decomposition of the faculty of feeling, or of any sensation in general." It is a simple "development" (*Ib.*, p. 56 et 338).

The Condillaquian analysis is therefore purely grammatical. It is carried out from the objective point of view of a physicist, who starts from a "fantastic model" (i.e. something to which nothing real corresponds). By assuming this hypothesis, no science dealing with the operations of the mind is conceivable from a real (i.e. *reflected*) point of view because "the nominal titles of faculties are no more than circumstances or characters of the same sensation which are really inseparable from it" (*Ib.*, p. 55).

In such a "middle method" placed between that of Descartes and that of Locke or Bacon, sensation is the common principle of the faculties and encloses or envelops them; it combines an external point of view and a kind of internal point of view: sensation is linked to the action of a foreign cause, for "although the external world does not yet exist for the statue, it is nonetheless supposed to be there, really existing; thus, we find ourselves, from the very first steps, in the method of objective experience" (*Ib.*, p. 335). Yet another kind of internal point of view is required.

> [if] the statue is, in the eyes of the one who has constructed it, and who observes it from the outside, a feeling being which receives the impression of an object, or of an odoriferous cause, it is, for itself, only its own modification, and nothing more. We are therefore placed in another kind of interior point of view, and obliged to seek the passage from this modification to the perception or representation of its cause or object, as Descartes seeks the passage from the primitive and reflective act which reveals to him only his own existence (considered as absolute), to the reality of foreign existences.
>
> (*Ib.*)

What does the phenomenologist Henry say about this Condillaquian beginning? He greets it and baptises it on the spot: the Condillaquian operation is nothing other than a "phenomenological reduction":

> the statue isolated from the world is a figure of phenomenological reduction, it delimits a sphere of absolute immanence where we stick to impressions as they arise in experience, independently of any idea or interpretation from elsewhere.
>
> (*Incarnation*, p. 198)[7]

On the basis of this first reduction, Condillac accomplishes a series of successive reductions.

Two words only about this Henryan interpretative presupposition: it is not only a perfect replica of the one made with regard to Biran himself, whose work is nothing other than a "vast phenomenological reduction" (*Philosophie et phénoménologie du corps*, p. 25),[8] but it also immediately breaks with Biran's interpretation of Condillac. While Henry praises the Condillaquian discovery of the sphere of immanence that characterises both subjective life and life in general (independent of, and antithetical to the transcendent mode of donation of the world), Biran does point out the hybrid character of such a beginning which implicitly supposes a foreign cause. While Condillac, according to Biran, "submits man to the Procrustean bed" (*Journal*, I, p. 184)[9] by cutting out what he cannot explain due to his purely logical method, he is, in the eyes of Henry, a phenomenologist before his time, similar to Descartes and Biran. He is in fact a better one, Henry claims, because he discovered ontological dualism, i.e. the ontological difference through which world and life are given to us: the latter without distance in the pure immanence of "self-affection," as opposed to the "ek-static transcendence" or exteriority of the world.

2.2 Questioning the "I" of the Statue

Initially limited to the sense of smell, the rose-smelling statue is unable to distinguish itself from the flower it smells (*A Treatise on Sensations*, Chapter 1, 174). Memory, however, is the persistence of an impression that the statue's attention is able to retain according to its degree of strength (*A Treatise on Sensations*, Chapter 2, p. 178). Soon, in fact, it "is never one smell without recalling that it was once another smell" (*A Treatise on Sensations*, Chapter 6, 200). And what about its "I"? "Its 'I' is only the collection of sensations it experiences, but of those its memory recalls" (*A Treatise on Sensations*, pp. 200–201). Thus, the statue cannot say "I" at the first moment of its existence, because to say "I" supposes the consciousness of a change and with it the judgement that it is the same as before: the self supposes the memory of impressions.

If what Biran calls the "identificatory becoming" [le devenir identificatoire] of the statue deprives it of the possibility of distinguishing itself from what it feels, it nevertheless feels itself as extended. According to Condillac, such a feeling corresponds neither to its greatness nor to its surface; it is a "vague impression of its extension" (*A Treatise on Sensations*, Chapter 11, p. 217). Condillac indeed asserts the existence of a "basic sentience" in the statue:

> Our statue... exists first by its sensitivity to the action of the various parts of its body on each other, and above all to respiratory movements: and there you have the lowest degree of sentience to which it can be

reduced. I will call this "basic sentience", because animal life begins and depends uniquely on this activity of the machine.
(*A Treatise on Sensations*, Part 2, Chapter 1, p. 225)

Condillac seems to assimilate, as to their origin, such a "basic sentience" to the "I" of the statue. In the *Treatise on the Sensations*, Condillac therefore affirms the existence of a kind of primitive spatiality of our own body, distinct from the actual extension of the body of the statue, which is due to the action of the organs on each other, basis of a "fundamental feeling" by which it feels itself to be in some way extended, a vague idea which allows several modifications to coexist within it: "It will be limited to basic sentience and it will know its own existence only by the vague impression that results from the movements to which it owes its life" (*A Treatise on Sensations*, p. 226).

Thus Biran finds in Condillac's *Treatise* the distinction between a vague extension and a circumscribed body, with the decisive nuance that the Biranian inner extension will be, though initially vague and unlimited, *relative to effort*.

3 Discovering Bodies

3.1 Touch

Does this feeling give a sense of the extension of the statue's body? Condillac's answer is negative:

> It will not sense at all that some parts are exterior to others and contiguous with them. It is as if it existed only at a point and it is not yet possible for it to discover that it has extension.
> (*A Treatise on Sensations*, p. 226)

Since sensation is not related to the body, how will the statue be able to acquire the knowledge of bodies in general from its own sensations—which are, for the statue, only states of its own being (*A Treatise on Sensations*, Part 2, Chapter 4, p. 230)?[10] How then, driven at first by instinct and without any knowledge of it, will the statue discover "that it has a body and that beyond it there are other bodies?" (*A Treatise on Sensations*, Part 2, Chapter 5, p. 233).

We know the Condillaquian answer: if instinctive movements allow the statue to learn that it has a body and to recognise itself in its solid and distinct parts, contiguity and continuity must wait for the sense of touch:

> It is only with extension that we can make extension as it is only with objects that we can make objects. For we do not see how there can be

contiguity among several nonextended things nor how as a result they can form a continuum.
(*A Treatise on Sensations*, p. 230)[11]

To the question of how we "find ourselves" in our organs, how the "I" can understand that the different parts of its body are different parts of *itself*, Condillac replies: when we know perfectly the nature of the mind and the mechanism of the human body, no doubt we will be able to explain readily how it is that the "I" which is only in the mind seems to be found in the body (*A Treatise on Sensations*, p. 231).

In any case, the statue will end up putting its hands on itself:

> The statue will only discover that it has a body when it distinguishes the different parts of that body and when it recognizes itself in each part to be the same sentient being; and it will discover that there are other bodies only because it does not find itself in those that it touches.
> (*A Treatise on Sensations*, p. 233)

Conversely, for the statue, the impossibility to "recognise" itself in other bodies will make it judge that there are bodies *distinct* from it. Only the *réplique du sentiment* makes it possible to distinguish between its own body and a foreign body (*A Treatise on Sensations*, p. 234).

For the statue to get the sensation of the body of its own, it must experience the sensation of solidity which makes us perceive the resistance that two bodies (or two parts of a body) have by mutually excluding each other. That is so because Condillac distinguishes felt solidity and judged impenetrability: we judge that two bodies are impenetrable, i.e. they mutually exclude each other from the proper place they occupy. The basis of this judgement is the sensation of solidity which, in the feeling of the pressure exerted, gives us sensitive access to this mutual exclusion. According to Condillac, the sensation of solidity cannot be confused with a modification (i.e. a state) of our own being (*A Treatise on Sensations*, p. 233). In Condillac's view, resistance therefore refers to the exclusive and reciprocal pressure felt in relation to two bodies. This means that resistance is what distinguishes bodies:

> Since the essence of this sensation of solidity is to represent at one and the same moment two things that exclude each other, the mind will not perceive solidity as one of those states in which it finds only itself.
> (*A Treatise on Sensations*, p. 233)

So, Condillac writes: "There you have then a sensation with which the mind proceeds from itself to outside of itself and we begin to understand how it will discover objects [corps]" (*A Treatise on Sensations*, p. 233).

Reductions and Radicalisation of Reductions 259

When the hand accidentally touches a part of the body, the statue finds itself necessarily in that part: "However, in distinguishing the chest from the hand, the statue will find its 'I' anew in each of them because it senses itself in both of them" (*A Treatise on Sensations*, p. 234). But this body is not yet an entire whole for the statue. Therefore, we are facing a statue that moves without knowing that it moves, without knowing that it has a hand, a statue that discovers, through touch, parts of a solid body that it makes out to be its own because they respond sensitively to it.

3.2 Continuity of Self/Contiguity

How will the statue know that this body, which replicates it perceptibly and in which it "finds its self," forms a single body, i.e. "a single continuum?" (*A Treatise on Sensations*, p. 234). In order to know this, the statue must experience the continuity of its body (identified by Condillac with the contiguity of its parts). *The following lines written by Condillac are decisive in this respect, and it is not by accident that both Maine de Biran and Michel Henry comment extensively on them*:

> But if the statue happens to move its hand the length of its arm and, without skipping over any intermediary part, onto its chest, its head, etc., it will experience a continuity of self as its fingerprints, so to speak; and this same hand that has brought together the formerly separated parts into a single continuum will thereby render extension more perceptible.
> (*A Treatise on Sensations*, p. 234, emphasis added)

Later Condillac adds:

> The statue learns then to recognize its body and to recognize itself in all the different parts that make it up because as soon as it places its hand on one of these parts the same sentient being responds, as it were, from the one part to the other "this is me". Let the statue continue to touch itself, and everywhere the sensation of solidity will represent two things that are mutually exclusive and at the same time contiguous, and everywhere also the same sentient being will respond from one to the other: "this is me, this is me again". The statue senses itself in all the parts of its body. Thus it will no longer confuse itself with its states: it is no longer heat and cold but it senses heat in one part of its body and cold in another.
> (*A Treatise on Sensations*, p. 234)

What is remarkable about this passage? The assertion that the continuity of touch ensures the continuity of the body and thus that of a self. The statue admits that other bodies replicated it only because it admitted emptiness, space. Condillac thus supposes that in the absence of a continuous touch, the statue, whose parts substantially replicate each other, feels "as much 'I' as it feels (in) different body(ies)":

> When touch circumscribes several distinct and coexisting sensations within limits where the "I" replies to itself, the statue takes cognizance of its body; when touch circumscribes several distinct and coexisting sensations within limits where the "I" does not respond to itself, the statue has the idea of a body different from its own.
> (*A Treatise on Sensations*, p. 235)

How will the statue discover the existence of bodies other than its own and consequently that it is not "as if it were the only thing that existed?" (*A Treatise on Sensations*, p. 234). The foreign body, unlike its own, does not respond sensitively: *"When touch circumscribes several distinct and coexisting sensations within limits where the 'I' does not respond to itself, the statue has the idea of a body different from its own"* (*A Treatise on Sensations*, p. 235). To give the idea of a continuum, touch must therefore be uninterrupted, uniform, and the statue's sensations must "continue" without interruption.

In this analysis, the status of one's own body [sa "mienneté"] remains an enigma. Because it is absolutely identical, in its "givenness"—except for the replica of feeling—to the body seen from the outside, whose parts touch each other, are not outside of each other. By discovering, by chance, its own body, the statue discovers "the pleasure of feeling extended," as well as the sensual pleasure of movement (itself determined by pleasure), which increases its feeling of existence:

> Thus the statue is not limited to loving only itself but its love for objects [son amour pour les corps] follows from the love it has for itself. It has no other goal in loving them than the search for pleasure or the flight from pain.
> (*A Treatise on Sensations*, 238)

4   Biranian and Henrian Criticism

First of all, Maine de Biran has no difficulty in showing the absurdity of the hypothesis that a movement operates without any effort. Where Condillac sees only the replica of feeling, Biran confronts him with effort. He writes about the statue's hand: "I do see there a universal module, an instrument that serves to know, to measure objects, but this instrument itself how is it known in the first place?" (*Mémoire*, p. 137).[12]

Condillac has not gone back far enough in his analysis: "how can any mobile organ been constantly directed without being known?" Condillac has confused the representative, secondary knowledge of the body with the primitive feeling of self. This feeling is given in the experience of effort, and as such is inseparable from the inner resistance of the body itself.

Here we are at the heart of Henry's Biranism: the phenomenologist quotes these lines over and over again whenever he wants to underline the prodigious character of Biran's discovery:

> The hand, the organ of the sensation of solidity, according to Condillac, is the instrument that allows us to determine the parts of our body, but this instrument itself, how is it first known? This is a decisive question, as we can see, and it leads back to the other question that Maine de Biran asked Condillac, still concerning the hand: "How has any mobile organ been constantly directed without being known?" The movement of the hand is undoubtedly not known in the sense that it is not constituted, but if it can be directed by us, is it not because we are instructed in it, because we possess a primordial knowledge of it, which is precisely that kind of knowledge in which no phenomenological distance intervenes, in which no constitution takes place? The movement of the hand is known without being apprehended in a world, it is immediately given in the internal transcendental experience that merges with the very being of this movement. Because it is not constituted, because it is a transcendental experience, the movement of the hand has nothing to do with any displacement in objective space or in any transcendental medium, the original and real movement is a subjective movement. For this reason, too, it is in my power, not at all in the sense that objects, for example, are subject to the grasp of a power that would be mine, but in the sense that it is itself this power, where it is itself that which has a grasp on things.
>
> (*Philosophie et phénoménologie du corps*, p. 82)[13]

Biran radicalised Condillac's initial reduction and his own genius lies in the discovery of effort which ruins the doctrine of transformed sensation. It is then with regard to the feeling of effort that the analysis of the senses can be carried out. The origin of the self lies with that of a first willed effort.

4.1 Henryan Radicalisation of Biranian Radicalisation

What are the phenomenological lessons drawn from Henry's move? (1) Before being an instrument, the hand raises the issue, phenomenologically speaking, of the original movement which is always already in our possession: the hand is not known as part of an external and subjective body but as something in my power, without any intentional movement intervening, no distance, even phenomenological, and no reflection: one's own body is the source of all power in its "original potentiality," says Henry. That original knowledge of one's own body is a primordial *practical* knowledge. It is given before and in the absence of the transcendent world or "milieu," which is not linked to a displacement in external space and which is not relative to an objective or transcendent world. This is what Henry calls "transcendental internal experience" which is the "very being of movement" that "I" am. "The hand...is the very ego!" (*Philosophie et phénoménologie du corps*, p. 11). My body is an "I," i.e. the self-affection of a power. *This is the Henrian radicalisation of the first Biranian radicalisation of the Condillaquian reduction. But it is only the first.*

(2) There is, in fact, prior to all intentional movement, an original affectivity whose form-content is purely impressional,[14] by which the individual and Life are self-experiencing and are given to themselves: a pure interiority whose concrete matter is the affective impressional or sensual flesh, and which is the foundation of a fleshy memory, as well as its praxis. This is where *the second Henrian radicalisation* comes into play. This radicalisation affects both Condillac's and Biran's analyses (Biran in fact never said that effort was an auto-affection in the strict sense).

4.2 The Biranian "Resistentis Continuatio": The Inner Expanse

It is therefore necessary to start, according to our two authors, from the experience of a movement, which is never "coming out" of itself, but supposes a "primordial knowledge" of itself. The important question here is to know what precisely this experience consists of.

The Biranian continuum is an *inner touch*, or a schema without any sensible or tangible analogue, which is only valid through the awareness that I "have" of it. Such a continuum has nothing to do with contiguity because my resisting body is a body whose parts touch each other only because they are animated by the same force of will (*Mémoire*, p. 432). Biran calls it a "continuously resisting interior extension":

> There is first of all a common effort in the general locomotion of the body considered as a single solidarily mobile mass. To the unique deployment of this common effort, to the uniformity or continuity of organic resistance must correspond the feeling of a kind of interior extension which is at first vague and unlimited, but which nevertheless has the first and fundamental condition on which depends in another sense the perception of the objective extension, I mean the continuity of resistance to the same desired effort: resistentis continuatio.
>
> (*Mémoire*, p. 432)

Reductions and Radicalisation of Reductions 263

The resisting body is the *immediate object* of the will, it is a mobilisable mass and solid in its points: in it everything touches each other, not because it is composed of contiguous parts that touch themselves, which would make it a simple extended being, foreign *de jure* to effort, but because in it everything holds together. This active holding and this active internal cohesion are immediately felt, without being seen or touched from the outside.

Consequently, it is the external or representative knowledge that the statue has of its body—what makes my body *mine* is, for Condillac, nothing other than the possibility of apprehending a contiguous thing—but Biran declares this to be secondary (*Ib.*, p. 137). Against Condillac, Biran intends to show that one's own body [le corps propre][15] is an immediate continuum while other bodies are a *mediated* continuum that can only be continuously perceived by means of a sense enclosed in the sense of effort: that is, the active external touch that has a double function—sensitive and motor. Composed extension does not constitute the essence of other bodies, and the "kind of composition" of the internal resistance is inseparable from the self.[16]

The outer extension is composed of and by our movements, while the inner one is only a "kind of composition," a composition resulting from effort. There is a major difference between these two extensions. The former is restricted to the "property of contiguous and juxtaposed parts" while the latter is not a matter of any juxtaposition of parts in a space. We thus gain two very different continuities: touch allows us to have a "continuous impression of a solid extension," but this is only because the external extension "applies to equally contiguous and juxtaposed sensible parts of our body" (Biran, 1990, p. 70).[17] In short, touch reveals the extension of external bodies, whereas the immediate apperception that the "I" has of itself in its own effort is inseparable from the experience of an inner continuity of resistance.

4.3 Replica of Effort and Replica of Feeling

Biran acknowledges along with Condillac that sensibility contributes both to a delimitation of the body itself with regard to foreign bodies (the feeling is redoubled in the case of the body itself and it is simple in the case of the foreign body) and to the knowledge of the forms, distances or situations of the touched parts. However, Biran is nevertheless keen to emphasise that the sensitive or passive tact composes the judgement of exteriority, which finds its foundation only in effort without creating it (*Mémoire*, p. 211). If there were no invincible or absolute resistance (coming) from foreign bodies, the ego would take itself for the soul of the world (*Mémoire*, p. 208).

4.4 Continuity of Self/Continuity of Body

Biran distinguishes between three things: (1) the primitive effort, (2) the active external touch and (3) the passive tact which composes the judgement of exteriority without constituting it (*Essai*, pp. 158–159). To make this explicit, Maine de Biran hypothesises a man whose hand would end "in a single finger entirely covered with a nail as sharp as one can imagine" (*Mémoire*, p. 205). This man would conceive of all outer existence in the form of a resistant point, without the idea of any extension, and therefore does not essentially receive the idea of body but rather that of resistance. Supposing—Biran continues—that

> this nail cannot move continuously but must jump from one point to another by a series of repeated actions, there would be the idea of a plurality of resistant points, or of repeated units which are still only the results of repeated acts of the same constrained force, but [there would] still no[t be and] idea of extension or composition by simultaneity.
>
> (*Mémoire*, p. 205)

Assuming now that he could slide continuously over the term resistant, he would have the idea of points that touch and continue (*Mémoire*, p. 206).

The essence of external bodies is constituted by the force of resistance, and consequently "we are finally neither more nor less certain of the reality of the foreign term than of that of the organic term, and consequently of the very existence of the subject of effort or of the self" (*Mémoire*, p. 207).

The sensibility of touch thus complicates the knowledge of the outer body without constituting it. Touch offers, in fact, the contrast between a redoubled and simple feeling in the respective cases of the application to a part that belongs to us or to a foreign part. Active touch thus clearly has a privilege in the knowledge of other bodies because it preserves us from sight and representation, that is to say, from the representative and secondary knowledge of the body.

Biranian inner extension, initially vague and unlimited, is therefore not, as in Condillac's case, the identification of the "I" with the world, for it is an extension *relative to* the effort, which consents to it and replicates it. In Condillac's case, the discovery of the solid and extended body—which is not yet the discovery of a space—is followed by the statue's "disquiet to know where it is and, if I may venture to express myself in this way, exactly up to what point it is" (*A Treatise on the sensations*, Part 2, Chapter 5, p. 235). Biran substitutes to such a disquiet *the question of knowing "how far" the will acts*. These two questions are very different. Where Condillac expresses an identification between the "I" and the world in terms of space, of expansion, and thus from an external point of view,

Biran expresses it from the point of view of effort: in the absence of the perception of outer bodies, I could believe that my *will* is everything.

It is only the inner extension that guarantees the distinct simultaneity of impressions, in an unrepresentable or unimaginable scheme. The hand cannot therefore be, as Condillac wrongly believed, what gives knowledge of the extension of the body itself, and the replica of feeling comes after the replica of effort. It is the active inner touch which is in itself a continuity inseparable from that of the inner resistance: "Je me touche moi-même intérieurement."[18]

5 The Henrian Revival of the Biranian Critique

Why is Biran's critique of Condillac "a move as brief as decisive in modern thought" (*Incarnation*, p. 198)? This is because it highlights the "pouvoir-se-mouvoir" immanent in the power to touch, without which the latter would be stripped of all power (*Incarnation*, p. 198). After recalling Biran's "decisive" question to Condillac—"what makes the power to touch a power?"—Henry continues:

> Because it stands in Life, the "moving itself" of the power to touch is an immanent movement, it is the movement that remains in itself in its very movement and takes itself with itself, that moves itself in itself—the self-movement that does not separate itself from itself and does not leave itself, not allowing any part of itself to be detached from itself, to be lost outside of itself, in any exteriority, in the exteriority of the world.
> (*Incarnation*, p. 203)

Henry's "power," a re-reading of the Biranian will, is not only given in immanence and capable of being actualised, but "constantly given, without any discontinuity" (*Incarnation*, p. 204). To the question of how an organ can be directed without being known, Henry replies: "Only the reduction to a radically immanent impressional subjectivity makes it possible to pose the problem in such a way as to remove the aporia" (*Incarnation*, p. 205).

Condillac had, at least, this immense merit. Henry agrees with Biran that the hand is not here the objective part of the objective body (nor is its movement a displacement in space); rather, it is the subjective power to touch and to take. However, according to the phenomenologist, this power is only given to itself, "put in possession of itself in the pathetic self-donation of life, in the flesh of our original corporeity" (*Incarnation*, p. 205). The concept of "flesh" by "enclosing within it the possibility of acting of each of our powers and its revelation" does name the possession of our powers (*Incarnation*, p. 205). For the "durable of the ego" [le durable de l'ego] of the Biranian effort, Henry substitutes the continuity of an original flesh, always given to oneself, without interruption, not even that of sleep.[19] And the durability of the Henrian ego owes its "permanence" only to a hyperpower or aprioristic possibility that Life gives him, which it gives him in the strict sense (*Philosophie et phénoménologie du corps*, p. 134). Such is the "permanent knowledge that is my very existence," the permanence of a power founded in our very being, which is no different from the being of our own body (*Philosophie et phénoménologie du corps*, p. 135).

Henry retains the material of the impression, to the detriment of the only voluntary movement. He maintains at the same time that the original impression is rooted in mobility and that it is a pathos: immediacy of a knowledge that never "leaves" itself, never escapes from itself, which he calls for that reason "revelation," which supposes the identification between the being given to itself and the self-donation itself.

5.1 The Question of Touch

As early as in *Philosophy and Phenomenology of the Body*, Henry denies the privilege given to touch in Biran's analysis and he attributes knowledge of external bodies to all the senses without discrimination (*Philosophie et phénoménologie du corps*, p. 114). Thus, touch loses the paradigmatic value it has had in Biran's work, and the capacity to touch, to grasp, that we are permanently in possession of, is only a pre-existing capacity of prehension that "dominates time" in an "Archi-Presence" of the body to itself.[20]

Henry substitutes the disposition of our powers for the (Biranian) idea of an "I" that inaugurates the life of relation, because he goes back upstream from this availability of our movements to the immemorial gift of Life. Consequently, it is the Henrian phenomenology of Life only that elucidates the "double presupposition" left untouched by Condillac's analysis, namely the relation of subjective movement to the objective displacement of the hand, and the relation that links this subjective movement to ourselves:

> To touch and feel, only the subjective power of touching can do this. On the one hand, it relates intentionally to what it touches. On the other hand, this intentional relation is only possible given to itself in the pathetic self-giving of Life.
>
> (*Incarnation*, p. 202)

In other words—and this is what makes for the whole heresy of Henrian phenomenology within Husserlian phenomenology—upstream of any intentional aim stands our flesh, which is given in pure affectivity. If Henrian touch is a pathos, it is because in the last instance all force is affective.[21] Biran, in criticising Condillac, happily leads us back to the "touching touch without which nothing touched would ever be for us" (*De la phénoménologie*, vol 1, p. 160). With Biran, the world is no longer an object of intellection and the subject ceases to be a rational subject as soon as our own body is installed at the principle of our experience of the world:

> The genius of Maine de Biran is to have understood that the type of experience according to which touch is in relation to itself as touching has nothing to do with that by which touching enters into relation with everything it touches.
> (*De la phénoménologie*, vol 1, p. 161)

While in the latter case the relation is intentional—the touch exceeds itself towards what it touches

> and reaches it as what resists it in such a way that what resists stands outside the force that comes to break against it. On the contrary, in the relation of the touching touch to itself, that allows this touching touch to be in possession of itself and to act, there is no intentional relation...
> (*De la phénoménologie*, vol 1, p. 162)

6   Henry, a Condillaquian? Condillac, a Phenomenologist?

By placing strong emphasis on the primitive knowledge of the hand, Henry downplays the role of "motility of consciousness."[22] Regardless of the legitimacy of the interpretation of Biranian effort as self-affection, the question arises whether one should consider the self-affection of the self, the "immanence of power-touch," as a replica of feeling or of effort. In fact, Henry absorbs under the term "powers" what is irreducible to the Biranian power to act, namely the multiple powers of being affected by an ego, which in turn are resorbed into the essential passivity or affectivity of Life itself. In short, is the self-impressionality of the Henrian ego not the first cousin of the Condillaquian replica of feeling?

Biran's feeling of power is then turned into the power of feeling. The "decisive connection," according to Henry, is indeed between affectivity and power:

> If power is only given to oneself in the pathetic given [self-donation] of Life, then all power is affective not because of the effect of circumstances that would be foreign to its own essence, but because it resides in this pathetic self-affection that, installing it in itself, gives it the possibility of exercising itself, of being the power that it is.
> (*Incarnation*, p. 204)

If Henry locates the deficiency of Condillac's analysis in his oblivion of effort, he does so to immediately interpret it as an oblivion of Life itself. He locates it here only to affirm, first of all, a pathetic determination internal to each of our powers or "bodily performances": "Here is easily recognised and becomes intelligible the unfounded presupposition of all Condillaquian analysis: the origin of all the movements of the statue in its pure impressional subjectivity according to the play of its impressions" (*Incarnation*, pp. 204–205). The Condillaquian phenomenological reduction, although unfounded, *is nonetheless true*: for it lies in the uncovering of pathetic self-impressionality, which neither Husserl nor Merleau-Ponty could see (*Incarnation*, pp. 222ff). Quite a strange and ironic verdict if we remember that Biran blames Condillac precisely for having forgotten life itself, for having forgotten that sensation presupposes the living as living (Biran, *Essai*, p. 211).

Where, then, is the Henrian overcoming of Condillaquian analysis? If the statue isolated from the world is a figure of phenomenological reduction, which "delimits a sphere of absolute immanence where one holds on to impressions as they are experienced themselves, independently of any idea or interpretation from elsewhere" (*Incarnation*, p. 200), the question is indeed to understand:

> where the possibility of accomplishing such movements [by which the statue reacts to the sensations it experiences] lies: will it be "in the impressions themselves?" It would be necessary to show this, which hardly seems possible as long as the sensations are considered as psychological data, passive modalities of our soul in the arrival of which the latter has nothing to do.
> (*Incarnation*, pp. 200–201)

The one and only error of Condillac was to be a sensualist:

> The phenomenology of impression, the centrepiece of the reversal of phenomenology, had persuaded us that the humblest impression carries within it a revelation of the Absolute. All of Maine de Biran's criticism of Condillac refers to an "inside" of sensation that sensualism never accounts for.
> (*Incarnation*, p. 238)

It is Biran, and not Condillac, who gave a model of the given of this *inside*, which is none other than immanent Life. Nevertheless, Condillac anticipated Henry's material phenomenology which emphasises impression.

At last we can assume that Henry would have been particularly sensitive to the final lines of Chapter VI of the *Treatise on Sensations* because they open up the scope of the human field of action in general (against all philosophy of meaning and ideality). Action is based on the subjective body and its powers, that is to say, on the primitive action exercised on one's own body, which, doing no more than the former, obeys "a simple interest in knowledge" (*Incarnation*, p. 237). But this action is the result of a sensitive, sensual teleology, which the phenomenologist calls no more and no less than the "auto-eroticism" (*Incarnation*, p. 237) of the statue.

The "fable of the statue" in its twofold direction (man's power over nature/sensitive or erotic possibilities of man's body) shows its shortcomings which a simple (i.e. Biranian-inspired) phenomenology of the flesh cannot resolve but requires a shift to a phenomenology of the Incarnation in which the flesh is "the place of perdition" but also of salvation (*Incarnation*, pp. 236–238).

7 Conclusion

Let us not be surprised that Henry's phenomenological reduction seems to us to be much closer to Condillac's than to Maine de Biran's: does not Henry rely, as early as in *Philosophie et phénoménologie du corps*, on Condillac to affirm that there would be a relationship prior to the primitive duality? All the commentators have noted this "misinterpretation" of a master who is no longer a disciple! (*Philosophie et phénoménologie du corps*, p. 176). For in the passage quoted by Henry, far from admitting a more primitive duality than the primitive duality itself, Biran affirms, in a gesture directed against Condillaquian decomposition, that in order to found personality, "some other condition than a completely passive affectivity" is necessary.[23] The primitive compound [le composé primitif] is not the "I" and the sensation, but the all-inclusive relationship between the force and the inner resistance of the body itself. For Henry, however, this relation "is instituted within subjectivity itself in the phenomenon of transcendental internal experience" and is "a relation which, to tell the truth, is no longer a relation, since it is the very negation...of all mediation, but which is the very being of absolute Life" (*Philosophie et phénoménologie du corps*, p. 176).

Against sensualism, which makes sensible data the raw material of the life of consciousness, Husserl argued that the flow of experience is not a flow of sensations or a set of hyletic data—the latter constitute a "matter which by itself is in fact meaningless and irrational, though certainly accessible to rationalisation."[24] In Husserl's view, the error of sensualism was to try to reconstruct the life of consciousness from sensations or hyletic data, non-intentional sensual elements, while neglecting acts or "intentional functions." According to Henry, such a hyletic phenomenology (to which he opposes the *material* phenomenology) "borders on sensualism" and is the "testimony of the unresolved problem of the being of subjectivity" (*Phénoménologie matérielle*, pp. 13–59). By placing the pure matter of affectivity, the "invisible phenomenological substance" (*Phénoménologie matérielle*, p. 7), upstream of all intentionality as its ultimate foundation — against the Husserlian hyle, —does not Henrian phenomenology designate itself as the illegitimate but distant daughter of sensualism? If Biran is the "prince of thought" (*Philosophie et phénoménologie du corps*, p. 12), Condillac at least deserves the title of "prince consort"!

Notes

1 Anne Devarieux (2018) *L'intériorité réciproque. L'hérésie biranienne de Michel Henry*, Grenoble: Millon.
2 Michel Henry never ceases to express his debt to Biran and to mobilize the key concepts of his thought.
3 Maine de Biran's, *Of Immediate Apperception* (2021) (translated by Mark Sinclair), Bloomsbury Academic, §2, 90. On the "phenomenal" self, p. 118.
4 Étienne Bonnot de Condillac (1982) *Philosophical Writings. Volume 2. A Treatise on Sensations* (Translated by Franklin Philip and Harlane Lane. London: Lawrence Erlbaum).
5 Maine de Biran (1988) *Œuvres*, vol. III, *Mémoire sur la décomposition de la pensée*, Paris: Vrin.
6 See also André Charrak (2003) *Empirisme et métaphysique*, Paris: Vrin, p. 28; pp. 59–61.
7 See A. Devarieux (2018) and B. Baertschi (1981).
8 Michel Henry (1965) *Philosophie et phénoménologie du corps, Essai sur l'ontologie biranienne*, Paris: PUF.
9 Maine de Biran, *Journal*, vol. I (Neuchâtel: La Baconnière).
10 "Si l'âme ne les apercevait que comme des manières d'être, qui sont concentrées en elle, elle ne verrait qu'elle dans ses sensations: il lui serait donc impossible de découvrir qu'elle a un corps, et qu'au-delà de ce corps il y en a d'autres" (Condillac, Étienne Bonnot de (1947–1951). *Œuvres philosophiques*, edited by George Le Roy, vol. I, Paris: PUF, p. 254).
11 [Nous ne saurions faire de l'étendue qu'avec de l'étendue, comme nous ne saurions faire des corps qu'avec des corps ," *Traité des sensations*, p. 253].
12 See also Maine de Biran (2001) *Œuvres*, vol. VII-1-2, *Essai sur les fondements de la psychologie et sur ses rapports avec l'étude de la nature*, pp. 287–288.
13 See also Michel Henry, *Incarnation*, §26, p. 210.
14 Michel Henry, *Phénoménologie matérielle* (1990), Paris: PUF, p. 58.
15 Biran invented the syntagma. See A. Devarieux (2021) "Maine de Biran et l'invention du corps propre," in *Corps ému, essais de philosophie biranienne—Corpo abalado, Ensaios de filosofia biraniana-*, coord. Luis Antonio Umbelino (Coimbra: University Press), pp. 27–59.
16 Such an analysis makes it irreducible to the sense of proprioception ignored by Biran and of course by Condillac. Indeed, what Biran describes is irreducible to a physiological phenomenon and designates the primitive fact of consciousness.
17 Maine de Biran, *Commentaires et marginalia, XVIIème siècle* (1990), vol. XI-1, Paris: Vrin, p. 70.
18 Maine de Biran, *Commentaires et marginalia XVIIème siècle*, (1990) vol. XI-1, p. 117.
19 Sleep appears, like the night of Henryan immanence, as the truth of our Life.

20 Michel Henry (2003) *De la phénoménologie*, vol I, *Phénoménologie de la vie*, Paris: Puf, p. 163.
21 Michel Henry (1985) *Généalogie de la psychanalyse. Le commencement perdu*, Paris: PUF, p. 217.
22 Maine de Biran, *Correspondance philosophique* (1996) t.XIII-2, Paris: Vrin, p. 328.
23 See Devarieux (2018), p. 170.
24 Edmund Husserl (1913) *Idées directrices pour une phénoménologie*, Paris: Tel Gallimard, p. 295. Our translation.

References

Baertschi, Bernard (1981). "L'idéologie subjective de Maine de Biran et la phénoménologie," *Revue de théologie et de philosophie*, Vol. 113, No.2, pp.109–122.
Charrak, André (2003). *Empirisme et métaphysique*, Paris: Vrin.
Condillac, Étienne Bonnot de (1947–1951). *Œuvres philosophiques*, edited by George Le Roy, vol. I, Paris: PUF.
Condillac, Étienne Bonnot de (1982). *Philosophical Writings*. Volume 2. *A Treatise on the Sensations*, translated by Franklin Philip and Harlane Lane, London: Lawrence Erlbaum.
Devarieux, Anne (2018). *L'intériorité réciproque. L'hérésie biranienne de Michel Henry*, Grenoble: Millon.
Devarieux, Anne (2021). "Maine de Biran et l'invention du corps propre," in *Corps ému, essais de philosophie biranienne—Corpo abalado, Ensaios de filosofia biraniana-*, coord. Luis Antonio Umbelino, Coimbra: University Press, pp. 27–59.
Henry, Michel (1965). *Philosophie et phénoménologie du corps, Essai sur l'ontologie biranienne*, Paris: PUF.
Henry, Michel (1985). *Généalogie de la psychanalyse. Le commencement perdu*, Paris: PUF.
Henry, Michel (1990). *Phénoménologie matérielle*, Paris: PUF.
Henry, Michel (2000). *Incarnation*, Paris: Seuil.
Henry, Michel (2003). *De la phénoménologie*, vol I, *Phénoménologie de la vie*, Paris: Puf.
Husserl, Edmund (1913). *Idées directrices pour une phénoménologie*, Paris: Tel Gallimard.
Maine de Biran, Pierre (1954). *Journal* (edited by Henri Gouhier), vol. I, Neuchâtel: La Baconnière.
Maine de Biran, Pierre (1988). *Mémoire sur la décomposition de la pensée*, vol. III, Paris: Vrin.
Maine de Biran, Pierre (1990). *Commentaires et marginalia, XVIIème siècle*, vol. XI-1, Paris: Vrin.
Maine de Biran, Pierre (1996). *Correspondance philosophique*, (1996), vol. XIII-2, Paris: Vrin.
Maine de Biran, Pierre (2001). *Essai sur les fondements de la psychologie et sur ses rapports avec l'étude de la nature*, vol. VII-1–2, Paris: Vrin.
Maine de Biran, Pierre, Alessandra Aloisi, Marco Piazza, and Mark Sinclair (2021). *Maine de Biran's of Immediate Apperception*, London. New York. Oxford; New Delhi. Sydney: Bloomsbury Academic.

Index

Note: Page numbers followed by "n" denote endnotes

activity 92–94, 96–99, 124, 126, 201, 238
active: attention as 83, 86, 97, 112; passive and 91, 93–94; sensation as 126, 127, 201–202, 263–265
agency 219–220, 241–242
Agüero, Juan Manuel Fernández de 190, 195, 197–199, 205–206
Alcorta, Diego 190, 195, 202–205
analogy 50, 113–114, 148, 225, 242; between human and nonhuman animals 162–163, 184; L'Épée and 67, 72, 75–76
analysis 1, 6, 244–245; in clinical medicine 102–113, 115–117, 202–203; Comte and the method of 139, 145–147, 149–150; of continuity of self 253, 255, 260–261, 266, 268; Cousin and 122–123, 128–129; ideas and 67, 90, 177–178, 194–195, 197, 199–200
analytic method 5, 73, 197; Alcorta and 203, 205, 206; Formey and 159, 161–162, 168; medicine and 102–104, 106–108, 112, 114, 115
animal(s) 4, 6, 143–144; "animal economy" 107, 109; human animal 70, 71, 162–165, 171–173, 175–185, 198–199; sentience and reflection 232–233, 235–236, 239
application 123, 128–130

Argentina 4, 191–195, 202, 207–208
association 196, 223, 224
attention 5, 83–85, 239, 241; De la Peña on 201; Laromiguière on 85, 87, 90–100, 128, 129
attraction 44–47, 51, 52–55, 57–58
Augustine, St. 68, 69, 216, 217
Augustinism 98, 221–222
auto-eroticism 269

Berkeley, George (bishop of Cloyne) 12, 15–17, 28–33, 37
Berlin Academy 4, 155–157, 158
Biran, Pierre Maine de see Maine de Biran, Pierre
Blainville, Henri-Marie Ducrotay de 139, 143–144
body 6, 199, 201, 269; passions in the 107, 109; representations of 232–233, 235–236, 238, 241–248, 253; sensation and the 19–20, 23–24, 26, 34, 35, 257–267; soul and 161, 162, 218, 225
bodily movements and manifestations 21–22, 65, 176, 198, 201, 225–226

Canabis, Pierre Jean Georges 86, 137, 191, 194, 195, 197–199, 203–206
canon, philosophical 1, 4, 191, 196, 205–206, 208
Cartesianism 2, 68–69, 112–113, 129–130, 192; Condillac and 87,

274 *Index*

88, 92–99, 122, 196, 206–207; Newtonianism and 46, 49, 54, 56
Châtelet, Émilie Du *see* Du Châtelet, Émilie
Cheselden, William 3, 29–31, 32–33, 163
clinical judgement 104, 105–106, 109, 112, 115
cognition 172, 173, 177, 178–181, 184; cognitive symptoms 104–106, 109–112, 115–116; *see also* metacognition
Comte, Auguste 5, 137–150
consciousness 91, 126, 137, 269; self-consciousness and 6, 233–236, 238, 239, 245–247
contiguity 257–258, 259, 262
continuity 237–238, 257, 259–260, 262–266
continuity thesis 172–173, 179–181, 182, 184
Cours d'études (Condillac) 3, 57, 59, 67, 71–72
Cousin, Victor 11, 85, 87, 95–96, 97–98, 137; "French School" and 119–122, 122–124, 124–125, 125–127, 127–128, 131, 132n1

deafness 3–4, 63–77, 77n1
De la Peña, Luis José 190, 195, 199–202, 205–206, 209n7
Degérando, Joseph-Marie 97–98, 121, 123, 127, 129–131
Descartes, René 1, 2, 5, 68–69, 133n26, 155, 171, 255–256; in Argentinian philosophy 192–193, 195–196, 198–199, 200, 202, 203, 206–207; Comte on Condillac and 142, 143–144, 149; Cousin on Condillac and 120–121, 126, 127, 130, 131, 133n17; Du Châtelet on 46, 48, 54; Laromiguière on Condillac and 88, 90–91, 96–98
Deschamps, Léger-Marie (Dom) 13, 22–26
development, human: theory of 4, 161, 172–181, 184, 185n2, 185n6, 235; of the mind 12, 83, 197; of the faculties 254–255; *see also* developmentalism

developmental: historical and 106, 109; view of science 58–59
developmentalism 5–6, 216, 220, 224–227
Diderot, Denis 11–18, 25, 30–31, 39, 74
dualism 5, 92, 98, 104, 132, 205, 256
Du Châtelet, Émilie 3, 45–47, 49–50, 52–54, 59

eclecticism 17, 85, 117, 119, 121–122, 127, 129–131, 167n30, 202
empiricism 2, 5, 17, 20–22, 25–26, 44–45, 48–49, 51–52, 58–59, 202
empiricist 12, 69, 77, 84, 122, 149, 156, 200
Enlightenment 12, 44–48, 55, 63–64, 76–77, 155–156, 191
epistemic 104, 109, 114, 117
epistemology 1, 11, 13, 44–48, 58–59, 89, 104–105, 115
error 111, 120, 159, 204
Esquirol, Jean-Étienne 99, 191, 202
An Essay concerning Human Understanding (Locke) 6, 28–31, 38, 222, 228
Essay on the Origin of Human Knowledge (*Essai sur l'origine des connaissances humaines*, Condillac) 1, 2, 4, 59, 100n1, 125, 173–174, 254; Argentinian reception of 196, 204, 205; Laromiguiere and 83–85, 87, 89, 91, 93–94, 98; materialism and 11–25; the Molyneux Problem and 28, 30–33, 36, 38–40; and philosophy of mind 103–104, 108, 111, 113–114; self-knowledge and 235–238, 240, 243–244, 247

feeling 95, 173–174, 198, 255–257, 260–265, 267
flesh 262, 265–266, 269
Formey, Jean Henri Samuel 4, 156–165
fragmentation 2
French philosophy 1, 5, 253; Argentina, influence in 190, 194, 195, 202, 206–207; foundation of psychology and

85–88, 94–95, 99, 103; French Enlightenment 12, 44–48, 55, 63–64, 76–77, 155–156, 191; the "French School" 119–122, 127–132, 142–143, 149–150; materialism and 3, 11; Molyneux Problem in 28, 30

Gall, Franz Joseph 5, 139–143

habit 113–114, 144, 159, 164, 174–176
Henry, Michel 5, 253, 255–256, 261–262, 265–269
Herder, Johann Gottfried 4, 172–173, 177–185
historiography 11, 86, 124, 126, 191, 202
history: of philosophy 18–19, 59, 87–88, 233; of psychology 104, 106–108, 115, 142, 216, 224, 229; of religion 216
human interior 215–216, 220, 225, 227, 229
humans *see* animal(s), human
Hume, David 4, 156
Husserl, Edmund 233, 266, 268–270
hybridization 2, 5
hypothesis 3, 44–59, 113–114, 145

idealism 2, 12–16, 18, 24–26, 119, 131
idéologie 1, 190–191, 193–198, 202, 205–208
Ideologist philosophy 102–105, 117, 119, 121, 123
Idéologues 1, 86, 88–89, 98–99
imagination 19–20, 22, 48, 58, 110–114, 163–164
Ingenieros, José 20, 190–194, 198, 202, 206–208
instinct 96, 144, 164, 174–176, 182–184, 198–199, 257

Jurin, James 29–31, 39

knowledge: children and animal cognition 173, 176–177, 199; Condillac's theory of 2, 11–19, 21–26, 83–89, 114, 159, 226–228, 254; Cousin on 123–125, 127–128; De la Peña and Alcorta on 201, 203–204; Descartes and 96; of external objects 34–35, 141, 253, 257, 261–266; hypothetical 49–50, 57–58; L'Épée and 69, 70; of normal functions 105–106; self-knowledge 232–236, 238–248

Lafinur, Juan Crisóstomo 190, 194–197, 202, 205–206
La Mettrie, Julien Offray de 3, 11–13, 18–22, 24–26, 30–31
language: Condillac's theory of the origin of 4, 71, 90, 171–181, 234–238; Formey on 159–160; Herder on 177–184; language of action 3, 64–65, 72–76, 77n5, 175–176, 243–247; language argument 171; language of calculation 147–150; L'Épée on 70; reflectivity and 239–242; science and 112, 115; *see also* sign language
Laromiguière, Pierre 5, 103; De la Peña and 200–202, 205, 206; the "French School" 120–123, 127–130; *Lessons on Philosophy* 86–99
law 44–47, 52–54, 56, 58, 199, 203, 224
Leibniz, Gottfried Wilhelm: and the human interior 218, 225–226; Leibnizian-Wolffian psych paradigm 4, 155–156, 158; *New Essays on Human Understanding* 39; Newtonianism and 46–48, 53–54
L'Épée, Charles-Michel, Abbé de 3, 63–74, 76–77
Leroy, Georges 139, 143–144
Lessons on Philosophy (Laromiguière) 86–99
life: Henry's phenomenology of 253, 256, 262, 265–269; human interiority and time 216–217, 219, 222–225, 228
Locke, John 2, 20, 69, 140–141, 156, 167n35, 222; Argentinian treatment of 191–192, 195–196, 198–203, 206; Cousin on Condillac and 125–126, 130,

133n16; on delirium 110–111, 115; *An Essay concerning Human Understanding* 6, 28–31, 38, 222, 228; L'Épée on 69–70; the Molyneux Problem and 28–34, 37, 39; on self-knowledge and memory 232–233, 235–237, 245–246, 248

Maine de Biran, Pierre 5, 87, 95, 99; criticism of Condillac's sensualism 253, 254, 256–257, 259–269
Malebranche, Nicolas 123, 128, 198, 203, 220–221, 224, 228
materialism 3, 77n2, 120; Condillac as materialist 92–93, 103, 131, 247; mid-eighteenth century 11–13, 18–22, 25, 232
mathematics 44–47, 53–58, 147–148
memory: attention and 83, 139; language and 174–175, 179; self-knowledge and 167n35, 233, 235–241; sensations and 113, 256, 262
metacognition 234, 239
metaphysical 2, 66, 68, 158
metaphysics 115–116, 203, 227; in Condillac's *Essay* 11–12, 18, 21–22, 25; Deschamps's 22–25; French nineteenth-century 85, 95–96, 120, 123–125, 128–131
metarepresentation 239
method: analytic 1, 90, 95, 102–108, 112, 114–117; in Argentinian philosophy 192, 194–200, 202–203, 206; Comte on Condillac's method 5, 139, 145–147; Condillac compared to Cousin on 122–126, 128, 130–131; of hypotheses 44–59; self-knowledge and 235, 244–245; sensation and 254–255
methodological 185n6; empirical orientation and 6, 25, 58; methodical signs 3, 63, 66–67, 70, 72–74, 76; unity 88
mind 71, 177–178, 224–225, 233, 237; attention and 83, 87, 90–93, 96–99, 111–112; Condillac and theory of 124, 128, 159, 174–175, 199–201, 203–205,

228; Ideologist philosophy of mind 103, 106, 109–112; materialism and development of the 11–12, 17–26; mind sciences 224, 229; self and 237–248, 258; sensation and 139–141, 233–235
Molyneux Problem 3, 28–34, 38–40
Montesquieu, Charles Louis de Secondat 222

naturalism 232–236, 241
naturalistic philosophers 172, 191, 233, 238–246, 248n13
naturalistic psychology 6, 232–234, 236, 243
nature: grace and 221, 223; humanity and 24–25, 172, 179, 180, 182–185; language produced by 64–65, 67, 73; laws of 44–45, 51, 58, 224; order in 227; philosophy of 50, 53
New Essays on Human Understanding (Leibniz) 39
Newtonianism 45
Newton, Isaac 44–46, 48, 51, 52–54, 56–59

organ: brain as 105, 108, 111, 113–114; direction of an 261, 265; *see also* senses
organic sciences 145–146
order: analytical method and 112, 115–116, 203; empirical 106, 109; reason and 179; time and 215, 219–222, 224–228

Pascal, Blaise 6, 160, 219–221
passive: active and 53, 91–94, 127, 201–202; tact 263–264
passivity 92–93, 126, 129, 201, 267
Peña, de la Luis José 190, 195, 199–202, 205–206
perception: Condillac's theory of 3, 6, 28, 31–34, 37–39, 71, 89, 198–199, 236, 242–243; La Mettrie and 21–22; of relief 38–39; sensation and 91–92, 204, 225, 247; visual 29, 31–34, 36
phenomenological reduction 255–256, 268, 269

Index 277

phenomenology 5, 31, 233, 253, 255–256, 261–262, 266–270
philosophy of mind *see* mind
phrenology 139–140
Pinel, Philippe 5, 102–112, 114–117, 191, 202–203, 232
predestination 217–223
proprioception 35–37, 270n16
psychology 4, 37, 95, 139; developmental 6, 216; experimental 5, 125; foundations of, and Condillac 85, 95, 98, 99, 104–108, 115–116, 126, 131, 160; leading up to Condillac 215–217, 220, 223, 225–227; naturalistic 6, 191, 232, 236–237, 243
psychopathology 3, 99, 105–107, 109, 115

rationalism 2, 59, 208
reason 4, 222; Condillac's concept of human 71, 75, 88–90, 113, 144, 148–149, 159, 171–173, 178–185, 196, 226–227, 243–244; in the "French School" 119, 123–124, 127–128; Newton's rule of reasoning 44–47, 52–54, 57–59
reception of Condillac 1–2, 173; Argentinian 4, 190–191, 206, 208; at the Berlin Academy 155, 157, 164–165; French 3, 5, 28, 85–86, 253; by L'Épée 63–67, 72; among materialists 12, 25; medical 103–104, 115–116; in phrenology 137, 138–139
reflection 64–65, 119, 126; in Condillac's *Essay* 2, 83, 84, 93, 174–175, 179; in Condillac's *Traité* 164, 172, 176; in humans and animals 175–177, 182, 199, 232, 235; on self 144, 236–238, 240–241, 245, 262
reflective abilities 172, 174–180, 235–236, 239
reflectivity 236–239, 241, 245
representation 71, 97, 161; of action 242–243, 247; of the body 232–233, 235–236, 238, 241, 245–246, 248; metarepresentation 239
Rousseau, Jean-Jacques 59, 128, 138, 178–179, 220, 222–223, 226–227
Royer-Collard, Pierre-Paul 87, 95

St. Augustine 68, 69, 216, 217
Saphary, Jean 120–122, 127–128, 130–131
self 24, 142, 144, 160; Biran and 254, 261–263, 265, 267–268; continuity of 259, 264
self-consciousness 6, 28, 233–234
self-knowledge 233–236, 238–242, 244–248
sensation: Alcorta on 204–205; Biran on 254–257, 268–269; Herder on 177–178; languages of action and 71–72, 74; Leibniz on 225; the Materialists on 19–26; the Molyneux Problem and 28, 31–33, 38–39; self and 238, 246–248; sensationalism 137–138, 149; "sensation of movement" 253; as source of knowledge 57, 127–129, 155, 162, 198–199, 201–202, 240, 248; touch and 34–37, 257–261; transformed 74, 84–85, 89, 91–95, 98, 138–143, 197, 204, 254, 261; will and 104–105, 108; *see also Treatise on Sensations* (Condillac)
senses 34, 69–70, 201; hearing 3–4, 63–77; sight 12–15, 28–33, 37–39, 64, 66; touch 29, 31–39, 141, 257–267
sensualism 2, 87; Argentinian reception of 191–192, 202, 207; Biran's critique of Condillac's 5, 253, 269–270; the "French School" and 119–120, 122, 124–125, 127, 130; materialism and 11, 103
signs 239–240
sign language 4, 63–69, 71–77, 175–176; *see also* language of action
skepticism 158
The Skeptic's Walk (Diderot) 13–14
solipsism 13–18, 24–25

spiritualism 2, 192, 137–138, 202, 205; Materialists and 1, 19–21, 92–99; in contrast with sensualism 84–87
Spiritualists 19, 119, 123, 131
species 4, 172–182, 184
system 87, 226–227, 254; critique of 4, 92, 127, 137, 157–158, 164; hypotheses and 3, 44–45, 48–45, 54–56, 58–59, 145, 192–193; Laromiguière's 95, 98; *see also* Treatise on Systems

time: development of reason in space and 181–185; human interiority and 216–220, 225, 226, 228–229; language and 74–76
Treatise on Sensations (*Traité des sensations*, Condillac) 2, 6, 11; and the Molyneux Problem 28, 31, 33–40; concept of attention and 84–85, 89, 91, 94; Argentinian reception 191; naturalism and 232–235, 237–238, 240–241, 244–246; influence on Biran 253–254, 256–257, 268
Treatise on Systems (Traité des systemes, Condillac) 3, 23, 31, 47, 50–51, 56–58, 85, 92, 126, 145, 157–158, 165

understanding: animal versus human 175–176, 180–181; Condillac's theory of 92–93, 104–106, 139; and will, dualism of 5, 96, 104, 107–112, 115–116, 140, 164; *see also* An Essay concerning Human Understanding (Locke)

Voltaire (François-Marie Arouet) 30–31, 32–32, 45, 132n4, 138

will: attention as an act of 93–96; Biranian 262–265; free will 65, 95, 219–220; language and 175; and understanding, dualism of 5, 96, 104–105, 107–112, 115–116, 140, 164
Wolff, Christian 13, 156, 158